EARLY MUSIC PRINTING
IN GERMAN-SPEAKING LANDS

The first century of music printing in Germany had its own internal dynamics, affected by political and social events such as the Reformation. Yet it also had an international dimension: German printers set up shops all around Europe, taking materials and techniques with them, or exporting necessary materials such as type. For the first time, this collection brings together the different strands that define the German music printing landscape from the late fifteenth to the late sixteenth century. From the earliest developments in music printing and publishing, to printing techniques and solutions, the commerce of music printing, and intellectual history, the chapters outline broad trends in the production of different genres of printed books and examine the work of individual printers. The book draws upon the rich information gathered for the online database *Catalogue of early German printed music/Verzeichnis deutscher Musikfrühdrucke (vdm)*, the first systematic descriptive catalogue of music printed in the German-speaking lands between c.1470 and 1550, allowing precise conclusions about the material production of these printed musical sources. The result is a highly original and varied picture of the beginnings of music printing in a geographical region that, until now, has been somewhat neglected.

Andrea Lindmayr-Brandl holds a chair of music history at the University of Salzburg, Austria. She studied music, musicology, philosophy and mathematics at her home university, at the Mozarteum Salzburg and at the Schola Cantorum Basiliensis. Her doctoral dissertation examined the sources of the motets of Johannes Ockeghem, and her habilitation studied Schubert's musical fragments. She has held the Austrian Chair Professorship at Stanford University, has been guest professor at the University of Vienna and is an active member of several academic institutions and organisations. She directs two research projects: one on the critical edition of works by Gaspar van Weerbeke, the other the project *Early music printing in German-speaking lands*.

Elisabeth Giselbrecht is an early career fellow at King's College, London, UK. She completed her undergraduate and Master's degrees in Vienna (including a term at New York University), followed by a PhD on the dissemination of Italian sacred music in German-speaking lands in early modern Europe at the University of Cambridge (2012). She then took up a post-doctoral position at the University of Salzburg, working on the project and database *Music printing in German-speaking lands.* Her current research project, entitled *Owners and Users of Early Music Books*, is funded by a Leverhulme Early Career Fellowship.

Grantley McDonald is a postdoctoral researcher and lecturer in the department of musicology, University of Vienna, Austria, where he directs the FWF research project *The court chapel of Maximilian I: between art and politics*. He holds doctoral degrees in musicology (Melbourne, 2002) and history (Leiden, 2011). Grantley has held postdoctoral fellowships at Wolfenbüttel, Tours, Leuven, Dublin, and the University of Salzburg, where he worked on the project *Early music printing in German-speaking lands*. His research has been distinguished with prizes from the Australian Academy of the Humanities (Canberra) and the Praemium Erasmianum Foundation (Amsterdam). He is author of *Biblical Criticism in Early Modern Europe: Erasmus, the Johannine Comma and Trinitarian Debate* (Cambridge, 2016).

Music and Material Culture

Series Editor

Laura Macy

Music and Material Culture provides a new platform for methodological innovations in research on the relationship between music and its objects. In a sense, musicology has always dealt with material culture; the study of manuscripts, print sources, instruments and other physical media associated with the production and reception of music is central to its understanding. Recent scholarship within the humanities has increasingly shifted its focus onto the objects themselves and there is now a particular need for musicology to be part of this broader 'material turn'. A growing reliance on digital and online media as sources for the creation and consumption of music is changing the way we experience music by increasingly divorcing it from tangible matter. This is rejuvenating discussion of our relationship with music's objects and the importance of such objects both as a means of understanding past cultures and negotiating current needs and social practices. Broadly interdisciplinary in nature, this series seeks to examine critically the materiality of music and its artefacts as an explicit part of culture rather than simply an accepted means of music-making. Proposals are welcomed on the material culture of music from any period and genre, particularly on topics within the fields of cultural theory, source studies, organology, ritual, anthropology, collecting, archiving, media archaeology, new media and aesthetics.

Recent titles in the series:

Senza Vestimenta: *The Literary Tradition of Trecento Song*
Lauren McGuire Jennings

Manuscript Inscriptions in Early English Printed Music
David Greer

Media, Materiality and Memory: Grounding the Groove
Elodie A. Roy

Late Medieval Liturgies Enacted: The Experience of Worship in Cathedral and Parish Church
Sally Harper, P.S. Barnwell and Magnus Williamson

Early Music Printing in German-Speaking Lands

Edited by
*Andrea Lindmayr-Brandl, Elisabeth Giselbrecht
and Grantley McDonald*

LONDON AND NEW YORK

First published 2018
by Routledge
2 Park Square, Milton Park, Abingdon, Oxon OX14 4RN

and by Routledge
711 Third Avenue, New York, NY 10017

Routledge is an imprint of the Taylor & Francis Group, an informa business

© 2018 selection and editorial matter, Andrea Lindmayr-Brandl, Elisabeth Giselbrecht, and Grantley McDonald; individual chapters, the contributors.

The right of Andrea Lindmayr-Brandl, Elisabeth Giselbrecht, and Grantley McDonald to be identified as the authors of the editorial material, and of the authors for their individual chapters, has been asserted in accordance with sections 77 and 78 of the Copyright, Designs and Patents Act 1988.

With the exception of Chapter 8, no part of this book may be reprinted or reproduced or utilised in any form or by any electronic, mechanical, or other means, now known or hereafter invented, including photocopying and recording, or in any information storage or retrieval system, without permission in writing from the publishers.

Chapter 8 of this book is available for free in PDF format as Open Access from the individual product page at www.routledge.com. It has been made available under a Creative Commons Attribution-Non Commercial-No Derivatives 4.0 license.

Trademark notice: Product or corporate names may be trademarks or registered trademarks, and are used only for identification and explanation without intent to infringe.

British Library Cataloguing in Publication Data
A catalogue record for this book is available from the British Library

Library of Congress Cataloging in Publication Data
Names: Lindmayr-Brandl, Andrea. | Giselbrecht, Elisabeth. | McDonald, Grantley
Title: Early music printing in German-speaking lands / edited by Andrea Lindmayr-Brandl, Elisabeth Giselbrecht, and Grantley McDonald.
Description: Abingdon, Oxon ; New York, NY : Routledge, 2018. | Includes bibliographical references and index.
Identifiers: LCCN 2017041980 | ISBN 9781138241053 (hardback) | ISBN 9781315281452 (ebook)
Subjects: LCSH: Music printing – German speaking countries – History – 15th century. | Music printing – German speaking countries – History – 16th century.
Classification: LCC ML112 .E3 2018 | DDC 070.5/7940943 – dc23
LC record available at https://lccn.loc.gov/2017041980

ISBN: 978-1-138-24105-3 (hbk)
ISBN: 978-1-315-28145-2 (ebk)

Typeset in Palatino
by Florence Production Limited, Stoodleigh, Devon, UK

Bach musicological font developed by © Yo Tomita

Contents

List of plates	ix
List of figures and music examples	x
List of tables	xiii
List of contributors	xiv
List of abbreviations	xvii

Introduction   1
Andrea Lindmayr-Brandl, Elisabeth Giselbrecht, and Grantley McDonald

PART I
Music printing and publishing in the fifteenth century   19

1   Early music printing and ecclesiastic patronage   21
       Mary Kay Duggan

2   German-speaking printers and the development of music printing
       in Spain (1485–1505)   46
       Margarita Restrepo

PART II
Printing techniques: problems and solutions   65

3   'Made in Germany': the dissemination of mensural German music
       types outside the German-speaking area (and vice versa), up to 1650   67
       Laurent Guillo

4   Printing music: technical challenges and synthesis, 1450–1530   84
       Elisabeth Giselbrecht and Elizabeth Savage

5   'Synopsis musicae': charts and tables in sixteenth-century music
       textbooks   100
       Inga Mai Groote

viii   CONTENTS

PART III
Music printing and commerce   121

6   Melchior Lotter: a German 'music printer'   123
     Elisabeth Giselbrecht

7   The music books of Christian Egenolff: bad impressions = good
     return on investment   135
     John Kmetz

8   The music editions of Christian Egenolff: a new catalogue and
     its implications   153
     Royston Gustavson

PART IV
Music printing and intellectual history   197

9   The cult of Luther in music   199
     Grantley McDonald

10   Theobald Billican and Michael's ode settings in print: notes on an
     exceptional transmission   225
     Sonja Tröster

11   Polyphonic music in early German print: changing perspectives in
     music historiography   245
     Andrea Lindmayr-Brandl

     Index   260

Plates

1   *Graduale Herbipolense*. Würzburg: Georg Reyser, 1496

2   *Obsequiale Eystettense*. Eichstätt: Michael Reyser, 1488

3   *Obsequiale Augustense*. Augsburg: Erhard Ratdolt, 1487

4   *Missale Cesaraugustanum*. Zaragoza: Pablo Hurus, 1485

5   *Processionarium Predicatorum*. Seville: Meinardo Ungut and Estanislao Polono, 1494

6   *Missale mixtum*. Toledo: Pedro Hagenbach, 1500

7   Decretals of Gregory IX (written in Bologna c.1300), later used as a frisket sheet

8   Printer's device of Erhard Ratdolt, from *Missale Pataviense*. Augsburg: Erhard Ratdolt, 1494

9   Detail of block for Pieter Bruegel the Elder, *The Dirty Bride (Wedding of Mopsus and Nisa)*

10   *Obsequiale Constantiense*. [Augsburg]: Erhard Ratdolt, 1510

11   *De dulcissimo nomine Iesu officium*. Mainz: Peter Schöffer the Younger, 1518

12   *Missale Wormatiense*. Speyer: Peter Drach III, 1522

13   *De dulcissimo nomine Iesu officium*. Mainz: Peter Schöffer the Younger, 1518

14   *Libellus ad omnes*. Leipzig: Melchior Lotter the Elder, 1522

15   *Evangelistarum quatuor passiones*. Leipzig: Melchior Lotter the Elder, 1533

16   *Libellus ad omnes*. Leipzig: Melchior Lotter the Elder, 1522

17   *Missale Brandenburgense*. Leipzig: Melchior Lotter the Elder, 1516

Figures and music examples

Figures

I.1	Geographical distribution of sources	6
I.2	Geographical distribution of sources	7
I.3	Distribution of source types as a percentage of the total production between 1501 and 1540	9
1.1	The impact of ecclesiastical patronage on incunabula of German lands with printed music or space for music	22
1.2	*Missale Augustanum*. Dillingen: Johann Sensenschmidt, 1489	27
1.3	*Antiphonarium Augustense*. Augsburg: Erhard Ratdolt, 1495	30
1.4	*Graduale Suecicum*. Lübeck: Steffan Arndes, 1493	32
2.1	Places of origin of German-speaking printers	47
2.2	Towns where German-speaking printers settled	49
2.3	*Missale Tarraconense*. Barcelona: Juan Rosenbach, 1499	53
2.4	*Lux bella* by Domingo Marcos Durán. Seville: Cuatro Compañeros Alemanes, 1492	55
2.5	Guillermo del Podio. *Ars musicorum* or *Comentario musices*. Valencia: Pedro Hagenbach and Leonardo Hutz, 1495	57
3.1	Diagram expressing a complex dissemination	68
3.2	Dissemination expressed by a classic 'arrow' diagram	68
3.3	Dissemination expressed by an 'area' diagram	69
3.4	Dissemination of types N° 1 and 4	70
3.5	Dissemination of types N° 2 and 5	72
3.6	Dissemination of types N° 3 and 6	74
3.7	Dissemination of types N° 7 and 8	76
3.8	Dissemination of types N° 9 and 10	78
3.9	Type 1 – Sigmund Salminger, *Cantiones quinque vocum*. Strasbourg: Peter Schöffer the Younger, 1539	82
3.10	Type 2 – Heinrich Finck, *Schöne auszerlesne lieder*. Nuremberg: Hieronymus Formschneider, 1536	82
3.11	Type 3 – Dominique Phinot, *Liber secundus mutetarum*. Lyon: G. & M. Beringen, 1548	82
3.12	Type 4 – Orlando di Lasso, *Moduli sex septem et duodecim vocum*. Paris: Le Roy & Ballard, 1573	82
3.13	Type 5 – Adrian Denss, *Florilegium omnis fere generis cantionum . . . ad testudinis tabulaturam*. Cologne: G. Grevenbruch, 1594	82

FIGURES AND MUSIC EXAMPLES   xi

3.14	Type 6 – Louis Desmasures, *Vingtsix Cantiques chantés au Seigneur*. Lyon: J. de Tournes, 1564	83
3.15	Type 7 – *La Philomèle séraphique, partie seconde*. Tournai: A. Quinqué, 1632	83
3.16	Type 8 – Orlando di Lasso, *Magnum opus musicum*. Munich: N. Heinrich, 1604	83
3.17	Type 9 – Lodovico Viadana, *Centum sacri concentus*. Frankfurt/Main: W. Richter, 1615	83
3.18	Type 10 – Hieronymus Praetorius, *Cantiones sacrae de praecipuis festis totius anni*. Hamburg: Ph. von Ohr, 1599	83
4.1	Title page of *Clarissima plane atque choralis musice interpretatio*. [Basel]: Michael Furter, 1501	90
4.2	*Clarissima plane atque choralis musice interpretatio*. [Basel]: Michael Furter, 1501	91
4.3	Diagram of Cancer, metal strips with type inset. Lazarus Beham, *Buch von der Astronomie*. Cologne: Nicolaus Götz, c.1476	93
4.4	One possible organisational scheme of *De dulcissimo nomine Iesu officium*. Mainz: Peter Schöffer the Younger, 1518	97
5.1	Gregor Reisch, *Margarita philosophica*. [Freiburg im Breisgau]: Johann Schott, 1504	103
5.2	Johannes Fries, *Synopsis Isagoges Musicae per Ioannem Frisium Tigurinum*. Zurich: Froschauer, 1552	106
5.3	Johannes Fries, *Brevis musicae isagoge*. Zurich: Froschauer, 1554	107
5.4	Gregor Faber, *Musices practicae Erotematum Libri II*. Basel: Petri, 1553	109
5.5	Christoph Praetorius, *Erotemata musices in usum scholae Lunaeburgensis*. Wittenberg: Schwertel, 1574	112
5.6	Valentin Goetting, *Compendium musicae modulativae*. Erfurt: Baumann, 1587	115
6.1	Distribution of subjects printed by Melchior Lotter the Elder	124
6.2	Church dioceses for which Melchior Lotter published liturgical books	127
6.3	*Hortulus musices practicae*. Leipzig: Melchior Lotter the Elder, [1514]	129
6.4	[*Breviarius Misnensis*]. Meissen: Melchior Lotter the Elder, 1520	130
6.5	Development of religious service books with music printed in German-speaking lands, 1500–1540	133
7.1	Albrecht Dürer, *The Publishing Bakery*, 1511	141
7.2a	Ox head watermark. Egenolff, *Reutterliedlin*, 1536	144
7.2b	Ox head twin watermark. Egenolff, *Reutterliedlin*, 1536	144
7.3	Poor registration of unnested, single impression type. Egenolff, *Gassenhawerlin*, 1535	144
9.1	Hans Baldung Grien, *Luther as an Augustinian friar*, from *Acta et res gestae, D. Martini Lutheri, in Comitijs Principum Vuormaciae, Anno M D XXI*. [Strasbourg]: [Johann Schott], [1521]	200
9.2	Title page from Petrus Sylvius, *Luthers vnd Lutzbers eintrechtige vereinigung*. [Leipzig]: [Michael Blum], 1535	201
9.3	*Ad Martinum Lutherum captivum lamentatio*. [Strasbourg]: [Johann Knobloch the Elder], [c.1521]	203
9.4	*Epithalamia Martini Lutheri Wittenbergensis*. [Dresden]: [Hieronymus Emser], [c.1525]	205

xii FIGURES AND MUSIC EXAMPLES

9.5 Petrus Sylvius, *Eyn erschreglicher und doch widderumb kurtzweylliger und nutzlich gesangk*. [Leipzig]: [Nickel Schmidt], 1526 — 210

10.1 Beginning of *Scriberis fortis* (alto and bass) from Theobald Billican, *De partium orationis inflexionibus*. [Augsburg]: [S. Ruff], 1526 — 229

10.2 Titlepage of Theobald Billican, *De partium orationis inflexionibus*. [Augsburg]: [S. Ruff], 1526 — 230

10.3 First pages of music section from *De partium orationis adcidentibus, compendium Aldi*. Marburg: [Franz Rhode], 1531 — 232

10.4 *Lydia dic per omnes* from Theobald Billican, *De partium orationis inflexionibus*. [Augsburg]: [S. Ruff], 1526 — 234

10.5 *Lydia dic per omnes* from *De partium orationis adcidentibus, compendium Aldi*. Marburg: [Franz Rhode], 1531 — 235

10.6 *Livor tabificum* from *De partium orationis adcidentibus, compendium Aldi*. Marburg: [Franz Rhode], 1531 — 236

10.7 *Livor tabificum* from *De partium orationis adcidentibus compendium Aldi, unà cum versificatoria Ioannis Murmellij*. Marburg: Franz Rhode, 1533 — 236

11.1 Increase of the number of titles known between 1 October 2013 and 21 December 2015 in course of the research project 'Early Music Printing in German-Speaking Lands (1501–1540)' — 247

11.2 Development of polyphonic printing in German-speaking countries, Italy and France — 252–253

11.3 Number of editions with printed music notation at Nuremberg — 256

Music examples

9.1 Anon., *Ad Martinum Lutherum captivum lamentatio* (1521) — 218–222

9.2 Anon., *Rhythmus die divi Martini pronunciatus* (1511) — 222

9.3 Hieronymus Emser, *Hymnus paranymphorum* (1525) — 222

9.4 Caspar Othmayr, *Mein himlischer vatter* (1546), beginning — 223–224

Tables

1.1	Music editions of Georg Reyser for Prince-Bishop Rudolf of Scherenberg, Würzburg	37
1.2	Music Editions of Johann and Lorenz Sensenschmidt for Heinrich IV von Absberg, Bishop of Regensburg; Ludwig von Helmstedt, bishop of Speyer; Heinrich Gross von Trockau, Prince-Bishop of Bamberg; Sixtus von Tannberg, Prince-Bishop of Freising; and Friedrich II, Prince-Bishop of Augsburg	38
1.3	Music editions of Erhard Ratdolt for Prince-Bishop Friedrich II, Count of Zollern, Bishop of Augsburg, Sixtus von Tannberg, Bishop of Freising, Melchior von Meckau, Bishop of Bressanone, Christoph von Schachner, Bishop of Passau, and Heinrich VI, Bishop of Chur	39
1.4	Liturgical editions of Steffan Arndes, with and without printed music	41
1.5	Liturgical editions of Conrad Kachelofen	42
1.6	Johann Prüss, Strasbourg; editions with printed staves, or notes and staves	43
2.1	List of German-speaking printers with locations, dates, and list of publications	60
2.2	Publications and printers by city	62
6.1	Publications with music by Melchior Lotter the Elder (and his son Michael in Wittenberg branch)	125
7.1	Selected music books by Egenolff. A summary of dates, titles, sizes, formats and exemplars	142
7.2	Prices paid for German music books in the sixteenth-century	146
7.3	Music manuscripts of the same or similar size as Egenolff's music books (i.e., 7.5 × 10.5 cm)	148
10.1	Overview of the publications containing Michael's ode settings	227
10.2	Musical contents of the publications containing Michael's ode settings	243
11.1	Development of polyphonic printing (number of editions) in German-speaking lands	249
11.2	Development of polyphonic printing (number of compositions) in German-speaking lands	251
11.3	Number of editions with printed music notation in German-speaking areas	255

Contributors

Mary Kay Duggan is a Professor Emerita at the University of California, Berkeley, where she taught in the School of Information and Department of Music. She received her undergraduate and Master's degrees (Musicology) from Ohio State University and PhD from UC Berkeley with a dissertation on Italian music incunabula which was revised and published in 1992 as *Italian Music Incunabula: Printers and Type* (University of California Press). The chapter in this book draws on the author's recent research on music incunabula in German-speaking lands, on which she is currently preparing a monograph. She has also published on fifteenth-century readers and the liturgy. Her research articles have appeared in the *Gutenberg-Jahrbuch, La Bibliofilia, Church History and Religious Culture*, conference papers and exhibition catalogues (see people.ischool.berkeley.edu/~mkduggan).

Elisabeth Giselbrecht completed her undergraduate and Master's degrees in Vienna, followed by a PhD at the University of Cambridge (2012) on the printed dissemination of Italian sacred music in German-speaking areas. She then took up a post-doctoral position at the University of Salzburg, working on the project and database *Early music printing in German-speaking lands*, before starting a Leverhulme Early Career Fellowship at King's College, University of London, in 2015. Her current project is entitled *Owners and Users of Early Music Books*.

Inga Mai Groote is Professor of Musicology at the Ruprecht-Karls-Universität Heidelberg. She studied musicology, medieval and modern history, and Italian philology at the University of Bonn (Dr. phil. 2005). She has been Wissenschaftliche Assistentin and Oberassistentin at the Universities of Munich and Zurich (Habilitation 2013), and Associate Professor of Musicology at the University of Fribourg (2014–15). Her current research focuses on early modern and late nineteenth-century music history, especially on the history of music theory in relationship with the pragmatics of knowledge and book history (project *Material Formations of Music Theory Concepts*, SFB 933).

Laurent Guillo – since passing his PhD at the École Pratique des Hautes Études in Paris (1986), Laurent Guillo has studied sources of printed or manuscript music from France, Geneva and the Spanish Netherlands, dating from the sixteenth and seventeenth centuries, with a particular focus on the Paris publishing firm Ballard. His studies have also extended to the history of early music libraries and collections, music typography, and the legal aspects of music publishing. His research attempts to synthesise the three basic dimensions of the history of books and publishing: the commercial, the technical and the intellectual elements.

Royston Gustavson joined the Australian National University in 2003 and has served as an Associate Dean (Education) since 2010, first in the College of Business and Economics and currently in the College of Arts and Social Sciences. He convenes the Learning and Teaching Network of the Australasian Council of Deans of Arts, Social Sciences, and Humanities. Additionally, he was interim Head of the School of Music for a year until August 2016. His published work has been divided between corporate governance and the history of music printing. His dissertation (University of Melbourne, 1998) dealt with the printer Hieronymus Formschneider and the music publisher Hans Ott.

John Kmetz is an an American businessman who received a PhD from New York University with a dissertation on *The Sixteenth-Century Basel Songbooks*. He has published three books and numerous articles and reviews on sixteenth-century German and Central European music. He has been a guest professor at Columbia University, New York University, The City University of New York, and at the Universities of Munich, Salzburg, Vienna and Zurich. Currently he is writing and teaching on the topic of 'Music, Money and Markets: A Socio-Economic Look at the History of Western Music'.

Andrea Lindmayr-Brandl holds a chair of music history at the University of Salzburg. She studied music, musicology, philosophy and mathematics at the University of Salzburg, at the Mozarteum Salzburg and at the Schola Cantorum Basiliensis. Her doctoral dissertation examined the sources of the motets of Johannes Ockeghem, and her habilitation studied Schubert's musical fragments. She has held the Austrian Chair Professorship at Stanford University, has been guest professor at the University of Vienna and is an active member of several academic institutions and organisations. Currently she directs two research projects: one on the critical edition of works by Gaspar van Weerbeke, the other the project *Early music printing in German-speaking lands*.

Grantley McDonald is a postdoctoral researcher and lecturer in musicology at the University of Vienna, where he directs the FWF research project *The court chapel of Maximilian I: between art and politics*. He holds doctoral degrees in musicology (Melbourne, 2002) and history (Leiden, 2011). Grantley has been awarded fellowships at the Herzog August Bibliothek (Wolfenbüttel), Centre d'Études Supérieures de la Renaissance (Tours), KU Leuven, Trinity College Dublin, and the University of Salzburg, where he worked on the FWF project *Early music printing in German-speaking lands*. Among his publications are a volume in the *Complete Works of Paul Hofhaimer* (Munich: Strube, 2014), *Biblical Criticism in Early Modern Europe: Erasmus, the Johannine Comma and Trinitarian Debate* (Cambridge: Cambridge University Press, 2016) and *Marsilio Ficino in Germany, from Renaissance to Enlightenment: a Reception History* (Geneva: Librairie Droz, forthcoming). He is also active as a performing musician.

Margarita Restrepo – the arrival and adoption of the madrigal in Spain was the topic of Margarita Restrepo's PhD dissertation from Brandeis University. She has also explored the adoption of European sacred music at the Santa Fe de Bogotá Cathedral, Colombia. Her edition of the three Requiem Masses of Juan de Herrera (1665–1738), a chapel master at the cathedral, was published in 1996 by the Fundación Vicente Emilio Sojo and the Instituto Colombiano de Cultura. Dr. Restrepo is on the faculty of the Walnut Hill School for the Arts, in Natick, Massachusetts.

xvi CONTRIBUTORS

Elizabeth Savage is 2015–18 British Academy Postdoctoral Fellow and Lecturer in Book History and Communications, Institute of English Studies, School of Advanced Studies, University of London, and By-Fellow of Churchill College, Cambridge. After taking her PhD (Cambridge), she was a member of the Centre for Material Texts, University of Cambridge; Visiting Fellow at the Warburg Institute, London; and Munby Fellow in Bibliography, Cambridge University. Her research into early modern printing techniques has been recognised with the Wolfgang Ratjen-Preis and awards from the Bibliographical Society of America and American Printing History Association. Her recent publications include *Printing Colour 1400–1700: Histories, Techniques, Functions and Receptions* (2015), which was recognised at the IFPDA Book Awards, and her recent academic curation includes exhibitions at the British Museum and Cambridge University Library.

Sonja Tröster studied musicology at the University of Vienna. Between 2008 and 2015 she worked with Stefan Gasch and Birgit Lodes on a catalogue of the works and sources of Ludwig Senfl, which will be published in 2017. In 2015 Tröster completed her dissertation on German polyphonic songs from the first half of the sixteenth century ('Stilregister der mehrstimmigen Liedkomposition in der ersten Hälfte des 16. Jahrhunderts und die Liedsätze Ludwig Senfls'). She is currently working in a research project at the University of Vienna: a new edition of the Renaissance composer Ludwig Senfl (*New Senfl Edition*), which will begin by publishing Senfl's motets. In addition to her musicological research, she also works as a violinmaker.

Abbreviations

ISTC	Incunabula Short Title Catalogue: http://istc.bl.uk
MGG^2	*Musik in Geschichte und Gegenwart*, Second Edition
New Grove^2	*New Grove Dictionary of Music and Musicians*, Second Edition
RISM	Répertoire International des Sources Musicales
USTC	Universal Short Title Catalogue: http://ustc.ac.uk
VD16	Verzeichnis der im deutschen Sprachbereich erschienenen Drucke des 16. Jahrhunderts: www.gateway-bayern.de/index_vd16.html
vdm	Verzeichnis deutscher Musikfrühdrucke / Catalogue of early German printed music: http://vdm.sbg.ac.at/db/music_prints.php

Introduction

Andrea Lindmayr-Brandl, Elisabeth Giselbrecht, and Grantley McDonald

Scholars who work on Renaissance music and its sources are confronted with questions that arise from the emergence of the new medium of music printing: why, how, when and where was the printing press used to make music available? How did music printing begin? How did it develop technically? How did printed music channel the dissemination of specific repertoires, and how did the increased availability of music affect the cultural world of the early modern period?

These questions are not new. Several scholars have already studied various aspects of early music printing. Investigation of the work of the 'inventor' of polyphonic music printing, Ottaviano Petrucci, began in the middle of the nineteenth century with Anton Schmid, and found its pinnacle in the recent *Catalogue raisonné* by Stanley Boorman.[1] Comprehensive books on a number of other Italian printing firms have been published, such as studies devoted to Antonio Gardano, the Scotto Press, Valerio Dorico, and a thesis on the dazzling figure of Andrea Antico.[2] Another cornerstone is the historical study and bibliographical catalogue of the French printer Pierre Attaingnant by Daniel Heartz, as well as studies of later printing entrepreneurs, such as Jacques Moderne, the Antwerp printer-publisher Tylman Susato or the English music publisher Thomas East.[3] Other scholarly work has focused on particular printing centres, such as Venice or Antwerp, or has provided a general overview of the early printing culture of an entire country.[4] Further studies have investigated specific topics such as printing privileges and contracts, the role of printer, editor and composer, patterns of dissemination, acquisition and collection of printed music, and studies of repertoire.

However, most scholarly work to date has concentrated on music printing in Italy and France, with scattered studies on the Netherlands, Spain and England. Until relatively recently, early music printing in German-speaking countries has attracted less attention. A few examples may be mentioned. One is the doctoral dissertation of the Australian scholar Royston Gustavson, on a motet collection printed at Nuremberg in 1537/38. However, this dissertation is unpublished and therefore difficult to access.[5] Another important, thematically concentrated study is the Habilitation dissertation of Birgit Lodes, which examines Mewes' 1507 edition of Obrecht's masses. Again, this is only partially published.[6]

---

1 Schmid, *Petrucci da Fossombrone*; Boorman, *Ottaviano Petrucci*.
2 Lewis, *Gardano*; Agee, *Gardano*; Bernstein, *Scotto Press*; Cusick, *Dorico*; Chapman 'Antico'.
3 Heartz, *Attaingnant*; Pogue, *Moderne*; Forney, 'Susato'; Meissner, *Susato*; Smith, *East*.
4 Bernstein, *Print Culture*; Schreurs and Vanhulst, *Music Printing in Antwerp*; Fenlon, *Music, Print and Culture*; Duggan, *Italian Music Incunabula*.
5 Gustavson, 'Hans Ott'.
6 Lodes, 'Gregor Mewes', published partially as 'An anderem Ort, auf andere Art'.

Lodes organised a conference in 2007 that concentrated on the beginnings of music printing north of the Alps. The proceedings of this conference record the state of research and demonstrate how much is still to be done in this area.[7]

There are several reasons why research on early music printing in German-speaking countries has lagged so far behind that of other European countries. The most important may be the fact that in the first decades of the sixteenth century no single printer dominated the German market in the same way as Petrucci or Attaingnant did, and there are thus few obvious subjects for a bio-bibliographical approach comparable to the studies of Boorman or Heartz. In German-speaking lands it was general printers who introduced the new media of music printing north of the Alps, not specialised music printers. Quite independently of each other, they experimented with various printing techniques specific to particular repertoires, in several different places. Hence, it took some time before a network emerged and technical knowledge and printing material spread through the German-speaking territories and beyond.

Another possible reason for the delayed development in the study of German music printing follows from the first one. Since there are no big names, it is more difficult to obtain an overview of printed production in the first decades of the sixteenth century. Many different firms each printed a small number of titles containing different kinds of music. Besides collections of polyphonic compositions by several authors (classified by RISM, the international repertory of musical sources, as 'collective editions' or 'Sammeldrucke') or by a single composer ('Einzeldrucke'), printers also produced many anonymous works or editions containing mainly text with isolated instances of musical notation.

Unfortunately, RISM does not provide a reliable summary of these various types of printed editions. What information is available must be retrieved from different volumes of RISM.[8] Not all these volumes are organised in chronological order, not all contain a chronological index, and not all distinguish titles according to place of printing or even broad geopolitical areas. A search in RISM online is still yet to overcome the problem of displaying individual musical works and musical sources on the same level.[9] Moreover, large groups of sources are not recorded in RISM, for example liturgical books containing plainchant, or lost editions. Liturgical editions must be identified with an online database (RELICS), but this resource, valuable though it is, is incomplete, and does not reliably indicate whether music is contained in a given edition.[10]

A third reason for the relatively small number of studies on early German printed music might be found in a national peculiarity. German historians of the nineteenth and early twentieth centuries were proud that it was a German who invented printing. Gutenberg was the great German cultural hero of the fifteenth century, and his life and invention were studied in minute detail. One high-profile journal in the history of the book, *Gutenberg-Jahrbuch*, promotes this pride by including his name in its title. By contrast, the fact that the so-called father of *music* printing, the Italian Ottaviano Petrucci, came from the 'land

---

7 Lodes, *NiveauNischeNimbus*.

8 *RISM: Series A*, 14 vols., I: *Notendrucke: Einzeldrucke vor 1800* (Kassel: Bärenreiter, 1971–2003); *Series B*, I: François Lesure, *Recueils imprimés XVIe–XVIIe siècles* (Munich: G. Henle, 1960); VI/1–2: François Lesure, *Ecrits imprimés concernant la musique*, 2 vols. (1971); VIII/1: Konrad Ameln, Markus Jenny, and Walter Lipphardt, *Das Deutsche Kirchenlied. Band 1, Teil 1: Verzeichnis der Drucke von den Anfängen bis 1800* (1975); special volumes (Kassel: Bärenreiter): Norbert Böker-Heil, Harald Heckmann, and Ilse Kindermann, *Das Tenorlied. Mehrstimmige Lieder in deutschen Quellen, 1450–1580* (= Catalogus musicus 9), *vol. 1: Drucke* (1979).

9 *RISM-OPAC* (https://opac.rism.info/metaopac/start.do?View=rism).

10 *Renaissance Liturgical Imprints. A Census* (http://quod.lib.umich.edu/r/relics/).

of music,' led to a perception that German music printers were mere epigones. This suspicion was supported by classic nineteenth-century accounts of Renaissance culture, such as those of Jacob Burckhardt and John Addington Symonds, that depicted this cultural movement as radiating outwards from its Italian homeland to ever less brightly illuminated climes.[11] The apparent pre-eminence of Italian music printers such as Petrucci may have discouraged German scholars from devoting much energy to recovering Germany's own contribution to this field.

But this attitude is born of an error. Petrucci did not invent music printing *tout court*; he only developed a viable way to print mensural notation from movable type. The privileged place given to Petrucci in the historiography of music printing is in part a figment of the perception that the history of music is primarily concerned with a teleological development of polyphonic composition. Looking beyond this limited perspective brings a much wider repertoire into view, including instrumental music, humanistic compositions, monophonic music for the liturgy, private devotions, or the dissemination of news or political propaganda. Once we cease to restrict ourselves to polyphony and allow for a broader understanding of musical production, it becomes clear that Germany actually played an important role in the development of music printing. The first known music book printed from movable type is an impressive folio gradual, printed somewhere near Constance in around 1473. The fact that so few details about the edition can be determined with certainty – the identity of the printer, the exact place of printing, and the precise date – should not diminish the importance of this event in German cultural and technical history. Moreover, there is a direct link between the workshops of Gutenberg and Peter Schöffer the Younger, a pioneer in early music printing whose music editions demonstrate a high level of technical proficiency and aesthetic sensitivity.[12]

Any further investigation of music printing in German-speaking lands has to be grounded in a thorough bibliographic survey of all publications including musical notation, a task undertaken by the *vdm* team, as will be described below. However, both in the collection of data as well as in the scholarly work arising from it, such as the articles in this volume, recent developments in book history have to be taken into account. This concerns, first of all, the discipline of bibliography itself. A heightened emphasis on distinguishing editions and different states of editions on the basis of seemingly small details has led to increased accuracy and brought an astonishing number of new editions to light.[13] Until quite recently, many bibliographies, including RISM, failed to distinguish multiple editions of the same book produced by the same printer in the same year. Complete collations, page measurements and accurate and complete transcriptions of title pages and colophons represent a necessary first step in distinguishing editions inadvertently conflated in earlier catalogues.[14] Accordingly, *vdm* provides data on these markers of identity, as far as they can be ascertained, and gives a diplomatic transcription of title page and colophon as accurately as the UNICODE character set will allow. Once the data is collected, they can be analysed in different ways to reveal various synchronic, diachronic, and geographical patterns,[15] as illustrated in Andrea Lindmayr-Brandl's chapter in the present book.

---

11 Burckhardt, *Die Cultur der Renaissance*; Symonds, *Renaissance in Italy*.
12 Lindmayr-Brandl, 'Peter Schöffer der Jüngere'.
13 Dane, *What Is a Book?*
14 Undorf, 'The Idea(l) of the Ideal Copy'. See also Lindmayr-Brandl, 'Identity'.
15 See Moretti, *Distant Reading*.

Going beyond the data, the bibliographical entity, the published book or sheet, is now understood as part of a network of influences that can be simplified to a triangle involving the producers, the text, and the reader or consumer of (music) books.[16] The processes involved in the production of a musical source have received considerable attention in recent years. In the study of music books, for example, the project on the Production and Reading of Music Sources (PRoMS) has analysed the decisions involved in designing a page, including layout, decoration, and the scribes (or types) of music.[17] Crucially, this project examined both manuscripts and printed books, highlighting the fluidity between these different media.[18] On the other hand, readers and users of music books have recently received more scholarly attention than ever before. Building on the work of book historians, Kate van Orden has examined readers and social contexts of individual copies of French chanson books.[19] Examination of early inventories, publishers' catalogues, library catalogues and bibliographies has revealed the titles of several editions that no longer exist – always a bittersweet discovery. Early catalogues are especially useful where large historical collections containing unique collections of regionally specific material – for example the old municipal library of Strasbourg or the university libraries of Utrecht or Breslau (Wrocław) – have been partially or completely destroyed or dispersed. They also reveal that earlier readers sometimes conceptualised items that we lump together as 'music books' in different ways, for example under the rubrics of *poetica*, *grammatica* or *liturgica*. Such conceptualisation can sometimes be inferred indirectly. For example, a collector's decision to unite several titles in a single binding can tell us much about the way they categorised the content of each title. Unfortunately, many composite collector's volumes were broken up in the nineteenth and twentieth centuries, and the individual titles rebound separately.

The project 'Early music printing in German-speaking lands'

In autumn 2012 we set out to remedy the relative lack of attention to German music printing with the project 'Early music printing in German-speaking lands: studies in technical and repertoire development,' funded by the Austrian Science Foundation (FWF). This three-year project focused on the first four decades of the sixteenth century (from 1501 to 1540). This period is of interest due to three events. First, a technical shift in the printing of music, from double impression to single impression, that took place in the 1530s, stimulated the market for printed music dramatically. Second, this period saw the beginning and first climax of the Reformation, in which printing was used as an important means for spreading political and theological propaganda. And third, this was the period when polyphonic music was first printed.[21]

---

16 Lewis Hammond, *Editing Music*. Herz, 'Ein neu aufgefundener Geschäftsvertrag'.

17 Thomas Schmidt, *PRoMS. The Production and Reading of Music Sources. Mise-en-page in manuscripts and printed books containing polyphonic music, 1480–1530*. Online database www.proms.ac.uk.

18 McKitterick, *Print, Manuscript and the Search for Order*.

19 Van Orden, *Materialities*.

20 The team of the FWF project P24075–G23 comprised the authors of this chapter and the editors of this book: Andrea Lindmayr-Brandl (project leader), Elisabeth Giselbrecht, and Grantley McDonald (project workers).

21 A follow-up project extends the time span forwards to the middle of the sixteenth century, and backwards to the beginning of music printing in the 1470s, to cover the first eighty years of music printing in German-speaking lands. The workers on this new project, 'Music printing in German-speaking lands: From the 1470s to the mid-sixteenth century' (P28353–G26), are Marianne Gillion, Moritz Kelber, and Grantley McDonald.

The geographical limits of the project are somewhat flexible. It covers not only modern-day Germany, Austria, and German-speaking Switzerland, but also border territories that now lie outside these modern countries. In the north, we included Low German-speaking areas, but not Dutch-speaking ones. In the east, we included Silesia as well as individual locations where there was a large German-speaking community, such as Lanškroun/Landskron (Bohemia) and Moravské Vlkovice/Fulnek (Moravia). To the west, we included Strasbourg. We cite editions from Kraków (where German was then one of the official administrative languages) only when a given book contains German text. While mindful of modern-day political sensitivities, we included these border areas in acknowledgement of the widespread use of German in the sixteenth century across the familiar borders of our time.

A distinctive feature of the project is its focus on the technical challenges of printing musical notation. Unlike other studies that focus on a specific musical genre, a music printer or a printing centre, we examine all kinds of sources containing printed musical notation: theoretical and pedagogical books containing musical examples, broadsheets and pamphlets with music, liturgical books, tablatures for all kinds of instruments, polyphonic music, hymn books, humanistic dramas with musical choruses, and so on. This broad approach provides a new and comprehensive insight into the varieties of musical production during this period, and leads to a better understanding of the influence and role of music printing in cultural history. Furthermore, our project is driven by a special interest in the history of the technology of a new media as well as in the materiality of individual printed objects.

The database *vdm*

To this point, the main obstacle to a study of this breadth has been the lack of bibliographical control over the relevant sources. To organise these different kinds of objects, we established the database *vdm* (*Verzeichnis deutscher Musikfrühdrucke/Catalogue of early German printed music*).[22] This open-access online database, which is constantly being updated, provides detailed information about each known edition. These data are intended to serve as a starting point for further research. Each entry provides basic information, brought together from various bibliographies and corrected through the examination of individual copies in original or reproduction. Moreover, it records additional bibliographical data, specific typographical features and detailed descriptions of the exemplars inspected. The *vdm* is constructed as a relational database on two levels: the main entry for each edition, based on an autopsy copy; and a detailed description of the individual copies as discrete material objects. Both levels are linked to each other, as well as to other items on the same level if there is a relationship between them, for example between different editions of the same work, or between individual copies bound together.[23]

---

22 The database can be found on the homepage of the project: www.vdm.sbg.ac.at. The siglum *vdm* indicates the close relationship to *VD16* (*Verzeichnis der im deutschen Sprachbereich erschienenen Drucke des 16. Jahrhunderts*), a retrospective national bibliography of German books printed between 1501 and 1600: www.gateway-bayern.de/index_vd16.html.

23 A relationship might consist for instance between earlier and later editions of the same work in the title level, or between different copies bound together in the copy level. The central relationship, however, is that between title and copies. Each copy can only be related to one title. The sum of all physical objects – individual exemplars of one edition – make up a title. See Figure 1 at Lindmayr-Brandl, 'Identity'.

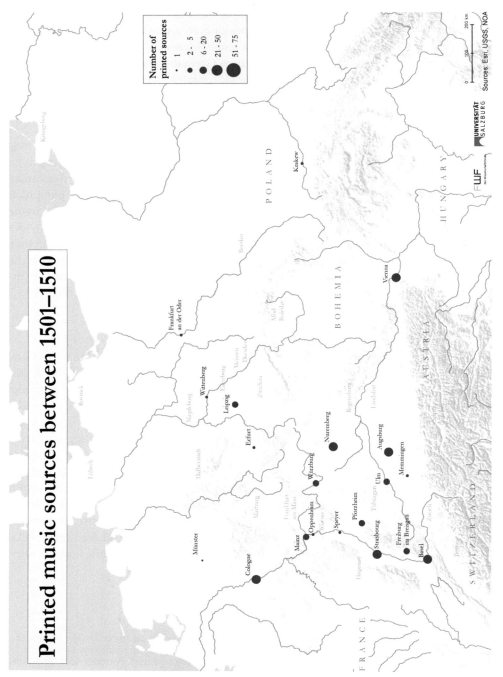

Figure I.1 Geographical distribution of sources

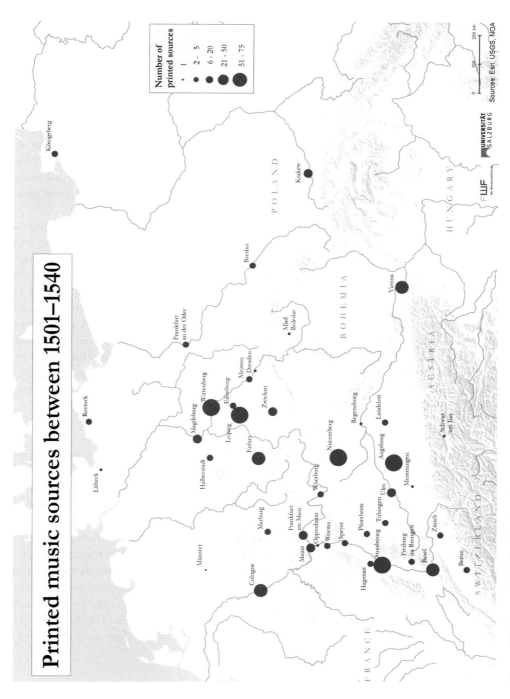

Figure I.2 Geographical distribution of sources

Mapping print production

This database also has additional features intended to serve as the starting point for further investigations. One of these is a tool to visualise the distribution of locations in the German-speaking lands where music was printed. Since there are too many items to gain a reliable impression of the geographical dispersion of the items from a simple data enquiry, we have developed a cartographic visualisation tool that displays printing centres on a map of the German-speaking area, with a visual indication of the cumulative number of editions printed in each place, indexed decade by decade. This map lacks political borders but displays rivers as the central trade routes. The cities are represented by circles of different sizes that represent the number of editions produced there (see Figure I.1). A visualisation of the output of music printing in the first decade of the sixteenth century shows clearly that the centre of this activity lay in the southwestern corner of the German-speaking territories, spreading along the Rhine and the Danube. Most of the cities where music was printed, such as Mainz, Strasbourg, Basel or Augsburg, already had a tradition of book printing. In relation to this central area, Cologne, Leipzig and Vienna seem like outposts.

Thirty years later, the map looks quite different (see Figure I.2). The number of editions produced in the existing print centres has grown considerably; Strasbourg, Augsburg and Nuremberg have developed remarkably. Moreover, there are also new cities on the map. The musical output of these new cities is mainly a result of the beginning of the Lutheran Reformation, centred at first in Saxony. The principal centres for printing related to the Reformation were Wittenberg and Leipzig. The new cities outside that circle produced only a few prints containing music: German hymn books or local church regulations (*Agenda* or *Kirchenämter*) for the newly established confessions. This is the case at Lübeck, Rostock, Königsberg, Breslau and Mladá Boleslav (Jungbunzlau), the centre of the Moravian Brethren (*Unitas Fratrum*). Vienna and Cologne, where the old church remained strong, did not share in the increase in printed music caused by the Reformation, even if they produced many polemical titles intended to discredit the Reformation.[24]

Distribution of source types

Another aspect that can be derived from the database is the distribution of source types during the first four decades in the sixteenth century. As already mentioned, the project does not concentrate on printed polyphonic music, but on all sources containing printed musical notation, regardless of their content. The items are sorted into eight distinct source types (see Figure I.3).

Calculated solely according to the numbers of titles containing printed music, the largest group—a third of the total number of titles in the database—comprises liturgical books, both Roman Catholic and Protestant. This is not only the most comprehensive group but also the most diverse. The books in this group vary greatly in their content and formats, ranging from large missals, graduals, and antiphoners in folio, to agendas and processionals in quarto, as well as even smaller breviaries and Lutheran church orders. The theory books make up the second largest group, comprising 19 per cent of titles. (Here we include only

---

24 To this point the various kinds of sources are depicted in increments of ten years. We aim to develop this program in a way that users can select the parameters 'type of source', 'printing technique' and 'format' as well as a given time span, in order to have a structured graphic overview of the editions of his research interest. The program can produce short animations to visualise changes of output over time. This tool will be integrated in our homepage for open access.

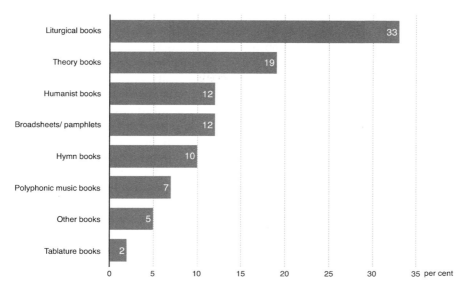

Figure I.3 Distribution of source types as a percentage of the total production between 1501 and 1540
Source: based on the data collected in the *vdm* database, 12 August 2016

books that contain musical notation, and exclude those that consist only of text.) This source type is dominated by pedagogical books that were produced for the newly established Latin schools in Protestant areas. Many of these titles were reprinted several times. The next largest groups, each with approximately equal numbers of titles, comprise humanist books on one hand, and broadsheets and pamphlets on the other. Each of these groups represents a 12 per cent share of the overall number of titles. Humanist books are mainly textbooks containing ode-settings or dramatic choruses within a play. Broadsheets and pamphlets form a discrete group because of their specific manner of production: both kinds of sources were printed on a single sheet of paper and sold either as a single broadsheet, usually printed on one side only, or as a small booklet of one gathering, printed on both sides of the sheet. The musical content of this source type is varied. It could be a monophonic or polyphonic song, sacred or secular, a devotional song or a hymn. In a few cases we even find polyphonic motets printed in this form. Hymn books, which first appear in 1524, represent 10 per cent of the editions. They are typically smaller items, often in octavo format, and contain monophonic German songs for the evangelical liturgy as well as for private religious gatherings. The fact that polyphonic music books do not exceed 7 per cent of the total number of titles is one of the most surprising insights of this project; the implications of this finding are explored in Andrea Lindmayr-Brandl's contribution in this volume. Most of these polyphonic books are in partbook format, and most were produced in the last decade of the period under consideration. The smallest group, at 2 per cent, or ten titles in absolute numbers, comprises tablature books, containing notation specific to stringed or keyboard instruments. The remaining books that cannot be sorted into one of the other categories are subsumed in the category of 'other books'. Here we find for example non-musical books that nevertheless contain musical notation as part of an illustrative title woodcut, or religious works, such as devotional books or theological treatises, that include musical notation.

From manuscript to print

Printed music differed from music transmitted in manuscript or orally in several ways. It is now widely accepted that all three forms of dissemination coexisted for decades. The 'switch' from manuscript to print happened very gradually, and was neither as complete nor as absolute as Elizabeth Eisenstein posited.[25] Nevertheless, the introduction of printing from moveable type did bring some significant changes. Most obviously, it permitted the production of multiple identical (or near-identical) copies of the same piece or group of pieces. This multiplication of copies greatly assisted both in the establishment of an international musical style in the sixteenth century, and in the dissemination of regionally specific styles over a broader geographic range than possible before. Next, it enabled the imposition of a uniform, authoritative and approved musical text. This was not only useful in the case of liturgical chant, but was also a precondition for the growing consciousness of individual compositions as musical works, carefully worked out by the composer to be preserved for posterity. In a letter of commendation printed at the outset of Arnolt Schlick's *Tabulaturen Etlicher lobgesang vnd lidlein* (1512), whose title-page proudly announces that it was printed at Mainz, the 'original home of printing', Schlick's son rejoiced that the press allowed authors to set out their knowledge to a hitherto unimagined public, and thus to achieve a kind of apotheosis of the faculty of reasoned discourse that separates humans from irrational animals, who merely follow their lower instincts and perish without a word. 'What is your art (*kunst*) if nobody knows what you can do (*kanst*),' Schlick's son asks pointedly.[26] Such a consciousness of the importance of the durability of the musical work, even after the author's death, is a central feature of the notion of *musica poetica*, first articulated in Nicolaus Listenius' *Musica* (Wittenberg: Rhau, 1533), which would become an important feature of German music theory, well into the seventeenth century.

Print also allowed for the cheap and easy production of ephemeral works that treated topical issues and were addressed to a broad audience, but that were not intended to be archived for later reference. The collecting habits of some early owners have fortunately preserved tantalising traces of such ephemeral editions, most of which were printed on single sheets, either as full-size broadsheets or folded as single-quire pamphlets. Some of these sources contain music that would otherwise be lost – often occasional or devotional songs. Many printed copies were adapted according their users' needs and expectations, in ways familiar from manuscript culture. Many users annotated or corrected their copies of musical editions, added chant to empty stafflines, or appended entire pieces. In such ways, individual copies of musical editions became personalised and distinguished from other 'identical' copies. Such alterations provide much valuable information about the ways in which these sources were perceived and used by their first owners.

Martin Luther was the first author to realise the full potential of the printing press to spread his message rapidly across the Holy Roman Empire and beyond. The Reformation also inspired a burst of musical creativity to meet the liturgical needs of the new rites. Music was also used to commemorate various events associated with the Reformation, such as the burning of the Lutheran sympathisers Hendrik Vos and Jan van Esschen at Brussels in 1523 (Luther's song *Ein neues Lied wir heben an*), or several musical pieces commemorating or criticising events in Luther's own life, as Grantley McDonald describes in his chapter. In such cases, music is not merely decorative, but serves a serious propagandistic aim.

---

25 Eisenstein, *Printing Press*.
26 See Lindmayr-Brandl, 'Peter Schöffer der Jüngere', 294.

Early printing techniques

Once a printer has decided to publish a certain œuvre, he (or in some cases she) had to decide how to realise this technically. How was the notation to be printed? Was it worth investing in a specific music font? Was it worth risking multiple runs of the same sheet through the press, or was a single impression less likely to result in misalignment and waste? Our work on the database and the articles presented in this volume shed new light on the technical aspects of printing music in the early sixteenth century. The database provided us with a way of seeing the 'bigger picture': the distribution of the different printing techniques and their development over time, as well as the general trends in printing different kinds of sources containing notation. At the same time, detailed examination of individual publications reminded us time and time again that no development is linear, and that individual printers found many different solutions to the same problem at hand. These findings are confirmed and illustrated in the chapters in this volume.

During the first decades of music printing, printers settled on two main solutions to the question of how to print staves and notes in the same space on the page: printing from woodblock and printing in multiple impressions. These two techniques were used simultaneously, as is clear from a search of *vdm*. Of the titles printed between 1501 and 1540 that we have examined to date, 328 were printed from woodblock, while 123 used multiple impression.[27] Each technique is associated particularly with certain types of publications: woodcut is used in particular for books of music theory, humanist books and ephemeral publications such as broadsheets; double impression is typically found in large liturgical books. Curiously, no German printer during this period used intaglio technique (engraving on metal plates, usually copper) to print music, even though this technique was well established for the production of graphic works, and brought to a high level of technical perfection during the later fifteenth century by artists such as Martin Schongauer and Israhel van Meckenem. The failure to take up this technical solution may be explained by the fact that printing engraved plates requires a high-pressure rolling press, a specialised piece of equipment that was not present in many print shops.

The printing of music from woodcut must be understood in the context of the printing of other visual material from the same medium. It made no real difference to the cutter whether he was dealing with music, diagrams or pictures. In fact, cutting musical notation required no specific musical knowledge. Researching music printed from woodcut throws up its own sets of questions. One of the most intriguing is the relationship of different woodcuts to each other. When printers re-issued books containing musical woodcuts, did they reuse the original woodcuts? Did they have the *Formschneider* cut new blocks to resemble the originals, or did they design and cut new blocks from scratch? The genre of didactic music books presents us with a particularly rewarding pool of material, as they were frequently published in multiple editions over many years, even over decades. The use of diagrams in music pedagogy is further explored in Inga Mai Groote's chapter.

A fascinating example is provided by the multiple editions of Andreas Ornitoparchus' music theory treatise. The first edition appeared in Leipzig in 1517 and contains several woodcuts, including some images printed in reverse (white lines on black background), such as a diagram of note values.[28] There was no musical reason to print these particular images in white-line rather than in the more standard black-line printing. Admittedly, it

---

27 Data taken on 13 September 2016.
28 *Musicae activae micrologus* (Leipzig: Valentin Schumann, 1517), vdm 506.

12 ANDREA LINDMAYR-BRANDL *ET AL.*

is much faster to produce white-line blocks than the more commonly used black-line ones; only the lines and notes have to be cut out of the block, whereas a black-line block requires all the white space to be removed, leaving only the lines and notes remaining on the woodblock. However, white-line blocks require much more ink and make for a messier result, which probably explains why this reverse technique was used relatively rarely.[29] The woodcuts in the second edition of Ornitoparchus' treatise, produced in 1519 by the same printer, Valentin Schumann, are printed from the same blocks.[30] Fourteen years later, in 1533, Johannes Gymnich in Cologne published an edition of this detailed and apparently popular book of music theory.[31] There we find the same woodcut images, including those printed in reverse. At first glance one might assume that Gymnich used the same woodblocks, but closer examination reveals that the blocks were actually re-cut very faithfully. Although there was no need to retain the reverse printing for the new edition, Gymnich either wished to stay close to the 'original' publication, or his block-cutter saw no need to vary from his model.

The story of re-cutting does not end there for this particular book: even when Ornitoparchus' treatise was republished in London in 1609 – translated into English by none other than John Dowland – the printer kept very close to the original edition.[32] The block-cutters probably had no knowledge of music, and often copied the same mistakes over many decades. And even though Dowland took great care to translate the text in this book, he did not update, change or correct the music examples. Once again the reverse printing is repeated in this edition, more than ninety years after the book was first published.

Printers could also print music from moveable type, in single or multiple impressions. The very first music printed from moveable type employed a multiple impression technique. A printer who wished to use the multiple-impression technique needed to take three factors into account: finding a way to print musical staff lines, cutting or acquiring a music font for the notes, and mastering the perfect superimposition of the second print run onto the first.

For the first requirement the solution seems to have been quite unproblematic, as printers had already printed straight lines for other publications. The results vary significantly, even in the work of individual printers, as can for example be seen in the work of Melchior Lotter, the focus of Elisabeth Giselbrecht's contribution to this book. The staff system could be printed by woodblocks, by shorter segments of type bearing four or five lines, or by long individual metal strips held together to create a complete staff. Cutting shorter segments of staff lines was a challenge if the printer wished to avoid gaps between the individual segments.

Acquiring music type could be a bigger challenge. On one hand, some of the earliest entrepreneurs, such as Erhard Ratdolt, did not have access to punchcutters with the relevant experience. On the other hand, a printer needed to be able to justify the outlay on such an

---

29 There are other examples, however, where use of white-line printing enhances the readability of the book. An example is a little-known edition of *Geistliche Lieder auffs new gebessert*, probably printed by Wolfgang Stürmer in Erfurt around 1540. It uses white-line and black-line woodblocks in turns to show the antiphonal performance of a litany. See *Geistliche Lieder auffs new gebessert* ([Erfurt]: [Wolfgang Stürmer], [c.1539–1540]), vdm 459. As the unique copy of this publication survives incomplete in D-B and without a colophon, precise publication details cannot be supplied. This aspect of early music printing will be explored further by Elisabeth Giselbrecht in an article currently in progress.

30 *Musicae activae micrologus* (Leipzig: Valentin Schumann, 1519), vdm 505.

31 In between a further edition was printed by Hero Fuchs in Cologne (vdm 528), which was not inspected in the preparation of this article. Gymnich also printed a second edition in 1535 (vdm 504).

32 Scans of the different editions can be found through IMSLP.

INTRODUCTION   13

investment, if a project requiring music type was not sponsored by a strong patron, a topic Mary Kay Duggan explores further in her chapter. Especially after the introduction of single-impression type, some printers began to purchase music fonts from others, even from different geographical areas, as Laurent Guillo shows in his contribution.

Finally, printers had to master the technical challenge of printing the music on top of the staff (or in some cases the other way round). In theory this should not have been too difficult, as superimposition was a technique that early printers practised when printing other kinds of material, as Elizabeth Savage and Elisabeth Giselbrecht describe in their chapter. In practice, however, solutions to this problem varied widely, and so did levels of success.

The first printers to use movable type needed to master these same three steps, whether printing chant or mensural music, yet the almost exclusive focus on the printing of mensural music in the previous literature has largely obscured the fact that printers had already solved the most important technical challenges of printing polyphony when trying to work out how to print chant. And although printers of mensural music from double impression have been the object of research for many years, our project has managed to add some new names to the list.[33] One of these is Simprecht Ruff of Augsburg, who printed a hitherto largely unknown edition of ode settings in 1526.[34] In her contribution, Sonja Tröster describes this printer's place in the context of a group of related publications.

The move from double- to single-impression printing is generally associated with Pierre Attaingnant in Paris in the 1530s. Although it did not replace woodcut printing, single-impression soon became the printing method of choice for mensural publications in German-speaking areas. The benefits of this technique are obvious and the downsides few: since each sort (piece of type) contains a full segment of staff as well as a note, rest, accidental or clef, printers no longer needed to pass the paper through the press in multiple runs. Music could now be set just like text. The obvious benefit of reducing the time and thus cost of production, even at the expense of aesthetic effect, was a major consideration for printers or indeed any business-minded craftsman, as will be explored further below in the case of Egenolff. Admittedly the appearance of music printed in single impression is often much messier than that printed in double impression, sometimes with gaps between the individual pieces, or a lack of alignment between the segments of staff on each sort. Particularly from the middle of the sixteenth century, the alignment of staves in many publications is quite uneven, which can even affect the readability of the music. Such gaps could be avoided, or at least minimised, by using the technique of 'nesting', in which a single sort contains a note (or rest, or clef, or some other notational detail) as well as between zero to five staff lines. The compositor then 'nested' these sorts into complete staves, filling in blank spaces with empty lines that ran the length of several sorts.[35] This technical solution, used by printers such as Johann Petreius to print polyphony from 1537 onwards, was first used by the Viennese printer Johann Winterburger to print chant, as in his *Graduale Pataviense* (1511). Melchior Lotter the Elder later used this technique in Ulrich Burchardi's *Hortulus Musices* (c.1514) to print staff lines, over which he then printed chant neumes in a second impression.

Stanley Boorman has shown that the spread of the single-impression technique was preceded by a use of individual sorts containing four staff-lines and a single neume that

---

33 A detailed documentation of the new printers is in preparation by Andrea Lindmayr-Brandl.
34 *De partium orationis inflexionibus compendium* ([Augsburg]: [Simprecht Ruff]), 1526, vdm 137.
35 For a fuller discussion, see McDonald, 'Printing Hofhaimer'.

were embedded in missals otherwise printed from double impression, as seen in Johann Winterburger's 1510 Vienna edition of the *Missale Salisburgense*. This composite single-/multiple-impression technique allowed Winterburger to render chant in two different versions simultaneously: in the regular, ferial form in which the singers performed only the notes printed in black, and in a more elaborate festal form, with optional notes suitable for more important feasts printed in red.[36] Work on the *vdm* database brought to light another use of this technique. We found several publications from the 1510s onwards that include instructions for the correct enunciation of Latin (and some Greek) texts. In some of these, such as the editions of Johannes Cochlaeus' *Grammatica* printed by Reinhard Beck at Strasbourg, the printer used musical notation to indicate long and short syllables in verse. In the many editions of Melanchthon's *Grammatica graeca*, the printers used musical notation to indicate the speech melody inherent to Latin and Greek. In another work, the *Exemplar in modum accentuandi* (1513), Winterburger used musical notation to indicate relative pitch of stressed and unstressed syllables when intoning lessons during the liturgy.[37] Here, Winterburger had a special sort cut that comprised a single staff line and a single punctum, less than 2 mm high, that could be turned either way to indicate a relatively high or low pitch. The musical sorts were placed above the text, which was itself set in a smaller text font, giving a combined body-height that was probably the same as that of Winterburger's main text font in this section. These three fonts (the main text type, the small text type and the musical sorts) were printed simultaneously in a single impression. Such cases represent the first examples of single-impression music printing, which was developed later under different circumstances.

Motivations and risks

Printers had many motivations to undertake the risks inherent in printing a book. For risks there were, and misjudging the market too often could easily lead to bankruptcy. Gutenberg was not only the first person to print a book from movable type; he was also the first person to go broke from the attempt. Among the very few printers who managed to make their fortunes from printing in the first century was Christian Egenolff. As the contributions of Royston Gustavson and John Kmetz show, his recipe for success was simple. The first element was maintaining a diverse catalogue. The historiographical focus hitherto on the 'great' music printers such as Petrucci, Attaingnant or Gardano has unwittingly created the misleading impression that printers in the sixteenth century who produced music books were usually specialists. In the German-speaking lands, this was far from the case. As already mentioned, music was far from being a dominant element in the catalogues of early German printers. Rather, it was part – indeed, a relatively small part – of a diverse portfolio that contained books for the professions of theology, law and medicine, literary works, vernacular vademecums in all kinds of subjects for popular consumption, occasional pamphlets and official ordinances. As John Kmetz has often repeated, the market for printed music was small and limited by several features.[38] A diversified catalogue was a way of spreading risk.

---

36 Boorman, 'Salzburg liturgy'.

37 *Exemplar in modum accentuandi secundum ritum chori ecclesiae Pataviensis* (Vienna: Johann Winterburger, 1513), vdm 636.

38 See Kmetz, 'Closed Market'.

The second element of Egenolff's winning formula was reprinting books that other printers had been able to sell successfully – even where this meant infringing on the privileges of other printers – and doing so as efficiently and cheaply as possible. Often this concern for economy involved shrinking the format of the originals. Egenolff's tiny songbooks in sedecimo format illustrate his ability to keep costs down by manipulating format. These tiny books were also a novelty, not only affordable but also fun to use, highly portable and easily lost: bad for the owner, but good for the bookseller.

Yet risk could also be distributed elsewhere along the chain of production. Mary Kay Duggan explores several cases in which bishops employed printers directly to print liturgical books, some of which contained music. The printers sometimes moved their workshop temporarily to the bishop's see, in some cases even within his palace, to facilitate the constant communication necessary to ensure that the final product corresponded to the patron's specifications. In many such cases, the edition was usually funded by the bishop to ensure a uniformity of liturgical practice within his diocese. In such cases, the printer ran little financial risk except the potential opportunity cost of losing other jobs. In other cases, such as that of Hans Ott of Nuremberg, the publisher was a capitalist who wished to make money by paying a printer (and in some cases an editor, if he did not possess the necessary skills himself) to produce a certain number of copies on his behalf, which he then planned to sell at a profit. Here, there was a risk that the printer would pull off a few more copies to sell on the side; in the case of Ott, such eventualities were forbidden expressly in the contract, as Royston Gustavon has shown. Risk could also be shared by creating a partnership with other printers. In her chapter, Margarita Restrepo explores the shifting dynamics of a group of German printers active in Spain in the fifteenth century, whose configuration changed over time as members of the group integrated into their new setting or moved on.

In other cases, printers took on the full financial burden of producing a musical edition, in the expectation of retaining all profits generated; in such cases, the roles of printer and publisher are united in one person. The printing of liturgical books was limited by local variations in the liturgy from diocese to diocese. Such variations were particularly acute in the case of propers for local saints. A liturgical book produced for one diocese might not be right for another. The printers Johann Prüss the Elder in Strasbourg and Johann Winterburger in Vienna solved this problem by producing large chant books that contained chants from several dioceses, which could be marketed more widely.[39]

As risk could be distributed along the chain of production, so too was the creation and exchange of value. Funding an edition attracted reputational value to the patron. Purchasing a copy of a printed music book converted cash into value of other kinds.[40] Acquiring printed music might enable the user to perform a liturgical act as was expected of him, to engage in an act of private religious devotion, to acquire cultural capital by mastering musical theory and skills, either alone or in a classroom setting, or to strengthen social bonds by participating in an enjoyable shared activity. The value of printed music should thus not be calculated simply by how much it cost. Assessment of its value must also consider what it made possible.

---

39 On Winterburger, see Merlin, 'Winterburger Antiphonar'.
40 See Gustavson, 'Competitive Strategy Dynamics'.

References

Agee, Richard J. *The Gardano Music Printing Firms, 1569–1611*. Eastman Studies in Music. Rochester: University of Rochester Press, 1998.

Bernstein, Jane A. *Music Printing in Renaissance Venice: The Scotto Press (1539–1572)*. Oxford: Oxford University Press, 1998.

Bernstein, Jane A. *Print Culture and Music in Sixteenth-Century Venice*. New York: Oxford University Press, 2001.

Boorman, Stanley. 'The Salzburg Liturgy and Single-Impression Music Printing'. In *Music in the German Renaissance*, edited by John Kmetz. Cambridge: Cambridge University Press, 1994, 235–253.

Boorman, Stanley. *Ottaviano Petrucci: Catalogue Raisonné*. Oxford: Oxford University Press, 2006.

Burckhardt, Jacob. *Die Cultur der Renaissance in Italien: ein Versuch*. Basel: Schweighauser, 1860.

Chapman, Catherine. 'Andrea Antico'. PhD dissertation, Harvard University, 1964.

Cusick, Suzanne G. *Valerio Dorico: Music Printer in Sixteenth-Century Rome*. Studies in Musicology 43. Ann Arbor, MI: UMI Research Press, 1981.

Dane, Joseph A. *What Is a Book? The Study of Early Printed Books*. Notre Dame, IN: University of Notre Dame Press, 2012.

Duggan, Mary Kay. *Italian Music Incunabula: Printers and Type*. Berkeley, CA: University of California Press, 1992.

Eisenstein, Elizabeth L. *The Printing Press as an Agent of Change: Communications and Cultural Transformations in Early Modern Europe*. Cambridge: Cambridge University Press, 1979.

Fenlon, Iain. *Music, Print and Culture in Early Sixteenth-Century Italy*. (The Panizzi Lectures 1994). London: British Library, 1995.

Forney, Kristine. 'Tielman Susato, Sixteenth-Century Music Printer: an Archival and Typographical Investigation'. PhD dissertation, University of Kentucky, 1978.

Gustavson, Royston Robert. 'Hans Ott, Hieronymus Formschneider, and the "Novum et insigne opus musicum" (Nuremberg, 1537–1538)'. PhD dissertation, University of Melbourne, 1998.

Gustavson, Royston. 'Competitive Strategy Dynamics in the German Music Publishing Industry 1530–1550'. In *NiveauNischeNimbus: 500 Jahre Musikdruck nördlich der Alpen*, edited by Birgit Lodes. Wiener Forum für ältere Musikgeschichte 3. Tutzing: Hans Schneider, 2010, 185–210.

Heartz, Daniel. *Pierre Attaingnant. Royal Printer of Music. A Historical Study and Bibliographical Catalogue*. Berkeley, CA: University of California Press, 1969.

Herz, Randall. 'Ein neu aufgefundener Geschäftsvertrag zwischen Sebald Schreyer und Johann Sensenschmidt über den Druck von 21 Bamberger Missalien auf Pergament'. *Archiv für Geschichte des Buchwesens* 68 (2013): 1–45.

Kmetz, John. '250 Years of German Music Print (c.1500–1750): A Case for a Closed Market'. In *NiveauNischeNimbus: Die Anfänge des Musikdrucks nördlich der Alpen*, edited by Birgit Lodes. Wiener Forum für ältere Musikgeschichte 3. Tutzing: Hans Schneider, 2006, 167–184.

Lewis, Mary S. *Antonio Gardano, Venetian Music Printer 1538–1569: A Descriptive Bibliography and Historical Study*. New York: Routledge, 1988–1997.

Lewis Hammond, Susan. *Editing Music in Early Modern Germany*. Aldershot: Ashgate, 2007.

Lindmayr-Brandl, Andrea. 'Early Music Prints and New Technology: Variants and Variant Editions'. *Fontes artis musicae* 64 (2017): 244–260.

Lindmayr-Brandl, Andrea. 'Peter Schöffer der Jüngere, das Erbe Gutenbergs und "die wahre Art des Druckens"'. In *NiveauNischeNimbus: Die Anfänge des Musikdrucks nördlich der Alpen*, edited by Birgit Lodes. Wiener Forum für ältere Musikgeschichte 3. Tutzing: Hans Schneider, 2010, 283–312.

Lodes, Birgit, ed. *NiveauNischeNimbus. Die Anfänge des Musikdrucks nördlich der Alpen.* Wiener Forum für ältere Musikgeschichte 3. Tutzing: Hans Schneider, 2010.

Lodes, Birgit. 'An anderem Ort, auf andere Art: Petruccis und Mewes' Obrecht-Drucke'. *Basler Jahrbuch für Historische Musikpraxis* 25 (2002): 85–111.

Lodes, Birgit. 'Gregor Mewes' "Concentus harmonici" und die letzten Messen Jacob Obrechts'. Habilitationsschrift, Universität München, 2002.

McDonald, Grantley. 'Printing Hofhaimer: a Case Study'. *Journal of the Alamire Foundation* 7 (2015): 67–79.

McKitterick, David. *Print, Manuscript and the Search for Order, 1450–1830.* Cambridge: Cambridge University Press, 2003.

Meissner, Ute. *Der Antwerpener Notendrucker Tylman Susato. Eine bibliographische Studie zur niederländischen Chansonpublikation in der ersten Hälfte des 16. Jahrhunderts.* Berliner Studien zur Musikwissenschaft 11. Berlin: Merseburger, 1967.

Merlin, David. 'Das von Johannes Winterburger gedruckte Antiphonar aus dem Jahr 1519: ein Antiphonale Pataviense?' In *Cantus Planus: Papers read at the 16th meeting, Vienna Austria 2011.* Vienna: Österreichische Akademie der Wissenschaften, 2012, 267–275.

Moretti, Franco. *Distant Reading.* London: Verso, 2013.

Pogue, Samuel. *Jacques Moderne: Lyons Music Printer of the Sixteenth Century.* Geneva: Droz, 1969.

Schmid, Anton. *Ottaviano dei Petrucci da Fossombrone, der erste Erfinder des Musiknotendruckes mit beweglichen Metalltypen, und seine Nachfolger im sechzehnten Jahrhunderte. Mit steter Rücksicht auf die vorzüglichsten Leistungen derselben, und auf die Erstlinge des Musiknotendruckes.* Vienna: Rohrmann, 1845.

Schreurs, Eugeen, and Henri Vanhulst, eds. *Music Printing in Antwerp and Europe in the 16th Century.* Yearbook of the Alamire Foundation 2, Leuven: Alamire Foundation, 1997.

Smith, Jeremy L. *Thomas East and Music Publishing in Renaissance England.* Oxford: Oxford University Press, 2003.

Symonds, John Addington. *Renaissance in Italy.* 7 vols. London: Smith, Elder, 1875–1886.

Undorf, Wolfgang. 'The Idea(l) of the Ideal Copy: Some Thoughts on Books with Multiple Identities'. In *Early Printed Books as Material Objects,* edited by Bettina Wagner and Marcia Reed. Berlin: Walter de Gruyter, 2010, 307–319.

Van Orden, Kate. *Materialities. Books, Readers, and the Chanson in Sixteenth-Century Europe.* Oxford: Oxford University Press, 2015.

Part I

Music printing and publishing in the fifteenth century

1

Early music printing and ecclesiastic patronage

Mary Kay Duggan

Printing was first established in Mainz, the seat of the archbishop who was the most important of the seven Electors of the Holy Roman Empire and head of the largest ecclesiastical province of that Empire, containing 17,000 clerics who made a perfect market for liturgical books.[1] The Council of Basel had ended in 1449 with the imperative to distribute newly reformed liturgical texts across Europe, and music was an integral part of those reformed texts. Although it appeared that the entire international church was behind the adoption of the conciliar reformed *Liber Ordinarius*, the Council of the Province of Mainz that met in 1451 voted against what was essentially a Roman liturgy, supporting instead a text offered by the archbishop of Mainz.[2] Despite the pope's threat to use military force if necessary, the council ended by sending bishops and abbots back to their homes to create unique reformed diocesan and monastic texts in a giant exercise in textual editing.[3] The publication of hundreds of editions of liturgical books – tens of thousands of copies – would have to wait.[4]

Music was in the middle of the struggle over textual orthodoxy. Every priest was required to have a missal, an enormous market for printers, and music was a necessary, if small, part of the genre, the fairly simple plainchant sung by the priest. On the other hand, choirbooks, agendas, services for the dead (*vigiliae, obsequiale*) contain melismatic chant on nearly every page, requiring complex neumes of music type designers. The crucial significance of choir music in the liturgical reform movement is demonstrated by the fact that music was first printed in choirbooks.[5] We know how the struggle for uniformity in liturgical texts ended. The international distribution of new books sought by council reformers and promised by the invention of printing would be the Roman liturgy authorised

---

1 Holy Roman Empire. Ecclesiastical Organization, c.1500. Map by Dr. Andreas Kunz. http://germanhistorydocs.ghi-dc.org/map.cfm?map_id=2814

2 Duggan, 'Politics and Text'. See also Duggan, 'Fifteenth-Century Music Printing'.

3 Budapest was said to have had its *Liber ordinarius* ready for printing in 1455. Polish canons were working on editing the text of the liturgy at Gniezno in 1433 and 1469. *Acta Capitulorum nec non Iudiciorum Ecclesiasticum*, ed. Bolesław Ulanowski, Monumenta Medii Aevi Historica Res Gestas Poloniae Illustrantia 13 (Cracow: Polska Akademia Umiejętności, 1894). As quoted in Nowakowska, *Church, State and Dynasty*, 75. In 1483 Bishop Jan Rzeszowski entrusted the Cracow breviary to the printing press, but no copy survives. See Ulewicz, *Wśród impresorów krakowskich*, 18–20.

4 Nowakowska, 'From Strassburg to Trent', lists 107 liturgical books commissioned by bishops before 1501. My own research identifies 252 liturgical books printed in German-speaking lands before 1501 of which 132 have music or space for it. I described 156 such books printed in Italy before 1501 (see Duggan, *Italian Music Incunabula*, esp. 17, Table 4.) For liturgical books printed in France, Spain, and England, see Weale, *Bibliographia Liturgica* and Bohatta, *Liturgische Bibliographie*.

5 *Graduale* [Southern Germany, about 1473], vdm 1107; *Graduale Romanum* (Parma: Damiano and Bernardo Moilli, 10 April 1477), ISTC ig00329800.

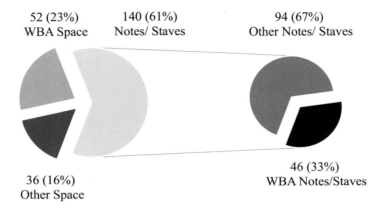

Figure 1.1 The impact of ecclesiastical patronage on incunabula of German lands with printed music or space for music. WBA = Würzburg, Bamberg, Augsburg

by the Council of Trent in the next century, but only after northerners had been allowed to see into print their regional texts and chant celebrating local saints and practices.

Bishops and abbots played a major role in bringing their reformed liturgy to print, investing large sums of money in the creation of impressive text and music types and in the printers able to compose such type. Solid evidence of relationships between ecclesiastical patrons and printers exists for liturgical printing in Würzburg and later Eichstätt with Georg and Michael Reyser, Bamberg with Johan Sensenschmidt, Steffan Arndes in Schleswig and Lübeck, and Augsburg with Erhard Ratdolt. Those printers alone published one-third of all fifteenth-century German liturgical books printed with notes and staves (46 of 140) and well over half of the liturgical books with space for music (52 of 88) (Figure 1.1).

Würzburg: Georg Reyser and Prince-Bishop Rudolf von Scherenberg

The first example of ecclesiastical sponsorship of liturgical printing is a contract for a territorial monopoly of the new technology of printing. The privilege awarded to the first printers in Würzburg by Prince-Bishop Rudolf von Scherenberg, the governing prince of his territory, just east of Mainz, is clearly described in a letter in the first book off the press, the *Breviarium Herbipolense* (after 20 September, 1479):

> The liturgical books of our Würzburg choir should be circumspectly examined, corrected, and improved with the utmost care by selected men whom we considered suitable for this task – which we have indeed found to have been carried out with utmost attentiveness – so, in order that the prelates and other priests and office holders of our city and diocese might in all future times benefit and prosper from this due correction and integral renewal of the books, we have therefore decided that nothing could be more proper and even opportune than that in accordance with the correction and improvement of the liturgical books their impression should be carried out and adapted by some outstanding masters in the art of printing. For which purpose we have come to an agreement with the following far-sighted men who are devoted to us in Christ and whom we sincerely esteem: Stephan Dold, Georg Reiser and Johannes Beckenhub, alias Mentzer – these being most experienced masters in this art – and we have brought them to our city of Würzburg on the basis of contracts and equal terms. To them alone and to no one else have we given the opportunity to print accurately and in the best possible way these liturgical books (as indicated above, including those for the choir). We have taken them and their families, their goods and chattels, under our dutiful and paternal

EARLY MUSIC PRINTING   23

protection and defense. Therefore, so that fuller faith might reveal itself to all thanks to such a printing of the books, we have ordered and allowed the master printers to decorate the canonical books which are to be printed in the manner mentioned above with the insignia of our Pontificate and Chapter.[6]

Bishop Rudolf invited Strasbourg residents Georg Reyser, Stephan Dold, and Mainz cleric Johannes Beckenhub to establish a printing shop in Würzburg, the central city within his duchy. Though Reyser had a thriving printing business in Strasbourg with his relative Michael and had acquired citizenship there in 1471, he left the town of 40,000 to move to Würzburg, a town of a few thousand, to accept a monopoly on printing with the primary goal of the production of reformed liturgical texts. There is no evidence that Reyser purchased property in Würzburg, and the terms of the contract – protection of goods and chattels – suggest that his home and printing shop were in the bishop's residence.[7] The first book to be issued in Würzburg was a folio breviary for the diocese, and Dold, Reyser and Beckenhub are listed in the colophon. The edition is dated after 20 September 1479, the date of the contract, but it is likely that it came off the press the following year.

Reyser printed thirteen editions of service books for Würzburg with two sizes of gothic plainchant type: nine missals, an agenda, a *Vigiliae mortuorum*, a gradual, and an antiphonal (see Table 1.1 in the Appendix). In addition he printed in 1482 the first missal for the diocese of Mainz. His Very Large Antiphonal type was created for the Würzburg choirbooks of the 1490s, spaciously laid out on nine staves per page (see Plate 1). The strong verticality and regularity of the neumes are proof that the bishop had made a good investment in the Strasbourg printers. Note the tightly abutting staff segments that make up the staves and the regularity of the double lines at the margins. Each of the punches for plainchant in an extant fifteenth-century set at the Plantin-Moretus Museum in Antwerp is six inches long, a size thought necessary for the large designs of a choirbook.[8] The engraver had to carve lines that extended to the very ends of the steel punch so that printed segments would abut, unlike most type characters such as the clef signs that were carved in the centre of a punch, to be surrounded by space on a piece of type.

Georg Reyser was the *Hofbuchdrucker* and as such probably wore the livery of the bishop on fine occasions, as did Gutenberg in Mainz. About one-half of his printed editions were devoted to government printing, broadsides or short pamphlets about laws and official news. His press and types would have been the property of the bishop and his work would have been done only upon the order of the bishop. Rudolph subsidised and controlled the press, and paid for the creation of two sets of music punches as well as alphabetic types of extremely fine design. Only after Rudolph's death was Georg awarded the right of citizenship by his successor, after which he printed a few songs and other works in German before his death in 1504.[9]

---

6 *Breviarium Herbipolense* ISTC ip01162400. The privilege is given in Latin, English and image in *Primary Sources on Copyright (1455–1900)*, eds L. Bently and M. Kretschmer, *www.copyrighthistory.org*, Identifier: d_1479.

7 Sigmund Freiherr von Pölnitz suggests that the printing shop was in the Hochstift within the walls of the residence, high above the city. See Chapter 5, 'Rudolf von Scherenberg. Vollendung der Reform', *Die bischöfliche Reformarbeit*, 124. Rudolph also commissioned an impressive copper engraving of himself, his arms and those of the Cathedral chapter that opened the five missals, two breviaries and an agenda, spreading the image of his authority and power in thousands of copies. Reproduced in Hubay, *Incunabula Würzburg*, Plate 11.

8 Duggan, 'Notendruck', Abb. 1.

9 The songs include *Mannslob. Ein Mannslob in der Briefweis [Lied]*, about 1500 (ISTC im00210500) and *Soffey. Historie des Grafen von Soffey (Savoy)*, about 1495 (ISTC is00612150).

Eichstätt: Michael Reyser and Prince-Bishop Wilhelm von Reichenau

Our next example is Michael Reyser, the relative of Georg who is described as the owner of the house in Strasbourg in which their printing shop was located. By 1479 Georg Reyser had moved to Würzburg to serve Rudolph. In that same year he was awarded citizenship in the duchy of Eichstätt, southeast of Würzburg. The bishop of Eichstätt commissioned Georg to print in Würzburg two breviaries for Eichstätt in 1483 and 1484.[10] But the bishop's plans for Georg seem to have changed, and Michael would move to Eichstätt instead of Georg.

Michael is not mentioned in Georg's contract with the Würzburg bishop, but we know that he was an important part of the printing operation there because of a letter written by Bishop Rudolph in 1480 (April 25) to the magistrate and city council of Strasbourg.[11] The letter requested that Michael Reyser, one of the journeymen (*Gesellen*) of the master printer Georg, be released from prison in Strasbourg because the important work of printing missals for Würzburg could not be completed without him. The following is an extract from the letter, with an approximate English translation:

Dasselbe werck [die Ordenung des gebets und der messebucher unnsers Stieffts] wir dann ettlichen personen die in Ewer Stat gesessenn sind, zu-volbringen gegonnet und dorauff bestalt die dann auch das also angefangen unnd ettlich zceythere mit Trucken gearbeyt und doch das noch biszanhere nicht zu ende haben bracht.

Nu lanngt uns durch die meistere der gemelten Truckerey in unnser Stat Wirtzburg an wie Michel Reyser der irer gesellen einer und zur Truckerey vast nutzbar sey, etlichs hanndels halbenn von euch zuverhefftigung bracht, Darnach uff einen bestalt zum Rechten ausz der gefengknuss gelassen unnd aber itzt wider doreyn gelegt wordin ist, villeicht uf die meynung gegen ime mit der tate zugebarn, das doch die Recht nicht erheischen, Dadurch wir zu volbringung unnsers furgenomen wercks [die Ordenung des gebets und der messebucher unnsers Stieffts] mangel haben.

Wann nu uns und unnserm Stiefft zu enffung des dinst gotes doran nit geringe Sundern gross und mercklichen ist gelegen wue wir durch die abwesennlichkeyt des gemelten Michels verhinderung haben Biten wir euch gar mit besundern vleiss gutlich ir wollet das furnemen das got dem Almechtigenn seiner Liebenn mütter maria und unnsern Lieben heyligen patronenn obgemelt zu Lobe unnd Ere beschiet auch unnsers Stieffts notdurfft und guttat so dorausz enstenn werden, ansehenn und den benanten Michel unns zugefallen ausz dem gefengknuss komen lassen, ine auch gegen der widerpartheye wue es die notdurfft erfordert zu Recht stellen und

We have permitted and subsequently ordered to complete the same work [The order of prayer and the missals of our foundation] certain persons resident in your city, who some time ago began to work on the printing but have not yet finished it.

Now it has been brought to our attention by the masters of the same print shop in our city of Würzburg how Michel Reyser, one of its journeymen, who is very useful to the print shop, was taken into custody at your command because of some business, was then released following a reversal of judgment, but has now been incarcerated again, perhaps because some believe that proceedings should be taken against him in a matter that the laws nevertheless do not demand. To complete the works we have undertaken [The order of prayer and missals of our foundation] we have need [of him].

Since we and our foundation are under no small responsibility, or rather under a very great and conspicuous one, of ensuring the reception of the divine service, which is impeded by the absence of the said Michel, we therefore entreat you kindly, with particular earnestness, that you consider this decision – to the praise and honour to God the Almighty, His dear mother Mary, and our above-mentioned holy patrons, and also in consideration of our foundation's plight and the benefits that would arise from this – and do us the favour of releasing the aforementioned Michel from prison, reverse the decision regarding the opposing party as

---

10 *Breviarium Eystettense*, ISTC ib01161000 and ISTC ib01161300.
11 The author thanks Prof. Elaine Tennant and Grantley McDonald for their advice on the translation. For a discussion of the letter, see Ohly, 'Der Brief des Würzburger Fürstbischofs'.

slewnigkeyt des Rechten verhelffen; wurde er nu gegen seiner widerpartheye umb obgemelte verhandelung im Rechten ichts verlußtig, das müßt er verbussen.

necessity demands and see that justice is done swiftly. If in the above-mentioned case he loses anything legally to the party opposing him, he must make that good.[12]

While we shall never know what caused Michael's imprisonment, or even why he had returned to Strasbourg, it is clear that liturgical printing in Würzburg had been halted by his absence and the bishop himself was moved to request his release. What was Michael's unique talent required for such books? Georg Reyser had already demonstrated competence in printing breviaries in Strasbourg[13] and then in Würzburg, so he would have been expert in two-colour printing in different sizes of type, but those breviaries did not include music. What is new in 1481 is the beginning of printing of liturgical books that do include music, the first of thirteen that would be issued in Würzburg. Is it possible that Michael Reyser was the music printer of the books assigned to Georg Reyser, that it was his expertise in setting music type that was required to complete the Würzburg liturgical books? Was he also the creator of the music types, cutting the designs in metal, a true music specialist? We now know from the letter written by the Würzburg bishop to get Michael out of prison that he had been working for Georg in Würzburg before April 1480, the date of the letter, and presumably during the entire period of Georg's residence in Würzburg. Apparently the bishop's plea was successful in releasing Michael to return to Würzburg to complete a trio of books with music, missals for Würzburg and Mainz, and an agenda for Würzburg. We also know that further liturgical books for Eichstätt were printed not by Georg but by Michael himself, in Eichstätt, so apparently Michael was able to secure a lucrative contract for himself in the process of being extricated from prison.

Michael's career as a printer of his own editions is known solely from those done in the service of Bishop Wilhelm of Eichstätt (1425–1496) between 1483 and 1494. His sixteen editions include the statutes of the diocese and three missals for the diocese (1486, 1489, 12 July 1494)[14] plus government broadsides and pamphlets.[15] Finally a music book, the *Obsequiale* of Eichstätt (1488),[16] was printed with music on 90 of 200 pages from a new music type (see Plate 2).

A comparison of Michael's music printing to that of Georg in his missals reveals many similarities of type designs and type composition. Both men print staves with uneven metal rules. They both print one red line at each side, placing clef and custos within those lines. The common note, the virga, is the same size and shape for both, as is the lozenge. While Georg's Large Missal type uses the custos for the F clef, Michael has a new distinctive F clef and many more designs. But the new Very Large Antiphonal Type used by Georg for his choirbooks of the 1490s with staff lines from cast metal segments is far advanced, the product of a more refined typecutter.

---

12 City Archives of Strasbourg, IV 16/97. On the reverse is the address to the 'Burgermeistern und Rate Straszpurger', and the letter ends 'Würzburg, Tuesday after Jubilate Sunday [the third Sunday after Easter (25 April)] 1480'.

13 *Directorium Argentinense*, commissioned in 1477 by Rupert, Duke of Bavaria, Bishop of Strasbourg, and Johannes de Helffenstein, Dean of the Chapter, ISTC id00261800, printed [1478]; *Breviarium Argentinense*, commissioned by Rupert, Duke of Bavaria, Bishop of Strasbourg, ISTC ib01146650, published 12 January 1478; *Breviarium Argentinense*, commissioned by Rupert, Duke of Bavaria, Bishop of Strasbourg], ISTC ib01146600, printed 12 January 1478.

14 1486: ISTC im00659300, 1489: ISTC im00659500, 1494: ISTC im00659600.

15 Michael Reyser had some difficulty printing a correct text of the Eichstätt missal. Schilf, 'Ein Druckfehlerverzeichnis'.

16 vdm 1108.

26 MARY KAY DUGGAN

Bamberg: Johann Sensenschmidt and Prince-Bishop Philipp von Henneberg

The printer of our next example of ecclesiastical patronage was not limited to the service of a single bishop. Like the Reysers and Erhard Ratdolt in Augsburg, Johann Sensenschmidt (1422/32–1491) started his career working independently, printing fifty-five editions in Nuremberg, including three editions of the Bible, two in Latin (1475, 1476) and one in German (between 1476 and 1478).[17] Perhaps because of an intense competition in the printing industry in Nuremberg, in 1479 he moved his printing establishment to Bamberg, east of Würzburg, in order to fulfil contracts to print liturgical books.

That move was at the request of Abbot Ulrich III Haug of the Benedictine Monastery of Michelsberg which belonged to the Bursfeld Congregation. Sensenschmidt established his print shop in the priory belonging to the monastery to print the first *Missale Benedictinum* (31 July 1481), which contains no music. He continued to print in Bamberg, issuing three liturgical books without music for Bamberg Bishop Philipp von Henneberg (1475–1487);[18] breviaries for Freising (1482–1483) and Metz (1485); a *Manuale* for Toul (about 1481?); and an *Obsequiale* for Freising with his partner Petzensteiner (1484 IV 3).[19] Did Sensenschmidt's print shop remain in the priory?

Sensenschmidt was a bookseller as well as printer. One piece of evidence of his participation in the distribution of his liturgical books comes from the copy of his 1490 *Missale Bambergense* which he sold to Nuremberg merchant Sebald Schreyer, who had it magnificently illuminated by a Nuremberg illuminator. Schreyer commissioned twenty-one vellum copies of the Bamberg missal from Sensenschmidt for use at St. Sebald's in Nuremberg.[20]

Not until 1485 did Sensenschmidt print with metal music type, not in Bamberg but in Regensburg, where he accepted a contract with Regensburg Bishop Heinrich von Absberg to print the first Regensburg missal, completed on 5 March 1485 (see Table 1.2). The bishop's foreword tells us that the edition was printed at the cost of the city of Regensburg ('expensis ad civitatem ratisponensem') with 'complete characters' ('hunc librum missalem imprimi. ac post impressionem caracteresque completos'). Does the reference to 'characters' allude to the new music type, thus commissioned by the city? It must have been at great cost that Regensburg brought Sensenschmidt's printing establishment to their city. Sensenschmidt's strong dark plainchant type fits well the cast staff segments (Figure 1.2). There are few music type designs (note the reuse of the punctum for the custos), but the demands of the syllabic chant to be sung by the priest did not demand a large notational set.

From 1484 until his death, almost all of Sensenschmidt's liturgical editions were done in collaboration with Heinrich Petzensteiner. An exception is the first edition that includes printed music. In that 1485 missal for Regensburg the bishop credits Johann Beckenhub (1440 to about 1491) as the printer along with Sensenschmidt: 'hunc librum per viros industrios Johannem Sensenschmidt et Johannem Bekenhaub dictum maguntinum opifices iussimus

---

17 Randall Herz, 'Sensenschmid(t), Johann(es)', *Deutsche Biographie, www.deutsche-biographie.de*, 31 March 2015.

18 *Agenda Bambergensis*, 1481; two breviaries, with Heinrich Petzensteiner, dated 21 February 1484 and 10 September 1484.

19 Herz says that the *Obsequiale* for Freising included printed red staff lines, but a review of the Munich BSB copy online (links on ISTC and GW) proves that no space for music was left in the edition. Sensenschmidt also printed broadside governmental work for Bamberg Bishop Heinrich and his successor, Heinrich Gross von Trockau (1487–1501). Sensenschmidt's early printing program in Bamberg of Horace, Cicero and Cato as well as some German pamphlets would seem to be his own entrepreneurial undertaking.

20 Herz, 'Ein neu aufgefundener Geschäftsvertrag'.

Figure 1.2 *Missale Augustanum*. Dillingen: Johann Sensenschmidt, 10 I 1489
Source: München, Bayerische Staatsbibliothek, 2 Rar. 201, fol. r1

et fecimus impressione decorari'.[21] Beckenhub was a native of Mainz who lived there at the time of the first printing in the 1450s. He was a cleric and an author, and is listed in the colophon of one printed book in Strasbourg with Georg Husner (Durand, *Speculum iudiciale*, 1473; GW 9148), though for that book his contribution seems to have been as publisher and corrector. He accompanied Georg Reyser to Würzburg in 1479 as part of Reyser's contract

---

21 *Missale Ratisponense*, vdm 1054, fol. π8^v.

with the bishop where he is listed as a master printer in the bishop's letter for the Würzburg breviary (see above). Beckenhub's only known connection to music printing is the Regensburg missal, but since it is the first music book printed by Sensenschmidt it seems significant that Beckenhub was brought in as a partner for the venture.

Let us review the chronology of music printing. Nothing is known about the publication of the first printed music in a gradual of about 1473, assigned to South Germany (Constance?).[22] The second printed music in Germany appeared in a *Missale Basiliense* dated 'not after 1481' and printed by Bernhard Richel, who died between 2 February and 8 June 1482.[23] Beckenhub accompanied Reyser to Würzburg in 1479, where the third printed music appeared 'after 8 November 1481'. Thus when Sensenschmidt and Beckenhub's printed music was issued 'after 5 March 1485' with the fourth music type, music printing was still in its infancy and very few typographers in Germany (one?) could have known how to create a font of music type and print with it. The presence of Beckenhub in Mainz at the time when printing began, and then again in both Würzburg and Regensburg when music fonts would have been cut and cast, is a remarkable coincidence. Beckenhub went on to win the right of citizenship as a bookman in Regensburg in 1487. From 1489 to 1491 he was a partner of Anton Koberger in Nuremberg.[24] The fact that Beckenhub is listed as an equal partner in the bishop's preface signifies that he played an important role in Sensenschmidt's first printed music book. That role was not as financial backer since the preface clearly states that the book was printed at the expense of the city of Regensburg ('expensis ad civitatem ratisponensem'). The preface states that the missal was printed once the characters had been finished ('hunc librum missalem imprimi. ac post impressionem caracteresque completos'), emphasising the new presence of complete type characters.[25] While there is no indication that Beckenhub was himself a typographer, as a cleric trained in plainchant he could certainly have advised on the music type designs that were cut for the book.

All but three of the next eleven fifteenth-century printed music books of Sensenschmidt and his successors included Heinrich Petzensteiner as partner or major printer (see Table 1.2). Petzensteiner had issued one book on his own, the first printed German arithmetic book[26] before joining Sensenschmidt and his successors from 1484 to 1494, after which he is unknown. The two missals for Olomouc (Olmütz) and the missal for Augsburg are the only music books not attributed to Petzensteiner as a partner.[27] Financial backing for missals for Olomouc and Prague was arranged through Peter Drach the Elder (1430–1489), as detailed in his account books.[28]

---

22 vdm 1107.

23 vdm 1436.

24 Ferdinand Geldner, 'Beckenhub (Beckenhaub, Bekenhub)', *Deutsche Biographie*, www.deutsche-biographie.de, 15 December 2015. Beckenhub identified Koberger as the printer of their 1491 (GW M32527) *Libri Sententiarum* of Peter Lombard ('Quo libri impressor Nurnberge Anthonius ipse Koberger tendat post sua fata precor') in a laudatory poem at the beginning of the volume. A letter by Nicolaus Tinctor to Beckenhub follows that poem, praising Beckenhub's scholarly work.

25 See note 21.

26 Bamberg, 1483 IV 15; GW M37209.

27 *Missale Olomucense* (04/03/1488) vdm 1058, *Missale Olomucense* (31/03/1488), vdm 1059.

28 After the death of Bishop Protasius of Olomouc in 1482, the cathedral chapter could not agree on a successor. John Filipec, Bishop of Várad, served as administrator of Olomouc from 1484 to 1489 but appears to have played no role in the publication of the Olomouc missals. A fragment of about a quarter of Drach's account books was found in 1957. It contains entries for five liturgical books with music (four with staves, two with notes and staves). Geldner, 'Das Rechnungsbuch'. Peter Drach the Elder opened a printing shop in Speyer about 1475, a business continued by his son Peter Drach the Younger (about 1456–1504). They worked as printers, publishers and jobbers with a network of over fifty agencies and outlets throughout Germany.

In 1482 Bishop Sixtus von Tannberg of Freising in Bavaria commissioned Sensenschmidt to produce liturgical texts for his diocese, and the printer issued in Bamberg that year a breviary, followed by an obsequiale in 1484. The bishop apparently was not completely satisfied because in the first missal for Freising he stated in the foreword that such an edition was only possible if the bishop and the print shop were in the same place. Thus Sensenschmidt had to move again, south to Freising in Bavaria, where the *Missale Frisingense* was finished on 31 August 1487.[29] Sensenschmidt was back in Bamberg to print two missals in 1488 for the bishop of Olomouc. Next the bishop of Augsburg requisitioned his services in Dillingen, the site of the episcopal residence, to print the first missal for Augsburg in 1489[30] at a time when Erhard Ratdolt did not yet have music type. Though Sensenschmidt is often called a peripatetic printer or *Wanderdrucker*, it was the demands of his ecclesiastic patrons that forced him to move.

Apparently Sensenschmidt's music type belonged to him rather than to a bishop. After his death in 1491 his son and his brother-in-law, Johann Pfeyl, would use it to print fifteen music books in fifteen years for dioceses from Augsburg to Olomouc and Prague in Bohemia.

Augsburg: Erhard Ratdolt and Bishops Johann II von Werdenberg and Friedrich von Hohenzollern

After an impressive printing career in Venice, Erhard Ratdolt (1447–1519) was brought back to Augsburg, the city of his birth, at the summons of Augsburg Bishop Johann II von Werdenberg (about 1430, reigned 1469–1486) to print liturgical books for the diocese of Augsburg, south of Würzburg (see Table 1.3). A letter from the bishop in Ratdolt's first liturgical edition in Augsburg (1487) describes their relationship and, since Johann died in 1486 (26 February), the year Ratdolt came to Augsburg, the contract extends to his successor, Friedrich von Hohenzollern (1449, reigned 1486–1505). One of the last books Ratdolt had printed in Venice was the first breviary for Augsburg, and it must have proven to the bishop that the printer was needed on the other side of the Alps. Unlike the liturgical printers brought to Würzburg and Eichstätt through ecclesiastical summons, Ratdolt continued to issue reprints of his Venetian editions and further first editions of important works, maintaining his professional identity and independence from the bishop's patronage while at the same time focusing on the production of commissioned liturgical works for Augsburg and eight other South German dioceses (Aquileia, Bressanone, Chur, Constance, Freising, Halberstadt, Passau, Salzburg). Perhaps part of the bishop's lure to bring Ratdolt north was the promise of a monopoly on texts for several South German dioceses.

Only after five years in Augsburg did Ratdolt use a metal music type. His three editions of the *Obsequiale Augustense* printed in 1487 use metal rules for staves plus woodcut gothic notation, a difficult combination since metal rules produce printed lines that are often wavy and irregular (see Plate 3).[31] Dissatisfaction with Ratdolt's woodcut music may have occasioned the commission in 1489 of the first missal for Augsburg from Sensenschmidt in Bamberg.

Ratdolt's music type finally appeared in the 1491 missal for Augsburg,[32] a superbly designed gothic plainchant, with many complex neumes and tightly abutting lozenges

---

29 vdm 1057.
30 vdm 1060.
31 *Obsequiale* (a): vdm 1071, *Obsequiale* (b) vdm 1072, *Obsequiale* (c) vdm 1073.
32 vdm 1074.

Figure 1.3 *Antiphonarium Augustense*. Augsburg: Erhard Ratdolt, 23 II 1495
Source: München, Bayerische Staatsbibliothek, 2 Inc. c.a. 3158, fol. LXV^v

(Figure 1.3). The delay of five years in acquiring a music type suggests that Ratdolt had some difficulty in securing the services of a music type specialist. He does not seem to have been himself a typecutter for either alphabetic or music types, since he introduced no new text types in Augsburg and printed with his Venetian rotunda types until 1522, by which time they were out of step with the types of other Augsburg printers.

Ratdolt first printed only eight staves on a folio page and no rules on the sides. He used the same music type for the larger imperial folio choirbooks, setting nine staves per page, with rules at the sides, for a spacious and Italianate look due to the rotunda text types. The clef designs are rounded alphabetic characters that blend with the rotunda of the text underlay. That blend of clefs to text raises the possibility that the music type may have come from Venice, or at least was cut by someone trained there.

Lübeck: Steffan Arndes and Laurens Leve

The career of Steffan Arndes as a music typographer and printer illustrates an intermediary step between ecclesiastical patronage and entrepreneurial activity, relying from about 1485 to 1494 on a private financial backer with strong ecclesiastical and governmental ties. His move about 1485 from Italy to the town of Schleswig, Denmark, to print the first missal for Denmark was presumably tied to the call of Helrich von der Wisch, bishop of Schleswig from 1474 to 1488, though no letter from him was printed in the missal. That book was financed by Laurens Leve and, with more help from Leve, Arndes moved to Lübeck, the capital of the Hanseatic League, to establish what would become the largest printing shop in northern Germany by the turn of the century. There he printed a Schleswig breviary (1489) and two books with printed music: a gradual for Sweden (1493), a missale for Viborg, Denmark,[33] and a missal for northern Franciscans (1504)[34] (see Table 1.4).[35]

Born about 1450 in Hamburg and active from 1477 to 1519, Arndes began his printing career in Perugia, Italy, where in a colophon he called himself 'Master Stephan Johannis from Hamburg in Saxony'.[36] Documentation of the early 1470s describing him as a typefounder and typecaster assisting a man named Crafto is now discounted as a case of mistaken identity with another German named Stephan de Maguntia. Nevertheless, documentation proves that he was a typecutter as well as a printer. In partnership with Johannes Johannis from Augsburg from 3 March 1478, he is cited as employed for the printing of books and cutting of type ('ad exercitium imprimendi libros et sculpendi licteras pro dicto exercitio impressorie librorum').[37] In Italy Arndes moved in high circles, both culturally at the University of Perugia, and financially. He was fortunate to have in residence a distinguished relative from his home town of Hamburg, Dietrich Arndes (1442/43–1506), who was attending the University (BA in 1461 from the University of Erfurt, doctorate in secular law in 1480 from the University of Perugia).[38] Dietrich would be the bishop of Lübeck from 1492 to 1506 when Arndes had his print shop there.

Also in Perugia in the middle of the 1470s lived the son of the man who would be Arndes's financial backer when he returned to Germany. Student Leve Leve, son of wealthy Laurens Leve, would become a chaplain at Lübeck's cathedral upon his return to Germany. Upon his father's death in 1495, Leve Leve was designated as the agent to terminate upon his death his father's formal contract with Arndes that had supported his print shop.[39] One wonders whether the early years in Italy of young Arndes had not been carefully choreographed for his later career in liturgical and vernacular printing in the north.

When Arndes returned north about 1485 to print the first missal for the diocese of Slesvig (Schleswig), he received financial backing from Laurens Leve, who was then a marshal

---

33 vdm 1091.

34 vdm 1017.

35 With the support of Laurens Leve, Arndes was able to pursue an ambitious independent publishing programme that included Bibles and prayerbooks in Low German and a spectacular *Hortus sanitatis* in Low German (*Gaerde der suntheit*) with 542 woodcuts, reminiscent of his elaborate Italian publications. Evidence of his financial stability is his marriage in March of 1493 to the widow Anneke Hog in a union that would produce a son Hans who would inherit the business upon his death. Bruns and Lohmeier, *Die Lübecker Buchdrucker*, 36–37, 69–73.

36 Lohmeier, *Missale Slesvicense 1486*, 25. Expertise in type design and creation is apparent in the roman and gothic rotunda types Arndes used in Perugia and the new gothic rotunda, gothic texture and music types that he used in the north.

37 Rossi, 'Dell'arte tipografica in Perugia', 171. Quoted in Lohmeier, *Missale Slesvicense 1486*, 27.

38 Dietrich Arndes then spent a remarkable few years with the Roman Curia where he was a notary and *familius* of Pope Sixtus IV and also a friend of Cardinal Francesco Todeschini-Piccolomini, later Pope Pius III. In 1482 Dietrich returned to Germany with a benefice at Speier conferred by the pope. Gatz, *Die Bischöfe*, 246.

39 The contract states that 'the print shop of the printed works' ('der druckerye offte prentewerckes eyne tidt her selschup tosamende gehatt'), had been in existence for some years ('etlicke jar'). Bruns and Lohmeier, *Die Lübecker Buchdrucker*, 36.

Figure 1.4 *Graduale Suecicum*. Lübeck: Steffan Arndes, 1493
Source: Stockholm, Kungliga biblioteket – Sveriges nationalbibliotek, 464 A, fol. aiii

(*Staller*) of the Danish king's council in Slesvig.[40] When the missal was complete, Arndes moved to Lübeck, where Leve provided the capital for the construction and maintenance of a printing shop.[41]

In 1493 Arndes published his musical masterpiece, a gradual for the diocese of Västerås in Sweden (Figure 1.4).[42] Arndes' impressive plainchant type is a roman design rather than the gothic design more common in northern Germany, though he cut a large formal Canon text type for his liturgical books with the narrow, angular characters common to the Upper Rhine Valley. Note the long-stemmed virga, kerned to fit with the spacing material below it and sometimes slightly bent. The only other fifteenth-century music type with such long-stemmed notes was used by Christoph Valdarfer in Milan in 1482, but there the stems appear to be separate metal pieces.[43] The lozenge created by Arndes is kerned so that it can be set very tightly with others for the descending climacus. Almost all of the neumes can be set abutting each other to create complex neumes (podatus next to diagonal of porrectus;

---

40 Christensen, *A Study of the Mass*, 31. Leve had been ennobled with a coat of arms by Pope Pius II in 1462.

41 A house was purchased in 1488 on the corner of Königstrasse and Fleischhauerstrasse, and in 1492 the enterprise was enlarged with the purchase of an adjoining house. Bruns and Lohmeier, *Die Lübecker Buchdrucker*, 36; Geldner, *Die deutschen Inkunabeldrucker*, I: 212.

42 ISTC ig00333000; 'Printer of the Graduale Suecicum'. The gradual brought into print Swedish music practice with its repertoire of saints and the chants associated with them. With the adoption of Lutheranism as the Swedish state church in the 1530s, copies of the gradual were soon destroyed or recycled as book covers. Vellum fragments used as book covers have been reassembled in a facsimile edition of the gradual, *Graduale Arosiense*.

43 For a type specimen of Valdarfer's roman plainchant type printed in the *Missale Romanum* of 1 September 1482, see Duggan, *Italian Music Incunabula*, 154–155 and Fig. 56.

podatus next to clivis). The square notes are cut with hairline touches at the corners in imitation of manuscript practice. The flat is an unusual design unique to this font. Arndes used his roman plainchant type one more time, in a missal of 1504 for northern Franciscans of the Province of Dacia (Denmark, Norway, Sweden, Slesvig, Finland, Estonia).[44]

Entrepreneurial music printers

In contrast to the careers of the printers discussed thus far, most early music printers of the 1490s were completely independent entrepreneurs. They were in business for themselves in urban centers where they could raise the capital to purchase property for a printing shop and its materials, assemble a set of types of alphabetic and music design, and decide on a publishing programme that would sell. The era of control of music printing by wealthy bishops who saw into production the first titles for their dioceses was replaced by a new generation of trained printers who had to seek a niche in a market economy for music publications that included the church and monastery but reached beyond to the general musically literate population.

Conrad Kachelofen, Leipzig

Conrad Kachelofen (about 1450–about 1529) gained citizenship in Leipzig in 1476 as a merchant of paper, groceries, and wine.[45] With a population of 25,000, a thriving university, and three annual fairs, Leipzig was a major center for the printing industry, with markets in central and southern Germany.[46] Kachelofen managed to open a print shop in 1483 and would become the city's most important printer of the fifteenth century. Between 1484 and 1501 he published at least ten editions of the liturgical psalter, a genre that, since it was based on the fixed text of the psalms, did not need the approval of ecclesiastical authorities and thus was open to entrepreneurial publishers (see Table 1.5). His first psalters merely left blank space for the entry of the text and notation of plainchant music that accompanied the psalms in the services of the Hours – incipits of antiphons, verses, and hymns – but Kachelofen did print at least the staves for music in a folio psalter of 1497.[47] In 1495, he finally had a gothic plainchant type for unauthorised missals for Meissen and Prague,[48] the last printed with his son-in-law, Melchior Lotter.

The first Prague missal had been printed without music in 1479 in Pilsen in Bohemia. Ten years later reprints began, first by Sensenschmidt and Petzensteiner, then by Georg Stuchs in Nuremberg, and five months later by Kachelofen, with his first printed music on forty-four pages. The title-page claims in entrepreneurial fashion that it was an amended addition, with many votive masses favoured by the cathedral chapter of Prague, with the calendar of the Prague diocese very usefully displayed, with new readings and commemorations and feasts.[49] Apparently none of the reprints were authorised by the bishop.

---

44 Fragments have survived as former archival book covers, housed today at the Uppsala University Library and the Royal Library in Copenhagen; Tveltane, 'Gamle bøker og bokbind', 60–61. Roelvink, *Franciscans in Sweden*, 161–162. The Franciscan missal was published by order of the well-known leader of the Observant movement, Anders Glob, who was in his fourth term of office as vicar provincial in Denmark, 1501–1504.

45 The entry in city archives refers to him as 'Contze Holtzhusen alis Kachelofen von Wartberg'. Knopf and Titel, *Der Leipziger Gutenbergweg*, 8.

46 Knopf and Titel, *Der Leipziger Gutenbergweg*, 4.

47 Folio psalter (1497), vdm 1094.

48 *Missale Misnense* (1495): vdm 1092, *Missale Pragense* (1498): vdm 1095, *Missale Misnense* (1500): vdm 948.

49 The woodcut artist even adds in words that the arms are those of the Prague diocese.

Johann Prüss, Strasbourg

Johann Prüss printed in Strasbourg, one of the largest cities in Germany with a population of 40,000, where he competed with many printing craftsmen for trade. Born about 1447, Prüss emerged in the 1480s as a printer, publisher, and bookseller, gaining the right of citizenship in 1490, and printing there until his death on 16 November 1510. During his career he owned some twenty alphabetic types, a music type, and numerous wood and metal initials.

With the encouragement of cathedral preacher Jean Geiler von Kaisersberg (1445–1510), a prominent Strasbourg humanist and preacher, Prüss entered upon a programme of liturgical printing without any bishop's approval.[50] Such independent editions between 1492 and 1510 include two agendas, two graduals, ten liturgical psalters,[51] two editions of the *Missale speciale,* and three diocesan missals – all entrepreneurial undertakings that had to pay for themselves by selling in a market that reached far beyond Strasbourg (see Table 1.6). When the archbishop of Cracow issued his own official edition of the Cracow missal in 1493, he complained about unapproved editions by 'avaricious and malicious persons'. By then two Strasbourg editions were already out, the one by Prüss about 1490, the other by Martin Schott in 1491.[52]

Prüss printed episcopal and monastic commissions as well: three agendas, for Strasbourg, Mainz (with music from woodcuts), and Wrocław (with music from metal); a gradual for Strasbourg (with music from metal), a *Vigiliae* for Mainz (with music from metal); a *Vesperale* for Metz (with music from metal), seven missals, for Constance, Mainz (two, with printed staves), Wrocław (space for music), Gniezo and Cracow, Cistercians, and Praemonstratensians; eight breviaries, for Mainz (two), Speyer, Halberstadt, Windesheim, the Teutonic Order (two), the Praemonstratensians; and one psalter, for the Premonstratensians (with staves for music).

Noteworthy among Prüss' non-liturgical editions are four issues of a scholarly treatise on plainchant by Hugo Spechtshart (*Flores Musicae Omnis Cantus Gregoriani;* 1488, 1490, 1492, undated).[53] He apparently chose the title well because it was a bestseller that required two reprints within six years. At this time Prüss possessed no metal music type and the ninety-two pages of plainchant neumes in Spechtshart's treatise were printed from woodcuts.[54]

---

50 Levresse, 'La datation'.

51 The liturgical psalters include eight quartos, six with staves for music; one sixteenmo; one folio with printed notes and staves from metal type.

52 Prince Frederick Jagiellon, Cardinal and Archbishop of Cracow and Gniezno, foreword to *Missale Cracoviense* ([not before 1493]), fol. π2[r]: In order that no avaricious or malicious person should dare to reprint this book, the most illustrious Prince Fryderyk . . ., together with his venerable canons of Cracow, hereby solemnly decrees that nobody may reproduce the Cracow missal for this diocese to the detriment of the aforementioned Johannes Haller, under pain of certain punishments. Latin: 'At ne eundem aliquis librum livoris avidus aut invidus. in eius detrimentum imprimere de novo audeat Illustrissimus princeps Fridericus . . . una cum suorum venerabilium canonicorum cracoviensium. cetu firm[i]ter sanxit: que non alter suarum diocesium quispiam de novo in prefati Johannis Haller detrimentum hoc missale cracoviensis rubrice imprimere audebit: sub certa indicta pena: in data desuper copia descripta.'

53 1488: *vmd* 1105, 1490: vdm 1106, 1492: vdm 865. Digital facsimiles of the copies of the 1488 and 1492 editions from the Bavarian State Library, Munich, can be found through links at GW and ISTC. See also Gümpel, *Hugo Spechtshart von Reutlingen.*

54 Three books of provincial statutes assigned to Prüss do not name a bishop but must have been printed at the dioceses 'command: *Statuta provincialia Moguntinensia* ([1484–1487?], ISTC is00749000; *Statuta Curiensia* (Chur), [about 1493–94?]; ISTC is00733800; BSB-Ink S-545 assigns the *Statuta Gnesnensia* (Gnesen) to Prüss, about 1489–91; GW and ISTC assign the edition to Peter Drach in Speyer, before 1500; ISTC is00739200; GW M43463.

Seven of Prüss's twenty-four liturgical publications contain music printed from metal type (Table 1.6): an agenda of about 1499, the *Vigiliae mortuorum ecclesiae Moguntinae*, dated 'after 1500', a folio psalter of about 1503, three graduals, a *Vesperale* for Metz, and two agendas for Wrocław.[55] He printed thirteen liturgical editions with metal staves for music.[56] In addition he printed a *Modus legendi et accentuandi epistolas* with examples from metal music type. The fifty-year-old printer finally cut music type and learned to set it, including the demanding melismatic chant of the gradual. Prüss knew music well since he was entrusted with the publication of four editions of the Spechtshart treatise on plainchant. His music type used a small, pointed notehead on a limited number of neumes that align well on the red staff lines.[57] The wavy rules at the sides, sloppy inking, and somewhat irregular designs deter from a polished appearance.

Conclusion

The model of ecclesiastical subsidy and control of early music printers contrasts sharply with the urban businessmen of the 1490s and later. Monopolistic control has both positive and negative effects, as can be seen in the business world of today. By contracting with some of the best printers of the time, wealthy bishops managed to maintain control of their professional lives, from the creation of types to the development of printing programmes to the very housing of their shops and homes. By completely subsidising the establishment of print shops, at times within ecclesiastical walls, and the process of type creation, a bishop gave his craftsmen a place, time and money to design excellent metal punches for the complex neumes of plainchant, and to lay out music staves on large, folio paper, often Imperial folio size, as well as vellum. Bishops assumed the financial risk of publication, the role of distribution, price fixing and collection of payment from their controlled market of diocesan clergy. The printers became the sole proprietors of printing in their dioceses, with a monopoly on titles and with no competition.

What did the early bishop's *Hofbuchdrucker* give up by accepting episcopal patronage? He was limited to printing liturgy and such government printing as was authorised by the bishop. The print shop and type belonged to the bishop. The printers recruited by bishops had to leave dynamic centres of printing – Strasbourg, Nuremberg, Venice – large trade centres with multiple book markets and developing technical ideas, as well as a labour supply of ambitious journeymen. Since Ratdolt was forced to print his first book with music from woodcuts, and he continued to use his Venetian text types through his career, it seems likely that he sorely missed the professional type craftsmen of Venice and took some time to find the right professional to create his music type for Augsburg printing.[58] In Würzburg, Bamberg and Eichstätt, music printers were completely dependent on the labour force they

---

55 The folio psalter is titled *Psalterium Constantiense* in GW M36294 and dated about 1503/1504(?). The unauthorized agenda of about 1499 (GW 457; ISTC ia00157620) has a variant incipit stating that it was for Chur, Switzerland.

56 Prüss continued in the sixteenth century to print liturgical genres without music: *Missale Moguntinum* (Strasbourg: Johann Prüss, between 1502 and 21 Dec. 1504), web facsimile of Trier StB, moves directly from Temporale, fol. CVII, to Sanctorale (no Canon); with blank space for chant above text ('Exultet iam' on three leaves following fols. CCXXVIII, ISTC im00675300. *Agenda sive Exequiale sacramentorum* (Strasbourg, 1505), VD16 A 616, BSB-Ink R-198. WWW facsimile of Munich, BSB, 4 Inc. s.a. 56 h.

57 Prüss used a special character (clivis) in the margin of his psalters to inform the chanter when to break the psalm tone.

58 In 1516 the Venetian music typecutter Jacobo Ungaro claimed to have worked there for forty years. Duggan, *Italian Music Incunabula*, 38–41.

36   MARY KAY DUGGAN

brought with them and their technical knowledge, though it is quite likely that they recruited and trained assistants in their new ecclesiastic surroundings. The bishop of Würzburg complained that liturgical printing was shut down when Michael Reyser was in prison. The man was irreplaceable, perhaps the only one around who could cut music punches and compose music type. While bishops' printers uniformly had proven themselves in previous careers of impressive, far-reaching programmes, they often gave up the right to break new ground in order to accept new manuscripts. By moving to small diocesan seats, they lost access to the distribution and trade networks of large cities.

What impact did the ecclesiastic contracts have on music printing? Since in Germany the first printed music from metal type was limited to liturgical books, the subsidisation of music type creation created a mature technology that would later be used by mensural type designers. By restricting the output of major excellent craftsmen to authorised plainchant, lesser figures remained to create type and print other kinds of music for the burgeoning culturally literate populace of merchant towns. By establishing monopolies on liturgical titles, bishops removed lucrative titles from the hands of entrepreneurs. While that was effective in Würzburg, Eichstätt and Bamberg, we have seen that once a diocesan first edition was printed, unauthorised reprints were not infrequent.

Did the control of major music craftsmen delay the move into mensural music printing? A glance at the specimens of plainchant type of such craftsmen should make it clear that they were quite able to cut the designs of mensural music into metal. By the 1490s song sheets and music theory books were being issued in commercial and university towns, but their music was printed from woodcuts rather than expensive music type. Proving that a market for non-liturgical music existed, one monophonic metrical German song went through three broadside editions between 1499 and 1506, certainly over a thousand copies.[59] The single polyphonic mensural music printed in Germany in the fifteenth century, a chorus for a humanistic dramatic piece, was printed from woodcuts in the small university town of Freiburg in Breisgau.[60]

But even our entrepreneurs – Kachelofen and Prüss – in the commercial centers of Leipzig and Strasbourg limited their music printing from metal type to liturgical music, with a guaranteed market. Creating a font of music type took months of laborious design and cutting of metal punches, followed by more time training a compositor to set that type, a man recruited as a knowledgeable reader of music notation as well as able to compose type. The finished products of the entrepreneurs could not compare with the subsidised accomplishments of a bishop's *Hofbuchdrucker*. Printers such as Kachelofen and Prüss had to compete with several printers in town. No wonder Kachelofen kept his shop in the Rathaus to sell paper, groceries and wine, and Prüss kept printing psalters with only metal staves for music. Is it any wonder that non-liturgical music printing from metal was initiated by Petrucci in Venice, a city of 100,000, with well-developed printing and typefounding industries, music specialists, and a far-reaching distribution network?[61] The scenario of prince-bishops who sought to continue the original Mainz pattern of containment, secrecy and control of printing within their governed territories would soon give way to modern well-financed

---

59 The sequence *Verbum bonum*, translated by Sebastian Brant as *Das wort ave lond uns singen* (Pforzheim: Thomas Anshelm, about 1500), ISTC iv00127600; [Pforzheim: Thomas Anshelm, about 1502–05], ISTC iv00127590; [Pforzheim: Thomas Anshelm, about 1506–09], VD 16 E-4286 (vdm 116, 120 and 122).

60 Friedrich Riedrer, after 5 November 1495; GW M18620.

61 For a discussion of Petrucci's music typefounder, Giacomo Ungaro, who had been cutting types in Venice for decades, see Duggan, *Italian Music Incunabula*, 30–41.

music printing specialists in major commercial centers. But credit must be given to those bishops who financed with the highest standards the technology of printing – including music – to accomplish their goal of providing reformed texts to dioceses.

Appendix

Table 1.1 Music editions of Georg Reyser for Prince-Bishop Rudolf von Scherenberg, Würzburg

Date	Title	Format	GW/VD16	ISTC/vdm	Pages with music
[About 1482–1486]	Psalterium	Royal folio	M36295	ip01046100 vdm **1040**	98
[After 1481 XI 8]	Missale Herbipolense	Royal folio	M24419	im00663900 vdm **1041**	42
[After 1482 II 6]	Agenda Herbipolensis	Chancery folio	463	ia00161000 vdm **1042**	62
[After 1482 III 18]	Missale Moguntinum	Royal folio	M24571	im00673600 vdm **1043**	17
[1484 II 19]	Missale Herbipolense	Royal folio	M24422	im00664000 vdm **1044**	33
[After 1491 II 1]	Missale Herbipolense	Royal folio	M24426	im00664500 vdm **1045**	36
[After 1493 X 1]	Missale Herbipolense	Royal folio	M24429	im00665000 vdm **1046**	38
[About 1495]	Missale Herbipolense	Royal folio	M24415	im00665800 vdm **1047**	38
[Between 1495–1498]	Vigiliae eccl. Herbipolensis	Chancery folio	M50441	iv00273565 vdm **1049**	57
1496 V 1	Graduale Herbipolense	Imperial folio	10984	ig00329730 vdm **1050**	306
[After 1497 VII 11]	Missale Herbipolense	Royal folio	M24432	im00666100 vdm **1051**	61
1498 VI 10; 1499 II 9	Antiphonarium Herbipolense	Imperial folio	2065	ia00773600 vdm **1052**	329
[After 1499 X 11]	Missale Herbipolense	Royal folio	M24435	im00666200 vdm **1053**	62
1503 VIII 14	Missale Herbipolense	195 × 320 mm printed area	M 5639	vdm **226**	

Table 1.2 Music Editions of Johann and Lorenz Sensenschmidt for Heinrich IV von Absberg, Bishop of Regensburg; Ludwig von Helmstedt, bishop of Speyer; Heinrich Gross von Trockau, Prince-Bishop of Bamberg; Sixtus von Tannberg, Prince-Bishop of Freising; and Friedrich II, Prince-Bishop of Augsburg

Date	Title	Place	Associated Printers, Publishers	Commissioner	Format	GW/VD16	ISTC/vdm	Pages with music
after 1485 III 5	Missale Ratisponense	Regensburg	With Johann Beckenhaub	Heinrich IV von Absberg	2°	M24660	im00686500 vdm **1054**	41
1487 III 14	Missale Spirense	Bamberg	With Petzensteiner	Ludwig von Helmstedt	2°	M24728	im00721900 vdm **1056**	44
1487 VIII 31	Missale Frisingense	Freising	[With Petzensteiner]	Sixtus von Tannberg	2°	M24388	im00660000 vdm **1057**	45
1488 III 4	Missale Olomucense	Bamberg	For Peter Drach		2°	M24582	im00677000 **vdm 1058**	42
1488 III 31	Missale Olomucense	Bamberg			2°	M2458250	im00677500 vdm **1059**	?
1489 I 10	Missale Augustanum	Dillingen		Friedrich II	2°	M24229	im00645450 vdm **1060**	25
1489	Missale Pragense	Bamberg	[With Petzensteiner]		2°	M24633	im00685000 vdm **1061**	32
1490 III 24	Missale Bambergense	Bamberg	With Petzensteiner	Heinrich Gross von Trockau	Royal 2°	M24241	im00646300 vdm **1062**	41
1491 I 15	Missale Bambergense	Bamberg	With Petzensteiner	Heinrich Gross von Trockau	Royal 2°	M24245	im00646500 vdm **1063**	41
1491 VIII 31	Agenda Bambergense	Bamberg	Lorenz with Petzensteiner, Pfeyl	Heinrich Gross von Trockau	4°	461	ia00160600 vdm **1065**	150
after 1492 I 20	Missale Ratisponense	Bamberg	Petzensteiner with Lorenz, Pfeyl	Heinrich IV von Absberg	2°	M24650	im00686600 vdm **1066**	41
between 1492–93	Missale Ratisponense	Bamberg	Petzensteiner with Lorenz, Pfeyl	Heinrich IV von Absberg	2°	M24657	im00686650 vdm **1067**	41
1497 XII 11	Missale Ratisponense	Bamberg	Johann Pfeyl		2°	M24653	im00687000 vdm **1068**	35
1499 V 29	Missale Bambergense	Bamberg	Johann Pfeyl	Heinrich Gross von Trockau	2°	M24237	im00647000 vdm **1069**	34
1500 XII 15	Missale Ratisponense	Bamberg	Johann Pfeyl		2°	M24655	im00688000 vdm **1070**	37
1507	Missale Babenbergense	Bamberg	Johann Pfeyl		2°	M 5558	vdm **685**	online scan
1510	Missale Ratisponense	Bamberg	Johann Pfeyl		2°	M 5617	vdm **680**	online scan
[1514]	Agenda Babenbergensis	(Bamberg)	(Johann Pfeyl)		4°	A 678	vdm **741**	
1518	Missale Ratisponense	Bamberg	Johann Pfeyl		2°	M 5619	vdm **682**	online scan

Table 1.3 Music editions of Erhard Ratdolt for Prince-Bishop Friedrich II, Count of Zollern, Bishop of Augsburg, Sixtus von Tannberg, Bishop of Freising, Melchior von Meckau, Bishop of Bressanone, Christoph von Schachner, Bishop of Passau, and Heinrich VI, Bishop of Chur

Date	Title	Place	Commissioner, Funder	Format	GW/VD16	ISTC/vdm	Music	Pages
1487 II 1	Obsequiale Augustense	Augsburg	Friedrich II	4°	M27375	io00001000 vdm **1071**	metal staves wood notes	7
1487 II 1	Obsequiale Augustense	Augsburg	Friedrich II	4°	M27379	io00001100 vdm **1072**	metal staves wood notes	7
1487 VII 1	Obsequiale Augustense	Augsburg	Friedrich II	4°	M27380	io00001500 vdm **1073**	metal staves wood notes	7
1491 IX 16	Missale Augustanum	Augsburg	Friedrich II	2°	M24223	im00645500 vdm **1074**	metal	31
1491 X 13	Vigiliae eccl. Augustensis	Augsburg		2°	M50445	iv00273525 vdm **1075**	metal	48
1492 III 31	Vigiliae eccl. Augustensis	Augsburg		2°	M50447	iv00273530 vdm **1076**	metal	51
1492 III 17	Missale Frisingense	Freising	Sixtus von Tannberg	2°	M24383	im 00660300 vdm **1077**	metal	53
1493 VIII 17	Missale Brixinense	Augsburg		2°	M24292	im00653000 vdm **1078**	metal	29
1493 X 18	Vigiliae eccl. Pataviensis	Augsburg		4°	M50461	iv00273580 vdm **1079**	metal	54
after 1493	Obsequiale Brixinense	Augsburg	Melchior von Meckau	4°	M27383	io00003000 vdm **1080**	metal	57
1494 I 21	Missale Pataviense	Augsburg	Christoph von Schachner	2°	M24617	im00683000 vdm **1081**	metal	44
1494 VI 20–1498 VI 30	Graduale Romanum	Augsburg		2°	10981	ig00331000 vdm **1082**	metal	248
1494 XII 23	Missale Aquileiense	Augsburg	Joh. Oswald Spetel	2°	M24216	im00645000 vdm **1083**	metal	
1495 II 23	Antiphonarium Augustense	Augsburg	Friedrich II	2°	[0]2062	ia 00773000 vdm **1084**	metal	178

Table 1.3 continued

Date	Title	Place	Commissioner, Funder	Format	GW/VD16	ISTC/vdm	Music	Pages
1496 II 1	Ordo Processionis	Augsburg	Friedrich II	2°	M2833310	if00320875 vdm **1085**	metal	1
1496 VI 10	Missale Augustanum	Augsburg	Friedrich II	2°	M24226	im00646000 vdm **1086**	metal	27
1497 VIII 11	Missale Curiense	Augsburg	Heinrich VI	2°	M24364	im00658300 vdm **1087**	metal	24
1498 XII 2	Missale Pataviense	Augsburg	Christoph von Schachner	2°	M24621	im00683500 vdm **1088**	metal	44
1499 26 XI	Obsequiale Augustense	Augsburg	Friedrich II	4°	M27381	io00002000 vdm **1089**	metal	8
about 1500	Missale Augustanum	Augsburg		2°	M2422620	im00646100 vdm **1090**	metal	?
1502	Obsequiale Constantiense	Augsburg	Hugo von Landenberg	4°	ZV 192	vdm **221**		
1502	Missale Frisingense	Augsburg	Philipp Wittelsbach	2°	M 5572	vdm **222**	digital facsimile	
c.1502	Vigiliae mortuorum secundum chorum ecclesiae Constantiensis	Augsburg	Hugo von Landenberg	2°	M50443	vdm **223**		
1503	Missale Pataviense	Augsburg	Wigileus Fröschl	2°	M 5605	vdm **229**	digital facsimile	
1504	Missale Constantiense	Augsburg	Hugo von Landenberg	2°	ZV 11021, 11022	vdm **230**	digital facsimile	
1505	Missale Constantiense (a)	Augsburg	Hugo von Landenberg	2°	M 5583	vdm **235**	digital facsimile	
1505	Missale Pataviense (a)	Augsburg	Wigileus Fröschl	2°	M 5607	vdm **780**	digital facsimile	
1505	Missale Pataviense (b)	Augsburg	Wigileus Fröschl	2°	M 5608	vdm **236**	digital facsimile	
1505	Missale Constantiense (b)	Augsburg	Hugo von Landenberg	2°	M 5582	vdm **635**	digital facsimile	
1510	Missale Augustense	Augsburg	Heinrich, bishop of Augsburg	2°	M 5554	vdm **258**	digital facsimile	
1510	Obsequiale Constantiense	Augsburg	Hugo von Landenberg	4°	ZV 193	vdm **740**	digital facsimile	
1512	Historia horarum canonicarum	Augsburg	Leonhard Dürr, abbot of Adelberg	2°	B 1184	vdm **280**	digital facsimile	
1515	Missale Ratisponense	Augsburg	Johann von Bayern	4°	M 5618	vdm **681**	digital facsimile	
1522	Quomodo se [. . .] sacerdos habere debeat (= Agenda)	Augsburg		16°	A 628	vdm **1003**	digital facsimile	

Table 1.4 Liturgical editions of Steffan Arndes, with and without printed music

Date	Title	Place	Financing	Format	GW/VD16	ISTC/vdm	Pages with music
1486	Missale Slesvicense	Schleswig	Laurens Leve	2°	M24724	im00721800	0
about 1489	Breviarium Slesvicense	Lübeck	Leve?	8°	0546310N	ib01180700	0
1493	Graduale Arosiense	[Lübeck]	Leve?	Imperial 2°	10983	ig00333000 vdm **1091**	256+ (fragmentary)
1497 III 22	Psalterium Romanum	Lübeck		8°	M36146	ip01055400	[lost]
1500 X 20	Missale Viburgense	Lübeck		2°	M24831	im00730400	0
1504	Missale Fratrum Minorum	Lübeck	Andreas Glob	2°	VD16 M5645	vdm **1017**	fragmentary

Table 1.5 Liturgical editions of Conrad Kachelofen

Date	Title	Place	Associate	Format	GW/VD16	ISTC/vdm	Pages with music
1485 VIII 24	Psalterium	Leipzig		4°	M36133	ip01045000	
1485	Psalterium	Leipzig		2°	M36131	ip01044800	
about 1485	Psalterium	Leipzig		4°	M36125	ip01045500	
about 1493	Psalterium	Ingolstadt	[Kachelofen?]	2°	M36110	ip01049420	
about 1493–95	Psalterium	Leipzig		8°	M36128	ip01049465	
about 1494?	Psalterium	Leipzig		8°	M36022	ip01049600	
1495 XI 9	Missale Misnense	Freiberg in Sachsen		2°	M24538	im00673400	
						vdm **1092**	37
about 1494?	Psalterium	Leipzig		8°	M3612850	ip01052250	
1497	Psalterium	Leipzig		8°	M36137	ip01056100	
1497	Psalterium	Leipzig		2°	M36135	ip01056000	
						vdm **1094**	Staves only
1498 VII 24	Missale Pragense	Leipzig		2°	M24638	im00686000	
						vdm **1095**	44
1500 IX 1	Missale Misnense	Leipzig	With Melchior Lotter	2°	M24540	im00673450	
						vdm **948**	47
about 1500	Psalterium	Leipzig		16°	M36124	ip01059260	
1501	Missale Misnense	Leipzig	With Melchior Lotter	4°	M 5597	vdm **756**	no copies are known

Table 1.6 Johann Prüss, Strasbourg; editions with printed staves, or notes and staves

Date	Author	Title	Format	GW/VD16	ISTC/vdm	Woodcut	Metal	Pages
1488	Spechtshart	Flores musicae	4°	M42916	is00637250/vdm **1105**	Notes/staves		82
about 1490?	Spechtshart	Flores musicae	4°	M4291910	vdm **1417**	Notes/staves		Fragment
about 1492	Spechtshart	Flores musicae	4°	M42920	is00637400/vdm **865**	Notes/staves		82
?	Spechtshart	Flores musicae	4°	M42921	is00637300/vdm **1106**	Notes/staves		82
about 1492		Agenda Moguntinensis	2°	[00]469	ia00163000/vdm **1097**	Notes/staves		28
about 1498		Psalterium	4°	M35969	ip01057500/vdm **1098**		Staves	49
about 1498		Psalterium	4°	M36071	ip01057620/vdm **1099**		Staves	
about 1499		Agenda sive Exequiale	4°	457	ia00158200/vdm **931**		Notes/staves	51
1499–1506?		Psalterium Praedicatorum	4°	M36066	ip01063800/vdm **1100**		Staves	
about 1500?		Psalterium	4°		ip01059280/vdm **1101**		Staves	53
after 1500?		Psalterium	4°		ip01059650/vdm **1102**		Staves	
after 1500?		Vigiliae eccl. Moguntinae	4°	M50451	iv00273575/vdm **1103**		Notes/staves	78
1501		Graduale secundum laudabilem cantum Gregorianum	2°	G 2725	vdm **660**			
1501		Graduale Argentinense		–	vdm **910**			
1502–1504		Missale Moguntinum	2°	M24569	im00675200/vdm **881**		Staves	23
1502–1504		Missale Moguntinum	2°	M24567	im00675300/vdm **883**		Staves	
about 1503		Psalterium cum antiphonis	2°	M36294	ip01059750/vdm 993		Notes/staves	
c.1503		Missale Moguntinum	2°	M24569/M 5589	vdm **881**		Staves	online scan
c.1503		Missale Moguntinum	2°	M24567/M 5590	vdm **883**		Staves	online scan
1504		Psalterium	4°	ZV 1646	vdm **1104**		Staves	
c.1505		Vesperale Metense	4°	–	vdm **234**		Notes/staves	
c.1505		Modus legendi et accentuandi epistolas	4°	M24991/M 5764, F 1854	vdm **742**		Notes/staves	online scan
1505		Missale ord. S. Johannes Jerosolemitani	2°	M 5646	vdm **1010**			
1509		Psalterium chorale	2°	ZV 1648	vdm **778**		Staves	
about 1510		Missale Praemonstratense	2°	M24182/M 5647	vdm **242**		Staves	14 online scan
1510		Graduale Gregorianum	2°	G 2726	vdm **659**		Notes/staves	online scan
1510		Agenda Wratislaviensis	4°	A 620	vdm **249**		Notes/staves	
1510		Festum divae virginis Mariae	2°	R 1064	vdm **251**			
1510		Agenda Wratislaviensis	4°	A 699	vdm **254**		Notes/staves	
1510	Wollick	Opus aureum musicae		RISM B/VI p. 900	vdm **389**			

References

Bohatta, Hanns. *Liturgische Bibliographie des XV. Jahrhunderts mit Ausnahme der Missale und Livres d'Heures*. Vienna: Gilhofer & Ranschburg, 1911.

Bruns, Alken and Dieter Lohmeier. *Die Lübecker Buchdrucker im 15. und 16. Jahrhundert: Buchdruck für den Ostseeraum*. Heide in Holstein: Boyens, 1994.

Christensen, Mark John. 'A Study of the Mass in the Diocese of Slesvig in the Late Medieval Period'. PhD dissertation, University of Notre Dame, 1993.

Duggan, Mary Kay. 'Fifteenth-Century Music Printing: Reform, *Uniformitas*, and Local Tradition'. In *NiveauNischeNimbus: Die Anfänge des Musikdrucks nördlich der Alpen*, edited by Birgit Lodes. Wiener Forum für ältere Musikgeschichte 3. Tutzing: Schneider, 2010, 17–31.

Duggan, Mary Kay. 'Politics and Text: Bringing the Liturgy to Print'. *Gutenberg-Jahrbuch* (2001): 104–117.

Duggan, Mary Kay. *Italian Music Incunabula: Printers and Type*. Berkeley, CA: University of California Press, 1992.

Duggan, Mary Kay. 'Notendruck. I. Bis 1500.' In *Die Musik in Geschichte und Gegenwart*. Kassel: Bärenreiter, 1997. Sachteil V: 433–442.

Freiherr von Pölnitz, Sigmund. 'Rudolf von Scherenberg. Vollendung der Reform'. In *Die bischöfliche Reformarbeit im Hochstift Würzburg während des 15. Jahrhunderts unter besonderer Berücksichtigung der übrigen fränkischen Diözesen*. Würzburg: Verlag für katholisches Schrifttum, 1941. Würzburger Diözesangeschichtsblätter, 8–9, 119–153.

Gatz, Erwin, ed. *Die Bischöfe des Heiligen Römischen Reiches 1448 bis 1648: Ein biographisches Lexikon*. Berlin: Duncker & Humblot, 1996.

Geldner, Ferdinand. *Die deutschen Inkunabeldrucker*. Stuttgart: Hiersemann, 1968–1970.

Geldner, Ferdinand. 'Das Rechnungsbuch des Speyrer Druckherrn, Verlegers und Grossbuchhändlers Peter Drach'. *Börsenblatt für den deutschen Buchhandel*, XVIII (28 Mai 1962), Nr. 42a, 885–978; reprinted in *Archiv für Geschichte des Buchwesens* 5 (1963): 1–196.

Graduale Arosiense, edited by Toni Schmid. Laurentius Petri Sällkapets Urkundsserie VII: 1–7. Malmö: Ljustrycksanstalt, 1959–1965.

Gümpel, Karl-Werner. *Hugo Spechtshart von Reutlingen. Flores musicae (1332/42)*. Mainz: Verlag der Akademie der Wissenschaften und der Literatur, 1958.

Herz, Randall. 'Ein neu aufgefundener Geschäftsvertrag zwischen Sebald Schreyer und Johann Sensenschmidt über den Druck von 21 Bamberger Missalien auf Pergament'. *Archiv für Geschichte des Buchwesens* 68 (2013): 1–45.

Hubay, Ilona. *Incunabula der Universitätsbibliothek Würzburg*. Wiesbaden: Harrassowitz, 1966.

Knopf, Sabine and Volker Titel, *Der Leipziger Gutenbergweg: Geschichte und Topographie einer Buchstadt*. Beucha: Sax-Verlag, 2001.

Levin, Otto. *Stephan Arndes og hans Forhold til Danmark: Fra Bogtrykkets Barndom Nyköbing*. Falster: Central-Trykkeriet, 1937.

Levresse, René. 'La datation des éditions inofficielles du ritual'. In 'Les Rituels incunables de Strasbourg'. *Archives de l'Église d'Alsace* 39 (1976): 63–102.

Lohmeier, Dieter. *Missale Slesvicense 1486: Ein Meisterwerk des Frühdruckers Steffen Arndes*. Kiel: Schleswig-Holsteinische Landesbibliothek, 2001.

Nowakowska, Natalia. 'From Strassburg to Trent: Bishops, Printing and Liturgical Reform in the Fifteenth Century'. *Past and Present* 213 (November 2011): 32–39.

Nowakowska, Natalia. *Church, State and Dynasty in Renaissance Poland: The Career of Cardinal Fryderyk Jagiellon (1468–1503)*. Burlington, VT: Ashgate, 1988.

Ohly, Kurt. 'Der Brief des Würzburger Fürstbischofs Rudolf von Scherenberg an den Strassburger Magistrat über Michael Reyser (datiert 25. IV. 1480)'. In *Aus der Welt des Bibliothekars. Festschrift für Rudolf Juchhoff zum 65. Geburtstag*. Cologne: Greven Verlag, 1961, 99–117.

Roelvink, Henrik. *Franciscans in Sweden, Medieval Remnants of Franciscan Activities (Scripta Franciscana)*. Assen: Van Gorcum, 1998.

Rossi, Adamo. 'Dell'arte tipografica in Perugia. Documenti estratti dalla Biblioteca Comunale.' *Giornale delle biblioteche* 2 (1868): 153–156, 162–163, 170–171, 180–182.

Schilf, Gertrud. 'Ein Druckfehlerverzeichnis zu Michael Reysers Eichstätter Missale von 1486'. *Beiträge zur Inkunabelkunde*, N. F. 11 (1938): 141–142.

Tveltane, Mattias. 'Gamle bøker og bokbind fra Bergan: noen tilleggsopplysninger'. *Nordisk Tidskrift för Bok- och Biblioteksväsen* 57 (1970): 49–62.

Ulewicz, Tadeusz. *Wśród impresorów krakowskich doby Renesansu*. Cracow: Wydawnictwo Literackie, 1977.

Weale, William Henry James and Hanns Bohatta. *Bibliographia liturgica: Catalogus missalium ritus latini ab anno MCCCLXXV impressorum*. London: Quaritch, 1928.

2

German-speaking printers and the development of music printing in Spain (1485–1505)

Margarita Restrepo

As late as 1470, printing had not yet been established in Spain, mainly due to the lack of expertise of native printers.[1] To fulfil the need for printed material, Spain had become dependent on imported books, coming from mostly France and Italy, prompting the Catholic Monarchs – King Ferdinand I of Aragón (r. 1479–1516), and Queen Isabella I of Castile (r. 1474–1504) – to put two initiatives into effect. They reduced taxes on book imports in order to increase these, but also offered an exemption from military service in the ongoing war against the Moors to attract foreign printers.[2]

A large group of printers who identified themselves as 'German' – their 'nationality' a distinctive feature advertising their expertise in an invention of German origin – began to arrive and not only established printing in the country, but soon dominated the industry.[3] Spain, with its absence of capable printers, offered the potential for employment and possible financial success that German-speaking provinces, with a saturation of competent printers, could not afford.

Among the newly arrived was Juan Parix of Heidelberg, responsible for the first known publication in Spain, *Sinodal of Aguilafuente* (Segovia, 1472), a compilation of the records of a synod celebrated at the church of Santa María of Aguilafuente in Segovia. Not surprisingly, some of these printers also played a pivotal role in the development of printed musical notation, for it was sixteen German-speaking printers who produced some of the earliest examples of printed musical notation in Spain.[4] Although their production has been the focus of scholars such as Conrad Haebler, John F. Norton, Antonio Odriozola, and Francisco Vindel, among others, this article examines them as a cohesive group, considering the available evidence on their lives and careers, beginning with their places of origin, in order to better understand their role in establishing and developing musical printing in Spain.[5]

While Jorge Coci, Thomas Glockner, Pedro Hagenbach, Leonardo Hutz and Meinardo Ungut simply identified themselves as 'German' in the colophons of their books, the rest

---

1 In 1472, three Spaniards, Antonio Martínez, Alfonso del Puerto and Bartolomé Segura, opened in Seville what may have been the earliest printing workshop in Spain. Their first publication, however, dates from 1477, *Sacramental* by Clemente Sánchez de Vercial.

2 López-Vidriero, 'The history of the book', 249.

3 Spain, however, was not unique in its reliance on German-speaking printers. Among several German-speaking printers settling in other European locations are Ulrich Hahn, Arnold Pannartz, and Konrad Sweynheym, who reached Rome in 1467, and Ulrich Gering, Martin Crantz, and Michael Friburger, who arrived in Paris in 1470.

4 Refer to Table 2.1 for a detailed list of printers with locations, dates and list of publications and Table 2.2 for publications and printers by city.

5 Haebler, *Early Printers* and *Tipografía ibérica*; Norton, *Printing in Spain and Descriptive Catalogue*; Odriozola, 'Tipógrafos alemanes' and Vindel, *Arte tipográfico*.

were more precise and provided their exact places of origin (see Figure 2.1). There is a great variety of locations, but most came from southern German-speaking towns, where the printing industry was more developed. Pablo de Colonia and Juan Rosenbach were from Cologne and Heidelberg respectively, while Jacobo Cromberger and Juan Pegnitzer came from Nuremberg. Seligenstadt was the hometown of Juan Gysser and the Hurus brothers, Pablo and Juan, appear in their colophons as 'Germans from Constance'. Somewhere on the river Fils was the place of origin of Magno Herbst. Fadrique Biel was from Basel, not yet part of the Swiss Confederacy, while Pedro Brun was from Geneva, although political changes in the region made him identify himself sometimes as 'German', at other times as 'Savoyard'. Juan Luschner, however, came from a northern town, Lichtenberg.

Information about their activities before they came to Spain is scarce, but since they were all competent printers upon arrival, they must have spent time working under experienced printing masters. There is evidence that Biel had been an employee of the renowned Michael Wenssler in Basel, as his name appears in one of Wenssler's volumes.[6] Incidentally, it has been reported that Hurus attended the University of Basel.[7] Although the nature of his studies is not known, it is possible he also learned the trade there. It can be surmised

Figure 2.1 Places of origin of German-speaking printers

---

6 This is *Liber Epistolarum* (1470) by Gasparino Barzizza of Bergamo, one of the first books printed in Basel. See Cuesta Gutiérrez, 'Tipógrafos extranjeros', 67.

7 Delgado Casado, *Diccionario*, vol. 1, 333.

that Brun, Colonia, Cromberger and Pegnitzer trained at their places of origin, as Geneva (Brun), Cologne (Colonia) and Nuremberg (Cromberger and Pegnitzer) were also important printing centers. The remaining could have travelled to towns that had established printing presses. Rosenbach, from Heidelberg, and Gysser, from Seligenstadt, could have moved to Mainz, while Luschner could have travelled from Lichtenberg to Leipzig, and Herbst from his town on the Fils to Basel.

Like other German-speaking printers, some either perfected their skill in Italy or made a stop there to purchase the types they were to use in Spain. Ungut worked in Naples with Mathaias Moravus, which explains his use of types in the Neapolitan style,[8] while the 'Cuatro Compañeros Alemanes' (Four German Friends), Colonia, Glockner, Herbst and Pegnitzer, spent time in Venice, where they purchased their Venetian typefaces.[9]

Their dates of arrival in Spain range from the 1470s, when the country was in dire need of their expertise, to the first decade of the 1500s, when opportunities for foreign printers had dwindled as competition from Spanish printers, some of whom they had trained, began to increase. Three are first reported in Spain in the 1470s: Pablo Hurus appears to have arrived in Valencia in 1474, but did not seem to have produced any publications there, as he starts his job as a printer in Barcelona a year later.[10] Biel may have reached Burgos in 1475,[11] and Brun is printing in Tortosa in 1477.[12] Only one arrived in the 1480s. In 1488, Juan Hurus was at the press established by his brother Pablo in Zaragoza.[13] A larger number reached Spain in the 1490s, possibly attracted by the success of the German-speaking printers already working in the country. A few opened workshops in Seville: 'Cuatro Compañeros Alemanes' in 1490[14] and Ungut a year later.[15] Others arrived in Valencia, Rosenbach in 1490,[16] and Hagenbach and Hutz in 1491.[17] Coci was in Zaragoza in 1492[18] and Luschner in Barcelona in 1495.[19] Only two arrived in the first decade of the 1500s. Gysser began his career in Salamanca in 1500,[20] and the first archival reference to Cromberger is in Seville three years later.[21]

---

8 Martín Abad, *La imprenta*, 51.

9 Hazañas y la Rua, 'Cuatro alemanes compañeros', 201.

10 Delgado Casado, *Diccionario*, vol. 1, 333. He works together with another German-speaking printer, Juan de Salzburga; their first volume is Niccolò Perotti's *Rudimenta Grammaticae* (Barcelona, 1475), one of the most popular modern Latin grammar texts and the earliest dated book coming out of Barcelona.

11 Delgado Casado, *Diccionario*, vol. 1, 70. His first dated work, however, is Andrés Gutiérrez Cerezo's *Grammatica Latina* (Burgos, 1485).

12 Revello Torre, *Orígenes*, 26. He begins his printing career associated with another German-speaking printer, Nicolás Spindeler. Their first book is the popular *Rudimenta Grammaticae* (Tortosa, 1477) by Niccolò Perotti.

13 Delgado Casado, *Diccionario*, vol. 1, 332. His first publication was a treatise on astronomy, *Sumario de astrología* (Zaragoza, 1487/88) by Bernat de Granollachs.

14 Hazañas y la Rua, 'Cuatro alemanes compañeros', 201 and 209. Their earliest volume is Alfonso Palencia's *Universal vocabulario en latin y en romance* (Seville, 1490).

15 Haebler, *Tipografía ibérica*, 49. Associated with Stanislao Polono, from Poland, their earliest print is *Defensiones Sancti Thomae* (Seville, 1491) by Diego de Deza.

16 Norton, *Descriptive Catalogue*, 39–40. His first known publication was Pedro Pascual's *Obra anomenada Biblia parva* (Barcelona, 1492).

17 Norton, *Descriptive Catalogue*, 366 and 450. Initially working together, their first known book is Juan Gerson's *Monyspreu del mon* (Valencia, 1493).

18 Delgado Casado, *Diccionario*, vol. 1, 145. He appears as an employee of Pablo Hurus in 1492, but his first volume is *Breviarium Hieronymitanum* (Zaragoza, 1499), which he published in association with Hutz and Lope Appetenger, the nephew of the Hurus brothers.

19 Norton, *Descriptive Catalogue*, 59. He is mentioned in Barcelona in 1494, in connection with Rosenbach. His first publication is *Grammatica* (Barcelona, 1495) by Bartolomé Mates.

20 Norton, *Descriptive Catalogue*, 194. His first work is Nicolás de Plove's *Tractatus sacerdotalis* (Salamanca, 1500).

21 Griffin, The *Crombergers*, 21. His earliest volume is Celio Sedulio's *Carmen Pascale* (Seville, 1504).

Although they were all attracted by the favourable employment opportunities offered in Spain, some were expressly invited to set up shop. The 'Cuatro Compañeros Alemanes' came at the request of Queen Isabella, who felt the need to have printers who specialised in producing academic textbooks.[22] Ungut, however, was invited by both Queen Isabella and her husband King Ferdinand, who were interested in having editions of works on civil and ecclesiastical law.[23] Others, however, were sponsored by fellow countrymen already established in the country. After achieving a certain level of success, Pablo Hurus brought his brother Juan to replace him while he travelled to Constance on a business trip.[24] Rosenbach was invited to Valencia by the successful German-speaking book seller, Hans Rix de Chur, who, like others in his trade, realised it would be less expensive to produce books in the country than importing them from other European locations.[25]

Once they arrived, they settled in university and commercial towns, where they could find capital and easy distribution (see Figure 2.2).[26] In the Kingdom of Aragon, ruled by King Ferdinand, they set up shop in Barcelona, the main port to the Mediterranean; Valencia, the most populous city, due to its lucrative textile industry; and Zaragoza, the capital city. In the Kingdom of Castile, ruled by Queen Isabella, they settled in Burgos, the capital city; Salamanca, a major university town; Seville, with easy access to water transportation, became a significant commercial centre that traded with Portugal and the New World; and Toledo, the seat of Spain's wealthiest cathedral.

Most, however, did not remain in one place for long, but moved around looking for better job opportunities. The most nomadic were Hutz and Rosenbach, who relocated five times. Hutz arrived in Valencia in 1491, moved to Salamanca in 1496, then Zaragoza in 1498 before returning to Valencia in 1505, where he ended his career as a printer, although he was documented back in Zaragoza, for the last time, in 1519.[27] Rosenbach arrived in Valencia in 1490, moved to Barcelona in 1492, to Tarragona in 1498, and Perpignan (then

Figure 2.2 Towns where German-speaking printers settled

---

22 López-Vidriero, 'The history of the book', 250.
23 Collantes de Terán, 'Un taller alemán', 147.
24 Delgado Casado, *Diccionario*, vol. 1, 332.
25 Sarría Rueda, 'Los inicios de la imprenta', 46. At his death in 1490, an inventory of Rix's possessions shows the scale of the book import business. It listed 5,265 volumes, mostly imported into Spain.
26 See Table 2.2 for a detailed list of printers and publications by location.
27 Delgado Casado, *Diccionario*, vol. 1, 335–337.

part of Catalonia) in 1500, before making a final return to Barcelona in 1506, where he became the leading printer until his death in 1530.[28]

A few, nevertheless, remained in one place, often dominating the printing industry in their location. Biel became the major printer in Burgos, where he resided until his death in 1517.[29] Coci settled in Zaragoza, took over the Hurus press in 1499, when Pablo left Spain for Constance, built up a reputation as the best printer in the city – explaining why several documents refer to him as 'master printer' and 'lord of the printing press' – and stayed until his death in 1546.[30] A remarkable case is that of Cromberger, the founder of a dynasty that dominated printing in Seville for three generations.

Regardless of where these men settled, the hazardous nature of the business made them associate with other German-speaking printers to finance their publications and spread the risk of loss. The best known partnership is that of 'Cuatro Compañeros Alemanes' – Colonia, Glockner, Herbst and Pegnitzer – who worked together from their arrival in Seville in 1490. These partnerships, however, were characterised by flux as job opportunities in the early years of printing in Spain were constantly changing. Colonia left the 'four friends' four years later.[31] The remaining three continued as 'Tres Compañeros Alemanes'. After Glockner's departure, Herbst and Pegnitzer operated under the name 'Dos Compañeros Alemanes,' but by 1502, only Pegnitzer remained.[32] To show how convoluted some of these partnerships are, it is worth mentioning that Coci worked with Hutz in Zaragoza. But before working with Coci, Hutz had partnered with Hagenbach in Valencia, and after that Coci and Hutz joined with Pablo Hurus back in Zaragoza.[33]

Their need to congregate with fellow German-speakers also led them to hire German-speaking employees. Juan de Ars identified himself as 'German' in legal documents and was employed by 'Tres Compañeros Alemanes',[34] while Ulrico Belch, from Ulm, worked for Luschner.[35] Wendel (or Vendelin) Rosenhayer also identified himself as 'German', and not only worked for Rosenbach, but also lived in the master's home.[36] His attachment to the family was such that before he died in 1528 he appointed Rosenbach as his executor and left his assets to Rosenbach's wife.[37]

Although they surrounded themselves by other German-speakers in their professional lives, those whose marriages are documented are known to have married Spanish women, which indicates that they were young and single when they arrived or that their wives died in Spain. Just to mention a few, when Rosenbach settled down in Barcelona, he married twice, each time to Spanish women, Isabel Rexach and Ursula Carreras.[38] Biel and Coci also married Spanish women, María Sánchez de la Sierra[39] and Isabel Rodríguez[40] respectively. It is not known whether this reflects a lack of German-speaking women in the country or the desire of these printers to integrate into Spanish society. Evidence of their possible assimilation is that all of those who are accounted for until their passing chose to remain in Spain,

---

28 Millares Carlo, 'La imprenta en Barcelona', 511–512.
29 See Cuesta Gutiérrez, 'Tipógrafos extranjeros', 67–70.
30 Delgado Casado, *Diccionario*, vol. 1, 145.
31 Hazañas y la Rua, 'Cuatro alemanes compañeros', 203.
32 Hazañas y la Rua, 'Cuatro alemanes compañeros,' 207 and 208.
33 Haebler, *Early Printers*, 25, 37–38.
34 Hazañas y la Rua, 'Cuatro alemanes compañeros', 206.
35 Haebler, *Tipografía iberica*, 75.
36 Rubio i Balaguer, 'Integración de los impresores alemanes', 120.
37 Rubio i Balaguer, 'Integración de los impresores alemanes', 115.
38 Delgado Casado, *Diccionario*, vol. 2, 610.
39 Cuesta Gutiérrez, 'Tipografos extranjeros', 69.
40 Delgado Casado, *Diccionario*, vol. 1, 145.

where they eventually died, except for Pablo Hurus, who returned to Constance in 1499.[41] At the time of their deaths, most had Spanish children and grandchildren, and some, such as Biel, Coci and Rosenbach, had spent more than thirty years in Spain, and likely felt a strong kinship with their adopted country.[42] Even their names reveal assimilation, as is the case with George Koch, whose Hispanicised name, Jorge Coci, left no traces of his German origin.

While there is a certain degree of diversity in their careers, their book production is characterised by similarities. As they were supplying the reading needs of a young nation, they all produced books on a broad range of subjects: from liturgical and devotional, to medical and legal, and from translations and adaptations of the classics, to poetry and fiction. Some are in Latin, others in the vernacular, Catalan, Spanish and Valencian. Indeed, some of their volumes are jewels in the history of Spanish printing. Biel is best known for having produced the first edition of *La Celestina* (1499) by Fernando de Rojas, one of the masterpieces of Spanish literature, Coci for the first edition of *Amadís de Gaula* (1508), an anonymous landmark work among chivalric romances,[43] and Cromberger for the earliest edition of Antonio de Guevara's *Libro Aureo del emperador Marco Aurelio* (1528), one of the most popular reads in sixteenth-century Spain.[44]

As can be expected for a large group of printers, some were more productive than others. Cromberger surpassed all, with 300 volumes, representing two-thirds of the books printed in Seville during his tenure.[45] Coci followed with 250,[46] while Biel produced about 120 books.[47] At the bottom of the list is Pegnitzer, who only printed two volumes after being left alone by his former 'Compañeros Alemanes'.[48] Cromberger, Coci and Biel, however, are also known for the quality of their books. Cromberger's 300 volumes are also considered some of the most beautifully printed in sixteenth-century Spain.[49]

A very remarkable group of volumes in the production of these sixteen printers are the twenty-three liturgical and eight theoretical books that contain the first examples of musical notation printed in Spain. The larger number of liturgical prints over theoretical volumes is explained by the fact that the Catholic Church was the first and best client of German-speaking printers. The Catholic Monarchs, who considered themselves as the restorers of the church after the integration of the 'reconquered' territories in the Kingdom of Granada in 1492, strengthened their authority and control by appointing new archbishops and bishops who embarked on a programme of reform that included the printing of liturgical volumes.[50] In fact, the twenty-three liturgical prints with musical notation represent only a small portion of a vast production, for even though the printing output of Spain during the fifteenth century was small, the production of liturgical texts was the highest in Europe.[51]

---

41 Haebler, *Tipografía ibérica*, 42. All are accounted for, except for those who leave the printing business, namely Brun, the 'Compañeros Alemanes', Gysser, Hutz, and Luschner.

42 They also had the longest careers of the printers mentioned in this article. Biel's lasted forty-two years, Rosenbach's forty and Coci's thirty-eight. The shortest career is that of Juan Hurus, who arrived in 1488 and passed away in 1491.

43 In circulation since the 1300s but arranged by Garci Ródriguez de Montalvo, the story of Amadís inspired four operas, by Jean-Baptiste Lully (1684), George Friedrich Haendel (1715), Johann Christian Bach (1779) and Jules Massenet (1922).

44 Whinnom, 'Best-seller', 194.

45 Martínez, 'Los Cromberger'.

46 Delgado Casado, *Diccionario*, vol. 1, 145.

47 Sarría Rueda, 'Los inicios de la imprenta', 63.

48 Hazañas de la Rua, 'Cuatro alemanes compañeros', 211.

49 Griffin, *The Crombergers*, 69.

50 Castillo-Ferreira, 'Chant, liturgy and reform', 282.

51 López-Vidriero, 'The history of the book', 249.

From 1479 to 1490, religious and monastic orders printed their own liturgical books, as did almost half of the dioceses. By 1529, all but five dioceses did so.[52] Unfortunately, an inventory of these liturgical volumes does not yet exist, but it is reasonable to speculate that there must be hundreds of such editions, particularly when we consider the number of different religious services, not only in a week but for the seasons of the year and all the feast days. It is important to clarify, however, that volumes of polyphonic music destined for practical performance began to appear after 1530 and were the work of Spanish printers.[53]

Missals, containing the texts to be said or sung at mass during the entire year, are the most numerous, accounting for thirteen publications. These volumes represented a lucrative portion of the business, as the printing process was slow and laborious, which, to the benefit of the printer, kept the presses busy for long periods of time. They contained a diversity of types in two inks, black and red, on both sides of the folios, woodblock illustrations, parchment or paper of excellent quality, and required careful correction of proofs.

The Hurus brothers are responsible for the production of three missals. The first, *Missale Cesaraugustanum* (Zaragoza, 1485), printed by Pablo (see Plate 4 in the colour section), is the earliest known volume containing musical notation. Its 350 copies, some in vellum, were commissioned by Alfonso de Aragón, Archbishop of Zaragoza and illegitimate son of King Ferdinand.[54] Of the 330 folios, the music occupies folios 191 to 198. Pablo printed the four-line staff in red, following the practice of medieval scribes, who copied the musical staff in red ink so that the black note heads would stand out more clearly for singers to read. The black note heads were filled in by hand, and this explains their irregularity in surviving copies. This Missal is also significant for using new letters combining five characters, depending on the importance of the text, and a few illustrations, decorated edges and capitals. Motivated by practical reasons, Pablo's brother, Juan, rebound unsold copies of this Missal in 1488 and sold it to the cities of Huesca and Jaca, *Missale Oscense et Jacense* (Zaragoza, 1488).[55] Ten years later, Pablo produced a newer version of the *Missale Cesaraugustanum* (Zaragoza, 1498), but this time both staff and notes were printed.

Like the Hurus brothers, Rosenbach, who produced a large quantity of books on a wide variety of subjects, although the exact count is not available, also printed three missals in his Barcelona workshop, for the dioceses of Gerona, Vic and Tarragona. His *Missale Tarraconense* (Barcelona, 1499) (see Figure 2.3) is considered his best work. Its 210 folios are printed in black and red using letters in three different sizes. Most of the folios with music in the copy digitised by the Biblioteca Virtual del Patrimonio Bibliográfico (originally the copy from Tarragona's Biblioteca Publica del Estado) only have the staff in red, with either no note heads added, or sometimes note heads added by an inexperienced copyist.

Hagenbach produced two missals, both for the Cathedral of Toledo, one of the wealthiest in Spain, *Missale Toletanum* (Toledo, 1499) and *Missale Mixtum* (Toledo, 1500). The *Missale Mixtum* (Toledo, 1500) is the first printed edition of the Mozarabic rite, the ancient chant

---

52 These are Canarias, and four territories recently recovered from the Moors, Cádiz, Málaga, Almería and Guadix-Baza. See Odriozola, 'Libros litúrgicos', in *Diccionario historia eclesiástica*, 1326. The number of copies varied from one diocese to the next, but frequently the copies fluctuated between 200 and 500, rarely 1,000 or more.

53 The first ever was Luis de Milan's *El maestro* (Valencia: Francisco Díaz Romano, 1536), a collection of vihuela works. The first vocal collection was Juan Vásquez's *Villancicos i canciones* (Osuna: Juan de León, 1551).

54 Romero de Lecea, *Introducción*, 100.

55 Romero de Lecea, *Introducción*, 100.

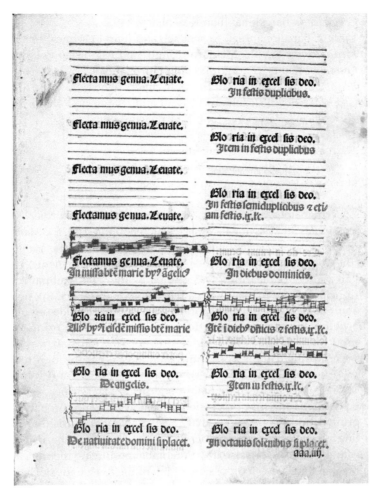

Figure 2.3 *Missale Tarraconense*. Barcelona: Juan Rosenbach, 1499
Source: Biblioteca Pública de Tarragona, I/132, fol. aaaIV[r] a / 2006 Minesterio de Cultura

tradition of Toledo practiced by Christians living under Muslim rulers (see Plate 6).[56] It uses five lines in red and printed notes in black. Commissioned by the powerful cardinal of Toledo, Francisco Jiménez de Cisneros, who, interested in legitimizing the process of 'reconquest' through the revival of this ancient tradition, assigned the Canon Alonso Ortíz to study a number of Mozarabic manuscripts, but made sure that the missal included elements of the Roman Rite as it was used in Iberia, particularly the preliminary prayers for the Mass.[57]

A complete list of missals gives a better idea of the number and variety of printing locations of these publications:

- *Missale Cesaraugustanum*. Zaragoza: Pablo Hurus, 1485;
- *Missale Oscense et Jacense*. Zaragoza: Juan Hurus, 1488;

---

56 The cathedral itself stands on the site of the Great Mosque of Toledo.
57 Odriozola, 'Libros litúrgicos', 1326.

- *Missale Gerundense*. Barcelona: Juan Rosenbach, 1493;
- *Missale Vicense*. Barcelona: Juan Rosenbach and Juan Luschner, 1496;
- *Missale Predicatorum*. Seville: Meinardo Ungut and Estanislao Polono, 1497;
- *Missale Cesaraugustanum*. Zaragoza: Pablo Hurus, 1498;
- *Missale Benedictinum*. Montserrat: Juan Luschner, 1499;
- *Missale Giennense*. Seville: Meinardo Ungut and Estanislao Polono, 1499;
- *Missale Tarraconense*. Barcelona: Juan Rosenbach, 1499;
- *Missale Toletanum*. Toledo: Pedro Hagenbach, 1499;
- *Missale Mixtum*. Toledo: Pedro Hagenbach, 1500;
- *Missale Legionense*. Seville: Jacobo Cromberger, 1504;
- *Missale Oscense et Jacense*. Zaragoza: Jorge Coci, 1504.

Besides missals, German-speaking printers also produced other liturgical volumes, such as manuals, processionals and passionals. Two worth mentioning are the *Manuale Toletanum* (Seville, 1494) and the *Processionarium Predicatorum* (Seville, 1494). The *Manuale Toletanum*, which contains the texts said or sung at other services, such as sacraments, visitation of the sick, burial and all manner of blessings, was printed by the 'Tres Compañeros Alemanes'; it is the first liturgical volume to print both a red-ink staff and black-ink notes. It consists of seventy-six unnumbered folios with decorated capital letters made out of wood blocks, and shows the abundant material of different sizes that these printers owned. The 'Compañeros' used the technique of double impression: the red staff was done first, and the black notes were printed the second time the paper went through the presses. The *Processionarium Predicatorum* (Seville, 1494), containing litanies and hymns for use in religious processions, was produced by Ungut and his Polish partner, Estanislao Polono. This significant volume is the first processional printed in Spain, probably the first processional ever printed, and the first book that consists solely of music (see Plate 5). Its 187 folios use four-line red staves done by rule across the page with note-heads printed in black.

German-speaking printers were also instrumental in producing theoretical volumes, for they were responsible for seven, and possibly eight, of the twelve music theory books that were printed in Spain between 1492 and 1510, listed below.[58]

- Domingo Marcos Durán. *Lux bella*. Seville: Cuatro alemanes compañeros (Pablo de Colonia, Juan Pegnitzer, Magno Herbst and Tomás Glockner), 1492;
- Guillermo del Podio. *Ars musicorum* or *Comentario musices*. Valencia: Pedro Hagenbach and Leonardo Hutz, 1495;
- Alonso Spañón. *Introducción muy útil e breve de canto llano*. Seville: Pedro Brun, 1504;
- Domingo Marcos Durán. *Súmula de canto de órgano*. Salamanca: [n. p.] (Juan Gysser?), 1504?;
- Domingo Marcos Durán. *Lux bella*, 2nd. ed. Salamanca: Juan Gysser, 1509;
- Domingo Marcos Durán. *Lux bella*, 3rd. ed. Seville: Jacobo Cromberger, 1509;
- Gonzalo Martínez de Bizcargui. *Arte de canto llano et de contrapunto* . . . Burgos: Fadrique Biel, 1509;
- Francisco Tovar. *Libro de música práctica*. Barcelona: Juan Rosenbach, 1510.

---

58 The remaining volumes are *De canto llano* (Salamanca: [n. p.], 1496) by Cristóbal Escobar, *Comento sobre Lux bella* (Salamanca: [n. p.], 1498) by Domingo Marcos Durán, *Portus musice* (Salamanca: [n. p.], 1504) by Diego del Puerto and *Arte de canto llano lux videntes dicha* (Valladolid: Diego de Gumiel, 1506?) by Bartolomé Molina.

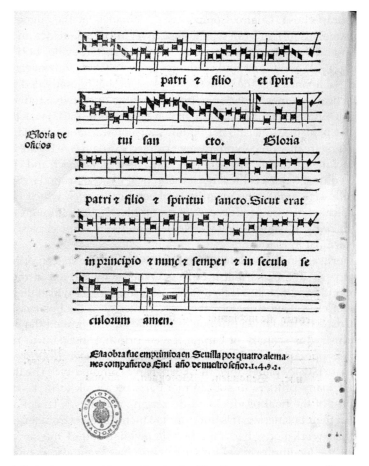

Figure 2.4 *Lux bella* by Domingo Marcos Durán. Seville: Cuatro Compañeros Alemanes, 1492
Source: Madrid, Biblioteca Nacional de España, Inc/2165(3), fol. [53ᵛ]

The possible eighth volume is Domingo Marcos Durán's *Sumula de canto de órgano* (Salamanca, 1504?), the first treatise on polyphony in Spanish, which may have been the work of Gysser, as it has been suggested that Gysser worked in one of the two anonymous print shops that operated in Salamanca.[59] *Sumula de canto de órgano* was Marcos Durán's third theoretical study; his first, which focused on plainchant, was *Lux bella* (Seville, 1492), the earliest theoretical treatise to be printed in Spain, the first written in Spanish and the first ever with printed staff and printed notes.[60] This significant volume consists of fourteen unnumbered folios, with eight containing printed music (see Figure 2.4). 'Cuatro Compañeros Alemanes,' who produced *Lux bella*, left the spaces for the examples blank, but printed them using woodcuts the second time the folios went through the presses. The use of woodcuts explains the lack of uniformity of the staff and note heads.

---

59 Delgado Casado, *Diccionario*, vol. 1, 315. It is believed that Antonio Nebrija, one of the most prominent humanists in the country, was behind both anonymous print shops. Not wanting to compromise his intellectual reputation by involving himself in a financial activity, Nebrija kept the name of printers anonymous. See Sarría Rueda, 'Los inicios de la imprenta', 71.

60 His second was *Comento sobre Lux bella* (Salamanca: [n. p.], 1498), an expanded versión of *Lux bella*.

It is likely Durán chose 'Cuatro Compañeros Alemanes' at the suggestion of Pedro Jiménez de Préxamo, his former professor at the University of Salamanca and the dedicatee of *Lux bella*, who had used them for his work *Floretum Sancti* (Seville, 1491).[61] For *Súmula de canto de órgano* (1504) and the second edition of *Lux bella* (1509), however, Marcos Durán chose the city of Salamanca and the presses of Gysser, probably motivated by the fact that these were didactical volumes intended to be used by the university students.

While Marcos Durán's *Sumula de canto de órgano* (Salamanca, 1504?) was the first treatise on polyphony in Spanish, Guillermo del Podios's *Ars musicorum* (Valencia, 1495), written in Latin, was the first treatise on polyphony ever printed in Spain (see Figure 2.5). Del Podio, employed by the Valencia Cathedral as choir master, chose Hagenbach and Hutz to produce this remarkable volume, which is the largest theoretical treatise printed in Spain.[62] It is 136 pages long in folio size, unlike the majority of theoretical works, which were printed in quarto. The musical staff was produced with wood blocks, but although the note heads were intended to be hand-copied, they were never entered in some copies, such as that in the Biblioteca Nacional in Madrid.[63]

Finally, it is worth exploring whether the productivity of these sixteen printers translated into financial success. It appears that it did not. When they arrived in the country they possessed talent and expertise, but lacked financial resources, for which they depended on the Spanish upper class. Unfortunately, the lack of interest in the business on the part of wealthy Spaniards, who disdained printing as manual labour, limited the development of the printing industry, as scarcity of capital forced printing in Spain to remain a small industry.[64] Printers operated with limited budgets, their restricted resources forcing them to borrow money to pay for paper, their most expensive commodity.[65] The limited capacity of presses forced many printers to subcontract parts of a book to make deadlines, thus increasing the cost of the final product and decreasing earnings.[66] To get a better idea of the modest size of their businesses, it is important to mention that Cromberger, who owned one of the biggest workshops, had four presses, while around the same time, Anton Koberger, one of the leading printers in Nuremberg, had twenty-four presses and more than 100 employees.[67]

What seems clear is that only those who diversified into other businesses made substantial profit. One such case was Pablo Hurus, who also acted as representative of the 'Great Trading Society', a commercial company in Ravensburg.[68] Among several commodities, the company traded paper made in mills north of the Alps, possibly the paper used by the Hurus press. Haebler speculates that Pablo perhaps also traded in saffron, as Zaragoza was the centre of trade for the spice, which was sold by travelling merchants in cities around Lake Constance.[69]

---

61 For biographical information on Marcos Durán, see Barrios Manzano, 'Domingo Marcos Durán', 91–127.

62 For biographical information on del Podio, see Villanueva Serrano, 'El tractadista Guillermus de Podio', 3–24.

63 Romero de Lecea, *Introducción*, 103.

64 Moll Roqueta, 'Valoración', 82. In fact, the limited capability of presses made it necessary for Spain to continue importing books, particularly the classics and academic textbooks.

65 Haebler, *Early Printers*, 435.

66 Moll Roqueta, 'Estudio de la edición', 18.

67 Marsá, *La imprenta*, 16.

68 Painter, 'First press at Barcelona', 142. His association with this trading society probably explains his frequent absences from Zaragoza (from 1478 to 1481, 1483 to 1484 and 1486 to 1490).

69 Haebler, *Tipografía ibérica*, 40.

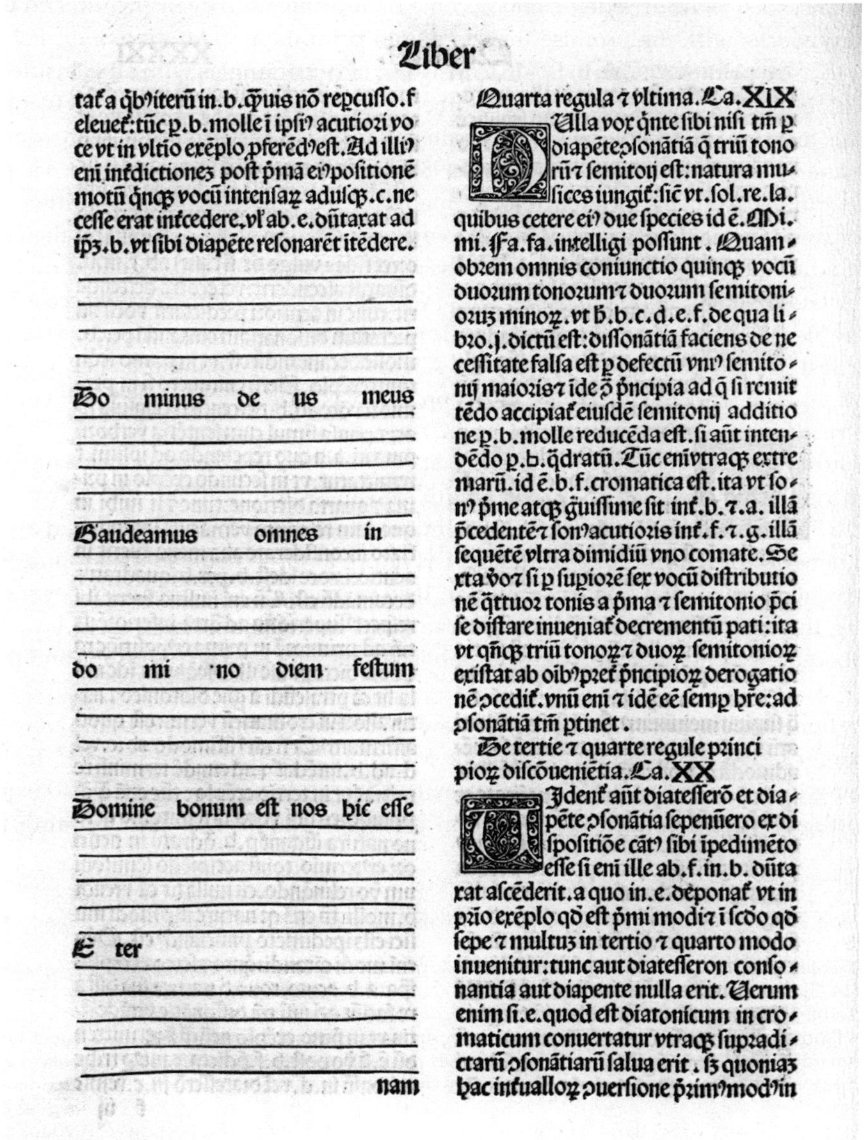
Liber

tar a q b? iterū in.b.q̄uis nō repcusso.f eleuet: tūc p.b.molle i ipsi? acutiori voce vt in vltio exēplo pferēd? est. Ad illi? eni intdictiones post p̄mā ei? positionē motū q̄nq3 vocū intensaz adusq3.c.necesse erat intcedere.vl' ab.e.dūtarat ad ip3.b.vt sibi diapēte resonarēt itēdere.

Do minus de us meus

Gaudeamus omnes in

do mi no diem festum

Domine bonum est nos hic esse

E ter

nam

Quarta regula 7 vltima. Ca. XIX

[N]ulla vox q̄nte sibi nisi tm̄ p diapēte 9sonātiā q̄ triū tonorū 7 semitonij est: natura musicos iungit: sic vt.sol.re.la. quibus cetere ei? due species id ē. Mi.mi. Fa.fa. intelligi possunt. Quam obrem omnis coniunctio quinq3 vocū duorum tonorum 7 duorum semitoniorū minoz. vt b.b.c.d.e.f. de qua libro.j. dictū est: dissonātiā faciens de necessitate falsa est p defectū vni? semitonij maioris 7 ide 9 p̄ncipia ad q̄ si remittēdo accipiat eiusdē semitonij additione p.b.molle reducēda est. si aūt intendēdo p.b.q̄dratū. Tūc eni vtraq3 extremarū. id ē.b.f. cromatica est. ita vt son? p̄me atq3 grauissime sit int.b.7.a. illā p̄cedentē 7 son? acutioris int.f.7.g. illā sequētē vltra dimidiū vno comate. Sexta vox 7 si p supiorē sex vocū distributionē q̄ttuor tonis a p̄ma 7 semitonio p̄cise distare inueniat decrementū pati: ita vt q̄nq3 triū tonoz 7 duoz semitonioz existat ab oib? p̄ter p̄ncipioz derogationē 9cedit. vnū eni 7 idē eē semp h̄re: ad 9sonātiā tm̄ ptinet.

De tertie 7 quarte regule principioz discōueniētia. Ca. XX

[V]identr aūt diatesserō et diapēte 9sonātia sepenūero ex dispositiōe cāt? sibi ipedimēto esse si eni ille ab.f.in.b. dūtarat ascēderit. a quo in.e. dēponat vt in p̄io exēplo qd est p̄mi modi 7 i scdo qd sepe 7 multu3 in tertio 7 quarto modo inuenitur: tunc aut diatesseron consonantia aut diapente nulla erit. Uerum enim si.e. quod est diatonicum in cromaticum conuertatur vtraq3 supradictarū 9sonātiarū salua erit. s3 quonia3 hac intualloz 9uersione p̄rim? mod? in

Figure 2.5 Guillermo del Podio. *Ars musicorum* or *Comentario musices*. Valencia: Pedro Hagenbach and Leonardo Hutz, 1495

Source: Madrid, Biblioteca Nacional de España, Inc/1518, fol. xxxxi[v]

Hurus' success not only allowed him to bring his brother, Juan, and nephew, Lope Appentegger in 1492, possibly to replace Juan, who had passed away in 1491, but also permitted him to finance some of the publications produced in his workshop.[70] His resources enabled him to play a decisive role in the intellectual life of Zaragoza. He befriended local intellectuals, such as Andrés de Li, and became their printer and even encouraged them to write new works with the promise that he would print them.[71] An innovator, Pablo was the first to use a printer's mark in Spain, consisting of two triangles with an H inside each.[72]

Pablo's books contained the largest number of illustrations of any Spanish incunabula. One of his most luxurious volumes is the Spanish translation of Bernhard von Breydenbach's *Peregrinatio in Terram Sanctam* (Zaragoza, 1498), a fifteenth-century bestseller.[73] He printed the illustrations from the original blocks made by the Dutch artist and printer Erhard Reuwich, who traveled with Breydenbach to make drawings of the sights, and then printed the first edition (Mainz, 1486). Some of these illustrations are highly detailed multi-block foldout plates of cities along the route. These woodblocks were transported across Europe, and were also used in Lyon.[74] Another significant work is *Ysopete historiado* (Zaragoza, 1482), the earliest translation into Spanish of Aesop's Fables, containing 191 woodblock illustrations. The work enjoyed wide diffusion as it was used in schools to teach youngsters how to read.

The most remarkable story, however, is that of Cromberger. Like other German-speaking printers, he started small. He took over Ungut's business around 1500, after he married his widow, a Spanish woman by the name of Comincia de Blanquis.[75] By 1508 he had organised a large network of distributors, from street vendors to large book shops around Spain.[76] He started to invest in real estate in 1510.[77] In 1525 he expanded his operation beyond Spain by using the extensive experience in international commerce of his son in law, Lázaro Nuremberger, who helped Cromberger establish trade with the rest of Europe and the New World.[78]

Since non-Castilians were forbidden by law to establish commerce with the New World, Cromberger sent a representative, Diego de Mendieta, to sell his books there.[79] In 1528 he was doing business in Santo Domingo, Mexico City, and Yucatán, but he also expanded into Portugal, after accepting an invitation by King Manuel I to start printing there.[80]

---

70 Lope Appentegger (Wolf Appentegger) was the son of Anna Hurus. See Delgado Casado, *Diccionario*, vol. 1, 39.

71 Haebler, *Tipografía ibérica*, 41. The Hurus press printed Li's *Tesoro de la passion* (1494), *Repertorio de los tiempos* (1495) and *Suma de paciencia* (1505).

72 Haebler, *Tipografía ibérica*, 41.

73 A landmark in the history of printing, *Peregrinatio* is the first printed illustrated travel book. The translation into Spanish was made by Martín Martínez de Ampies, but *Peregrinatio in Terram Sanctam* (Mainz: Erhard Reuwich, 1486), printed over thirteen times before 1500, was also translated into German, French and Dutch.

74 National Library of Scotland, at www.nls.uk/collections.rare-books/collections/breydenbach.

75 Griffin, *The Crombergers*, 24. Although the first archival evidence of him in Seville is in 1503, he must have arrived earlier. His son Juan legally accepted the deed of gift of the Cromberger press in 1525 and must therefore have been at least twenty-five years old, so it is possible that Jacobo married in 1500. (Ungut had passed away in 1499.)

76 Griffin, *The Crombergers*, 38–41.

77 Martínez, 'Los Cromberger'.

78 Lázaro was married to Jacobo's only daughter, Catalina. A native of the Nuremberg area, he first appears in Sevillian documents in 1522, but had been living in Lisbon as a factor of the Hischvogel trading company of Nuremberg. See Griffin, *The Crombergers*, 56–63.

79 Griffin, *The Crombergers*, 60–61.

80 Griffin, *The Crombergers*, 66 and 41.

In fact, he died in Lisbon in 1528, his estate, including several properties, valued at 12,000 ducats.[81] Juan, his son, took over the business and ran it successfully until 1540. Juan is best known for having introduced the printing press in the New World, setting up a workshop in Mexico City in 1539.[82]

Jacobo Cromberger's case, however, was exceptional as none of the children of the remaining printers took over the family presses. Most of their workshops passed into Spanish hands, sometimes their own workers, who had learned the trade from them. Just to mention a few, after Biel's death in 1517, his workshop went to Alonso de Melgar, who had worked with him and had married his daughter.[83] Carles Amoros, of French origin, bought the Luschner workshop in 1505, becoming the boss of Luschner's son, Joanot, who lacked the ability to run the family business.[84] Such was also the fate of the lucrative Cromberger business, which decayed under the leadership of Jacobo's grandson, Jácome. Overwhelmed by debts, Jácome closed the business in 1559, and moved to the New World, where he died around 1560.[85]

As their careers ended, so did the domination of German-speaking printers in Spain. In their fifty years of activity, from 1475 to 1525, this group of printers not only established the industry in Spain, but also left a lasting legacy. Although their professional lives were characterised by flux and mobility, due to the risky nature of the business, their shared contribution, besides the beautiful books they produced, was the training of a new generation of Spanish printers who took over the business and eventually produced the first examples of vocal and instrumental books intended for amateur musicians living in major urban centres.

---

81 Martínez, 'Los Cromberger'.

82 Juan was born and bred in Seville, so as a Castilian he could do business in the New World. The earliest printed volume was a Catechism in Spanish and Nahuatl, *Breve y mas compendiosa doctrina christiana* (Mexico City, 1539) by Juan de Zumárraga, the first bishop of Mexico City. See Griffin, *The Crombergers*, 85.

83 Cuesta Gutiérrez, 'Tipógrafos extranjeros', 70.

84 Rubió Balaguer, 'Integración de los impresores alemanes', 116. Amoros was one of several French printers working in the country. The most prominent was Arnaldo Guillén de Brocar, based in Alcalá de Henares, where he printed the *Biblia Políglota*. Commissioned by Cardinal Francisco Jiménez de Cisneros, Archbishop of Toledo, the *Biblia Políglota*, printed between 1514 and 1520, was one of the most challenging printing jobs in Spain at the time. This was a six-volume version of the Bible in Latin, Greek, Hebrew and Aramaic. It utilised several Latin, Gothic and Roman types, as well as a Greek alphabet made expressly for the work and considered as one of the best examples of its kind.

85 Griffin, *The Crombergers*, 117.

Appendix

Table 2.1 List of German-speaking printers with locations, dates, and list of publications

Name	Locations and dates	Publications
Fadrique Biel (Friedrich von Biel)	Burgos (1475–1517)	• *Manuale Burgense* (Manual of Burgos). Burgos, 1501. • *Passionarium Burgense* (Passionary of Burgos). Burgos, 1501. • Gonzalo Martínez de Bizcargui. *Arte de canto llano et de contrapunto. . .* (The Art of Plainchant and Counterpoint) Burgos, 1509.
Pedro Brun (Peter Brun)	Tortosa (1477) Barcelona (1478–c.1483/84) Seville (1492–1506)	• Alonso Spañon. *Introducción muy útil e breve de canto llano* (Useful and Brief Introduction to Plainchant). Seville, 1504.
Jorge Coci (Georg Koch)	Zaragoza (1499–1537)	• *Processionarium Cesaraugustanum* (Processional of Zaragoza) (with Leonardo Hutz). Zaragoza, 1502. • *Missale Oscense et Jacense* (Missal of Huesca and Jaca). Zaragoza, 1504. • *Passionarium Cesaraugustanum* (Passionary of Zaragoza). Zaragoza, 1504.
Compañeros Alemanes (Pablo de Colonia Thomas Glockner Magno Herbst Hans Pegnitzer)	Seville (1490–1502)	• Domingo Marcos Durán. *Lux bella* (Beautiful Light) (Cuatro Compañeros Alemanes). Seville, 1492. • *Manuale Toletanum* (Manual of Toledo) (Tres Compañeros Alemanes). Seville, 1494.
Jacobo Cromberger (Jakob Cromberger)	Seville (1503–1528)	• *Missale Legionense* (Missal of León). Seville, 1504. • Domingo Marcos Durán. *Lux bella,* 3rd. ed. Seville, 1509.
Pedro Hagenbach (Peter Hagembach)	Valencia (1491–1496) Toledo (1498–1502)	• *Missale Toletanum* (Missal of Toledo). Toledo, 1499. • *Missale Mixtum* (Complete Missal). Toledo, 1500. • *Manuale Toletanum* (Manual of Toledo). Toledo, 1503.
Juan Gysser (Hans Giesser)	Salamanca (1500–1509)	• Domingo Marcos Durán. *Súmula de canto de órgano* (Summary of Counterpoint). Salamanca, 1504? • Domingo Marcos Durán. *Lux bella,* 2nd. ed. Salamanca, 1509.

Table 2.1 continued

Name	Locations and dates	Publications
Pablo Hurus (Paulus Hyrus) Juan Hurus (Hans Hyrus)	Barcelona (1475) Zaragoza (1477–1499) Zaragoza (1488–1491)	• *Missale Cesaraugustanum* (Missal of Zaragoza). Zaragoza, 1485. • *Missale Oscense et Jacense* (Missal of Huesca and Jaca). Zaragoza, 1488. • *Missale Cesaraugustanum* (Missal of Zaragoza). Zaragoza, 1498.
Leonardo Hutz (Leonhardt Hutz)	Valencia (1491–1495) Salamanca (1494–1497) Zaragoza (1499–1504) Valencia (1505–1506) Zaragoza (1519)	• Guillermo del Podio. *Ars musicorum.* (The Art of Musicians) (with Pedro Hagenbach). Valencia, 1495.
Juan Luschner (Hans Luschner)	Barcelona (1495–1498) Montserrat (1499–1500) Barcelona (1501–1505)	• *Missale Benedictinum* (Benedictine Missal). Montserrat, 1499. • *Hymnorum Intonationes* (Intonations of Hymns). Montserrat, 1500. • *Officia Defunctorum* (Office for the Dead). Montserrat, 1500. • *Processionarium Benedictinum* (Benedictine Processional). Montserrat, 1500.
Juan Rosenbach (Johannes Rosenbach)	Valencia (1490) Barcelona (1492–1498) Tarragona (1498–1500) Perpignan (1500–1503) Barcelona (1506–1530)	• *Missale Gerundense* (Missal of Gerona). Barcelona, 1493. • *Missale Vicense* (Missal of Vic) (With Juan Luschner). Barcelona, 1496. • *Missale Tarraconense* (Missal of Tarragona). Barcelona, 1499. • Francisco Tovar. *Libro de música práctica* (Book of Practical Music). Barcelona, 1510.
Meinardo Ungut (Meinhardt Ungut)	Seville (1491–1499) Granada (1496)	• *Processionarium Predicatorum* (Processional for Dominican Use) (with Estanislao Polono). Seville, 1494. • *Missale Predicatorum* (Missal for Dominican Use) (with Estanislao Polono). Seville, 1497. • *Missale Giennense* (Missal of Jaén) (with Estanislao Polono) Seville, 1499.

62 MARGARITA RESTREPO

Table 2.2 Publications and printers by city

City	Publication and printer
Barcelona	*Missale Gerundense*. Juan Rosenbach, 1493.
	Missale Vicense. Juan Rosenbach and Juan Luschner, 1496.
	Missale Tarraconense. Juan Rosenbach, 1499.
	Francisco Tovar. *Libro de música práctica*. Juan Rosenbach, 1510.
Burgos	*Manuale Burgense*. Fadrique Biel, 1501.
	Passionarium Burgense. Fadrique Biel, 1501.
	Gonzalo Martínez de Bizcargui. *Arte de canto llano et de contrapunto* . . . Fadrique Biel, 1509.
Montserrat[a]	*Missale Benedictinum*. Juan Luschner, 1499.
	Hymnorum Intonationes. Juan Luschner, 1500.
	Officia Defunctorum. Juan Luschner, 1500.
	Processionarium Benedictinum. Juan Luschner, 1500.
Salamanca	Domingo Marcos Durán. *Súmula de canto de órgano*. Hans Gysser?, 1504?
	Domingo Marcos Durán. *Lux bella*, 2nd. edn. Juan Gysser, 1509.
Seville	Domingo Marcos Durán. *Lux bella*. Cuatro Compañeros Alemanes, 1492.
	Manuale Toletanum. Tres Compañeros Alemanes, 1494.
	Processionarium Predicatorum. Meinardo Ungut and Estanislao Polono, 1494.
	Missale Predicatorum. Meinardo Ungut and Estanislao Polono, 1497.
	Missale Giennense. Meinardo Ungut and Estanislao Polono, 1499.
	Missale Legionense. Jacobo Cromberger, 1504.
	Alonso Spañon. *Introducción muy útil e breve de canto llano*. Pedro Brun, 1504.
	Domingo Marcos Durán. *Lux bella*, 3rd. ed. Jacobo Cromberger, 1509.
Toledo	*Missale Toletanum*. Pedro Hagenbach, 1499.
	Missale Mixtum. Pedro Hagenbach, 1500.
	Manuale Toletanum. Pedro Hagenbach's workshop, 1503.
Valencia	Guillermo del Podio. *Ars musicorum*. Pedro Hagenbach and Leonardo Hutz, 1495.
Zaragoza	*Missale Cesaraugustanum*. Pablo Hurus, 1485.
	Missale Oscense et Jacense. Juan Hurus, 1488.
	Missale Cesaraugustanum. Pablo Hurus, 1498.
	Processionarium Cesaraugustanum. Jorge Coci and Leonardo Hutz, 1502.
	Missale Oscense et Jacense. Jorge Coci, 1504.
	Passionarium Cesaraugustanum. Jorge Coci, 1504.

Note: Luschner was asked to temporarily move to Montserrat to print material for the Benedictine monks at the Santa María de Montserrat Abbey.

References

Barrios Manzano, María del Pilar. 'Domingo Marcos Durán, un teórico extremeño del Renacimiento: Estado de la cuestión'. *Revista de Musicología* (1999): 91–127.

Castillo-Ferreira, Mercedes. 'Chant, liturgy and reform'. In *Companion to Music in the Age of the Catholic Monarchs*, edited by Tess Knighton. Leiden: Brill, 2017, 282–322.

Collantes de Terán, Francisco. 'Un taller alemán de imprenta en Sevilla en el siglo XV'. *Gutenberg-Jahrbuch* (1931): 145–165.

Cuesta Gutiérrez, Luisa. 'Los tipógrafos extranjeros en la imprenta burgalesa, del alemán Fadrique de Basilea al italiano Juan Bautista Varesio'. *Gutenberg-Jahrbuch* (1952): 67–74.

Delgado Casado, Juan. *Diccionario de impresores españoles: siglos XV–XVII*. Madrid: Arco, 1996.

Diccionario de historia eclesiástica de España, vol. 2. Madrid: Instituto Enrique Flórez, 1972.

Griffin, Clive. *The Crombergers of Sevilla: The History of a Printing and Mercantile Dynasty*. Oxford: Clarendon Press, 1988.

Haebler, Conrad. *The Early Printers of Spain and Portugal*. London: Bibliographical Society at the Chiswick Press, 1897.

Haebler, Conrad. *Tipografía ibérica del siglo XV*. The Hague: M. Nijhoff, 1902.

Hazañas y la Rua, Joaquín. 'Cuatro alemanes compañeros impresores de Sevilla 1490–1503'. *Gutenberg-Jahrbuch* (1931): 201–211.

López-Vidriero, Maria Luisa. 'The history of the book in the Iberian Peninsula'. In *The Oxford Companion to the Book*, vol. 1, edited by Michael H. Suarez, S. J. and Henry R. Woudhuysen. Oxford: Oxford University Press, 2010, 248–256.

Marsá, Maria. *La imprenta en los siglos de oro*. Madrid: Laberinto, 2001.

Martín Abad, Julian. *La imprenta en Alcalá de Henares (1502–1600)*. Madrid: Arco, 1991.

Martínez, Luisa. 'Los Cromberger: Una imprenta de Sevilla y Nueva España', 2003, at www.azc.uam.mx/publicaciones/tye/loscrombergerunaimprentadeseville.htm.

Millares Carlo, Agustín, 'La imprenta en Barcelona en el siglo XVI'. In *Historia de la imprenta hispana*. Madrid: Imprenta Nacional, 1982, 491–643.

Moll Roqueta, Jaime. 'Para el estudio de la edición española del Siglo de Oro'. In *Livres et librairies en Espagne et au Portugal, XVIᵉ–XXᵉ siècles*. Paris: Centre National de la Recherche Scientifique, 1989, 15–25.

Moll Roqueta, Jaime. 'Valoración de la industria editorial española del siglo XVI'. In *Livre et lecture en Espagne et en France sous l'Ancien Régime*. Paris: Association pour la diffusion de la pensée française, 1981, 70–84.

Norton, Frederick John. *A Descriptive Catalogue of Printing in Spain and Portugal, 1501–1520*. Cambridge: Cambridge University Press, 1978.

Norton, Frederick John. *Printing in Spain, 1501–1520*. Cambridge: Cambridge University Press, 1966.

Odriozola, Antonio. 'Los tipógrafos alemanes y la iniciación en España de la impresión musical (1485–1504)'. *Gutenberg-Jahrbuch* (1961): 60–70.

Painter, George D. 'The first press at Barcelona'. *Gutenberg-Jahrbuch* (1962): 136–149.

Revello Torre, José. *Orígenes de la imprenta en España y su desarrollo en América Española*. Buenos Aires: Institución Cultural Española, 1940.

Romero de Lecea, Carlos. *Introducción a los viejos libros de música*. Madrid: Joyas Bibliográficas, 1976.

Rubio i Balaguer, Jordi. 'Integración de los impresores alemanes en la vida social y económica de Cataluña y Valencia en los siglos XV–XVI'. *Spanische Forschungen der Görres-Gesellschaft* 20 (1962): 103–122.

Sarría Rueda, Amalia. 'Los inicios de la imprenta'. In *Historia del libro español*, edited by Hipólito Escolar. Madrid: Fundación Germán Sánchez Ruipérez, 1994, 35–93.

Vindel, Francisco. *El arte tipográfico en España durante el siglo XV*. Madrid: Dirección de Relaciones Culturales del Ministerio de Asuntos Exteriores, 1940–1954.

Villanueva Serrano, Francesc. 'El tractadista Guillermus de Podio: Bases pera la construcció d'una Biografia'. *Anuario musical* (2010): 3–24.

Whinnom, Keith. 'The Problem of the "best-seller" in Spanish Golden-Age Literature'. *Bulletin of Hispanic Studies* 57 (1980): 189–198.

Part II

Printing techniques

Problems and solutions

3

'Made in Germany'

The dissemination of mensural German music types outside
the German-speaking area (and vice versa), up to 1650

Laurent Guillo

During the period 1500–1650, around 150 to 200 music typefaces were used in Europe to print polyphonic music. Since the 1950s, some of these typefaces have been described in studies that focus on individual printers or areas, but no definitive census of these typefaces has yet been made. Descriptions and measurements must be sought in many studies, written by several scholars using different methods of description. While writing studies on music typography in France, Switzerland, and the Spanish Netherlands over the last thirty years, I noticed that some fonts made in these countries were exported abroad, while others made elsewhere were imported into these same territories.[1] Similar fonts were used in towns separated by thousands of kilometres, even more than a century after their punches were first cut. My goal in the present study will be to trace the source and direction of such transfers from one town to another, within and outside the German-speaking area, in France, England, Scotland, the Netherlands, Italy, Poland, Denmark and Sweden.

The most ambitious study of music typefaces within this area to date is a paper by Donald Krummel, published in 1985.[2] Here Krummel described twenty-seven music typefaces used in the German-speaking lands from the beginning until about 1650, and traced their dissemination. Here he limited himself to types used in part books. He emphasised the dominance of Nuremberg in the manufacture of the first typefaces that enjoyed an international distribution, and the dense network of music printers who used these characters right across the German-speaking territories, denser than that in France or Italy. His article was part of a larger project that was intended to cover all Europe, but he did not live to complete his plan. In my own publications I have been able to add two stones to Krummel's foundations by describing the situation in Lyon-Geneva and the former Low Countries. Although Krummel's objective still seems judicious thirty years on, it is difficult to use his work. Although he provided many interesting data, he did not follow a systematic method when describing the typefaces, their dimensions or use.

Some points of methodology

While comparing music typefaces used in various places, I encountered two major problems. To describe fonts, I follow the well-known Vervliet-Heartz method, based on three

---

1 See Guillo, *Les éditions musicales*. Music types are described under n° 121–144 (Lyon and Geneva); Guillo, 'Les caractères', 183–235 (Spanish Netherlands) and Guillo, *Ballard*, vol. I, 199–234 (Paris).

2 Krummel, 'Early German Type Faces'.

measurements and additional description when needed.[3] Unfortunately, the literature on music typefaces does not always give precise measurements. It is regrettable that studies such as those of Robert Steele (English typefaces), Donald Krummel (English or German typefaces), Åke Davidsson (Nordic typefaces), or Ernst-Ludwig Berz (Frankfurt typefaces up to c.1630) gathered so many data without giving reliable measurements, even if illustrations sometimes compensate for this lack of accuracy.[4] Comparing typefaces can therefore be risky, and it may be necessary to check results against real music books.

The second problem I encountered was the difficulty of graphically representing the dissemination of the fonts on a map. This dissemination can arise through different processes:

1. the sale of a music font from a type founder to a printer (this is the normal process of dissemination);
2. transfer of a font from one printer to another through sale or inheritance;
3. transfer arising when a printer moved from one town to another, with his fonts, tools, printing press and other equipment.

In most cases we do not know precisely how a given font was disseminated, though individual cases might be traced through archival research. But whatever the process was, we can discuss how to represent this dissemination on a map. The following three diagrams show first, what happens in a fictitious case (three primary transmissions from the type founder in town 1 to printers in towns 2, 3 and 6, then two secondary transmissions to printers in towns 4 and 5) which cannot be represented because of lack of sources (Figure 3.1); second, a classic 'arrow' diagram giving an approximate representation of this dissemination (Figure 3.2); and third, an 'area' diagram giving another approximate representation (Figure 3.3).

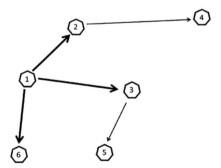

Figure 3.1 Diagram expressing a complex dissemination

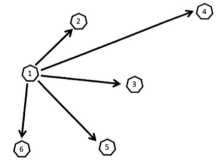

Figure 3.2 Dissemination expressed by a classic 'arrow' diagram

---

3 Three basic measurements are given: the total height of a five-line staff, the length of a minim whose head is on the external line, another whose head is on the external interline. Design of mensuration signs, clefs, and custodes must be described. Measures are made using mechanical or electronic calipers on moderately inked and non-broken types. The method is described by Guillo, *Les éditions musicales*, 377–378, after Heartz, 'Typography and Format'.

4 Steele, *English Music Printing*; Krummel, 'Early German Type Faces' and Krummel, *English Music Printing*; Davidsson, 'Das Typenmaterial' or Berz, *Frankfurt am Main*.

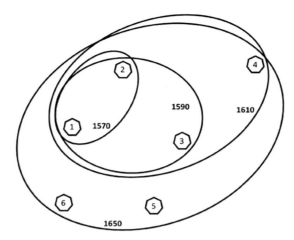

Figure 3.3 Dissemination expressed by an 'area' diagram

The 'area' diagram is more difficult to draw than the 'arrow' diagram, but it is more respectful of the historical reality, since it does not imply that all transfers originated from the first place the typeface is found. Although I shall use arrow diagrams in this study for their simplicity, we must keep in mind that they may not always reflect historical reality.

Ten music typefaces used within and outside the German-speaking area

When compiling data and measurements from the available literature on music printing, I found only ten music typefaces used both within and outside the German-speaking area. I will describe them here in chronological order. Illustrations of each typeface are given towards the end of this chapter (Figures 3.9–3.18).

N° 1: Guillo 1997 'Schöffer.' Double impression. Dimensions: 10.0 / 11.2 / 11.2 mm.
Use within the German-speaking area: Mainz 1512–1518, Worms 1525–1526, Strasbourg 1530–1539.
Use outside the German-speaking area: Antwerp or Kampen, c.1535 (*Kamper Liedboek*).

The first typeface was used by Peter Schöffer the Younger in three different places (Mainz, Worms, and Strasbourg) from 1512 to 1539.[5] It is a double-impression type, using the 'Petrucci process' in which the staves are printed first, then the notes. It obviously resembles the Petrucci type.

The font was used again around 1535 in the Netherlands, in the famous *Kamper Liedboek*, perhaps in Kampen (a small town near Amsterdam) but more likely in Antwerp, as David Fallows has suggested.[6] Nobody knows who brought this font there, but by the time the book was printed, it was already an old-fashioned typeface: in many places in Europe, new music fonts using the single-impression process initiated by Pierre Attaingnant in Paris (1528) were already in use (see Figure 3.4, dotted lines).

---

5 On this printer, see Lindmayr-Brandl, 'Peter Schöffer der Jüngere', with a reproduction of the typeface, 301.
6 See Fallows, 'Songbook at Kampen'.

Figure 3.4 Dissemination of types N° 1 (dotted lines) and N° 4 (plain lines)

N° 2: Krummel 1985 n° 2 'Formschneider' = Davidsson 1957[7] Tab. I type 1 (fig. n° 3, 7, 11, 12) = Davidsson 1962T Abb. 3 = Collijn 1952[8] pl. LXXXV. (Not included in Guillo 1997). Single impression. Dimensions: 10.4 / 8.4 / 8.9 mm.

Use within the German-speaking area: Nuremberg 1534–1555; Wittenberg 1538–; Leipzig 1552–; Jena 1557–; Magdeburg 1570–; Dresden 1570–; Ülzen 1575; Frankfurt/Oder; Stettin (Szczecin) 1578–; Rostock 1579–; Greifswald 1582–; Eisleben 1580–; Praha 1580–; Altdorf 1586–; Thorn (Toruń) 1587–; Kassel 1603; Hamburg 1613–; Frankfurt/Main 1617–; Halle 1634–; Danzig (Gdańsk) 1658–.

Use outside the German-speaking area: Stockholm 1594–; Copenhagen 1603–; Antwerp 1597–.

This typeface uses the Attaingnant process (single impression, with the staves cut in slices). It originated in Nuremberg, where it was first used by Hieronymus Formschneider from 1534 to 1555. From 1538, Georg Rhau used it in his presses at Wittenberg.

Very soon, fonts of this typeface were disseminated to many German towns north of Nuremberg. This process lasted until the middle of the seventeenth century. These fonts were used at Stockholm from 1594 by Gutterwitz; by his successors Mattsson and Reusner from 1634; at Antwerp in 1597; and at Copenhagen by Henrik Waldkirch, from 1603 or 1607. These types probably reached the Nordic countries through Rostock or Greifswald, or perhaps through Danzig (Gdańsk) (see Figure 3.5, plain lines).

N° 3: Guillo 1991 n° 124 = Guillo 1997 'Petreius small' = Krummel 1985 n° 3 'Petreius small' = Davidsson 1962T n° 1 p. 78 = Nielsen 1934[9] pl. XLVIII n° 21. Single impression. Added solmisation letters: Vervliet 2000[10] n° M 9.2. Dimensions: 9.2 / 7.8 / 8.0 mm. Nested typeface. Fifty matrices are kept in Antwerp, Museum Plantin-Morteus (MPM): MA 92.a.

Use within the German-speaking area: Nuremberg 1537–1655; Augsburg 1540–; Basel 1547–1582; Breslau (Wrocław) 1555–; Vienna 1561–; Frankfurt/Main 1565–; Heidelberg 157X; Dillingen 1575–; Lauingen 1584–; Strasbourg 1605–; Coburg 1608–; Freiburg im Breisgau 1651.

Use outside the German-speaking area: Lyon 1547–1559, 1641; Geneva 1550–1562; Antwerp 1551–1561; Copenhagen 1569–1592; London 1604?

The third typeface also originated in Nuremberg, and was used there by Johann Petreius from 1537. It is designed for nesting, which allowed the punchcutter to cut fewer punches than usual. Since cutting one punch required about one day of work, cutting a nested typeface resulted in significant savings of effort and money.

Fonts of this typeface were disseminated very quickly in many directions simultaneously. One font of this typeface was used at Lyons by the printers Godefroy and Marcelin Beringen, who came from Basel. They used a new font, which gives their music books a very neat look. This distinguished them from the old-fashioned, poor-quality typography of Jacques Moderne.

Some fonts subsequently reached Geneva (through Lyon), where the famous punchcutter Pierre Haultin added small solmisation letters to make the font suitable for printing psalm books. Consequently, this typeface was used in some editions of the Genevan Psalter. It also reached Antwerp, where it was used by Tielman Susato; Copenhagen, where it was

---

7 Davidsson, *Studier rörande svensk.*
8 Collijn, *Svensk Typografisk Atlas.*
9 Nielsen, *Dansk Typografisk Atlas.*
10 Vervliet, 'Printing Types of Pierre Haultin' describes twelve music types cut between 1554 and 1575.

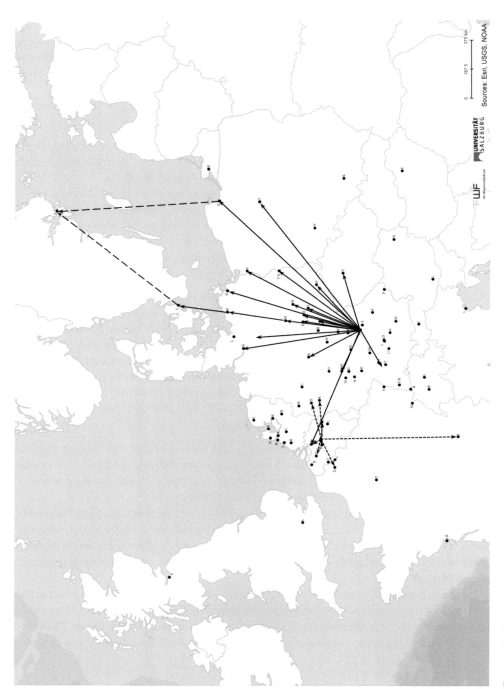

Figure 3.5 Dissemination of types N° 2 (plain lines) and N° 5 (dotted lines)

used by Lorentz Benedicht; and perhaps London, by way of Antwerp.[11] The presence of a set of matrices kept in the Museum Plantin-Moretus means that fonts could also disseminate from Antwerp (see Figure 3.6, plain lines).

N° 4: Guillo 2003 'MMF1' = Noailly 1988 n° 16 = Krummel 1985 n° 4 'Petreius Large' = Davidsson 1957 Tab. I type 3. Dimensions: 10.5 / 9.5–9.6 / 10.0–10.1 mm. Single impression. Nested typeface.
Use within the German-speaking area: Nuremberg 1538–1558; Bern 1553–; Erfurt 1572–; Wien 1574–; Königsberg (Kaliningrad) 1579–; Augsburg 1581–; Wasungen 1587–; Innsbruck 1588–; Coburg 1604–; Dillingen 1604–; Lübeck 1617–; Linz 1619–.
Use outside the German-speaking area: Paris 1553–ca 1600; Venice 1557–; Eger 1571–; Kraków 1580–; Praha 1586–; Stockholm 1619–1733.

This typeface also originated from the Petreius workshop in Nuremberg. Its punchcutter was probably working in Nuremberg. It is also a nested type, larger than the previous one and more suitable for books printed in quarto format. After its first use at Nuremberg in 1538, it was disseminated very quickly in many directions simultaneously.

A font of this typeface was used in Paris by the Le Roy and Ballard workshop from 1553 until 1600. We suggest that Guillaume I Le Bé, the type founder who worked for Le Roy and Ballard, whose workshop was situated just across the street from theirs, purchased a set of matrices. This would allow him to cast as many types as were needed by the active workshop of Le Roy and Ballard. Some other fonts also reached Venice, Kraków and Prague, then Stockholm, where it was used by many printers.

This typeface was imitated in Geneva around 1578, when some Genevan printers, such as Jean Le Royer, began to print Protestant contrafacta of music by Orlando di Lasso and Guillaume Boni, copied from Parisian prints by Le Roy and Ballard.[12] The typeface was also copied in Germany in the last quarter of the sixteenth century, though increasingly these copies show more differences from the original design, in clefs, signatures, alterations and other details (see Figure 3.4, plain lines).[13]

These four music typefaces were the first ones used in their respective workshops. The next six were mostly the second or third typefaces in the workshop, used to print smaller or larger books than those previously produced by a given workshop, or to replace older typefaces.

N° 5: Guillo 1991 n° 135 = Guillo 1997 'Phalèse Moyenne' = Vervliet 1968[14] n° M14 = Krummel 1985 n° 24 'Phalèse.' Single impression. Dimensions: 10.7 / 11.7 / 11.2 mm. Nineteen matrices in Antwerp MPM: MA 101b.
Use outside the German-speaking area: Leuven 1552–1578; Maastricht 1554; Lyon c.1556–1567; Douai 1578–1633; Antwerp 1582–1708; Brussels 1590; Ghent 1651–1689.
Use within the German-speaking area: Düsseldorf 1555–1589; Köln c.1593–1603.

This typeface was cut outside the German-speaking area. It originated in 1552, in the famous Phalèse workshop at Louvain (Leuven). It was disseminated to the Spanish Netherlands until the end of the seventeenth century.

---

11 On its possible use in London, see Krummel, *English Music Printing*, 89.
12 The dimensions of the Le Royer copy (Guillo, *Les éditions musicales*, n° 144) are very close: 10.7 / 10.0 / 10.2 mm.
13 See Krummel, 'Early German Type Faces', n° 11, 'Post Petreius'.
14 Vervliet, *Sixteenth Century Printing Types*.

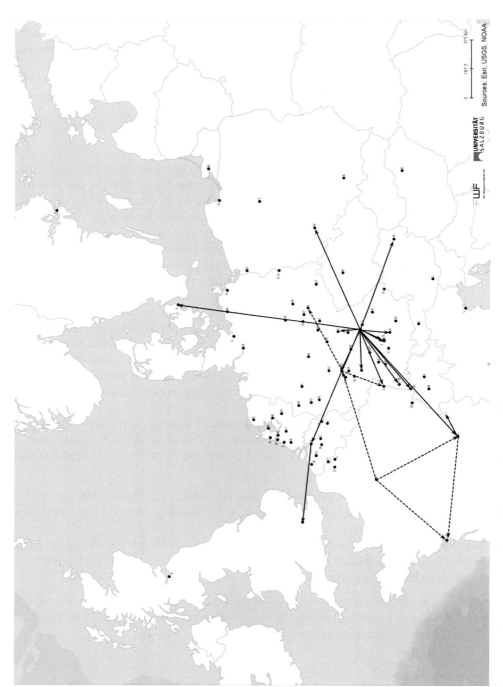

Figure 3.6 Dissemination of types N° 3 (plain lines) and N° 6 (dotted lines)

It was also disseminated southwards as far as Lyon, perhaps through Germany or Basel. There it is called 'note de Louvain à longue queue' (music type from Leuven with a long stem). It was used at Lyon once only, in 1567.[15] However, it was mentioned there as early as September 1556 in the inventory of Godefroy Beringen.[16] It was also disseminated eastwards to Düsseldorf and Köln, until the end of the sixteenth century. The Museum Plantin-Moretus keeps nineteen matrices, probably acquired from the Susato workshop (see Figure 3.5, dotted lines).

N° 6: Guillo 1991 n° 130 = Berz 1970 'D' = Noailly 1988 n° 7 = Vervliet 2015[17] n° 3. Not included by Krummel 1985. Single impression. Dimensions: 7.0 / 6.5 / 6.5 mm. Forty punches are kept in Antwerp MPM: ST 72.
Use outside the German-speaking area: Paris 1556–1588; Lyon 1560–1610; La Rochelle 1563.
Use within the German-speaking area: Frankfurt/Main 1570; Strasbourg 1587; Leipzig 1608.

This typeface was probably cut by the famous punchcutter Robert Granjon while he was working in Paris. Its punches now are kept in the Museum Plantin-Moretus in Antwerp. It was first used by Nicolas Du Chemin in Paris from 1556 to 1568, and by a few other printers there, such as Léon Cavellat and Marc Loqueneux. In Lyon, it was used heavily from 1561 to 1581 by Jean I and Jean II de Tournes, and by a few other printers from 1560 to 1610. It was used again by Barthélémy Berton in La Rochelle in 1563. It is possible that Pierre Haultin took it there.

The typeface was disseminated to Frankfurt/Main in 1570, Strasbourg in 1587, and as far as Leipzig, where it was used in the famous treatise on proofreading by Hieronymus Hornschuch, printed by Lantzenberger in 1608. This type probably reached Strasbourg and Leipzig through Frankfurt/Main (see Figure 3.6, dotted lines).

N° 7: Guillo 1991 n° 137 = Guillo 1997 'Granjon' = Krummel 1975 Type 8 = Vervliet 2015 n° 7. Single impression. Dimensions: 7.0 / 6.4 / 6.7 mm.
Use outside the German-speaking area: Antwerp 1565–1667; Ghent 1565–1574; London 1567–1654; Leiden 1578–1653; Rotterdam 1582–1644; Utrecht 1598–1613; Alkmaar 1604; Brugge 1609–1662; Amsterdam 1613–1700; Lyon 1615–1710; Valenciennes 1616–1631; Haarlem 1629–1759; Tournai 1632–1640; Leeuwarden 1634–1717; Edinburgh 1635; Deventer 1640; Bruxelles 1642; Enkhuizen 1668; Montbéliard etc.
Use within the German-speaking area: Wesel 1567; Würzburg 1662.

This typeface, cut by Robert Granjon around 1565, perhaps in Lyons or Antwerp, is famous in the history of music printing. It was disseminated rapidly from Antwerp. Its legible design allowed printers to use it in many psalm books in printed in sextodecimo or duodecimo format. Solmisation letters were added around 1570–1574 by Ameet Tavernier in Antwerp.

According to Krummel, several fonts of this typeface were distributed from Frankfurt/Main after the end of the sixteenth century, in addition to the dissemination from Antwerp.[18] Krummel stated that it appears a dozen times in Germany, but extra research is necessary here, since he did not give any detailed information. Some dissemination into Germany is

---

15 Giovanni Antonio Di Mayo, *Primo libro di madrigali* (Lyon: Antoine Cercia, 1567), USTC 120126–8, 203529; Guillo, *Les éditions musicales*, n° 81, RISM M 1487.
16 See Baudrier, *Bibliographie lyonnaise*, 35–36.
17 Vervliet, 'Granjon's music founts'.
18 See Krummel, *English Music Printing*, 51.

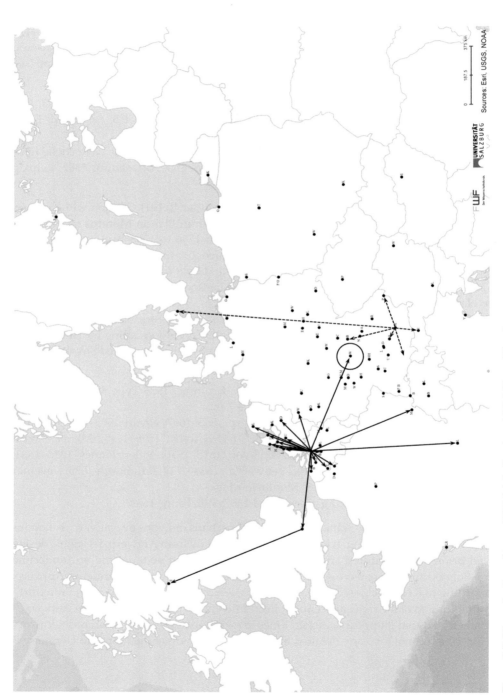

Figure 3.7 Dissemination of types N° 7 (plain lines) and N° 8 (dotted lines)

very likely since this is one of the most widely used music typefaces in Europe; I have verified that it was used by Christophe Küchler at Würzburg in 1662 (see Figure 4.7, plain lines).

N° 8: Krummel 1985 n° 16 'Nenninger' = Davidsson 1962D[19] (fig. 10 and 13). Single impression. Dimensions: 11.3 / 10.0 / 10.6 mm. Nested type.
Use within the German-speaking area: Passau 1602–; München 1604–; Ravensburg 1626–; Bamberg 1628–; Innsbrück 1640–; Augsburg 1655–;
Use outside the German-speaking area: Copenhagen 1646–.

This typeface originated in 1602 in Passau, where it was used by Matthäus Nenninger. Later it was used by Nikolaus Heinrich in Munich, for example in Lassus' *Magnus opus musicum*. It was disseminated in many places in south Germany throughout the seventeenth century, probably from Munich.

According to Davidsson, it is found later in Copenhagen, used by Melchior Martzan around 1646, then Christian Wering around 1655 (see Figure 3.7, dotted lines).

N° 9: Berz 1970 type 'L' = Schaefer 1975[20] type 'A' = Krummel 1985 n° 17 'Kieffer.' Single impression. Dimensions: 11.3 / 9.7 / 10.3 mm. Nested type.
Use within the German-speaking area: Frankfurt/Main 1609, Tübingen 1622–; Würzburg 1623–; Ulm 1644–; Stuttgart 1644; Wien 1648–; Schwäbisch Hall 1650–; Luzern 1651–; Giessen 1685; Basel; Darmstadt; Mainz.
Use outside the German-speaking area: Liège 1668–.

The dimensions of this typeface are very close to the previous one, and as a result these typefaces have sometimes been confused. It seems to have originated in Frankfurt/Main in 1609, under Wolfgang Richter's press, where it was used until 1631.

It was used in many places in Germany in the seventeenth century, distributed from Frankfurt/Main by the type founder Johann Adolph Schmidt. It is found again in Liège in 1668, used by Hendrik Streel (see Figure 3.8, plain lines).

N° 10: Krummel 1985 n° 14 'Van Ohr' = Davidsson 1957 Tab. I type 2. Single impression. Dimensions: 13.4 mm. Not to be confused with Krummel 1985 n° 15 'Holwein.'
Use within the German-speaking area: Hamburg 1597–; Rostock 1599–; Lüneburg 1621–.
Use outside the German-speaking area: Stockholm, 1622.

This typeface is used in the north of Germany, from 1597 until the end of the first quarter of the seventeenth century. It is found again briefly in Stockholm, used in 1622 by Christoffer Reusner (see Figure 4.8, dotted lines).

Some conclusions

These ten typefaces illustrate the major characteristics of the trade in music types during the sixteenth and the seventeenth centuries. First of all, it is obvious that the trade of music fonts was already an international business in its first half-century of existence. The fonts (and sometimes the matrices) could cross many borders for decades after the punches were cut. From this point of view, the types N° 3 'Petreius small' and N° 4 'Petreius large' are

---

19 Davidsson, *Danskt Musiktryck*.
20 Schaefer, *Die Notendrucker und Musikverleger*.

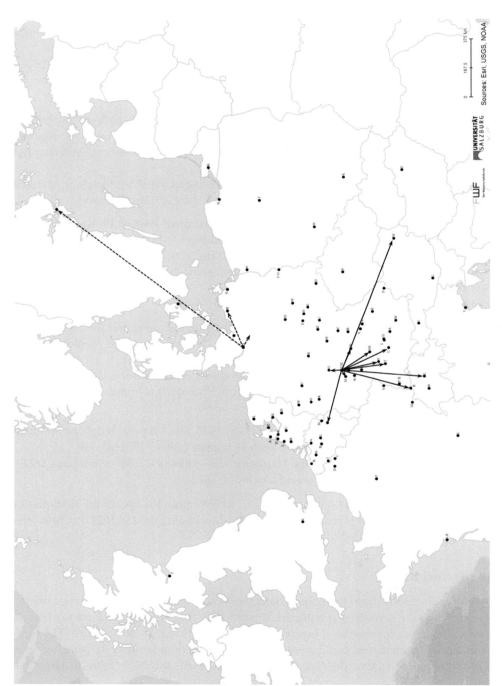

Figure 3.8 Dissemination of types N° 9 (plain lines) and N° 10 (dotted lines)

very significant: less than fifteen years after their first appearance, fonts cast from their matrices are found far away from Nuremberg, used by famous music printers such as Beringen in Lyon, Ballard in Paris, Pietrasanta in Venice, Nigrinus in Prague, and Susato in Antwerp. This can only be the result of efficient and international marketing of these products.

Furthermore, we note that the German-speaking area was a net exporter of music typefaces up to *c.*1650: seven typefaces were exported out of the German-speaking area, but only three were imported. During the first half of the sixteenth century, there are only exportations, and in foreign places these music fonts are used by workshops that printed 'modern books' as opposed to 'gothic books', that is, books with roman and italic types and elegant layout of the title page. In Lyon, such a transition is marked by the introduction of N° 3 'Petreius small' by the Beringen brothers, who were in competition with the old Jacques Moderne. In Paris this transition is marked with the introduction of N° 4 'Petreius large' by the Le Roy and Ballard workshop, at a time when the production of Attaingnant's workshop was in decline.[21]

Such rapid and distant sales of music fonts coming from Germany (mostly Nuremberg, Munich and Frankfurt/Main) prove that the production of German punchcutters of this time was of international quality and interest. Their design was modern, several of them were nested, and therefore less expensive, and many music printers may have found some immediate profit in buying and using some of these fonts. It is likely that the excellent quality of such production was a consequence of the great metallurgical expertise of some German towns of this time. Several punchcutters were sons of goldsmiths, or even goldsmiths themselves, such as Robert Granjon, and there is an evident link between goldsmithing expertise and the production of high-quality types. Nuremberg was particularly famous during the Renaissance for its production of armour as well as for high-quality goldsmithing and silversmithing, and its production was traded on an international scale.[22] We can guess that some music matrices and fonts may have reached foreign printers through the same commercial networks as armoury and goldsmith.

The first half of the sixteenth century was a kind of Golden age for German music punchcutting. However, by the second half of the century, a number of important music punchcutters were working outside the German-speaking area, such as Robert Granjon, Guillaume I Le Bé, Hendrik Vanden Keere, Pierre Haultin, and Jean Jannon. As a result, punchcutting became less of a German specialty than it had been in the first half of the century. Demand for German types elsewhere dropped off, since good types were sometimes available closer to home.

In this short study, we did not try to identify the precise origin of the music types mentioned above. Literature on punchcutting is scarce; on music punchcutting it is almost nonexistent, so further archival research is needed before we can reach any conclusions.[23] We think it would be better to devote time and energy to refining and completing the census of music types begun by Krummel, Berz, Schäfer and other scholars in order to determine the solid and exhaustive contribution of Germany to the European census of music types.

---

21 Among other music types, such as Noailly, 'Claude Goudimel'. Music types are described in vol. 3, 348–384, n° 7, 8, 10, 11, and 16.

22 Voit, *Die Nürnberger Gold- und Silberschlägerei*.

23 See Bauer, *Chronik der Schriftgießereien*; Bruckner, *Schweizer Stempelschneider und Schriftgießer*; Diehl, *Frankfurter Schriftproben*; Fritz, *Geschichte der Wiener Schriftgießereien*; Mori, *Das Schriftgießergewerbe in Süddeutschland*; Mori, *Die Egenolff-Lutherische Schriftgießerei*; Mori, *Schriftproben deutscher Schriftgießereien*; Mori, *Die Anfänge des Schriftgießereigewerbes*; McMurtrie, 'Types and Typefounding'.

80 LAURENT GUILLO

The few maps we have drawn above show that a proper appreciation of the historical significance of the trade in music types will require a census that will necessarily be an international project.

References

Baudrier, Henri-Louis and Julien. *Bibliographie lyonnaise: recherches sur les imprimeurs, libraires, relieurs et fondeurs de lettres de Lyon au XVIe siècle*. Troisième série. Lyon, Brun, Paris: Picard et fils, 1897.

Bauer, Friedrich. *Chronik der Schriftgießereien in Deutschland und den deutschsprachigen Nachbarländern*. Offenbach: Verein Deutscher Schriftgießereien, 1928.

Berz, Ernst-Ludwig. *Die Notendrucker und ihre Verleger in Frankfurt am Main von den Anfängen bis etwa 1630: Eine bibliographische und drucktechnische Studie zur Musikpublikation. Catalogus musicus 5.* Kassel: Bärenreiter, 1970.

Bruckner, Albert. *Schweizer Stempelschneider und Schriftgießer*. Münchenstein: Haas'sche Schriftgießerei, 1943.

Collijn, Isak. *Svensk Typografisk Atlas: 1400–och 1500–talen*. Stockholm: Hugo Gebers förlag, 1952.

Davidsson, Åke. 'Studier rörande svenskt musiktryck före år 1750 = Studien über den Swedischen Musikdruck vor 1750'. PhD dissertation, University of Uppsala, 1957.

Davidsson, Åke. 'Das Typenmaterial des älteren nordischen Musikdrucks'. *Annales academiae scientiarum Upsaliensis* 6 (1962): 76–101.

Davidsson, Åke. *Danskt Musiktryck intill 1700-talets mitt*. Uppsala: Almquist & Wiksell, 1962.

Diehl, Robert. *Frankfurter Schriftproben aus dem 16. bis 18. Jahrhundert*. Frankfurt: Stempel AG, 1955.

Fallows, David. 'The Printed Songbook at Kampen'. In *NiveauNischeNimbus: die Anfänge des Musikdrucks nördlich der Alpen*, edited by Birgit Lodes. Wiener Forum für ältere Musikgeschichte 3. Tutzing: Hans Schneider, 2010, 347–354.

Fritz, Georg. *Geschichte der Wiener Schriftgießereien 1482–1923*. Wien: Berthold, 1924.

Guillo, Laurent. 'Les caractères de musique employés des origines à *c*.1650 dans les anciens Pays-Bas'. *Yearbook of the Alamire Foundation* 2 (1997): 183–235.

Guillo, Laurent. *Les éditions musicales de la Renaissance lyonnaise*. Paris: Klincksieck, 1991.

Guillo, Laurent. *Pierre I Ballard et Robert III Ballard, imprimeurs du roy pour la musique (1599–1673)*. 2 vols. Sprimont, Mardaga; Versailles, CMBV, 2003.

Heartz, Daniel. 'Typography and Format in Early Music Printing with Particular Reference to Attaingnant's First Publications'. *Notes* (1967): 702–706.

Krummel, Donald W. 'Early German Part Book Type Faces'. *Gutenberg Jahrbuch* (1985): 80–98.

Krummel, Donald W. *English Music Printing 1553–1700*. London: Bibliographical society, 1975.

Lindmayr-Brandl, Andrea. 'Peter Schöffer der Jüngere, das Erbe Gutenbergs und "die wahre Art des Druckens"'. In *NiveauNischeNimbus: die Anfänge des Musikdrucks nördlich der Alpen*, edited by Birgit Lodes. Wiener Forum für ältere Musikgeschichte 3. Tutzing: Hans Schneider, 2010, 283–312.

McMurtrie, Douglas C. 'Types and Typefounding in Germany: the Work of Christian Egenolff and His Successors in the Development of the Luther Foundry'. *The Inland Printer* 73 (1924): 564–569.

Mori, Gustav. *Das Schriftgießergewerbe in Süddeutschland und den angrenzenden Ländern, ein Abschnitt aus der Geschichte des deutschen Schriftgießergewerben*. Stuttgart: Schriftgießerei Bauer & Company, 1924.

Mori, Gustav. *Die Anfänge des Schriftgießereigewerbes in Frankfurt am Main*. Frankfurt/Main: Klimsch, 1928.

Mori, Gustav. *Die Egenolff-Lutherische Schriftgießerei in Frankfurt am Main*. Frankfurt/Main: D. Stempel AG, 1926.

Mori, Gustav. *Schriftproben deutscher Schriftgießereien und Buchdruckereien aus den Jahren 1479–1840.* Frankfurt/Main: Verein Deutscher Schriftgießereien, 1926.

Nielsen, Lauritz. *Dansk Typografisk Atlas, 1482–1600.* Copenhagen: Gyldendal, 1934.

Noailly, Jean-Michel. 'Claude Goudimel, Adrian Le Roy et les CL psaumes: Paris, 1562–1567', 3 vols. Ph.D. dissertation, Université de Saint-Étienne, 1988.

Schaefer, Hartmut. *Die Notendrucker und Musikverleger in Frankfurt am Main von 1630 bis um 1720.* 2 vols. Kassel: Bärenreiter, 1975.

Steele, Robert. *The Earliest English Music Printing: A Description and Bibliography of English Printed Music to the Close of the Sixteenth Century.* London, Bibliographical Society: Chiswick Press, 1903. Reprint: Meisenheim, 1965.

Vervliet, Hendrik D. L. 'Granjon's Music Founts'. *De Gulden passer* 93/2 (2015): 127–159.

Vervliet, Hendrik D. L. 'Printing Types of Pierre Haultin (*c*.1510–87). Part II: Italic, Greek and Music Types'. *Quærendo* 30 (2000): 173–227.

Vervliet, Hendrik D. L. *Sixteenth Century Printing Types in the Low Countries.* Amsterdam: Brill, Hes & De Graaf, 1968.

Voit, Hans. *Die Nürnberger Gold- und Silberschlägerei in historischer und sozialpolitischer Beleuchtung.* Nuremberg: B. Hilz, 1912.

Figure 3.9 Type 1 – Sigmund Salminger, *Cantiones quinque vocum*. Strasbourg: Peter Schöffer the Younger, 1539. Beginning of first page of Discantus partbook
Source: München, Bayerische Staatsbibliothek, Mus.pr. 48

Figure 3.10 Type 2 – Heinrich Finck, *Schöne auszerlesne lieder*. Nuremberg: Hieronymus Formschneider, 1536. Beginning of *In Gottes namen*
Source: München, Bayerische Staatsbibliothek, Mus.pr. 35/1

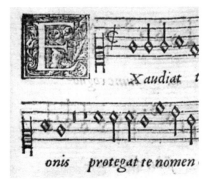

Figure 3.11 Type 3 – Dominique Phinot, *Liber secundus mutetarum*. Lyon: G. & M. Beringen, 1548. Cantus, beginning of motet 1
Source: München, Bayerische Staatsbibliothek, 4 Mus.pr. 194/3

Figure 3.12 Type 4 – Orlando di Lasso, *Moduli sex septem et duodecim vocum*. Paris: Le Roy & Ballard, 1573. Beginning of Superius, fol. 4^v
Source: München, Bayerische Staatsbibliothek, Mus.pr. 9678

Figure 3.13 Type 5 – Adrian Denss, *Florilegium omnis fere generis cantionum . . . ad testudinis tabulaturam*. Cologne: G. Grevenbruch, 1594. Beginning of fol. 8^r
Source: München, Bayerische Staatsbibliothek, 2 Mus.pr. 93

Figure 3.14 Type 6 – Louis Desmasures, *Vingtsix Cantiques chantés au Seigneur*. Lyon: J. de Tournes, 1564. Cantus, beginning of Cantique XXI
Source: München, Bayerische Staatsbibliothek, Mus.pr. 41/1

Figure 3.15 Type 7 – *La Philomèle séraphique, partie seconde*. Tournai: A. Quinqué, 1632, p. 15
Source: München, Bayerische Staatsbibliothek, Mus.pr. 27-1/2#2

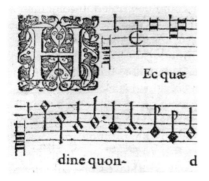

Figure 3.16 Type 8 – Orlando di Lasso, *Magnum opus musicum*. Munich: N. Heinrich, 1604. Cantus, first page of music
Source: München, Bayerische Staatsbibliothek, 2 Mus. pr. 68

Figure 3.17 Type 9 – Lodovico Viadana, *Centum sacri concentus*. Frankfurt/Main: W. Richter, 1615. Cantus, first page of music
Source: München, Bayerische Staatsbibliothek, 4 Mus.pr. 830

Figure 3.18 Type 10 – Hieronymus Praetorius, *Cantiones sacrae de praecipuis festis totius anni*. Hamburg: Ph. von Ohr, 1599. First page of music
Source: München, Bayerische Staatsbibliothek, 4 Mus.pr. 4331/2

4

Printing music

Technical challenges and synthesis, 1450–1530

Elisabeth Giselbrecht and Elizabeth Savage

Johannes Gutenberg, a goldsmith from Mainz, is celebrated for having invented printing around 1450. The press itself was not a novelty to his contemporaries, as screw presses had long been used, for example to make cider and wine. His breakthrough was movable type: these cast metal *sorts* or *types* (individual pieces) allowed for the creation of potentially infinite texts from a finite set of materials. Copies could be produced at unprecedented speed. Metal moveable type quickly expanded beyond text and was combined with other materials, including woodcut and metalcut, so that texts could be printed in combination with pictorial material, including images, printers' ornaments, decorative initials, diagrams and music. Each kind of content presented printshops with specific challenges.

For music, printers had to find ways to precisely superimpose notes upon staves, or vice versa. The development of a simpler and more commercially viable method of printing music in the 1530s, involving moveable music type that combined staves and notes on a single sort, enabled printers to set and print music in a single run through the press (like text).[1] In the eight decades between the invention of moveable text type and the invention of moveable music type, printers developed many solutions for printing music. Most involved two or more superimposed impressions *in register* (the printers' term for 'in alignment'). For music, this required at least two formes (one with staves, one with notes), which were printed in two (or more) runs through the press. In the musicological literature, the mastery of printing in register has been celebrated as an outstanding feat unique to music printing, and it has been posited that there might even have been a need for specially trained 'music printers'. However, few, if any guild systems in the early decades of the press could have accommodated this trade, nor would there have been any need for such specialised jobbing printers. As Joseph Dane has pointed out, this 'profession' is a recent academic invention, wholly unattested in contemporary and later records.[2]

Printing in register

Printing in register was used for a broad variety of textual and pictorial material. From the printer's perspective, the content was irrelevant. Whether they printed on both sides of a sheet, initials in red within lines of text in black, or a key block (outline) in black over colourful tone blocks, printers had to print in register. It did not matter whether the printed areas of successive impressions are adjacent (e.g. red initials next to black text) or overlap

---

1 For a discussion of the terminology, in particular single and double impression printing, see below. For the so-called 'single impression' technique, see the chapter by Laurent Guillo in this volume.

2 Dane, 'Two-Color Printing', 137.

(e.g. a black outline over a background tone), as they all involve running the paper through the press more than once.

Printing in register is often equated with printing in colour, and colour impressions account for a vast amount of early material printed in register. Margaret Smith and Alan May estimated that roughly 15 per cent of incunabula include text printed in red and black,[3] and tens of thousands of impressions of sixteenth-century book illustrations and single-sheet woodcuts were printed in more than one colour, with one run through the press per colour.[4] However, this does not mean – as is often tacitly assumed in art historical scholarship – that all material printed in register is necessarily in two or more colours. There are many instances of overlapping impressions in black, for example in diagrams or, indeed, in printed music. While there are many instances of music printed in two colours (red and black), predominantly in books of liturgical music, there are also many where black notes were printed on black staves. Regardless of the colour, however, music had to be printed in register, normally from two formes (staves and notes) as this was the way to achieve the superimposition of notes and staves.

In this sense, the earliest attempts at printing music in register around 1465 were neither novel nor specific to music. Instead, music was only one of the many uses for a basic skill that is attested from the first printed book, the Gutenberg Bible of c.1455, of which some copies contain rubrics printed in red within columns of text in black.[5] The materials would also have been familiar: printing music involved the same paper/parchment and standard relief printing inks (typically a binding medium of oil varnish, often boiled linseed oil, with colourants such as lampblack for black and vermillion or red lead for red ground in). Because all of these 'special methods' involved printing in register, effectively every early modern printer had the skills to print music.

Music has been largely excluded from technical histories of printing and of colour printmaking in fields including bibliography to art history. On the other hand, historians of music printing are yet to acknowledge the technical parallels between printing music and other kinds of content. However, it is no coincidence that early printers who printed music in register (in black, or in black and red) also printed, for instance, bicolour initials, images, and printers' devices, using the same materials (printing inks) and technique (in register). Because the key skill for music printing is not a mysterious trade secret but is essential to presswork, even if the music is printed entirely in black, the early history of music printing cannot be considered in isolation. Instead, it requires a multidisciplinary approach with reference to other categories of printed content.

This chapter demonstrates that early techniques of printing music, particularly printing in register, were neither exceptional nor specific 'music-printing techniques' per se, but stock-in-trade skills. Rather than focusing on the accident of content (that is, whether the printed elements comprise text, image, diagrams, musical notation, etc.), it explores the underlying printing techniques that shaped the development of music printing in the first generations of the press. As not all music printed in register was produced in the same way, it uses close visual analysis to deduce the various means by which printers achieved the same outcome. Drawing on case studies that locate music printing within a broader

---

3 The estimate of incunabula with text printed in red and black comes with the usual caveats regarding unknown losses. Smith and May, 'Early Two-Colour Printing', 1.

4 Savage, 'A Printer's Art', 93.

5 In these copies, rubrics are printed in red on fols. 1^r, 4^r, 5^r, 129^r and 129^v. Schwenke, 'Untersuchungen', 50–51.

context of printing in general, particularly colour printing, it provides step-by-step guides for identifying techniques that were used to print music. Many of the examples are liturgical books, since they constitute the majority of early printed books containing music and conventionally follow manuscript tradition with red staves and black notes. In particular, it discusses those printed by Erhard Ratdolt (Augsburg 1442–1528), a leading printer of liturgical music and the first major colour printer, since his oeuvre demonstrates the connections between printing genres across modern disciplinary boundaries. It challenges scholarly consensus by demonstrating that the limiting factor for early music printing was the availability of *materials* such as music type, not the acquisition of specialist *skills*.

Working methods and modern reconstructions

Printing from multiple formes and printing with more than one colour increases the complexity of the printing process. Before printing can begin, a batch of paper must be dampened to take the ink well, and a *frisket sheet* (protective mask) must be prepared. It is sandwiched between the forme and the sheet to protect unprinted areas, such as margins, from being fouled by stray ink and to prevent the paper from falling onto the sticky inked forme. For jobs in a normal format (octavo, quarto, etc.) in all black, the standard frisket sheet looks like a modern window pane, with strips that protect the margins from stray ink. If the areas of printing are small or irregular, for example with only a few initials in red, a new frisket sheet must be cut for each sheet to provide an appropriate configuration of holes (see Plate 7).[6]

Two pressmen stand at each press: the *beater*, who handles the ink, and the *puller*, who handles the paper and pulls the bar of the press. Before printing each batch, the puller secures the correct frisket sheet in the frisket frame, then the beater applies a film of ink with inking balls while the puller places a fresh sheet of paper onto the pointes of the *tympan*. He folds the frisket down onto the paper so that only the areas to be printed show through the frisket sheet's windows, then he lowers both the frisket and tympan over the forme. This positions the frisket sheet between the forme and the paper, so it protects the margins while preventing the paper from falling down onto the sticky inked surface. The tray is pushed underneath the *platen* (weight of the press), the platen is lowered (and, in earlier presses, raised so the rest of the tray can be moved underneath it, and lowered again to print the second half of the sheet); the tray is pulled out and the tympan and frisket unfolded; and the puller replaces the paper with a fresh sheet as the beater re-inks the forme for the next run.

When multiple formes must be superimposed, jobs are typically batched by forme. All impressions from one forme would be taken, then all of the second, then of the third, etc. The more runs through the press, the more difficult the timing, as paper must be damp to take the ink but that dampness makes it expand and then contract unpredictably as it dries. To ensure good registration, all successive runs must be printed after the previous film of ink has dried but while the paper remains damp. If the paper dries or is re-dampened, it can warp and ruin even the best efforts at achieving register. Hence, each additional run through the press adds risk to the process.

---

6 On the production and survival of early modern frisket sheets, see Upper (Savage), 'Red Frisket Sheets'.

The order(s) of printing

When multiple formes are involved, the question arises in which order they might have been printed. For music, for example, we often wonder whether the notes or the staves were printed first, particularly when they were printed from two colours. For the production of text, it is often assumed that the order of printing necessarily followed manuscript book production, with the majority of the content (in black) followed by details (in red), but this was not always the case. Some sheets are mostly, or exclusively, printed in red ink; images were normally printed lightest to darkest, with black last to preserve the outline. For Erhard Ratdolt's printer's device, which had a tone block in red and a text and a key block (outline) in black, the red was necessarily printed first and the black second (see Plate 8). If the black outline were printed first and then partially obscured by red ink, the visual effect could be sloppy or, at least, less clear. Of course, there are exceptions. Some printers' earliest attempts at printing woodcuts in colour show a thick red ink film over the black outline, which reduces the clarity of the image. However, certain iconographies, such as crucifixion scenes with red blood on a black-printed cross, may require red to be printed over black.[7] And in some single-sheet woodcuts, the darkest ink was printed first, with lighter inks layered on top to modulate tonal contrast.[8] For music, preserving contrast was less of a consideration, and the order of printing was less of a concern than precise registration.

What appears to be obvious visual evidence of the order of printing may be deceptive. Even if it looks like red staves were printed over black noteheads, the order of printing cannot necessarily be identified as red–black. Even on the same side of a single folio, one area may look obviously red–black, another black–red. The first impression could disrupt the topography of the page by leaving pronounced peaks (*ink squash*, or a raised rim around the printed area) and indented 'valleys' in the paper that, in turn, could interrupt the second impression. Consequently, what may look like a line of red on top of a black notehead (black–red) may instead be the opposite (red–black): in some cases, the black ink of the second impression may not be impressed into a red 'valley' (where the red staff line was pressed deeply into the sheet). Additionally, printing ink can adhere more strongly to fresh paper than to a layer of dried printing ink, so what may seem compelling visual evidence of red staves printed onto black notes (black–red) may instead be caused by the flaking or lack of adhesion of the black ink film over the red (red–black). Finally, the order may vary in copies of publications, within gatherings in a single copy, or on certain sheets within a gathering. Hence, despite appearances and claims to the contrary, it is often difficult to determine which colour was printed first.

Because each run normally provides only one colour, the number of colour inks is generally equated with the number of runs through the press. In music, however, exceptions abound, and the number of colours cannot be equated with the number of formes and press runs. For example, staves may be printed in black from one forme in one run (from either individual metal strips or blocks of staves) with notes from moveable type printed in black from another forme in another run. Neither, as discussed above, can one assume the order in which different colours were printed.

---

7 Stijnman and Savage, 'Materials and Techniques', 17, fig. 1.4.
8 Stiber Morenus, 'The Chiaroscuro Woodcut', 125.

Identifying workshop practices through visual analysis

Although most printed music before the 1530s required at least two runs through the press, printing in register was achieved through various working methods.[9] Presenting these techniques in the chronological order of the first known appearance of each technique would be misleading, as we cannot know what has been lost. Moreover, many techniques were invented independently several times, in several places, before emerging on a larger scale. They are therefore listed here in order of relative complexity, as indicated by the minimum number of runs through the press. Following scholarly consensus and common sense, we assume the quickest and easiest method by estimating the minimum number of formes and press runs based on overlapping content, whether deliberate or accidental. If the text, music, and staves do not overlap and are in the same colour, we presume that they were printed from one forme in one run through the press. If two categories are designed to overlap (e.g., staves and notes), we assume that the sheet was printed from two formes in at least two runs. The order presented in this discussion is not to indicate increasing progress or complexity in practice but to provide a conceptual framework to facilitate discussion.

Before we turn to printing that involved more than one run through the press, two early approaches to music printing that do not require superimposition must be mentioned.

Omitting music

The easiest way to print music is to not print it but imply that it should be inserted manually by the user or a professional scribe. Music was included in the second book ever printed from moveable type, the 1457 Mainz Psalter, but only conceptually. The printers, Johann Fust and Peter Schöffer the Elder, set type around blank areas reserved for music, leaving space for a musically literate scribe to insert both the staves and notes. Other would-be fifteenth- and sixteenth-century music printers printed only staves (or, rarely, only notes).[10] If only the staves were printed, metal strips (whether long or short) would presumably have been set between lines of *quads* (blanks), which were locked in a forme along with any text and printed in a separate run from the music. Staves can be identified as metal strips rather than woodcut if they have a uniform thinness and straightness and a tendency to bend and acquire nicks. In contrast, cracks, random breaks, and irregular staves indicate woodcut.

The whole or partial omission of music is often understood to result from a lack of materials and skills. While that may be true in some instances, it would not explain why such omissions are found in books printed through the sixteenth century. Such a supposition also overlooks key aspects of the early book market. First, leaving the music to scribes may have been a practical option, not a necessary constraint. From the printer's perspective, omitting music would have been cheaper and faster than investing in a font of music type (if one was available) or commissioning the design and cutting of many non-reusable music woodcuts. It could also have been an effective marketing strategy, as it allowed scribes to insert notes according to local traditions and thus increase each book's catchment area. Second, omitting content is not, in itself, exceptional. Printers omitted other non-textual elements, including diagrams and initials (sometimes indicated by guide letters), so that

---

9 Dane, 'Two-Color Printing' and Smith and May, 'Early Two-Colour Printing', 1–4.

10 For example, *Missale Maguntinum* (Mainz: Johannes Schöffer, 1507), vdm 239. For Italian examples see Duggan, *Italian Music Incunabula*.

they could be supplied by professionals to the requirements, taste, and budget of each client, be they a bookseller ordering in bulk or an end consumer commissioning a bespoke luxury. Leaving space for this specialist content may be parallel to reserving space for illuminators to provide illuminations. In some cases, it may not indicate a lack of materials and skills so much as a market structure in which printers supplied the bare bones for their end users (or their agents) to elaborate.

One forme, one run, one colour

One way to print music in just one run through the press is by using woodcut, a solution attested as early as the 1480s.[11] Especially for books requiring shorter sections of music, this would have been viable and economical: the woodcut would have been locked into the forme along with moveable type for the text, and the whole would be printed in one run. For longer passages of notation or entire books of polyphony, the design and cutting of woodcut music would have been increasingly cumbersome, labour-intensive and expensive. It could at times also have been geographically limiting, as different areas used their own systems of notation. As a result, very few music books used woodcut extensively; a notable exception is Andrea Antico's *Liber quindecim missarum* (Rome: Andrea Antico, 1516).[12] Despite these limitations, music was printed from woodcut throughout the sixteenth century, especially for short examples in theoretical treatise, often alongside woodcuts for other purposes, including ornament, diagrams and illustrations.

It has often been assumed in the musicological literature that music presented even highly skilled blockcutters with a difficult challenge, but this is far from the case.[13] As long as a musically literate scribe was available, the design, blockcutting and printing of a woodcut that happened to show music would be as simple and straightforward as one that showed an initial, diagram or image. A music woodcut would be produced like any other: the scribe/designer would produce a design (the notes and staves), either directly on a prepared block of wood or on a sheet of thin paper to be pasted onto it (in both cases, in reverse), and a professional blockcutter would then cut it from the woodblock. Just as the blockcutter would not have needed to understand the theological implications of certain attributes in order to cut a design of a saint, he would not have needed to be musically literate to cut a music design. Neither would the cutting itself be particularly demanding. Just as the scribe or designer considers the black lines, the blockcutter considers the white space. As blockcutting for music would involve cutting away large, straight areas of white from long, straight black lines with gouges and knives, blockcutters could have quickly cleared the large spaces between the staves and the smaller spaces between notes.

Many fifteenth- and sixteenth-century woodcuts of text and image (e.g. blockbooks) or of images alone would have been far more difficult to cut than even very complex music. The partially cut block for Pieter Bruegel the Elder's design for a woodcut of the *Dirty Bride* (*Wedding of Mopsus and Nisa*), c.1566, for example, shows the intricacy of the cutting required for a design of typical complexity (see Plate 9). To depict shade with crosshatching, a draughtsman lays down perpendicular lines, i.e. verticals and horizontals. But to a blockcutter each minute square of intersecting lines requires at least eight cuts: two on both sides of each of the four lines, possibly others to void the interior of the rectangle. Repeated

---

11 For examples also see the chapter by Mary Kay Duggan in this volume.
12 Chapman, 'Andrea Antico'.
13 See Boorman, 'Printing and Publishing'.

hundreds of times, thousands of tiny, individual cuts could be required to translate a design to a woodblock. Cutting noteheads, stems and staves would require far less work and skill than even the relatively simple foliage above the plumes of a hat (see Plate 9).

Woodcut music can be easily identified by the inconsistency of repeated elements (e.g. the width and length of staff lines, of certain note forms), the relative coarseness of a design ('fat' lines) and the presence of cracks. As the blockcutter cuts away everything except the design, the stems and staves are left unprotected. The resulting narrow, raised strips of wood can be prone to cracking or breaking.

It must not be overlooked that woodcut music was rarely the only kind of woodcut in a musical publication, or assumed that a printer's materials were limited to the skills of local producers. Woodcut images, initials, and/or musical passages within a single publication could have been acquired readymade or commissioned from various workshops.

Figure 4.1 Title page of *Clarissima plane atque choralis musice interpretatio*. [Basel]: Michael Furter, 1501, vdm 358
Source: München, Bayerische Staatsbibliothek, 4 Mus.th. 1257, fol. A1r

The title vignette of Michael Keinspeck's treatise *Lilium musicae planae*,[14] for instance, depicts Pythagoras and the personification of Music. A few pages later, a woodcut diagram explains the hexachords, and the main corpus of the book includes multiple short musical examples. Based on the consistent style of the design and the cutting, it is likely (but not certain) that one designer or workshop produced all the woodcuts, including the diagrams, music and title vignette. In other cases, the design and cutting of the title vignette and music show strikingly different skill levels. As in Prasperg's *Clarissima plane atque choralis musice interpretatio*,[15] the discrepancy between the finely executed, elaborate title vignette and the crudely cut music suggest the involvement of different hands (Figure 4.1 and 4.2).

The use of woodcut music through the sixteenth century both north and south of the Alps should not be surprising, as it was an obvious and practical solution rather than an indicator of poor quality. Let us now turn to examples of printing music with multiple runs through the press.

Figure 4.2 *Clarissima plane atque choralis musice interpretatio*. [Basel]: Michael Furter, 1501, vdm 358
Source: München, Bayerische Staatsbibliothek, 4 Mus.th. 1257, fol. C1ʳ

---

14 Michael Keinspeck, *Lilium musicae planae* (Augsburg: Johann Froschauer, 1500), vdm 482.
15 Balthasar Prasperg, *Clarissima plane atque choralis musice interpretatio* ([Basel]: Michael Furter, 1501), vdm 358.

Two formes, two runs, one colour

The main benefits of printing music from woodcut are cost and ease of use. Depending on their complexity and quantity, commissioning woodcuts may have been cheaper than purchasing a set of metal note types. As staves and notes could be printed together in one run, necessarily in the same colour (black), the use of woodcuts increased the speed and ease of printing music. However, when Erhard Ratdolt wanted to print black notes with red staves in the *Obsequiale Augustense* of 1487, he had to find a different solution (see Plate 3).[16] The staves run the width of the page with no interruptions, are uniformly extremely thin and straight, and have acquired small nicks and bends but not breaks or cracks, so they must have been printed from metal rules. This is neither an innovation nor unique to music; the use of metal rules rather than woodcut to produce long lines is attested from the 1470s, mainly for diagrams. In Lazarus Beham's *Buch von der Astronomie* (Cologne: Nicolaus Götz, c.1476), for example, woodcut was used for diagrams with a coarser design but metal strips for those that required long, fine lines, such as the long, thin lines delineating the words Leo and Cancer in this diagram (Figure 4.3).[17]

If the staves are broken into regular, shorter lengths, shorter rules would have been used. If there are small gaps between the narrow sections of staves flanking each note, the lines are straight, and the noteheads and stems are consistent, the music was set from metal type in which each sort comprises a section of staff lines and a note.

In the *Obsequiale*, the designs of the individual notes are irregular and there is no consistency in the appearance of repeated elements such as the virga, which indicates that they were cut from a woodblock. Because the staves occupy the same space on the page as the notes but are in a different colour, Ratdolt must have printed two formes, in two runs: metal strips (in red) and woodcut music (in black). The order of printing cannot be determined. As printing in register added time, risk and labour costs, Ratdolt's answer seems to defeat the ease and speed of printing music from woodcut.[18] But it allowed him to print music in two colours without investing in moveable metal type, which in any case may not have been available to him yet. This edition, as well as Ratdolt's other two editions of the *Obsequiale Augustense* of 1487, is the only known example of music printed from woodcut notes and typeset staves. Shortly afterwards, Ratdolt obtained metal music type.[19]

It may be no coincidence that Ratdolt arrived at this solution in the same year that he printed what was until recently thought to be the first figurative colour woodcut, a portrait of Heinrich von Absperg, Bishop of Regensburg, with the arms of the Bishopric of Regensburg and his family as the frontispiece to the *Breviarium Ratisponense*.[20] It is in four colours: red, yellow, green (now browned) and black. (Blue must have been intended for the azure field on the bishopric's arms, but difficulties with blue ink may explain why it was supplied by hand until he developed a workable recipe in the 1490s.)[21] The full order of printing cannot be ascertained in this case, but black was certainly printed last. This

---

16 *Obsequiale Augustense* (Augsburg: Erhard Ratdolt, 1487), ISTC io00001000.

17 Lazarus Beham, *Buch von der Astronomie* (Cologne: Nicolaus Götz, c.1476), ISTC ib00296700. Further, see Baldasso, 'La stampa'.

18 See Mary Kay Duggan's contribution in this volume.

19 See Mary Kay Duggan's contribution in this volume.

20 *Arms of Bishop Johann II, Count of Werdenberg, and the Bishopric of Augsburg*, colour woodcut from three blocks, frontispiece to *Breviarium Augustanum* (Venice: Erhard Ratdolt, 30 April 1485), ISTC; Savage, 'Colour Printing in Relief', 31, fig. 2.6 (Augsburg: Erhard Ratdolt, 1487 and January 1488), ISTC ib01176500.

21 On another early printer's difficulties with blue ink, see Ikeda, 'The Fust and Schöffer Office'.

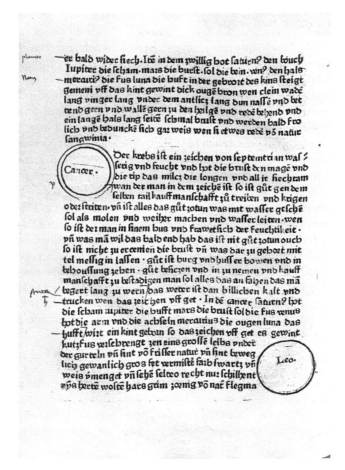

Figure 4.3 Diagram of Cancer, metal strips with type inset. Lazarus Beham, *Buch von der Astronomie*. Cologne: Nicolaus Götz, c.1476
Source: München, Bayerische Staatsbibliothek, Rar. 314, fol. 55ᵛ

four-colour woodcut, which presumably would have been a five-colour woodcut if Ratdolt had been able to develop a workable blue printing ink, was the most complex image ever printed up to this point. By achieving near-perfect register from four blocks in four runs through the press with newly invented recipes for yellow and green oil-based printing inks, Ratdolt's new and innovative combinations of otherwise standard materials expanded the possibilities of the press.

Ratdolt's technical advancements in printing music and images may be closely related. In 1487, he had just returned from Venice to Augsburg at the invitation of Johann von Werdenberg (1431–86), Bishop of Augsburg, on the basis of his extraordinary skill in printing. If the books he printed in 1487 are considered his launch into a new market (the German-speaking lands) with a new product line (liturgical books), the importance of demonstrating his unique innovations and skills becomes clear. Whether or not he developed these unprecedented approaches for printing music and images to communicate the same message to his new local audience, they followed from the same kind of technical experimentation.

Two formes, two runs, two colours

Before the invention of 'single-impression type', in which each sort comprises one note and a note-width section of staff, most music printed from type was printed in two runs: one for notes in cast metal type, one for metal strips. This process is usually referred to as 'double impression' in musicological literature, as two impressions were required, but this term is avoided in this study because it may incorrectly imply that both impressions were from the same forme. 'Double impression', in a literal sense, is attested in woodcuts that were run at least twice through the press, each time with different areas revealed by a customised frisket sheet and printed in a different colour of ink.[22] The term 'double run' is also avoided, as it is used when the same forme/block/plate is run through the press twice without re-inking.

The earliest known example of moveable type for the notes is found in a liturgical book, a *Graduale* ([Southern Germany (Constance?): Printer of the Constance Breviary, *c.*1473?]).[23] Each noteform is identical – for example, the virgas on the top line – and the stems are consistently thin and straight, with no cracks, so it has long been accepted that the notes were printed from moveable type. Nicks and bends confirm that the staves are from metal rules. Since the notes and staves overlap, they must have been printed from separate formes in two runs through the press. Thus, the process of superimposing two separate formes was used in the production of the earliest printed books of polyphonic music.

Increasing complexity

Most printers could achieve the desired effect with two runs through the press, one in black and one in red. But, in some cases, black notes and text/initials overlap and thus must have been printed in separate runs – possibly from separate formes. Why would some printers increase their workload and the risk of misregistration to print one sheet in two colours from *three* runs?

One-colour, three-forme printing is attested in some liturgical publications and early polyphonic music books, most notably those printed by Ottaviano Petrucci.[24] But it is not as rare as is currently believed. The overlapping black notes and black text in Ratdolt's *Obsequiale*, printed for Constance in Augsburg in 1510, would be possible only if they were printed separately, hence in two black runs.[25] We assume that the red staves were printed in a third run. Elsewhere in the book, elements do not overlap but are so close that they cannot have been set together in a single forme. For example, both ends of the descending stroke above the word '*Hic*' come so close to the letters that the text and notes cannot have been set in the same forme (see Plate 10), and must therefore have been printed in two black runs. The decision to print the text separately might have been driven by a need to save space by setting the notes and music very close together. However, the potential time savings that could be gained by this procedure may have been too small to justify the time lost to the workaround. It may seem baffling today, but Ratdolt once again added technical complexity to his music printing by applying innovations he was using to print bicolour initials and multi-colour images.

---

22 For an example, see Savage, 'Colour Printing in Relief', 40, fig. 2.13.
23 Boorman, 'Printing and Publishing'.
24 See Boorman, *Petrucci*.
25 *Obsequiale Constantiense* ([Augsburg]: Erhard Ratdolt, 1510), vdm 740.

The potential use of three formes is more evident in those publications where only one staff line, usually the f-line, or rarely the c-line, is printed in red. Following manuscript tradition, this would have facilitated sight-reading enormously for the singers. The f-note was not fixed on a specific location as it normally is in modern notation, so indicating its placement would have allowed them to easily identify the semitone step in the scale even when the clef changed line. However, contemporary performers were used to singing without having this line highlighted, so it would not have been a necessity. It seems extraordinary that a printer would go to the trouble of adding another run through the press to provide these red lines. At a minimum, two formes would have been printed in three runs: one forme with text and staves (printed in a black run and a red run); one forme with notes (printed in a black run). In practice, many more steps seem to have been involved.

It has been thought that the only German example of a red staff line is Peter Schöffer the Younger's *Responsoria Moguntina* (Mainz, 1518; vdm 261),[26] but four others have been identified. The music in Schöffer's folio *De dulcissimo nomine Iesu officium* (Mainz, 1518; vdm 972) was also printed with staves in red and black (Plate 11).[27] Other printers also provided a red staff line, such as Peter Drach in his 1522 Missal for Worms (Plate 12)[28] and Thomas Anshelm in a 1520 Missal for Strasbourg.[29] A Psalter for Speyer, which is credited in the preface to Drach,[30] but that Helmut Claus attributed to Schöffer the Younger, also has a red staff line.[31] Curiously, all four staff lines are printed in red in the *Pater noster* later in the publication.

As in Plate 13, a detail from *De dulcissimo*, the red initials are several millimetres too low. As they are out of registration with both the black initials and the red staff lines (which are in near-perfect register), they cannot have been printed in the same run (or set in the same forme) as the red staff lines, nor can they have been printed in the same run as the black initials (though they may have been set in the same forme). Schöffer must have used at least three formes, one each for the notes, staves and initials. Formes printed in two colours would have needed two runs through the press, so the text and staff formes would each have been printed in two runs (red and black). That adds up to five runs to print in two colours: 1) text in black; 2) staves in black; 3) notes in black; 4) text in red; 5) staves in red (in no particular order). This process seems implausibly, unnecessarily complicated, but two or even three runs for one colour have been recorded.

How did these printers achieve the red line? Its addition has been considered exceptional, something out of keeping with their usual working methods. Royston Gustavson assumed that it was printed last, as it often appears to sit on top of the black notes.[32] As explained above, however, unaided visual analysis does not necessarily provide conclusive evidence of the order of printing, even if the order seems obvious at first glance. Nor was the

---

26 Gustavson, 'Competitive Strategy Dynamics', 197.

27 We would like to thank Royston Gustavson and David Paisey, who independently brought the unique copy in GB-Lbm to our attention.

28 *Missale Wormatiense* (Speyer: Peter Drach III, 1522), vdm 767.

29 *Missale Argentinense* (Hagenau: Thomas Anshelm, 1520), vdm 730.

30 Expositum est nobis, fratres in Christo charissimi, honestum virum Petrum Drach scultetum nostrum Spirensem fidelem dilectum proposuisse, si cum assensu nostro fieri possit, psalterium, mortuorum vigilias, commune sanctorum et alia quedam generalia eorumque appendices ad cantum et notas iuxta usum ecclesie nostre Spirensis, qualia prius nondum habuimus, et ea quidem maioribus formis ac litteris impressioni tradere velle. Psalterium Spirense (Mainz: Peter Drach III & [Peter Schöffer the Younger], [1515]), vdm 729, fol. 1ᵛ.

31 *Psalterium Spirense* (Mainz: Peter Drach III & [Peter Schöffer the Younger], [1515]), vdm 729.

32 Gustavson: 'Competitive Strategy Dynamics', p. 197 fn 52.

employment of a detail such as a single red staff line inconsistent with printers' ability to achieve register in complicated layouts or when printing in multiple colours, as their sheets of text in black and red and decorated initials attest. Nevertheless, it seems extraordinary that they would have added another run through the press just to add a red line. Might there have been a simpler working method?

In all instances we measured, the distance between a red staff line and its black neighbours was consistent, i.e. equidistant, even if other red elements were out of register. Such consistency would be effectively impossible if the black and red staves were printed in two runs, whether two formes were used or one forme was used for two runs (i.e. in layouts that would allow for the staves to be set in one forme, divided with a frisket sheet, and printed separately in black and red runs). It seems improbable that the bicolour staves would have been printed from one run, but this possibility must be considered.

If that were the case, there would be two options. One possibility is that all staves were set in the forme, the red elements removed, the rest of the forme inked in black, the removed staves inked in red and reinserted, and the whole printed in one black-and-red run. Conceptually, if not practically, this would have been similar to jigsaw printing, which Fust and Schöffer the Elder first used in 1457 for the bicolour initials in the Mainz Psalter. However, inserting a small, malleable metal strip covered with sticky printing ink into a tight space seems highly impractical. Alternatively, the printers may have kept all metal strips in the forme and used small ink daubers (or brushes?) to ink some in black and others in red. This would represent the earliest expression of a technique later known as *á la poupée* (lit: with the 'dolly', or ink ball, which was stuffed with rags like a doll), that is, applying different inks to a single printing surface for simultaneous impression. It is attested in only several woodcuts and intaglio prints in the 1400s and 1500s, before it emerged on a larger scale from the 1680s as a way to produce 'printed paintings' for intaglio.[33] It is impossible to distinguish between these methods based on the end result, as there is no opportunity for impressions of the black and red staves to overlap. Neither seems plausible, but there seems to be no simpler way in which Schöffer could have achieved these results.

Further complexity?

Visual evidence from other folios in Schöffer's 1518 *De dulcissimo nomine Iesu officium* suggests that the entire publication may not have been produced with the three-forme, five-run method suggested above. The possibility of even more runs may beggar belief, but it must be considered, since the same visual evidence can also be convincingly interpreted as requiring three formes in four runs, perhaps even up to four formes in six runs.

In that book, the following categories of content can be identified: the vertical rules; the red staves; the black staves; the black notes; the black text; the red text; the four-line red initials, and the three-line black initials (see Figure 4.4). One forme included the black staves, another included the notes. The red staves are aligned with the black staves, but not with the other red elements, so they must have been in the staff forme. The occurrence of duplicated elements, caused by too-large windows in the frisket sheet, proves that black and red text was set together but printed in two runs. The three-line initials must have been set in the same forme as the text because they sit at the same level. As those initials

---

33 Stijnman and Savage, 'Materials and Techniques', 15, fig. 1.2.

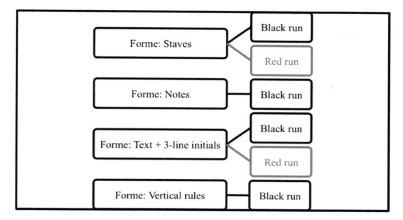

Figure 4.4 One possible organisational scheme of *De dulcissimo nomine Iesu officium*. Mainz: Peter Schöffer the Younger, 1518. Formes and colour runs shown in no particular order

overlap with the black staff lines and sheets in apparently perfect register and notes are placed so close to letters that a note sort would have to occupy the position of the shoulder of a letter sort, or vice versa, the text must have been set in a third forme. Note sorts, staves, and a black historiated initial overlap with the vertical rules, so they must have been set in a fourth forme. So far, this tally counts separate formes for notes (in black), staves (in red and black), text (in red and black) and vertical rules (in black), totalling two colours printed from four formes in six runs. But Occam's razor does not allow for such an elaborate workshop method. Schöffer's *tour-de-force* of printed music exemplifies the complexity of music-printing methods in the early modern German lands, the applicability of a range of general and specialist skills to music printing, the possible variability of method within a single project, and the limits of modern deductions of workshop methods based on visual analysis.

How can things become so complicated? First, in all likelihood, the man credited as the printer in the colophon inhabited a role we would now call 'publisher' or 'organiser'.[34] He may have overseen projects, managed clients and jobbing printers who worked the presses in the printshop he owned, and ensured overall quality for all the (overlapping) projects under his name. This was increasingly the case by the mid-sixteenth century. 'His' method may instead combine the methods practised by any number of hands in his employ. Second, pressmen were paid by output, not by time, so they would have used whatever solution seemed best at the moment. Neither the named printer nor the men who worked his presses aimed to adhere to specific approaches over time, following an order that later scholars could identify as a logical, step-by-step progression. Third, many of the books in this discussion required a great many folios. Rather than being printed in page order, different sections could be printed concurrently on several presses within a printshop. This means that one method may have been used on one sheet, another method on another sheet, and a different ad hoc solution on a third. It cannot be assumed that the working method was identical from sheet to sheet or even from quire to quire. At one point, it may

---

34 Stijnman, *Engraving and Etching*, 76.

have made sense to a beater/puller pair to set a new forme with only metal rules for every fourth staff line and to take an additional impression with red ink, but that does not imply that they would have continued in this way. Presumably, they simply adopted whatever solution seemed best in the moment.

Said another way, our assumption of the fewest formes and runs through the press could be incorrect, and it may be impossible to distinguish conclusively between three-, four-, five-, even six-run printing if the registration is excellent and no categories of content overlap. Also, the working methods may vary significantly within a publication. Scholars have struggled to explain technical inconsistencies in music printing from sheet to sheet, quire to quire, or edition to edition, but such inconsistencies are to be expected.

Conclusions

Before the invention of single-impression music type in about 1530, approaches to printing music varied from place to place, year to year, printshop to printshop, even within individual workshops. It is tempting to organise them by increasing technical complexity, but, as this discussion of techniques indicates, there was not a line of advancement and progress. Instead, related trends developed and ebbed in different places and different times. Printing music, like printing text, images, or diagrams, would often involve more than one run through the press. It could involve two impressions of the same forme, but with different areas masked off; impressions of different formes, printed either in red and black or in black and black; or any other permutation. Music was just one of the many categories of contents that shaped and developed, and was shaped and developed by, the ever-changing possibilities of printing in the early decades of the press. Future research into music printing techniques and workshop methods may help to identify a given printshop's 'fingerprints', refining attributions and leading to a better understanding of how the available materials and techniques determined how music could be printed.

References

Baldasso, Renzo. 'La stampa dell' editio princeps degli elementi de Euclide (Venezia, Erhard Ratdolt, 1482)'. In *The Books of Venice*, edited by Lisa Pon and Craig Kallendorf, Miscellanea Marciana 20. New Castle, Delaware, and Venice, Italy: Oak Knoll Press, Biblioteca Nazionale Marciana, and La Musa Talìa, 2009, 61–100.

Boorman, Stanley. 'Printing and Publishing of Music', *New Grove Online*. www.oxfordmusiconline.com.

Boorman, Stanley. *Ottaviano Petrucci. Catalogue Raisonné*. Oxford: Oxford University Press, 2006.

Chapman, Catherine. 'Andrea Antico'. PhD dissertation, Harvard University, 1964.

Dane, Joseph A. 'Two-Color Printing in the Fifteenth Century as Evidenced by Incunables in the Huntington Library', *Gutenberg-Jahrbuch* (1999), 131–146.

Duggan, Mary Kay. *Italian Music Incunabula: Printers and Type*. Berkeley, CA: University of California Press, 1992.

Gustavson, Royston. 'Competitive Strategy Dynamics in the German Music Publishing Industry 1530–1550'. In *Niveau Nische Nimbus. 500 Jahre Musikdruck nördlich der Alpen*, edited by Birgit Lodes. Wiener Forum für ältere Musikgeschichte 3. Tutzing: Hans Schneider, 2010, 185–210.

Ikeda, Mayumi. 'The Fust and Schöffer Office and the Printing of the Two-Colour Initials in the 1457 Mainz Psalter'. In *Printing Colour 1400–1700: History, Techniques, Functions and Receptions*, edited by Ad Stijnman and Elizabeth Savage. Library of the Written Word – The Handpress World 41. Leiden: Brill, 2015, 65–75.

Savage, Elizabeth. 'A Printer's Art: The Development and Influence of Colour Printmaking in the German Lands, *c.1476–c.1600*'. In *Printing Colour 1400–1700: History, Techniques, Functions and Receptions*, edited by Ad Stijnman and Elizabeth Savage. Library of the Written Word – The Handpress World 41. Leiden: Brill, 2015, 91–102.

Savage, Elizabeth. 'Colour Printing in Relief before c.1700: A Technical History'. In *Printing Colour 1400–1700: History, Techniques, Functions and Receptions*, edited by Ad Stijnman and Elizabeth Savage. Library of the Written Word – The Handpress World 41. Leiden: Brill, 2015, 23–41.

Schwenke, Paul. *Untersuchungen zur Geschichte des ersten Buchdrucks. Festschrift zur Gutenbergfeier.* Berlin: Königliche Bibliothek, 1900.

Smith, Margaret and Alan May. 'Early Two-Colour Printing', *Bulletin of the Printing Historical Society* 44 (1997): 1–4.

Stiber Morenus, Linda. 'The Chiaroscuro Woodcut Printmaking of Ugo da Carpi, Antonio da Trento and Niccolò Vicentino: Technique in Relation to Artistic Style'. In *Printing Colour 1400–1700: History, Techniques, Functions and Receptions*, edited by Ad Stijnman and Elizabeth Savage. Library of the Written Word – The Handpress World 41. Leiden: Brill, 2015, 123–139.

Stijnman, Ad and Elizabeth Savage. 'Materials and Techniques for Early Colour Printing'. In *Printing Colour 1400–1700: History, Techniques, Functions and Receptions*, edited by Ad Stijnman and Elizabeth Savage. Library of the Written Word – The Handpress World 41. Leiden: Brill, 2015, 9–22.

Stijnman, Ad. *Engraving and Etching 1400–2000: A History of the Development of Manual Intaglio Printmaking Processes.* London: Archetype, 2012.

Upper (Savage), Elizabeth. 'Red Frisket Sheets, *c.1490–1700*: The Earliest Artefacts of Colour Printing in the West', *Papers of the Bibliographical Society of America* 108, no. 4 (December 2014): 477–522.

5

'Synopsis musicae'

Charts and tables in sixteenth-century music textbooks

Inga Mai Groote

Tables, charts and diagrams constitute a conspicuous feature of music theoretical treatises and music textbooks, and an important means for presenting pedagogical material. The following chapter will examine a number of such large charts and tables. These often exceed the format of the volume to which they belong. Some were even issued and sold separately as broadsheets that could be hung on a wall. As printed objects, the charts profited from the technical expertise and conceptual knowledge available in the context of print production, and they combined features of music textbooks with those of other kinds of scientific and pedagogical books. Tables and broadsheets could adapt forms of visual presentation current in other disciplines, or for other purposes such as catechetic instruction.[1] From a book-historical point of view, the production of printed music textbooks shows distinct relationships with that of textbooks in other disciplines. At the same time, printed music textbooks also drew on longstanding traditions of visualisation in manuscript music treatises. Certain elements taken over from manuscript into print culture were integrated in more complex and comprehensive tables and synopses. The recurrence of designs in several publications by the same printer or editor, resulting from the reuse of printing materials, created traditions of illustrations. Charts and synoptic tables for music are usually related to music textbooks by the same author, and thus can illustrate the elaboration of different levels of pedagogical material in different kinds of printed media. From a more general perspective, these tables are prominent examples of the adaption of 'modern' pedagogical tools for musical instruction.

In this chapter I examine synoptic music charts as a special tool for the circulation of musical knowledge. These developed partly as a result of pedagogical innovation, and could be especially helpful in contexts where music was to be integrated into general education, as in early-modern schools. Against this functional background, musical charts constitute highly condensed digests of music theory or of music teaching. They may represent the minimum knowledge that students at a certain institution were expected to master, or the issues that teachers considered most in need of repetition. They show how abstract theoretical concepts and practical knowledge were combined. They help us to grasp techniques of musical instruction. Moreover, since such charts and tables were usually addressed to students or readers who were not yet specialists in music, they allow us to identify the musical content and concepts that reached a broader public. Examining such

---

1 For examples see Ferguson, 'System and Schema'. See also Ferrell, 'Page Techne'. On catechetical broadsheets, see the material presented in Watt, *Cheap Print and Popular Piety* (e.g. Charles Gibbons' *A premonition for euery disposition*, 1588, or William Perkins' *Armilla aurea*, 1590).

sources thus helps us to understand better how the transmission of musical ideas to non-professionals worked in practice.

Despite their conceptual richness, music charts and broadsheets have received little attention by researchers, and no full census has yet been undertaken.[2] Some may have been overlooked, as they are often poorly catalogued. Like all broadsheets, they are excluded from the VD16, a quirk of bibliographical history that has prevented an easy overview of these materials.[3] These items are also fragile and liable to damage: a single sheet associated with a book could be folded and bound with the main text, but because of its size it was at risk of being damaged during use or torn out.

Production of music textbooks and charts

As is well known, the production of music textbooks flourished in German-speaking lands in the sixteenth and early seventeenth centuries. This was caused by the systematic inclusion of music in the school programs and by the tendency of teachers to publish or edit their own books for local demand.[4] Several authors published different texts on the same subject: re-editions, emended versions, or new texts intended for a different readership. Differences may be seen in the language (German for beginners, Latin for proficient readers) as well as in the structure of the book. Music textbooks usually covered the scale, solmisation, intervals, the modes, mensural notation, and in some cases also the rules of singing and counterpoint, but an author might limit his treatment to the first parts in order to present a basic introduction. Tables and broadsheets, then, can help to condense the content of a book further and render it more easily understood and remembered. As such, they illustrate the elaboration of different levels of pedagogical material in different genres of text. Some are closely linked to textbooks by the same author, but others are independent. Consequently, the borders between autonomous broadsheet presentations and charts associated with a book are blurred.

Compared with editions of plain text, music textbooks are generally characterised by a relatively high number of graphic elements, and the inclusion of music examples in different kinds of notation, which could be produced with different printing techniques (woodcut or type).[5] The same applies to larger-scale music charts: the content could combine elements printed from woodcut or metal type, such as lines, circles and so on, together with type for text and music. The production of musical diagrams and charts did not pose the printer

---

2 The *vdm* database lists folding charts in Gregor Reisch, *Margarita philosophica* (Strasbourg: Johann Grüninger, 1515), vdm 490, and Johannes Frosch, *Rerum musicarum* (Strasbourg: Peter Schöffer the Younger and Matthias Apiarius, 1535), vdm 564 and 637. For a sample of sixteenth- to seventeenth-century examples, cf. Owens, 'You Can Tell a Book by Its Cover', esp. 362–or 364, including: *Monochordum. Regula musica* ([*c*.1550], D-Mbs 2 Mus.pr. 156–11, urn:nbn:de:bvb:12-bsb00090648–3); Sigmund Salminger, *Gradatio, sive scala principiorum artis musicae* (Augsburg: Philipp Ulhard, [*c*.1545]; D-Mbs 2 Mus.pr. 156–1/8, urn:nbn:de:bvb:12-bsb00090645–6), vdm 1183. Only one example is listed in *Deutsche illustrierte Flugblätter*, vol. 3, Nr. 160, 312.

3 A similar problem may be experienced with digitised copies if charts have not been unfolded during the process of scanning.

4 For an overview of the text production, cf. Niemöller, 'Deutsche Musiktheorie im 16. Jahrhundert'.

5 Cf. Florea, 'Virtus scriptoris', and Balensuela, 'Transformation of Music Theory Illustrations', although his statements on p. 107 that print simplified the relationship between text and images, and that an author had more control over the arrangement in print than in manuscript culture, seem simplistic. While it is true that a printed text fixes one arrangement of text and visual elements, it is not necessarily the author alone who decides. His claims, also on p. 107, about the difficulty of potential 'mental juggling' in determining the relations between text and image seem likewise slightly overstated.

102 INGA MAI GROOTE

problems any different from those involved in illustrating other kinds of books, such as geographical, geometrical or mathematical texts. As the larger charts integrate types of illustration also found in printed textbooks, we shall also note the various visual elements usually present in music theoretical textbooks.

Visual elements in musical texts

Diagrams and illustrations in books, as well as charts and broadsheets, visualised abstract concepts and also served as mnemonic aids. This latter function can be traced back to medieval usage. Tree diagrams in particular were used to structure information,[6] while buildings or similar structures could be used to develop artificial memory. However, the mnemonic aspect seems not to have been very important for the musical tables, perhaps because of the relative simplicity of the content to be memorised, at least in comparison with difficult juridical or philosophical material.

Some early elaborate frontispieces, such as those for the *Margarita philosophica* of Gregor Reisch, also make use of elaborate mnemonic topologies (see Figure 5.1). The frontispiece of the *Margarita* uses a tower to represent the system of disciplines.[7] The title page for the book on music exists in various editions in two different versions. Both represent a kind of classroom setting, in which figures surrounding an allegory of 'Lady Music' handle various musical instruments and learn music.[8] Even if primarily allegorical, the representation of a scene of musical instruction is relevant for our purposes, since it depicts the use of a board with notated musical examples (in this case, in chant and mensural notation) that could be read by a group of pupils. In the *Margarita* image, this board is held by the figure of Musica.

An important item is the *manus*, long associated with music or musical knowledge, notwithstanding the long tradition of mnemonic hands used for different purposes.[9] The frequent occurrence of the Guidonian hand on the title pages of music textbooks suggests that it was perceived as a strong visual marker for musical material. The presence of hands on broadsheets from the various groups thus can fulfil a double function: it is of course useful as a central pedagogical representation, but it also identifies the broadsheet visually as a 'musical product'.

Besides the Guidonian hand, several other *figurae* were used widely to visualise the mathematical aspects of music theory. Intervallic proportions were usually represented as distances on lines, evoking in a more or less realistic way the monochord as the appropriate instrument for measuring those relations,[10] for example in the diagrams accompanying Boethius' *De Musica*.[11] That the parallel use of different forms could be considered as relevant in a printed edition is demonstrated by Glarean's 1546 edition of Boethius, printed by Petri at Basel, which includes abstract and pictorial versions of the monochord side by side in book IV, chapter 18.[12]

---

6 For examples from the medieval manuscript tradition, see Smits van Waesberghe, *Musikerziehung*.

7 Büttner, 'Die Illustrationen der Margarita Philosophica'. See also Schmid, 'Darstellung der Musica'.

8 The version of the first edition can be found in all editions from Freiburg and Basel (vdm 485, 487, 489, 488, 650, 491). The second version was introduced in Grüninger's Strasbourg editions (vdm 492, 486 and 490). The Strasbourg *Margarita nova* of 1512 (vdm 492) has an additional title illustration for the added *musica figurata* part; it shows a group of putti holding a sheet bearing mensural notation.

9 Forscher Weiss, 'Symbols of Learning Music'.

10 Cf. Florea, 'Virtus scriptoris', 87–88.

11 Cf. Mellon, 'Inscribing Sound', esp. chapter 3.

Figure 5.1 Gregor Reisch, *Margarita philosophica*. [Freiburg im Breisgau]: Johann Schott, 1504 (vdm 487)
Source: München, Bayerische Staatsbibliothek, Res/4 Ph.u. 116 a, fol. n7^v

The encyclopaedic textbook *Quadratum sapiencie* by Johannes Foeniseca (Mader) (Augsburg, 1515) illustrates an intermediary state between abstract diagram and pictorial representation. It includes different types of diagrams used in the various disciplines, such as elaborate geometrical demonstrations.[13] Some of the technical diagrammatic representations in the chapter on music (a six-page digest) are combined with realistic shapes. While Foeniseca's monochord is abstract, he uses the shape of an organ pipe and a lute in other diagrams.[14] The Guidonian hand also appears, inscribed with the names of poetic metres alongside the index finger, thus serving as a memory aid for both musical and poetic theory.[15] Foeniseca's publication also included a larger sheet for diagrammatic demonstrations, but this is limited to items not related to music.[16]

---

12 *Boethi opera* (Basel: Heinrich Petri, 1546), vdm 1333.
13 Johannes Foeniseca, *Quadratum sapientiae* (Augsburg: Johann Miller, 1515), vdm 436.
14 Foeniseca, *Quadratum*, fol. [ccvi^r].

104   INGA MAI GROOTE

Another typical visual element is the sequence of note names and solmisation syllables, usually labelled as the 'Scale of Guido' ('Scala Guidonis'). It can take different shapes, usually resembling a ladder, but it is sometimes combined with more pictorial representations, such as an organ.[17] When accompanying a book in small format, the *scala* was sometimes issued separately on a larger sheet in order to give a more accurate representation of the distances. This is the case in some editions of Reisch's *Margarita philosophica*, and also in later texts. For Thomas Freigius' *Paedagogus* (1582), the *scala* was printed on a separate leaf, with a rubric that it referred to page 162 of the text.[18] Freigius' book is part of a series of texts printed by the Petri firm in Basel, all of which include larger diagrams for the Scala Guidonis. This series apparently began with the *Epitomes* of Glarean, but a nearly identical version appears later in the aforementioned musical part of Freigus' *Paedagogus*, and one year later in a re-edition of Gregor Reisch's *Margarita*, for which the woodcuts were recut.[19] We can assume that at least in the Petri/Henricpetri workshop, editors decided consciously to reuse sheets of this kind for several musical works.

Types of charts

The existing sheets may be distinguished into those that contain figures and those that do not.[20] Three main types of charts can be distinguished, though the visual presentation and content varies, and some examples combine characteristics of the other forms: the synoptic broadsheet, which combines different visual elements, like those also occurring in normal music textbooks; the stemmatic table, which structures and visualises the content in an abstract (often dichotomic or bifurcating) form; and finally, the pictorial broadsheet, which integrates different elements into a more elaborate, and sometimes non-musical, imagery.

Synoptic charts

In most cases, the synoptic broadsheet can be interpreted as a digest of a textbook, and thus as a tool closely related to certain pedagogical practices and habits. An early example of a large-format sheet that combines commonly occurring features is the *Principium et ars tocius musicae* by a certain Johannes Franciscus Ferrariensis, printed first in Italy and later in Antwerp.[21] This chart, which includes some pictorial elements, represents a type of

---

15 Foeniseca, *Quadratum*, fol. cciiii^r; 'da-cty-lus' clearly corresponds with the phalanges, 'spo[n]-de[us]' is given with the two upper ones (probably implying that they are of equal length); left of the highest one appears 'pyrrhi[chius]', horizontally orientated, which could refer to the fingertips of index and middle finger for short syllables).

16 D-As 4 Phil. 124.

17 Cf. the frontispiece to Franchino Gaffori, *Theorica musice* (Milan: Philippus de Mantegatiis, 1492), ISTC ig00006000.

18 Johannes Thomas Freigius, *Paedagogus, hoc est libellus ostendens qua ratione prima artium initia pueris quàm facillimè tradi possint* (Basel: Sebastian Henricpetri, 1582), VD16 F 2581: 'SCALA GVIDONIS ARETINI / ad paginam 162 referenda'; the passage on p. 162 reads 'Quis est autor illius maximi systematis? Guido Aretinus: quem Matthias Palmerius scribit sub Henrico secundo uixisse anno Domini 1018. Cuius hic typum habes cum signo.† † †.'

19 *Musicae epitome ex Henrici Glareani Dodecachordon*, ed. by Johannes Ludwig Wonnegger (Basel: Heinrich Petri, 1557), VD16 L 2614 (a second edition appeared in 1559 [VD16 L 2615]); Johannes Reisch/Oronce Finé, *Margarita philosophica, hoc est, habituum seu disciplinarum omnium, quotquot philosophiae syncerioris ambitu continentur, perfectißima κυκλοπαιδεια. Nunc vero innumeris in locis restituta* [. . .] (Basel: Sebastian Henricpetri, 1583), VD16 R 1042; cf. the copy in D-Rs (urn:nbn:de:bvb:12-bsb11109617–5).

20 For some useful thoughts on distinctions, cf. Ferguson, 'System and Schema', 12–14.

'SYNOPSIS MUSICAE': CHARTS AND TABLES   105

synoptic chart used for general instruction in music. A Guidonian hand is situated in the centre of the sheet, surrounded by boxes and scrolls with text and notation. The layout does not suggest a prescribed direction of reading. For example, in the upper part, a demonstration of note values under different mensurations (printed in two layers in one staff) is given above simple scales, probably intended to illustrate solmisation: ascending and descending hexachords by steps, thirds, fourths, fifths, and finally sixths. These two lines of notation are surmounted by mnemonic verses on psalmody.[22] A scala-diagram with brevis heads arranged on organ pipes is placed halfway up the right side of the sheet, combined with a scroll that provides the title of the sheet (*Principium* . . .). In the lower part, note values and examples of ligatures are followed by solmisation exercises. This arrangement juxtaposes elements that usually belong to different chapters in a treatise: solmisation is part of the introduction to the system of music, while notes and ligatures appear in the chapters on mensural notation. The reason for this placement on the sheet may be merely technical: both examples can be written in lines that use the whole width of the sheet. In a layout of this kind, the relatively large Guidonian hand in such a prominent position will have identified the sheet immediately as an exposition of music theory. The presentation would not help autodidacts much, and presupposes further explanation by a teacher. Such a sheet can best be understood either as a mnemonic device, or as a supplement to classroom instruction.

Johannes Fries, an influential humanist teacher in Zurich,[23] published a large single-sheet *Synopsis musicae* in 1552, produced by Froschauer, the most important printer in Zurich at that time (Figure 5.2).[24] Fries had been awarded a bursary by the chapter of the Grossmünster that allowed him to study in Bourges, Paris and Basel. In 1537 he returned to Zurich, where he worked as schoolmaster until 1563. Fries's *Synopsis* was printed in two columns on two folio sheets that were to be stuck together.[25] The dedication to Jacobus Ammianus (Ammann) is dated 1 February 1549. The title of this broadsheet associates it closely with the school at the Grossmünster, where Fries taught ('in studiosorum adulescentium Gymnasij Tigurini gratiam'). In his 1532 order for this school, Heinrich Bullinger prescribed the singing of psalms and *carmina* (i.e. metrical settings of poems or hymns) at the end of every school day.[26] In 1554, Fries published an amplified version of his poster in book form, under the title *Brevis musicae isagoge*.[27] It is printed in oblong octavo, and Fries comments on the change from broadsheet to book in his preface to the *Isagoge*: he had compiled a short digest from 'good authors', but so far it had only been presented in the form of a 'tabula' for the pupils, that is, the *Synopsis*. Now the printer Froschauer had decided to publish it as a small book ('libellus'), 'for the greater convenience of the students'.[28] The title of the chart, *Synopsis*

---

21 For a detailed description and discussion of this publication (463 × 307 mm), see Schreurs and Van der Stock, 'Principium Et Ars Tocius Musice'. A later, engraved version by Balthasar Caymox († 1635) was issued as late as 1600: urn:nbn:de:bsz:24-digibib-bsz3314056871.

22 The verses occur already in fourteenth-century texts, cf. for an identical version *The Berkeley Manuscript*, 82, and at the end of the fifteenth century in Bonaventura da Brescia.

23 The most recent account of his life is Bührer, 'Johannes Fries (1505–1565)'.

24 Reske, *Die Buchdrucker*, 1039–1040.

25 Johannes Fries, *Synopsis isagoges musicae* (Zürich: Johann Froschauer, 1552), not in VD16 (63.5 × 42.5 cm); www.zb.uzh.ch/ausstellungen/mam/ausstellung_5482/000006704.jpeg.

26 'Ze end der Schul vmb die 4. mit einem psalmen enden, aber an Zinstag, Donstag und Samstag sol man ie carmina singen wie bisher gebracht', cit. after Bührer, 'Johannes Fries', 205.

27 Johannes Fries, *Brevis musicae isagoge* (Zurich: Johann Froschauer, 1554), not in VD16, copy CH-Zz: http://dx.doi.org/10.3931/e-rara-684.

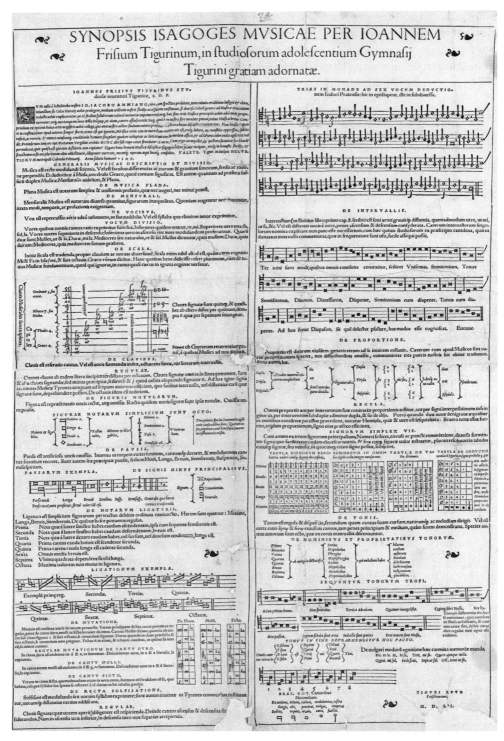

Figure 5.2 Johannes Fries, *Synopsis Isagoges Musicae per Ioannem Frisium Tigurinum*. Zurich: Froschauer, 1552. Woodcut, 61.5 × 40.4 cm
Source: Zentralbibliothek Zürich, Graphische Sammlung: EDR III 1552 Fries, 1

isagoges musicae, that is, a synoptic presentation of the *Isagoge* (*Introduction*) *to music*, shows that the book and broadsheet were conceived as two versions of the same work. This suggests that the broadsheet was conceived as a companion to a book that was yet to be printed. Furthermore, a remark on the title page of the *Isagoge* highlights the newly added material, namely metrical settings (*carmina*), based on Tritonius' melodies and set *ad aequales* by Fries's friend Heinrich Textor.[29] The broadsheet was thus converted into a music book in the form of a set of partbooks with an extended text section in the tenor booklet ('Generalis musica descriptio & divisio'), which constituted the *Isagoge* itself. The *Isagoge* could also have stood alone as a typical schoolbook, even without the *Synopsis*. That the function of the textbook seems to have been the most important for some users is illustrated by the fact that two surviving copies (those in Zurich and Wolfenbüttel) consist only of the tenor partbook.[30] For their possessors, it seems that the instructional text was at some point in time the only really useful part of the book, or at least the part they considered most worthy of conservation.

The production of both publications show their close links. The book is in oblong format, but the forme used to set the book was slightly narrower than the width of the columns on the broadsheet, so the line breaks are not identical. Nevertheless, it is clear that the book was intended to reproduce the various parts of the broadsheet closely. The woodcuts were printed from the same blocks, whereas the diagrams printed from type, including parts of the *scala* diagram, have been re-set. In order to fit into the new layout of the pages of the book, the staves of the examples of the ligatures seem to have been cut into segments and rearranged (see Figure 5.3).

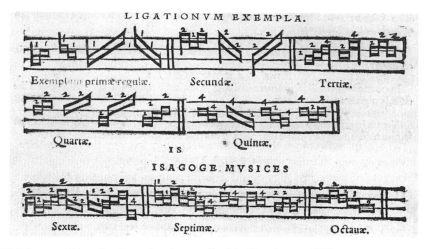

Figure 5.3 Johannes Fries, *Brevis musicae isagoge*. Zurich: Froschauer, 1554
Source: Zentralbibliothek Zürich, Alte Drucke, 5.399, A. Drucke Rara

---

28 'Composui ante quadriennium totius Musicae breve compendium ex optimis huius artis magistris collectum, quod tum temporis omnibus huius disciplinae amatoribus solum in tabula ad discendum proponebatur. Nunc vero visum est nostro FROSCHOVERO typographo insigni, & meo patrono singulari, illud denuo parvo libello maioris discipulorum commoditatis gratia typis excudere', Fries, *Isagoge*, fol. AA2ᵛ.
29 Fries, *Isagoge*, title page: 'Accessuerunt priori aeditioni omnia Horatij carminum genera: item Heroica, Elegica &c. quatuor vocibus ad aequales, in studiosorum adolescentum gratiam composita.'
30 D-W 23 Musica Helmst.

The *Synopsis* includes two longer notated examples, the mnemonic melody *Ter trini sunt modi*, and the second *Agnus* from Josquin's *Missa Hercules Dux*. (The latter has an inscription that resembles that in Glarean's *Dodekachordon*, which was evidently Fries's source.) Both have been rearranged for the *Isagoge*, and take each one line more than on the broadsheet. The choice of the latter piece suggests that the pupils at the Zurich Gymnasium in the mid century were introduced to pieces by Josquin that presuppose a certain level of musical proficiency. Furthermore, they learned aspects of the modal system in a way consistent with Glarean's recent theory, but limited to eight modes. At the end of the *Synopsis* (and the *Isagoge*), a curious item is added, a moralising musical rebus ascribed here to Erasmus, labelled as a poem addressed to the cantors of emperor Maximilian.[31] It uses the note shapes for the last words of each phrase (e.g. 'Ex minimis surgit seditio [maxima]') and thus may have been considered by Fries as an interesting item for inculcating the names of note values in playful form. The ascription to Erasmus may have made it still more attractive for the learned teacher. With these two elements, the Zurich pupils encountered two great authorities, Josquin and Erasmus, in their simple introduction to music theory. Implicitly, the work promotes a connection between music and language and evokes an intellectual context. Fries's *Synopsis* thus stands halfway between the blackboard inscription and a digest personalised with individual elements, addressed to students with a strong literary background.

Stemmatic tables

The stemmatic tables rely above all on a systematic, rigorous arrangement of information. This format became especially popular in the second half of the sixteenth century for 'methodical' presentation in the wake of pedagogical Ramism, even if similar diagrams were already widely used earlier. From the middle of the sixteenth century on, various 'divisiones musicae' were produced in the form of single sheets. A first peak in the production occurred in the 1550s, with highly elaborate 'divisiones' by Gregor Faber and Michael Voigt. In the following decades, a growing number of tables with strictly dichotomic representations were produced by authors such as Christoph Praetorius, Friedrich Beurhusius, Johannes Thomas Freigius and Valentin Goetting, in which the single theoretical issues (chant/mensural music, signs, modes, etc.) are represented by pairings. Here, the *tabula* (which Leibniz would describe a century later as an instrument for showing ordered knowledge at a glance) becomes the frame for arranging information on musical issues in the well-known form of 'Ramist' *schematismi*.[32] These divergent pairs are usually structured by curly brackets or lines, but they could also be rendered typographically by arranging short text blocks in columns separated by spacing. In their application of dichotomic presentation, these examples should sometimes be considered more as a tribute to current pedagogical trends than to a strictly logical application of the principle to music.

Gregor Faber's *Erotemata* (1553), a text directed at university-level readers, is remarkable in that it opens with an elaborate description of the different branches of philosophy, among which music is considered as a part of *philosophia theoretica*.[33] The stemmatic table printed

---

31 *Collected Works of Erasmus*, vol. 85: *Poems*, 368, No. 136 (*Erasmus cantoribus Maximiliani*) and vol. 86, 724–726; elsewhere, it is ascribed to Caelius, cf. Johannes Lauterbach, *Aenigmata [. . .] Additis simul Nicolai Reusneri [. . .] Aenigmatis. Griphologia sive sylvula logogriphorum* [ed. by Nicolaus Reusner] (Frankfurt/M.: Palthen, 1601 [VD17 39:139851S]), 157.

32 Cf. the definition, 'Tabula est in qua plura ordine exhibentur uno conspectu', Leibniz, *Collectanea*, cit. after Siegel, *Tabula*, 65.

33 Gregor Faber, *Musices practicae erotemata* (Basel: Johann Petri, 1553), VD16 F 55.

with the book (*Schema divisionem musicae continens*, see Figure 5.4) refers to the difficulties of presentation evoked in the beginning of the main text.[34] In his chapter on the nature of music ('Quid est musica?', fol. A4r), Faber does not define music according to one of the familiar *formulae* taken up from Boethius or Augustine (i.e. the art of measuring relations between sounds or the art of singing well), but by evoking the plurality of possible significations. Having stated this difficulty, Faber asserts that the chart with the *partitio musicae* is more helpful for understanding than the textual explications: 'Since musical

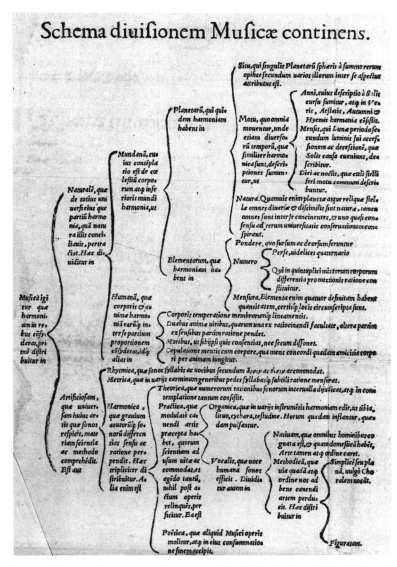

Figure 5.4 Gregor Faber, *Musices practicae Erotematum Libri II*. Basel: Petri, 1553. Folding chart: 'Schema divisionem musicae continens'
Source: Universitätsbibliothek Basel, AN V 59

---

34 It is preserved in the Basel copy, CH-Bu AN V 59.

110   INGA MAI GROOTE

reasoning is said to consist in various things, it will be easier to see from its divisions in the following diagram the part which we have undertaken to explain in these books.'[35]

Faber's *tabula*, together with the philosophical introduction, covers a much broader content than the main text, which elaborates on the traditional elementary practical topics contained in a music textbook. The table is not strictly dichotomic, but also includes some threefold distinctions: for example, *musica harmonica* is divided into *theorica*, *practica* and *poetica*.[36] It uses curly brackets, and has relatively long definitions for each point. Thus it is less an assembly of catch-words for quick orientation than a predecessor of the modern mind-map, making clear the relationships between the different levels of definition.

Another broadsheet that aims to present the whole range of music is Michael Voigt's *Definitio, divisio musices, & eius subdivisio*, printed at Basel by Petri in 1557.[37] An entry in the contemporary catalogue of the musical materials in the Amerbach-Iselin library at Basel probably also corresponds to this sheet.[38] This synoptic broadsheet includes a *divisio* of music, diagrams, text-blocks, and even a pictorial element: a figurative frieze displaying the mythological inventors of music. The sheet also bears dedicatory and laudatory poems by members of Voigt's personal network, such as Adam Sieber and Philipp Melanchthon, who provided advice on the layout.[39] Material was also supplied by Georg Fabricius,[40] who put Voigt in contact with Petri in Basel to organise the printing of the *Definitio* and a smaller book on music, which seems however not have to come into being.[41] Voigt dedicated the broadsheet to the city of Torgau, where he worked from 1551; this suggests that the *Definitio et divisio* was used to teach pupils at the local school.

The middle part of the right half is occupied by a *divisio* of music in a bracketed stemma. Here, bipartite distinctions prevail: music is either theoretical or practical; practical music can be instrumental or vocal, and so on. This scheme is more elaborate than others in that it includes instrumental music with its social functions, and distinguishes 'musica vocalis' into *mousiké*, in the sense that we would understand music, and *poietiké*, that is, versification. Similar to the source-texts quoted on the left side of the sheet, there is another text field beneath the *divisio*, with Proclus' explanation of the three harmonic genera from his *Commentary on the Timaeus*, and a composite diagram explaining the three genera in the lowest tetrachord (*tetrachordon hypaton*) by three parallel bars. This corresponds to Glarean's 'rationalisation' of the older circular diagram tradition in his edition of Boethius'

---

35 Gregor Faber, *Erotemata*, fol. A4^r: 'Nam cum uarijs in rebus musica ratio uersari dicatur, ex eius partitione, quam sequens tabula continet, melius perspicietur quam partem his libris susceperimus explicandam.'

36 Furthermore, an intermediate level is introduced (*practica* is either *organica* or *vocalis*, *vocalis* can be subdivided into *nativa* and *methodica*, the latter comprising *musica plana* and *musica figurativa*).

37 Michael Voigt, *Definitio, et Diuisio Musices, & eius subdiuisio* (Basel: Johann Petri, 1557), not in VD16 (http://daten.digitale-sammlungen.de/bsb00089937/image_1).

38 The entry in the catalogue by Conrad Pfister describes the item as 'Musicae doctrinae folia quatuor patentia Basilea per Henrichum Petri aº 1557 edita', listing the names and chapters appearing on the print, cf. *Philosophicae facultatis bibliothecae Amerbachianae Iselianae [. . .] index* (A.R. I), cit. after Kmetz, *Basel Songbooks*, 17.

39 Melanchthon, *Opera quae supersunt omnia*, vol. 7, col. 873 (19.12.1551).

40 Georg Fabricius, 'Clari musici in quadam cithara', in: Johannes Bartholomaeus *et al.*, *Poetae Germani & exteri* [. . .] (Görlitz: Ambrosius Fritsch, ²1574), VD16 F 341, 72–73.

41 'Quod ad te pertinet, vellem libellum simplicissimum προγυμνασματικὸν. colligeres, in quo prima elementa digna demonstratione artis, sed tamen cum praeceptorum explicatione necessaria traderes, sed ad captum eorum, qui primum inchoant eam artem. Deinde adderes secundum eum ipsum, in quo fundamenta extruis, quem mihi superiori anno iudicandum mittebas. Postea suo tempore progrederis longius, donec ad eum artis usum, qui iam in tot vocum varietate consistit, pervenires. Si idem sentis tu, facile efficiam, ut priores duo Basileae ab Henrico Petro, viro studiosissimo, exprimantur.' Reproduced after Schreber, *Vita clarissimi*, 115–116.

'SYNOPSIS MUSICAE': CHARTS AND TABLES   111

De institutione musica,[42] a scheme that Petri used repeatedly in the music treatises he published, from Glarean's *Dodekachordon* on.[43] Musical notation and the forms of practical vocal music are illustrated by two short pieces, similar to those found on Fries's *Synopsis*. These examples have a double function: they demonstrate real examples of notation, and could also be sung.

The *definitio* is placed on the left side, with paragraphs concerning the etymology, scope and causes of music, information on its relationship with other mathematical disciplines, and a diagram comparing the proportions of arithmetic with those of music. This presentation reproduces the information typically given in an introductory chapter of a music treatise, but is more elaborate than on other broadsheets, and employs philosophical terminology as well as Greek. The presence of quotations in Greek (Plato and Nicomachus) indicates that this sheet was aimed at pupils who were already quite advanced.

The sheet presents a balanced optical impression, with the rounded diagrams placed in the upper right and the lower left, with the square tetrachord diagram at the bottom balancing the woodcut with the inventors of music in the upper register. It combines various visual elements: technical, figurative and musical. Since this sheet presents advanced material, it lacks some basic elements present on other sheets, such as the emblematic Guidonian hand, thus creating a more technical and sophisticated impression. The replacement of the traditional arcs on the tetrachord diagram by straight lines may be interpreted as a modernising element.

In 1575, Voigt edited another single-sheet print, the *Stoicheiosis harmonica* (*The elements of harmony*), dedicated to the pupils ('studiosa iuventus') at Torgau.[44] Unlike the *Definitio*, the *Stoicheiosis* prominently presents a Guidonian hand in the left part, with the octave and its proportions depicted on the palm. Notwithstanding these references to elementary music knowledge and learners, the right side of the sheet contains relatively long sections of text, explaining proportions and the harmonic mean with citations from ancient Greek authors such as Plutarch and Plato, together with Latin translations. While the hand identifies the subject of the sheet unambiguously as music theory, the content of the sheet far exceeds the level of beginners. The left part includes two elements that emphasise the connection of music and learning: a poem by Georg Fabricius in honour of the author (who expounds music with its miraculous powers, familiar from ancient myths), and a short bilingual extract from Athenaeus' *Deipnosophistae*, which praises music as a treasure for the learned and well-educated. These elements assume that the intended users of this sheet were conversant with Latin and Greek, and inclined to link technical knowledge (such as the calculation of proportions) with ideas about the ethical power of music. The high level of technical proficiency assumed by the presence of such elements explains the lack of more basic musical definitions.

Also in 1575, the Wittenberg printer Johann Schwertel produced another music chart, this time in truly stemmatic form: Christoph Praetorius' large *Musices generalis typus*, a general account of music theory, that was issued in conjunction with Praetorius' textbook *Erotemata musices in usum scholae Lunaeburgensis* (1575) (see Figure 5.5). Praetorius studied

---

42 Cf. *Boethi opera* (Basel: Heinrich Petri, 1546), vdm 1333, 'quae hic latè tribus figuris dicuntur, hac unica perspicacius conspicis.' This edition includes the three older circular forms for each genus separately as well as Glarean's composite bar diagram.

43 Cf. (without the numbers) Wonnegger (ed.), *Epitome* (1557), 20 and *errata* sheet, or (in a simplified form) Faber, *Erotemata*, 14.

44 Wittenberg: Crato, 1575, F-Pn Rés. 1646 (this copy is glued on a sheet together with a copy of Voigt's *Insigne*.

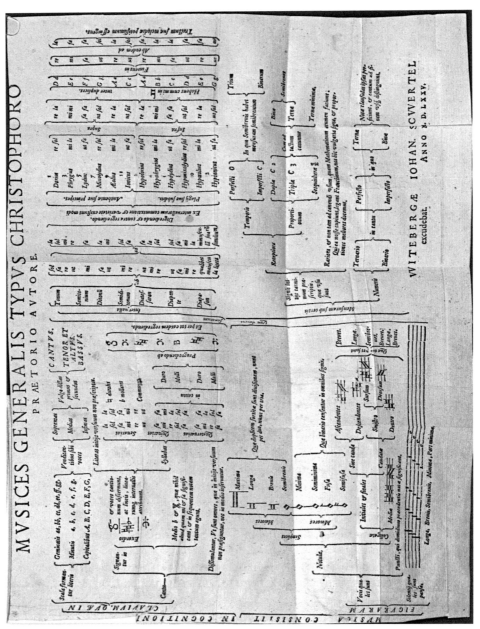

Figure 5.5 Christoph Praetorius, *Erotemata musices in usum scholae Lunaeburgensis*. Wittenberg: Schwertel, 1574. 'Typus musices' Source: Universitätsbibliothek Rostock, Dd-24.1

'SYNOPSIS MUSICAE': CHARTS AND TABLES   113

in Wittenberg and then became *cantor* at the Johanneum in Lüneburg, where he took up a
local tradition by reworking the successful textbook *Erotemata musicae practicae*, by his
predecessor Lucas Lossius.[45] Lossius published his *Erotemata* in 1563 for use at the school
at Lüneburg, and it was reprinted several times.[46] A chart devised by Praetorius is included
in a 1570 re-edition of Lossius' book, and is specifically mentioned as an important addition
on the title page, as a 'learned table containing a summary of the art of music'.[47] The
description of this chart as a 'summa' indicates that it was meant to contain everything in
condensed form. In 1574, Praetorius published his own textbook, *Erotemata musices*, which
clearly differs from Lossius' book in content and arrangement, and which likewise includes
a chart.[48] Visually, Praetorius' 1575 broadsheet *Typus* is more clearly structured than the
other examples discussed so far, and makes generous use of brackets, combined from small
pieces of type, in dihaeretic structures. This means that the material of the discipline is
presented in a series of distinctions, most often dichotomic ones. Praetorius' *Typus* includes
a few more elements than the chart he provided earlier to accompany Lossius' work. The
left and right halves of the unfolded sheet show two series of dichotomies. On the left-
hand side are explanations of the signs and names for basic categories of duration and pitch
of sound ('Musica consistit in cognitione figurarum/clavium'). On the right-hand side, each
group is differentiated further: *claves* teach intervals and modes, the *figurae* indicate the
mensuration ('quae docent sonorum mensurae/intervalla'). Solmisation is treated in an
interesting way: while in textbooks it is normally demonstrated in connection with a
diagram linked with the *scala* in order to show the connections between *claves* and *voces*,
Praetorius only explains *voces* in relation to the rules for solmisation and mutation points.
Readers could probably only understand this explanation if they knew the rules from the
corresponding chapter in the book.[49]

In some instances, the dichotomic principle breaks down. In the section on the pitches
('claves'), Praetorius' desire to create systematic and thoroughgoing dichotomies sometimes
forces him to introduce distinctions in which one term is effectively void. For example, he
writes that pitches in a piece ('claves in cantu') are either marked with accidentals ('signatae')
or not so marked. For the *signatae*, alteration through accidentals can be brought about either
through a key signature at the start of a system or by the application of accidentals within
a system. Notes that are not affected by accidentals may be so unaffected at the beginning
of a system or within a system. Here too Praetorius introduces a void term ('Dißimulatur,
Vt sunt omnes, quæ in initiis versuum non praefiguntur, nec in medio inseruntur'). In
another instance, where the tabular presentation does not allow much space to explain
extravagant mensurations, a cross-reference refers interested readers to Gaffurius' books
for more detail. (In a similar way, Lossius' *Summa* had referred readers to Heyden for further
information on this topic.[50]) In the upper right quarter of the sheet, the dichotomic ordering

---

45 Praetorius' publications are backed up by the local authorities as well, with a preface to the reader
by Albert Lenicer, then rector of the Johanneum, and a dedication to some sons of Lüneburg patricians by
Praetorius himself; Lenicer was also the author of the Lüneburg school order of 1570/77.

46 For a detailed list of editions, cf. Onkelbach, *Lucas Lossius*, 139–159.

47 Lucas Lossius, *Erotemata musicae practicae, ex probatissimis quibusque huius divinae [. . .] artis scriptoribus,
accuratè & breviter selecta, & exemplis ad puerilem institutionem [. . .] accomodatis illustrata. Ad usum scholae
Luneburgensis [. . .] olim à Luca Loßio in lucem edita: Iam verò recens ab eodem diligenter recognita. Cum tabella
erudita summam continente artis Musicae, autore Christophoro Praetorio [. . .]* (Nuremberg: Gerlach, 1570), VD16
ZV 17280. This is also the imprint for Praetorius' table, cf Onkelbach, *Lucas Lossius*, 262.

48 On Christoph Praetorius' book, with a second edition from 1581, see Onkelbach, *Lucas Lossius*,
261–265.

49 Cf. Praetorius, *Erotemata*, fol. D$^{r/v}$.

50 Onkelbach, *Lucas Lossius*, 262.

is modified, and the principle of distinguishing phenonema into increasingly fine levels of detail is not observed strictly. The left half of this quadrant refers to the intervals in general, whose combinations then constitute the modes, explained in the right half. Elsewhere, pairings continue over a number of levels, though the distinctions are not maintained on each level. For example, when discussing mensuration, Praetorius creates a series of three pairs when he distinguishes *numerus* into *ternarius* or *binarius*, corresponding to cantus *perfectus* or *imperfectus*, which are notated with *notae ternae* or *binae* respectively, yet these pairs are not subordinate to one another like the other distinctions. Such small inconsistencies of arrangement are integrated optically by the use of brackets.

In some cases, authors and printers also used stemmatic tables to articulate the content of a book. In this context, we shall briefly consider the so-called Ramist influences in the later sixteenth century. The ideas of Petrus Ramus (1515–1572), an important French logician and educational reformer, were received in Germany with great interest. He attempted to overcome problems with the way Aristotelian philosophy was taught at that time by establishing dialectic as the overarching method for all sciences.[51] This resulted in a strictly 'logical' ordering of material in any subject, often expounded by means of bifurcating charts. Ramus' name is also linked with school programs designed to teach a wide variety of disciplines in a relatively short time. Since his program was to be realised by 'methodical' teaching, his bifurcating tables 'invaded' schoolbooks, and his method was sometimes ridiculed when it was applied mechanically and inappropriately. Consequently, some writers on music showed strong interest in Ramus' techniques. Johannes Thomas Freigius (1543–1583), who lived among other places at Basel and Altdorf, edited some of Ramus' texts, and wrote books that treated different disciplines and subjects systematically by applying Ramist tables of definitions and divisions.[52] In 1582, he published an encyclopedia intended for private study, *Paedagogus*, which opens with a stemmatic chart delineating the system of disciplines.[53] This chart shows the shift of music into the realm of physical disciplines typical of the later sixteenth century. He introduces dichotomies for the different disciplines, but not for music, including only the aforementioned large sheet with the *scala* diagram. The absence of a Ramist methodology in Freigius' treatment of music may be explained by the fact that his chapter on music is based on a text by Conrad Stuber that came out of a teaching tradition without Ramist influences.

Other authors in Freigius' circle also used stemmatic tables to articulate the structure of their treatment of music. Freigius knew Friedrich Beurhusius in Dortmund, another well-known follower of Ramist methods, and Beurhusius received a dedicatory poem in Valentin Goetting's *Compendium musicae modulativae* (1587).[54] Beurhusius introduced his book on music, *Musicae erotematum libri duo* (1591), with a table entitled 'Typus Musicae' that shows the structure of the book, before the main text begins in erotematic (question-and-answer) form.[55] Beurhusius' strictly dichotomic presentation is not dialectical throughout, but includes some forced dichotomies that function as mere 'rhetorical dispositions'.[56]

---

51 Ong, *Ramus, Method, and the Decay of Dialogue.*

52 Rother, 'Ramus and Ramism in Switzerland', esp. 17–21.

53 Johannes Thomas Freigius, *Paedagogus, hoc est libellus ostendens qua ratione prima artium initia pueris quàm facillimè tradi possint* (Basel: Henricpetri, 1582).

54 Valentin Goetting, *Compendium musicae modulativae* (Erfurt: Georg Baumann, 1587), not in VD16.

55 Friedrich Beurhusius, *Erotematum musicae libri duo, ex optimis huius artis scriptoribus vera perspicuaque methodo descripti* (Nuremberg: Katharina Gerlach/heirs of Berg, 1580 [VD16 B 2363]; from this edition on, the book includes preface by Johannes Thomas Freigius). Book 1 is on 'musica elementaria' (the fundamentals: tone system, intervals, tempus), book 2 on 'musica harmonica' (melodia: cantus and modus, counterpoint).

56 Kotzakidou Pace, 'Ut dialectica musica', esp. 221–222.

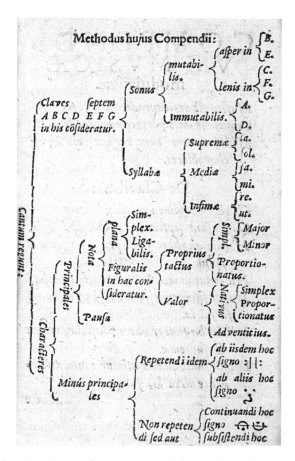

Figure 5.6 Valentin Goetting, *Compendium musicae modulativae*. Erfurt: Baumann, 1587
Source: Brussels, Bibliothèque royale de Belgique - Koninklijke Bibliotheek van België, Fétis 5.465 A (RP), fol. [B 7ʳ]

Goetting's *Compendium*, a relatively simple introduction to music, opens with a page-size table arranged in bracketed subdivisions, labelled 'The method of this *Compendium*' ('Methodus huius compendii', see Figure 5.6), a term typical of a Ramist style of presentation. The preface to the book (written by Henning Dedekind) elaborates on the pedagogical value of this method:

> Truth herself will commend this method [of Goetting's *Compendium*] more accurately than our speech. However, truth, the queen and protector of this method, commands us to affirm this one thing: that to this point nothing has appeared more succinct in its brevity, more plain in its rules, clear in its order, or more precise; [the *Compendium*] defines and divides the art duly, enunciates individual rules with words laden with meaning, and submits examples that lay out in full the practices that teachers should follow.[57]

---

57 Goetting, *Compendium*, fol. B1ᵛ–B2ʳ: 'Methodum hanc rectius ipsa veritas, quam nostra commendabit oratio, illud tamen hujus regina & tutrix veritas unum affirmare nos jubet: brevitate concinnius praeceptis clarius ordine accuratius facilitate exactius hactenus visum esse nullum, artem definit dividitque legitime, praecepta singula verbis enunciat significantibus, exempla subjicit omnem & totum praeceptorum usum exhibentia.'

116 INGA MAI GROOTE

However, the subdivisions are simple. *Cantus* needs *claves* and *characteres*, and both groups are subdivided further: *characteres* are divided into *principales* and *minus principales*, corresponding to the signs for notes and accessorial signs (repeat signs, *signa congruentiae* and so on) respectively. The *claves* are distinguished by means of dichotomy into letters and solmisation syllables. Despite their simplicity, tables of this kind appealed to contemporary readers, for their appearance claimed to transmit verified knowledge.[58] These tables, produced primarily for a readership of learners, exemplify the adaption of 'modern' pedagogic tools to musical instruction, in smaller and in larger formats. They could support the rearrangement of the disciplines, from the old scheme of the liberal arts to a more diversified one, and could make theoretical knowledge more easily digestible.

Pictorial broadsheets

The pictorial broadsheet is rarer, but is a good example of cross-disciplinary connexions or even applied emblematic thought. This last kind would, especially in the seventeenth century, develop further into highly elaborate examples such as Robert Fludd's *Templum musicae* from the *Utriusque cosmi majoris scilicet et minoris metaphysica, physica, atque technica historia*, which expressed forms of emblematic thinking in a universalist manner. Some sheets depicted instruments realistically in order to demonstrate tuning or playing techniques.[59] Pictorial broadsheets could draw on a range of imagery. Those used for teaching music employed images more or less closely related to the topic. Unlike in the examples discussed above, the optical presentation of such broadsheets was determined less by considerations of utility and practical needs than by the desire to create a visually attractive result. That musical content was nevertheless presented in pictorial form perhaps reflects a change of style. Just as birfurcating Ramistic diagrams showed that the desire to promote a particular style of presentation could trump the need to organise the material according to strict principles, visual considerations were often more significant in pictorial charts than the advantageous arrangement of the material.

A good example of such pictorial charts may be found in Christofle de Savigny's *Tableaux accomplis de tous les arts* (1587).[60] The author, fearing that learning was in danger of neglect, tried to find ways to present the arts and sciences to a non-specialist reader from among the means offered by synoptic tables.[61] On an abstract level, Savigny confronts us again with the problem of knowledge in general education. His tables were descendants of the dichotomic tables mentioned above, though here this structure served more to frame a presentation with rich visual associations.[62] Each page presents a summary of a discipline, arranged within a distinctive decorated frame, which typographically unifies the appearance and suggests coherence. For the printer, this was also a good way to produce a visually appealing book.

---

58 'Graphics imparted a particular look – orderly, verifiable, demonstrable to concepts on the page.' Ferrell, 'Page Techne', 14–15.

59 Hauge, 'The Temple of Music'. For a discussion of two elaborate philosophical examples, cf. Berger, 'Visualization of Logic'. On instruments, cf. Fabris, 'Lute Tabulature Instructions'.

60 Christofle de Savigny, *Tableaux accomplis de tous les arts libéraux, contenans brievement et clerement, par singulière méthode de doctrine, une générale et sommaire partition des dicts arts, amassez et réduicts en ordre pour le soulagement et profit de la jeunesse* (Paris: François de Gourmont, 1587).

61 '[...] ie n'ay peu me garder de lamenter & deplourer grandement la misere & malheur de ce temps [...] considerant ces doctrines & sciences tant excellentes & necessaires di-je pour l'instruction, regle & conduite de la vie, estre auiourd'huy ainsi méprisées, & negligées principalement presques de la plus grande part de ceux qui portent le tiltre de Gentilshommes [...].' Savigny, *Tableaux*, dedicatory letter (unpaginated).

62 On Savigny's project, cf. Siegel, *Tabula*, esp. chap. IV/V; it is also mentioned passingly in Stevens, 'Hands, Music, and Meaning', 89.

'SYNOPSIS MUSICAE': CHARTS AND TABLES   117

Starting with philosophy, Savigny explicates a system of disciplines enlarged to encompass applied arts such as meteorology and topography. Music is included among corporeal, physical matters, under the rubric of Hearing. The sheet for music mixes different levels. The page prominently displays two objects: the *manus*, and a chain of four bells. Elsewhere, Savigny used scrolls for tables with numbers; here the scrolls bear elements of notation. He then provides rudimentary information about the hexachords and intervals. In his expositions of the physical sciences, Savigny displays a number of real objects associated with each area of knowledge. For cosmography, there is an armillary sphere and highly emblematic diagrams for the system of the spheres and the climatic zones of the earth, diagrams of the kind familiar to anyone who had read a post-Ptolemaic geographical introduction. On the sheet for music, he displays more or less contemporary musical instruments and slightly stylised bells. These typical objects were evidently intended as visual triggers for each discipline.

In another broadsheet for elementary music instruction by Wolf Preisegger, dated to 1598, the content is simpler, but the pictorial aspect more complex, as it uses a non-musical visual idea, a double-headed eagle.[63] The identity of the author is provided in the musical system at the bottom of the page, in a code that relies on the correct association of notes and pitches.[64] Preisegger lived in Nuremberg, and the double-headed eagle may refer to the city's heraldic device, which included the imperial eagle. Although at first sight there seems no connexion between the pictorial motif and the instructional content, Preisegger uses the anatomy of the eagle, with its two heads and two wings, to suggest the fundamental musical distinction between *cantus durus* and *cantus mollis*. The body of the eagle, its wings, and the insignia it bears are likewise deployed as frames. The sceptre displays the *claves* and clefs, the rules of mutation are displayed across the wings, while on the body and tail are displayed the essence of mutation and the signs for notes and rests. The motto 'wine and music rejoice the heart of man' ('Vinum et musica laetificant cor hominis', Ecclesiasticus 40:20) is probably reflected in the inscription on the wine-cup ('crater vini') on the vessel that replaces the orb in the eagle's left claw.

A broadsheet of this kind does not seem very useful as a means for instruction: the information contained is limited to the rudiments of music, and the seemingly elaborate notation at the bottom of the sheet is not a meaningful piece of music, but an encrypted inscription of the author's identity. Even if the sheet perhaps served the needs of Preisegger, a Nuremberg town clerk, to represent his own inventiveness, the artefact nevertheless attests to the appeal of musical subjects in general.[65] For the owners of the sheet, it could become a decorative object that showcased their musical education.

Conclusion

Technically, printed music charts combine elements that also occur in regular textbooks. For this reason, the single elements are usually not larger than the page of a book. A broadsheet provided the space to present several such elements simultaneously. They also provided space for the inventiveness of authors and printers in very different ways. Further

---

63 Wolf Preisegger, *Der lieben Jugent auch andern Personen so lust vnnd Lieb, zur lernung der loblichen Kunst Musica haben, zu gutem an den Tag geben, ANNO 1598. TYPVS MVSICAE* ([Nuremberg]: [n. p.], 1598), D-Mbs Einbl. XI,81, not in VD16 (urn:nbn:de:bvb:12-bsb00098907–9).

64 For the solution, cf. Blumenberg, 'Bildrätsel'.

65 Cf. Blumenberg, 'Bildrätsel', 165.

118   INGA MAI GROOTE

research would be necessary to determine whether the considerable number of large-scale didactic sheets for music exceeds those produced for other disciplines; perhaps the nearest rival in terms of numbers of editions is religious broadsides. The mere existence of such relatively large numbers of musical charts may be interpreted as an indicator of the special position enjoyed by this discipline. Musical instruction consisted in theory and practice, and could take place in different contexts, both formal and informal. It seems likely therefore that music was especially inclined to develop a variety of forms for the presentation of didactic material.

The format of the music theory broadside could be interpreted, at least in the case of the synoptic pieces, as a counterpart to the choir-book format used for *musica practica*, which enables, and even implies, simultaneous use by multiple readers. Such broadsides could be consulted by groups of pupils, even at the same time. If placed in an accessible space, it could function as a reference work of which a single, stationary copy was sufficient for a number of users. The large size of some stemmatic tables in books arose from practical constraints: in order to produce the tables in a readable size, the author (and printer) needed more space than was offered by the format of the book in which the table was contained. The visual presentation of short text blocks (or signs and images) in a clear structure also helps readers to navigate around the content, and appeals to visual memory, since a table can act on a different level from connected prose in a textbook. The use of dichotomic representations in different disciplines supports certain shared reading (and learning) habits, a phenomenon reinforced by the high number of similar books printed for use in different subjects. Especially when tables were used in combination with erotematic texts, the structure of table and text reinforced each other. It is plausible that the dichotomies were memorised, as has been suggested for textbooks in grammar and rhetoric.[66] The pictorial broadsides, finally, are a further elaboration of the various manners of representation present in other kinds of printed materials. They allow for the transposition of information and visualisation strategies specific to music into contexts in which they had a value that was more symbolic, at least as long as music was still considered an important element of education. All of these items attest to strategies for visualising musical knowledge, drawing on the means made available by print.

References

Balensuela, C. Matthew. 'Ut hec te figura docet: The Transformation of Music Theory Illustrations from Manuscript to Print'. *Yearbook of the Alamire Foundation* 6 (2008): 97–110.

Berger, Susanna. 'Philander Colutius's *Logicae universae typus* (1606) and the Visualization of Logic'. *Word & Image* 31 (2015): 265–287.

The Berkeley Manuscript, edited and translated by Oliver B. Ellsworth. Greek and Latin Music Theory, vol. 2. Lincoln: University of Nebraska Press, 1984.

Blumenberg, Heike. 'Ein musikalisches Bildrätsel'. *Die Musikforschung* 45 (1992): 163–165.

Bührer, Peter. 'Johannes Fries (1505–1565). Pädagoge, Philologe, Musiker – Leben und Werk'. *Zürcher Taschenbuch 2002*, Neue Folge 122 (2001): 151–231.

Büttner, Frank. 'Die Illustrationen der "Margarita Philosophica" des Gregor Reisch. Zur Typologie der Illustration in gedruckten enzyklopädischen Werken der Frühen Neuzeit'. In *Sammeln, Ordnen, Veranschaulichen: zur Wissenskompilatorik der frühen Neuzeit*, edited by Frank Büttner *et al.* Pluralisierung & Autorität 2. Münster: LIT, 2003, 269–300.

---

66 Ramus, *Scholae in liberales artes*, X.

Collected Works of Erasmus, vols. 85–86: *Poems*, translated by Clarence H. Miller, edited and annotated by Harry Vredeveld, Toronto etc.: Univ. of Toronto Press, 1993.

Deutsche illustrierte Flugblätter des 16. und 17. Jahrhunderts, edited by Wolfgang Harms vol. 3: *Die Sammlung der Herzog-August-Bibliothek in Wolfenbüttel. Theologica, Quodlibetica. Bibliographie, Personen- und Sachregister*. Munich: Kraus International Publications, 1989.

Fabris, Dinko. 'Lute Tabulature Instructions in Italy: A Survey of the "Regole" from 1507 to 1759'. In *Performance on Lute, Guitar, and Vihuela: Historical Practice and Modern Interpretation*, edited by Victor Coelho, Cambridge: Cambridge University Press, 1997, 16–46.

Ferguson, Stephen. 'System and Schema. "Tabulae" of the Fifteenth to Eighteenth Centuries'. *Princeton University Library Chronicle* 49/1 (1987): 9–30.

Ferrell, Lori Ann. '"Page Techne": Interpreting Diagrams in Early Modern English "How-to" Books'. In *Printed Images in Early Modern Britain. Essays in Interpretation*, edited by Michael Hunter, Farnham: Ashgate, 2010, 113–126.

Florea, Luminita. '"Virtus scriptoris": Steps towards a Typology of Illustration Borrowing in Music Theory Treatises of the Late Middle Ages and the Renaissance'. *Yearbook of the Alamire Foundation* 6 (2008): 77–96.

Forscher Weiss, Susan. '"Disce manum tuam si vis bene discere cantum": Symbols of Learning Music in Early Modern Europe'. *Music in Art* 30/1–2 (2005): 35–47.

Kmetz, John. *The Sixteenth-Century Basel Songbooks: Origins, Contents, Contexts*. Publikationen der Schweizerischen Musikforschenden Gesellschaft II, 35. Bern etc.: Haupt, 1995.

Kotzakidou Pace, Elizabeth. '"Ut dialectica musica": Artificial and Natural Category Structures in Musical Treatises of the German Renaissance', PhD dissertation, Columbia University, 2006.

Melanchthon, Philipp. *Opera quae supersunt omnia*, edited by Karl Gottlieb Bretschneider and Heinrich Ernst Bindseil. Corpus Reformatorum 1–28. Halle: Schwetschke, 1834–1860.

Mellon, Elizabeth. 'Inscribing Sound. Medieval Remakings of Boethius' "De institutione musica"', PhD dissertation, University of Pennsylvania, 2011.

Niemöller, Klaus Wolfgang. 'Deutsche Musiktheorie im 16. Jahrhundert: Geistes- und institutionsgeschichtliche Grundlagen'. In *Deutsche Musiktheorie des 15. bis 17. Jahrhunderts. I: Von Paumann bis Calvisius*, edited by Theodor Göllner *et al.* Geschichte der Musiktheorie 8/I. Darmstadt: Wissenschaftliche Buchgesellschaft, 2003, 69–98.

Ong, Walter. *Ramus, Method, and the Decay of Dialogue: From the Art of Discourse to the Art of Reason*. Cambridge, MA: Harvard University Press, 1958.

Onkelbach, Friedhelm. *Lucas Lossius und seine Musiklehre*. Kölner Beiträge zur Musikforschung 17. Regensburg: Bosse, 1960.

Owens, Jessie A. 'You Can Tell a Book by Its Cover: Reflections on Format in English Music "Theory"'. In *Music Education in the Middle Ages and the Renaissance*, edited by Russell E. Murray, Jr., Susan Forscher Weiss, and Cynthia J. Cyrus, Bloomington, IN: Indiana University Press, 2010, 347–385.

Ramus, Petrus. *Scholae in liberales artes*, with an introduction by Walter J. Ong. Hildesheim: Georg Olms Verlag, 1970.

Reske, Christoph. *Die Buchdrucker des 16. und 17. Jahrhunderts im deutschen Sprachgebiet*. 2nd, extended edition Wiesbaden: Harrassowitz, 2015.

Rother, Wolfgang. 'Ramus and Ramism in Switzerland'. In *The Influence of Petrus Ramus: Studies in Sixteenth- and Seventeenth-Century Philosophy and Sciences*, edited by Mordechai Feingold *et al.* Basel: Schwabe, 2001, 9–37.

Schmid, Manfred Hermann. 'Die Darstellung der Musica im spätmittelalterlichen Bildprogramm der "Margarita philosophica" von Gregor Reisch 1503'. *Hamburger Jahrbuch für Musikwissenschaft* 12 (1994): 247–261.

Schreurs, Eugeen and Jan Van der Stock, ' "Principium Et Ars Tocius Musice": An Early Example of Mensural Music Printing in the Low Countries (*c*.1500–1508)'. *Yearbook of the Alamire Foundation* 2 (1997): 171–182.

Siegel, Steffen. *Tabula. Figuren der Ordnung um 1600*. Berlin: Akademie Verlag, 2009.

Smits van Waesberghe, Joseph. *Musikerziehung: Lehre und Theorie der Musik im Mittelalter*. Leipzig: Deutscher Verlag für Musik, 1969.

Stevens, Jane R. 'Hands, Music, and Meaning in Some Seventeenth-Century Dutch Paintings'. *Imago Musicae* 1 (1984): 75–102.

'The Temple of Music' by Robert Fludd, edited by Peter Hauge. Farnham/ Burlington: Ashgate, 2011.

Watt, Tessa. *Cheap Print and Popular Piety, 1550–1640*. Cambridge: Cambridge University Press, 1993.

Plate 1 *Graduale Herbipolense* (Würzburg: Georg Reyser, 1 V 1496), vdm 1050. Universitätsbibliothek Erlangen-Nürnberg, H62/INC 1203, fol. 1ʳ

Plate 2 Obsequiale Eystettense (Eichstätt: Michael Reyser, 1488), vdm 1108. München, Bayerische Staatsbibliothek, Rar. 772, fol. e7[v]

Plate 3 *Obsequiale Augustense* (Augsburg: Erhard Ratdolt, 1 II 1487), vdm 1072. München, Bayerische Staatsbibliothek, 4 L. impr. membr. 8, fol. XXXIX

Plate 4 Missale Cesaraugustanum (Zaragoza: Pablo Hurus, 1485). Archivo de Música de las Catedrales de Zaragoza. Archivos Catedralicios (La Seo y El Pilar), sig. 16-4, fol. 195[r]

Plate 5 Processionarium Predicatorum (Seville: Meinardo Ungut and Estanislao Polono, 1494). Madrid, Biblioteca Nacional de España, Inc/1268, fol. m1[r]

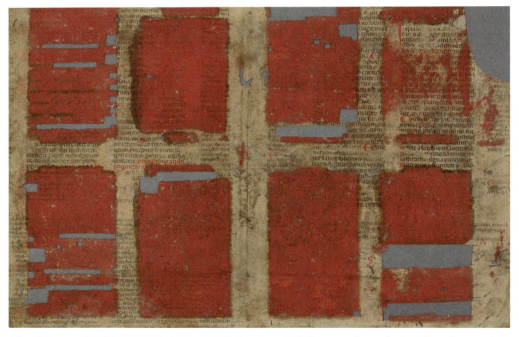

Plate 7 Decretals of Gregory IX (written in Bologna c.1300), later used as a frisket sheet for printing in red and a pasteboard inside a binding (both mid-sixteenth century), parchment, red printing ink and paste residue, 423 × 277 mm. Oxford, Bodleian Library, Broxb. 97.40. Photo: Bodleian Library, University of Oxford, 2016

Omniū offerentiū. CCXXVI

tē. Cū patre et filio adorandū et cōglorificandū. Qui locutꝰ est p ꝑphetas: et vnā sanctā catholicā et apostolicā ecclesiā. Confiteor vnū baptisma i remissionē pctōꝝ Expectamus resurrectionē mor moꝝ et vitā vēturi seculi. Amen. Post hec frāgat pbr eucha ristiā in mediū: τ ponat me dia parte in patena: τ de alia parte faciat quinqꝛ particu las τ ponat ī patena. τ acci piat aliā parte τ faciat qtuor particulas τ ponat ī pateria siliter per ordinē facte per ꝑ scriptas rotas. Et statiz pur get bene digitos. τ coopto calice faciat memēto pro vi

uis. Et perfecto simbolo di cat pbr ad orōnem dnicam equaliter.   **Oratio.**
Remꝰ apło tuo iacobo dne edocēte ꝑmonemur: vt si qs nrm indiget sapientia: postulet a te: q das oibus af fluenter: et nō improperas. Sed qꝛ ad te peruenire cupi mus per xpm: q est virtꝰ tua τ sapiētia: id agere ꝑobsta mus. Poscētes clementiā tu am: vt per eū qui apud te ad uocatꝰ factus est noster. Et peruēire nos ad te facias: et orōnez quā ipo dno instruē te didicimꝰ: ad te introire ꝑ mittas: ꝑclamātes e terris.

Pater noster qui es in celis. ℞. Amen. Sanctificetur nomen tuum. ℞. Amē. Adueniat regnū tuū. ℞. Amē. Fiat volūtas tua sicut in celo et in terra. ℞. Amen. Panem nostrum quotidianū

Plate 6 Missale mixtum (Toledo: Pedro Hagenbach, 1500). Madrid, Biblioteca Nacional de España, Inc/15, fol. ccxxxi[r]

Plate 8 Printer's device of Erhard Ratdolt (Mercury bearing the caduceus), two-colour woodcut (red, black), 140 × 100 mm (image)/245 × 347 mm (sheet). From *Missale Pataviense* (Augsburg: Erhard Ratdolt, 1494), vdm 1081. München, Bayerische Staatsbibliothek, Rar. 331, fol. CCLXI^v

Plate 9 Detail of Pieter Bruegel the Elder, *The Dirty Bride (Wedding of Mopsus and Nisa)*, c.1566, drawing in pen and ink on white-prepared, partially cut applewood block, 26.4 × 41.6 × 2.9 cm. New York, Metropolitan Museum of Art, Harris Brisbane Dick Fund, 1932 (32.63). Photo: www.metmuseum.org

Plate 10 *Obsequiale Constantiense* ([Augsburg]: Erhard Ratdolt, 1510), vdm 740. München, Bayerische Staatsbibliothek, Res/Liturg. 1459b, fol. LIIr (= g iiij^r)

Plate 11 *De dulcissimo nomine Iesu officium* (Mainz: Peter Schöffer the Younger, 1518), vdm 972. London, The British Museum, Department of Prints and Drawings, 159 a 20, fol. 3^v

Plate 12 Missale Wormatiense (Speyer: Peter Drach III, 1522), vdm 767. München, Bayerische Staatsbibliothek, Res/2 Liturg. 313, first page of music (unnumbered, after layer m)

Plate 13 Detail from *De dulcissimo nomine Iesu officium* (Mainz: Peter Schöffer the Younger, 1518), vdm 972. London, The British Museum, Department of Prints and Drawings, 159 a 20, detail of fol. 3^v

Plate 14 Libellus ad omnes (Leipzig: Melchior Lotter the Elder, 1522), vdm 322. Staatsbibliothek zu Berlin – Preußischer Kulturbesitz, Abteilung Historische Drucke, Dt 5030, fol. lxix^r

Plate 15 *Evangelistarum quatuor passiones* (Leipzig: Melchior Lotter the Elder, 1533), vdm 866. Wrocław, Zakład Narodowy im. Ossolińskich (Ossolineum), XVI.Qu.1627 adl., fol. c2^v

Plate 16 *Libellus ad omnes* (Leipzig: Melchior Lotter the Elder, 1522, vdm 322. Staatsbibliothek zu Berlin – Preußischer Kulturbesitz, Abteilung Historische Drucke, Dt 5030, fol. CXLIX^v

Plate 17 [*Missale Brandenburgense*] (Leipzig: Melchior Lotter the Elder, 1516), vdm 16 760). Staatsbibliothek zu Berlin – Preußischer Kulturbesitz, Abteilung Historische Drucke, 2° Dg6614, Qiii^r [fol. 132^r (pencil numbers)]

Part III

Music printing and commerce

6

Melchior Lotter

A German 'music printer'[1]

Elisabeth Giselbrecht

Between 1496 and 1537 Melchior Lotter the Elder printed close to 1000 books. Among them were thirty-three publications that contained notation, none of which was polyphonic music. Thus, Lotter might seem to be an unlikely focus for a book on music printing. However, it will be argued in this chapter that he was what could be described as the 'typical music printer' in German-speaking areas in the first half of the sixteenth century.

Up to this point Melchier Lotter the Elder has not been acknowledged as a printer of music; neither of the two standard encyclopaedic works in musicology (The *New Grove Dictionary of Music and Musicians* and *Musik in Geschichte und Gegenwart*) grant him an entry, and his name is rarely mentioned in the literature on music printing. But even though he clearly was not a music printer in the same way as his better-known contemporaries Ottaviano Petrucci or Pierre Attaingnant,[2] Lotter's biography, printed output, technical solutions to the challenge of printing music and the links of his business to the Reformation show him as exemplary of printers who published music north of the Alps during this period.

Lotter's publications

The name Melchior Lotter first appears in printed books beside that of his master, Konrad Kachelofen, at the end of the fifteenth century.[3] Lotter was an apprentice to Kachelofen until marrying his daughter, Dorothea. As in many comparable cases, this ensured Kachelofen continuity of his firm, and provided his new son-in-law with the inheritance of a flourishing business. Melchior Lotter successfully led this printing enterprise until 1537, when he is last mentioned in a colophon, and died twelve years later.[4] He and his wife had three sons, two of whom (Melchior the Younger and Michael) became printers.

Two events had a major influence on Lotter's life and business: the threat of plague in Leipzig, and the Reformation and associated rise of Wittenberg as a centre of printing. To avoid the plague, Lotter briefly moved his business to Meissen in 1520. There, according to the colophon of the Breviary he published there, he found a temporary home in the rooms

---

1 The research for this chapter was made possible by funding from the Austrian Science Fund (FWF) for the project P24075–G23.

2 Their body of printed music is substantial enough to warrant independent studies. See Boorman, *Petrucci* and Heartz, *Attaingnant*.

3 For the best overview of his early publications see the *Universal Short Title Catalogue* (*USTC*).

4 *USTC* lists four publications; Reske, *Buchdrucker*, suggests this to be the final one: Philipp Michael Novenianus, *Ein schöne vorordenung vnd Regiment* (Leipzig: Melchior Lotter the Elder, 1537), VD16 N 1920.

of the archbishop.⁵ In 1517, Martin Luther asked Lotter to set up a branch of his business in Wittenberg and Lotter sent his son Melchior the Younger, who was later joined by his brother Michael. The latter went on to become a successful printer in Magdeburg.⁶ In this chapter we will consider the work of Melchior the Elder in Leipzig and those books published by his sons in Wittenberg, whose work represented an extension of their father's business.

The Universal Short Title Catalogue (USTC) lists 970 titles printed by the firm of Lotter in Leipzig and Wittenberg, with the majority (755) appearing in Leipzig. They fall into various categories of content as distinguished by the USTC (Figure 6.1). Books with a religious content (both Roman Catholic and Protestant) account for more than half of Lotter's output. In terms of quantity they are followed by writings of classical authors, educational books, poetry and drama.

Only a very small number of Lotter's publications contain printed notation: thirty-three titles printed by Melchior in Leipzig, and four that appeared in Wittenberg (Table 6.1). Lotter was capable of printing music, but evidently did not make it a priority. Printing notation was simply one of the many technical challenges this early printer faced, alongside printing diagrams, images and text.

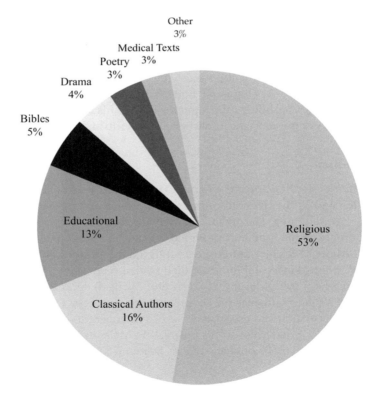

Figure 6.1 Distribution of subjects printed by Melchior Lotter the Elder
Source: data taken from *USTC* on 15.08.2016

---

5 The colophon states: 'Tempore pestilitatis excusus Misne in aula episcopali: per prouidum Melchiorem Lottheri Calcographum Lipsiacum. Anno domini Millesimo Quingentesimo Vigesimo. Die vero.xiiij. Mensis Februarij.' [*Breviarius Misnensis*] (Meissen: Melchior Lotter the Elder, 1520), vdm 299.

6 For a biography see Reske, *Buchdrucker*, 580.

Table 6.1 Publications with music by Melchior Lotter the Elder (and his son Michael in Wittenberg branch)

Title (standardised)	Year of publication	Printer	Type of source	Format	Music printing	vdm number
Psalterium Davidis cum hymnis	1498	Melchior der Ältere	liturgical	4	only staves printed	952
Psalterium cum hymnis	1499	Melchior der Ältere	liturgical	4	not inspected	1232
Psalterium cum hymnis	1499	Melchior der Ältere	liturgical	8	not inspected	1407
Missale Misnense	1500	Melchior d. Ä. & K. Kachelofen	liturgical	2	multiple impression	948
Agenda sive benedictionale	c.1500	Melchior der Ältere	liturgical	4	only staves printed	929
Agenda	1501	Melchior der Ältere	liturgical	4	only staves printed	834
[Missale Misnense]	1501	Melchior d. Ä. & K. Kachelofen	liturgical	[4]	no copies known	756
[Missale Merseburgense]	1502	Melchior der Ältere	liturgical	2	multiple impression	882
[Missale Misnense]	1502	Melchior der Ältere	liturgical	2	multiple impression	758
Scaenica progymnasmata	1503	Melchior der Ältere	humanist book	4	woodcut	101
[Missale Posnaniense]	1505	Melchior der Ältere	liturgical	2	multiple impression	886
Agenda sive benedictionale	1507	Melchior der Ältere	liturgical	4	only staves printed	238
Psalterium Davidis cum hymnis	1509	Melchior der Ältere	liturgical	4	only staves printed	951
[Missale Misnense]	1510	Melchior der Ältere	liturgical	4	multiple impression	876
[Diurnale Misnense]	1511	Melchior der Ältere	liturgical	8	not inspected	264
[Benedictionale Misnense]	1512	Melchior der Ältere	liturgical	4	multiple impression	279
Agenda sive benedictionale	1513	Melchior der Ältere	liturgical	4	not inspected	759
Hortulus musices	1514	Melchior der Ältere	theory book	4	multiple impression	417
[Missale Misnense]	1515	Melchior der Ältere	liturgical	2	multiple impression	757
Psalterium Davidis cum hymnis	1516	Melchior der Ältere	liturgical	2	only staves printed	953
[Missale Brandenburgense]	1516	Melchior der Ältere	liturgical	2	multiple impression	760
Isagoge in Musicam	1517	Melchior der Ältere	theory book	4	multiple impression	761
Hortulus musices practicae	1517	Melchior der Ältere	theory book	4	multiple impression	420
Psalterium Davidis cum hymnis	1518	Melchior der Ältere	liturgical	4	only staves printed	1380
Hortulus musices practicae	1518	Melchior der Ältere	theory book	4	multiple impression	421
[Missale Misnense]	1519	Melchior der Ältere	liturgical	2	multiple impression	956
[Vesperale Misnense]	1520	Melchior der Ältere	liturgical	2	multiple impression	303
[Breviarius Misnensis]	1520	Melchior der Ältere	liturgical	8	woodcut	299
Psalterium Davidis cum hymnis	1521	Melchior der Ältere	liturgical	2	only staves printed	955
[Missale Pragense]	1522	Melchior der Ältere	liturgical	2	multiple impression	324
Libellus ad omnes	1522	Melchior der Ältere	liturgical	8	multiple impression	322
[Agenda Mindensis]	1522	Melchior der Ältere	liturgical	4	multiple impression	278
Deudsche Messe und Ordnung	1526	Michael Lotter	liturgical	4	multiple impression	315
Deudsche Messe und Ordnung	1526	Michael Lotter	liturgical	4	multiple impression	316
Deudsche Messe und Ordnung	1526	Michael Lotter	liturgical	4	multiple impression	317
Deudsche Messe und Ordnung	1526	Michael Lotter	liturgical	4	multiple impression	1014
Evangelistarum quatuor passiones	1533	Melchior der Ältere	liturgical	4	multiple impression	330
[Agenda Posnaniensis]	1533	Melchior der Ältere	liturgical	4	multiple impression	329

126 ELISABETH GISELBRECHT

In this, he is not what might be called a 'music printer' – if such a profession existed[7] –
at least not in the sense that we have come to describe some Italian and French printers who
focussed on the publication of music. He is, however, more typical of music printers in
German-speaking areas in this period: a capable and versatile entrepreneur who printed
books of vastly different contents, exploring different techniques to achieve a particular
outcome. As mentioned above, Lotter did not publish any polyphony. Instead, his musical
œuvre consists mainly of liturgical books (predominantly missals), a few editions of music
theory and a humanist book containing music. This distribution represents the typical musical
landscape in German-speaking areas around 1500. The number of books with music printed
in German-speaking areas between 1500 and 1540 registered in *vdm* is constantly growing
(by now far exceeding any original estimations and hopes). Thus, to give any precise
numbers in writing would render this publication incorrect by the time it goes to press. However, it is safe to say that of all publications described in the database only a small percentage
(less than 10 per cent) contain polyphonic music. The largest group is, as it is with Lotter,
that of liturgical publications (of different denominations), followed by books of music
pedagogy, humanist dramas and others.[8] Thus, Lotter's output can be seen as representative
of this distribution.

Let us take a closer look at his publications. Among his thirty-one liturgical titles we find
ten missals, the majority (six) for his own diocese, Meissen. That he printed in the archbishop's
rooms in 1520 suggests a good rapport with the ecclesiastical authorities.[9] Additionally, he
was also the only printer in Leipzig in this period to print music from moveable type, and
was thus the obvious choice as a printer to publish missals, which were commonly printed
in that way. He was also known beyond his own diocese, and also published missals for
Poznań, Brandenburg, Prague and Merseburg, as can be seen in Figure 6.2.

For the diocese of Meissen he also printed other liturgical books, such as agendas
containing liturgies and prayers for specific occasions. The breviary and vesperal printed
in 1520 are some of the few examples of these types of service books to contain musical
notation.

While the business in Leipzig was closely linked to the Catholic church and its authorities,
the Wittenberg branch focussed on books associated with the new evangelical faith. From
this period, at least four editions of Luther's German Mass with music printed by Lotter
in Wittenberg survive. These are very similar, with no substantial variations in the text
between them, apart from some corrections. Only close comparison of the title pages and
the setting of each page shows that each edition was newly set. Inspection of more copies
may lead to the identification of further distinct editions. The name of the printer is not
given in any of these four editions, and has to be deduced through the identification of
typefaces. The place of publication, Wittenberg, is mentioned proudly on the title page, to
distinguish these editions from others printed the same year in Nuremberg, Augsburg,
Erfurt and Zwickau, and to make claim of authority – after all, Wittenberg was the home
of the famous reformer and author. That so many editions were printed in close succession
points to a high demand for these small books, most of which consisted of twenty-four
leaves in quarto format. Alongside other writings by Luther, they presented a new
opportunity for many printers, including Lotter and his sons. Evidently Lotter did not pick
sides in the debate over different religions, at least not in relation to his business. Instead,

---

7 For a discussion of this question see Giselbrecht/Savage in this volume.
8 Further on this also see Andrea Lindmayr-Brandl's contribution in this volume.
9 For more on this topic also see the chapter by Mary Kay Duggan in this volume.

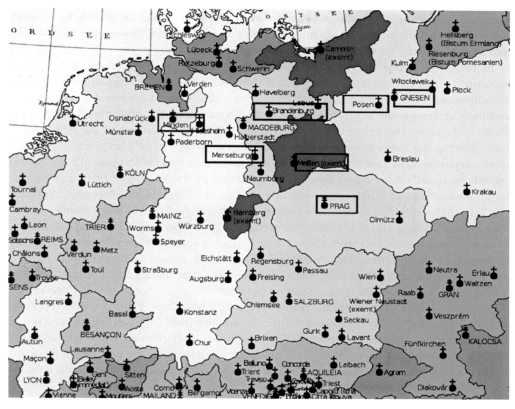

Figure 6.2 Church dioceses for which Melchior Lotter published liturgical books
Source: Gustav Droysen, *Allgemeiner historischer Handatlas*, Bielefeld, Verlhagen & Klasnig, 1886

as a business man he seized the opportunities that presented themselves. These involved printing for Catholic authorities as well as quenching the new thirst for evangelical books.

Beyond liturgical publications we also find music in four pedagogical books: three editions of *Hortulus musicus*[10] by the Leipzig theologian Ulrich Burchardi, a book entitled *Isagoge in Musicam* by St Bernard of Clairvaux, and Reuchlin's *Scaenica progymnasmata*, which contains musical choruses.

Technical innovation and flexibility

When looking at the work of early (music) printers we often unintentionally assume a simplistic and teleological approach: that once a printer has found a technique for bringing music onto the page, he (or she) would stick to it, at least for specific types of publications. He would, for example, print missals in the same way (usually using two runs through the press and with moveable type) and use woodblocks to insert small music examples in theory books. If anything, he would develop his favoured technique to simplify the process or

---

10 Additionally, it is unclear whether another edition, *Hortulus musices practicae* ([Leipzig]: [W. Stöckel], [1514]), vdm 418, was really printed by Wolfgang Stöckel, as stated in VD16. The differences with those editions published by Lotter are minor, and given that Stöckel is not known to have possessed any music type at this point, it seems more plausible to attribute it to Lotter.

128   ELISABETH GISELBRECHT

improve the appearance of the publication. What we see in the work of Melchior Lotter, however, is that the situation was more complex and that he used a variety of techniques and approaches to find solutions for the same problem.

In principle, Lotter had two ways of printing music: by printing staves and notes separately from two formes (the so-called double impression technique) and by using woodblocks. The former he used mainly in the publication of liturgical books, as was common in this period. For some publications, in particular the multiple editions of the *Psalterium cum hymnis* printed between 1498 and 1518, he only supplied the empty stave lines, leaving the notes to be added by hand. For most others, he also printed the notes from a separate forme. He had at least two different music fonts with musical type. For his missals he usually used a font that can be identified by the lengths of its two *virgae*, the larger measuring 10.5–11mm and the shorter 7.5–8mm.[11] The *Libellus ad omnes . . . circuitus* (1522) is, as the title already suggests, a handy pocket book and thus of much smaller format than most of Lotter's liturgical publications, requiring a smaller type. There, the two lengths of *virga* measure 8mm and 5mm respectively.[12] In addition to the 'usual' sorts for printing monophonic chant, Lotter also needed sorts for printing simple mensural music notated as *cantus fractus*, a rhythmicised form of plainchant that allows for a simple form of homophony. For these pieces he displayed the four voices in succession (see Plate 14).

Some of Lotter's titles using moveable type might have been printed with even more runs through the press, but this is often difficult to determine.[13] Overlapping text and music in the *Evangelistarum quatuor passiones* (1533) suggest at least three runs through the press. In Plate 15, for example, we can see how the descending stroke of the note above the word 'venisti' overlaps with the i-dash in the text. Hence, the elements printed in black (notes and text) could not have been printed at the same time.

In the books Lotter printed from two formes, the variety of approaches to printing the staff lines is striking. Particularly in early publications we see irregular lines that display little bends. There, Lotter used individual metal strips or rules, setting them individually with spacers between, as can be seen in Plate 16. In other publications he uses cast metal lines, either the width of one column or spanning the whole page. Judging from their perfect appearance with no bends and the equal distances between the individual lines, all four lines seem to have been cast as one metal sort. When he needed to display an initial in the space where the lines would otherwise appear, a section of staff of the required size was probably masked in the first run through the press to leave space for the initial, which was then printed in the second run. Apart from full-width segments of staff lines, Lotter also used combinations of shorter segments, a technique used by several other printers. Plate 17 exemplifies how he combines ten pieces, each measuring 16.5mm in length.

He also had a piece of 8mm available, which allowed him to interrupt the staves for rubrics. Finally, we find instances of what might be described as an early use of nested type: short cast segments of various lengths, some of which have fewer than four lines, which are then put together like a jigsaw puzzle, as can be seen in Plate 15. This snapshot of just one aspect of his printing technique displays the high degree of flexibility in Lotter's approach to music printing. Evidently, he used whatever option was available at the time

---

11 The following publications from Table 6.1 (indicated by their *vdm* number) made use of this font: 758, 279, 417, 757, 760, 761, 421, 303, 278. The virgae were measured with a digital caliper from the lowest to the highest point.

12 Measurement taken from the copy in A-Wn, shelfmark MS 5505 8°.

13 On this topic also see the chapter by Giselbrecht/Savage in this volume.

of printing a particular title, rather than laying down a specific technique for all publications that included notation.

Lotter also used his music font in music textbooks. The use of multiple impressions is less evident in these, since both the lines and notes are printed in black. While the combination of red lines and black notes in the liturgical books make it immediately evident that notes and lines could have not been printed at the same time, this is much less clear when everything is printed in the same colour. However, a closer look leaves no doubt about the technique. The staff lines were printed from shorter segments that have small gaps between them. In many cases the notes appear on top of these gaps, which indicates that they were printed separately. In Figure 6.3, for example, the note above the word 'cantus' sits exactly on top of a gap.

The uniformity of the notes and signs (such as the custos) shows that Lotter used moveable type. This is unusual for books of music theory in this period, in which the few musical examples are more commonly printed from woodcuts, which were frequently re-used for later publications. This way, such titles could also be printed by those who did not have any music type.

Figure 6.3 *Hortulus musices practicae*. Leipzig: Melchior Lotter the Elder, [1514] (vdm 417)
Source: München, Bayerische Staatsbibliothek, Mus. Th. 236, fol. A4[v]

Figure 6.4 [*Breviarius Misnensis*]. Meissen: Melchior Lotter the Elder, 1520 (vdm 299)
Source: Universitätsbibliothek Leipzig, Off.Lips.:Lo.152, fol. A8^v

Lotter did also use woodblocks for music in at least two of his publications: the four monophonic choirs in Reuchlin's *Scaenica progymnasmata* are all reproduced in this way, as in most editions of this book. Lotter also printed the *Breviarius Misnensis* (1520) from woodblocks, while in temporary lodgings in Meissen. Although he had clearly brought his music type with him to Meissen, and used it to print the *Vesperale*, he only needed to print very short sections of notation in the breviary, often near the margins (see Figure 6.4). He evidently calculated that it was more practical to set these short sections from blocks rather than from type.

The use of woodcuts, even when type was available, was not uncommon. In fact, woodblocks were still very popular, particularly for theory books, for much of the sixteenth century. In almost half of all entries currently registered in *vdm* (for music printed in German-speaking lands between 1500 and 1540), music was printed using woodblocks. And just because a printer made use of type at one point did not necessitate him doing so later on. An interesting example is Michael Lotter: while he and his brother printed music from type at Wittenberg, he later used woodcuts in all the musical publications he produced at Magdeburg. Hence, the teleological assumption of a development from woodcut to moveable type should be rejected.

Reformation – an agent of change?

As mentioned above, one major factor that determined the fortune of Lotter's business was the advent of the Reformation. The link between the Reformation and the rise of the printing press is complex. The rather simplistic view held by Elizabeth Eisenstein in the 1970s, according to whom the printing press was the precondition for the rise of the Reformation, has been questioned. Eisenstein claimed that the 'Reformation was a movement that was shaped at the very outset [. . .] by the new powers of the press'[14] and that it 'provided the stroke of magic by which an obscure theologian in Wittenberg managed to shake Saint Peter's throne'.[15] Today, it is widely accepted that the powers of this 'magical' printing press were less extensive. Many have disputed Eisenstein's insistence that the printing press signified a clear change from one kind of literate culture (the manuscript) to another (print).[16] It has been shown that manuscript and oral transmission still played a hugely significant role in the dissemination of the Reformation, particularly through preaching, singing and reading aloud. Moreover, Matthew Hall and Andrew Pettegree have demonstrated how our understanding of the connection between printing and the Reformation has to be revised as soon as we look beyond German-speaking areas, or after the initial decade of Lutheran dominance.[17]

Yet there clearly was a strong link between printing and the Reformation, one that went in both directions. On one hand, the ability to reproduce and distribute texts (cheaply?) unquestionably affected how messages were spread, how reform agendas were implemented and how disputes between theologians were conducted. And what is particularly striking is the impact the Reformation had on printers and printshops, how it transformed the landscape of early printing in German-speaking lands.

Andrew Pettegree has pointed out how the Reformation turned the small city of Wittenberg into an important centre for printing.[18] Between 1520 and 1525 Wittenberg's bookmen alone published 600 editions; the growth of the German printing industry as a whole was even more spectacular: in these six years German presses turned out 7764 editions – an increase of 340 per cent on the ten years previously and more than four times as many books as were published in Italy during these same years.[19] Pettegree names at least thirty-four towns and cities where the Reformation controversies were responsible for the establishment of a printing press.[20] No city felt the impact of this more profoundly than Wittenberg. In the incunabula period this town had hardly any importance for printing. With only around 2000 inhabitants, it was economically far less significant than other towns along the Rhine and Danube.[21] It was not a major centre of printing, since the majority of local printing was done in nearby Erfurt and Leipzig, which had a number of established printing firms (Melchior Lotter among them), was the location of the book fairs and had a generally thriving book industry. However, by the middle of the sixteenth century Wittenberg had become a major centre for book production, driven by enthusiasm for the Reformation and particularly for Luther's writings. As Pettegree has pointed out, the

---

14 Eisenstein, *Printing Press*, 303.
15 Ibid., 310.
16 A concise overview of the reactions to Eisenstein's book can be found in McNally, 'The Eye of the Beholder'.
17 Hall and Pettegree, 'The Reformation and the Book'.
18 Pettegree, *The Book in the Renaissance*.
19 Ibid., 101.
20 Ibid., 105.
21 Ibid., 91.

132   ELISABETH GISELBRECHT

type of publication required by the Reformation was exactly right for quick success: small, inexpensive to produce and with a high turnover.

Changes in the firm of Melchior Lotter illustrate the impact of the Reformation on individual printers. As early as 1518, the publication of Luther's work represented a significant fraction of their output. In the years to 1521, Melchior the Elder published fifty books by Luther. The most profound impact the Reformation had on the Lotter family was the opening of a new workshop in the house of Lucas Cranach the Elder in Wittenberg. The impulse to do so came from no other than Martin Luther himself, who specifically asked the Leipzig printer to come to Wittenberg.[22] Melchior the Elder sent his son, Melchior the Younger, to be in charge of this new branch. Initially a successful endeavour, the young printer soon fell into disgrace with some important members of Wittenberg's society, among them Lucas Cranach himself. In 1524 he was found guilty of torturing an apprentice and was fined a considerable sum.[23] Later, Luther apparently came to regret his decision to give considerable business to Melchior the Younger, and in his Table Talk from 1532 he expressed his disapproval of Lotter the Younger, who had 'made a lot of money' by printing his books, making an 'ungodly and intolerable profit'.[24]

The shift (or at least diversification) of Lotter's attention from Leipzig towards Wittenberg indicates a more general change in the centres of printing, for music and more generally. The data from *vdm* makes this particularly evident, especially in the realms of liturgical and polyphonic music. Comparing the locations where polyphonic music was issued between 1500 and 1540, a shift is noticeable around 1520. Before this time, the main centres for printing polyphony were Augsburg, Mainz, Basle and Cologne. After the beginning of the Reformation, Lutheran cities such as Nuremberg, Frankfurt, Strasbourg and Wittenberg took over. This change is strongly connected to the movements of individual printers. In Wittenberg we can observe how printers originally attracted to the town for its potential in the market of Reformation books later issued other kinds of publications there. An example is Georg Rhau, who was among the first to print non-liturgical books with music in Wittenberg. However, the Reformation was not the only determining factor in this shifting printing landscape. Changing economic considerations, the existence of paper mills, or the proximity of universities and schools also contributed to these shifts. The ways in which the musical needs of the Reformation opened up new possibilities for printers have not been fully acknowledged until now. In many cases, the Reformation prompted printers to change their physical location and their output, both the content as well as the types of publications they printed.

One major impact of the Reformation on music publishing was the introduction of new kinds of source. Before 1520 the only musical sources to include religious music were either Catholic liturgical books or a small number of polyphonic books containing masses or motets. Both kinds were difficult and expensive to produce, and were issued by only a relatively small number of printers. The Reformation, however, ushered in a range of new types of sources. First, the new churches need their own service books, such as Luther's German mass, and over time new church orders (*Kirchenordnungen*) were written for Protestant towns or areas, often including some music. Second, hymn books, with or without music, appeared in increasing numbers. And finally, numerous single-sheets or small pamphlets were published for the new faiths. These pamphlets, which mainly contained German psalm settings, presented great opportunities for printers who had never

---

22 Ibid., 993.
23 Reske, *Buchdrucker*, 994.
24 Ibid., 994.

published any music up to that point. They were cheap to produce and could be reprinted on demand. They present entirely different publications from elaborate polyphonic music books or Catholic liturgical publications.

In Wittenberg, the Lotter firm printed another 109 of Luther's publications between 1520 and 1525.[25] Many artists, among them also Lucas Cranach, despite his geographical proximity to the centre of the Reformation, continued to work for both Catholics and Lutherans. Similarly, after 1520 the Lotter firm did not print Lutheran material exclusively. Although its output changed with the onset of the Reformation, Melchior the Elder in Leipzig continued to publish books connected to the Roman Catholic church, while his sons focused on Protestant publications. The impact of the Reformation is clear when one considers their musical output: as can be seen from Table 6.1, neither branch of the Lotter firm is known to have produced a single Catholic liturgical book between 1520 and 1533. The only liturgical publications with music from this period are the four editions of Luther's German mass printed in Wittenberg. This dip in the production of Catholic service books, which had been a lucrative and relatively stable business up to that point, is consistent with general trends in German music book production. Figure 6.5 shows the development of religious service books with music printed in German-speaking areas between 1500 and 1540.

While Catholic service books had steadily been produced in the fifty years leading up to the Reformation, hardly any were printed in the 1520s. Instead, large numbers of evangelical liturgical books appeared. At a first glance, this seems logical: the new religion needed new books. However, large parts of German-speaking areas (and adjacent regions, which also had their books printed in Germany) remained Catholic, and these areas surely still needed some new service books, even if the market was already well saturated. It seems that the presses were busy printing the new formats and were also at this point less economically dependent on commissions from bishops to print their missals. Instead, they

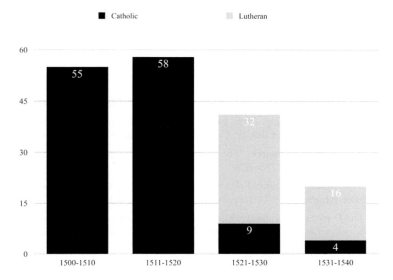

Figure 6.5 Development of religious service books with music printed in German-speaking lands, 1500–1540
Source: data taken from *vdm* on 15.08.2016

---

25 For an overview see *USTC*.

134 ELISABETH GISELBRECHT

produced large numbers of Lutheran agendas and numerous editions of the German mass. These appeared in very different formats with vastly differing requirements. While missals are usually in folio format, with often more than 300 folios, editions of the German mass are generally printed in quarto on no more than thirty folios. To finance these upfront would have constituted a relatively small financial risk. Moreover, they could easily be printed more or less on demand, as setting these for another print-run was less labour-intensive than a complete missal. The relative ease with which these re-editions were produced is illustrated by the four almost identical editions of the German mass printed by Lotter in Wittenberg in 1526 alone. Apart from slight variations and the corrections of mistakes in previous editions, the four editions are almost indistinguishable, which has led earlier bibliographers to fail to distinguish all four editions as being separate.[26]

These four (or perhaps even more) editions of the German Mass published in 1526 were the only editions containing music that Michael Lotter printed in Wittenberg before he moved to Magdeburg. There he would establish himself as an influential printer, particularly of Reformation books, including some hymn books with music. His brother would, as we have seen, next appear only in the disparaging remarks made by Luther a few years later, marking the rather inglorious end of his career. Melchior the Elder on the other hand continued to publish books for another ten years, including Catholic liturgical books containing music, predominantly for dioceses to the east, such as Prague and Poznań. Even late in his career, he was still expanding into new markets.

In conclusion, the firm of Melchior Lotter has been chosen here to represent the typical early music printer in German-speaking lands. He did not print any polyphony. Yet, in his output we find just over thirty publications including musical notation, a significant contribution to the corpus of musical sources from this early period in music printing. His technique for printing music was neither new nor unusual. What renders it remarkable, though, is the flexibility in his approach, as demonstrated by his range of techniques for printing staff lines. Developments in his life and business illustrate the influence of the onset of the Lutheran Reformation, one of the major forces that shaped the situation of early music printing north of the Alps.

References

Boorman, Stanley. *Ottaviano Petrucci. Catalogue Raisonné*. Oxford: Oxford University Press, 2006.

Eisenstein, Elizabeth. *The Printing Press as an Agent of Change: Communications and Cultural Transformations in Early Modern Europe*. Cambridge: Cambridge University Press, 1979.

Hall, Matthew and Andrew Pettegree. 'The Reformation and the Book: A Reconsideration'. *The Historical Journal* 47/ 4 (2004): 785–808.

Heartz, Daniel. *Pierre Attaingnant. Royal Printer of Music. A Historical Study and Bibliographical Catalogue*. Berkeley and Los Angeles, CA: University of California Press, 1969.

McNally, Peter. 'The Eye of the Beholder: Opinions Concerning Elizabeth Eisenstein and the Printing Press as an Agent of Change'. In *The Advent of Printing: Historians of Science Respond to Elizabeth Eisenstein's 'Printing Press as an Agent of Change'*, edited by Peter McNally. Montreal: McGill University, 1987, 1–7.

Pettegree, Andrew. *The Book in the Renaissance*. New Haven, CT: Yale University Press, 2010.

Reske, Christoph. *Die Buchdrucker des 16. und 17. Jahrhunderts im deutschen Sprachgebiet*. 2nd, extended edition, Wiesbaden: Harrassowitz, 2015.

---

26 RISM VIII and VD16 both only name three editions.

7

The music books of Christian Egenolff

Bad impressions = good return on investment

John Kmetz

For Andrea, Elisabeth, and Grantley:
The Creators and Custodians of vdm.sbg.ac.at[1]

In 1983, a blockbuster film was released about seven American test pilots who were selected to be the astronauts for Project Mercury, the first attempt at manned spaceflight by the United States. The film was entitled The Right Stuff: How the Future Began. It won many Oscars, produced many memorable scenes, and gave us many quotable lines. One of those quotes, which like a Wagnerian Leitmotiv is heard several times in the film, was actually a simple, yet profound, answer to what was intended to be a complicated question. The question was: 'What makes these rockets go up?' Astronaut Gus Grissom's answer: 'Funding makes these rockets go up. No bucks, no Buck Rogers.'

If Johann Gutenberg were alive today and watched the film, I'm sure he would agree with astronaut Grissom. Actually, without funding, without capital, or simply without cold hard cash in hand, few inventions in the history of mankind, or for that matter few of the monuments of early printing we today so admire, would probably ever have gotten off the ground. Without the funding of Johann Fust, would Gutenberg's 42-line bible and the so-called Gutenberg Galaxy ever have seen the light of day?[2] Without the financial backing of Maximilian I – or should I say without the backing of Jacob Fugger, who funded all things Maximilian – would the *Theuerdank*, the *Triumphzug*, or the *Weisskunig*, ever have seen their way into print?[3] And what about Andrea Vesalius and his magnificent *De humani corporis fabrica*? If it wasn't for the backing of his risk-averse publisher Johannes Operinus and the backing he ostensibly received from Charles V, who like his grandfather Maximilian relied on Fugger money to fund all things Charles, would this magnificent, astronomically expensive illustrated book of human anatomy ever have rolled off that Basel press?[4]

---

1 I would like to take this opportunity to sincerely thank Andrea Lindmayr-Brandl, Elisabeth Giselbrecht and Grantley McDonald (my so-called 'Goldstück Club') for their help and encouragement in the preparation of this article. Aside from providing me access to the information they had on the Egenolff music books resident in their wonderful database, and doing it well before their site went live in July 2015, they brought me up to speed on the value and the pitfalls of USTC and VD16. Without their generous support and advice, this article would never have been written.

2 Among the many books that discuss Fust's financial backing of Gutenberg and his press, see Pettegree, *The Book*, 29–32; Kapr, *Johann Gutenberg*, 156–159 and 171–179 and the enthralling novel by Alix Christie, *Gutenberg's Apprentice* (New York: Harper Collins, 2014) which although a fictional account of Gutenberg and his relationships with Fust and Peter Schöffer is well-grounded in serious research.

3 On Jacob Fugger as a businessman, patron, and financier to the Hapsburg dynasty, see Steinmetz, *The Richest Man* and Strieder, *Jacob Fugger the Rich*. On these magnificent volumes, see Silver, *Marketing Maximilian* and Scholz Williams, 'The Arthurian Model'.

4 On the production and marketing of the Vesalius, see Steinmann, *Johannes Oporinus* and Clark, 'Foiling the Pirates'.

136   JOHN KMETZ

The answer to these questions is probably not. Funding, along with technology, and a good dose of vanity, made these monumental folios of early printing happen. But what happens to a publisher, or for that matter an author, when funding is not available? When the bottom line of a book's publication is not necessarily to brand a publishing house for the first time, nor to celebrate the life and achievements of a Holy Roman Emperor, nor to document every muscle in the human body for the medical community, but rather to simply provide the publisher with a good return on his or her investment. Yes, what happens then when it simply becomes a question of ROI (namely, return on investment)? What happens? A business happens! A business that requires the publisher to deal with the economics of paper, ink and type, with the thorny issues of debt and credit, with the threat of market saturation, or, on the flip side of that coin, with the constant pressure to acquire new texts, but only after answering the questions as to what books sell, where do they sell, and to whom? It is also a business that requires the publishers to think in terms of cost containment. How much capital might be left after you pay the printer, pay the editor, procure the reams of paper, and get the book in the hands of the booksellers? And what about format? Should it be a folio, quarto or octavo, or should the publisher have his printer save time and money by folding sheets multiple times to produce small, if not tiny books in duodecimo or sextodecimo formats? And what if the book is a first edition or a reprint, how many copies should be issued? And of those copies, what accounting principle should be deployed with the inventory at a time when inflation is running rampant?[5] Finally, how much money should the publisher expect to net on an individual copy or on a print run, and how many free copies, if any, does the author receive, assuming that the author is even aware that his book is being published for the first time or reprinted for a second or third?

These types of questions are ones that are all too familiar to scholars of early printing,[6] and certainly must have been questions that were commonly asked by anyone of the dozen-odd German publishers and printers who issued books of music, or books about music in the first half of the sixteenth century.[7] Among those Germans with surnames such as Öglin, Schöffer, von Aich, Klug, Petreius, Formschneider, Lotter, Rhau, Ott, Kriesstein, Egenolff, and Berg & Neuber,[8] I have chosen to focus my attention on the Frankfurter Christian

---

5 I am thinking particularly of the two accounting methods known as 'First in First Out' (FIFO), and 'Last In First Out' (LIFO). These methods are used to determine the value of unsold inventory and the cost of goods sold. FIFO is when goods placed first in an inventory are sold first, and unsold goods remain in the inventory to the end of a fiscal year. LIFO, on the other hand, is when goods placed last in an inventory are sold first. LIFO, unlike FIFO, allows inventory valuation to be lower in inflationary times as we shall see when we discuss print runs and profitability factors for Egenolff's music books. In short, if costs for labour and materials are increasing, as they were indeed doing during the sixteenth century, books produced first at lower inflationary levels are going to be cheaper than those produced later at higher levels. Consequently, it is not surprising that some publishers warehoused books produced at lower costs, and then sold them later for higher profits.

6 On the question of financing the publication of music books, see particularly Gustavson, 'Competitive Strategy Dynamics', Bernstein, *Print Culture*, 73–83; Blackburn, 'The Printing Contract' and Boorman, 'Early Music Printing'.

7 Although little correspondence has survived documenting the concerns of early printers of music, we do have an extraordinary treasure trove of letters written by the Basel printer, Johann Amerbach (1440–1513), ed. Alfred Hartman as volume 1 in the series, *Die Amerbachkorrespondenz*. The correspondence has been translated into English by Halporn, *The Correspondence*. Halporn's translations of the original Latin and German are exemplary, as is the content of the letters themselves for scholars of early printing. Books for teaching, books as a commodity, the prices of books, books as gifts or as compensation for services rendered, and even information on the sale and marketing of books are just a few of the many topics that are discussed by Johann Amerbach in this priceless correspondence.

8 For biographical information on these German publishers and printers and for a list of the music books they issued, see the relevant entries in *New Grove*[2] and the *MGG*[2]. For further information on these printers, particularly with regard to the many other books they published that had nothing to do with music, see Reske, *Buchdrucker*.

THE MUSIC BOOKS OF CHRISTIAN EGENOLFF   137

Egenolff, who seemed not only to ask the right questions, but also to have had the right answers.

Egenolff the Rich

The reason I believe that Christian Egenolff asked the right questions is simply because when he died in 1555, his estate was valued for tax purposes at 16,000 gulden, which in the Renaissance was a lot of money.[9] In 1530 he bought a home in Frankfurt, the Haus zum Falkenstein on the fashionable Sandgasse, for 550 gulden. In 1545, he purchased two adjoining buildings on the Grosse Kornmarkt for 800 gulden, and in 1549 closed the deal on two additional buildings in Frankfurt's city center for 800 gulden each. Actually, he owned sixteen houses in downtown Frankfurt, as well as vineyards and open fields of land in the Frankfurt countryside, and even a paper mill, which upon his death was storing no less than 1,418 reams of paper worth 4,200 gulden (a ream was valued at 3 gulden). Bottom line, this man, Christian Egenolff, was a successful businessman, even when one compares his net worth to that of the richest man in the western world in the sixteenth century, namely Jacob Fugger.[10] So what did Egenolff do as a publisher to amass this kind of wealth? I can assure you it was not by publishing a dozen music books. Actually, it was by publishing almost everything else, and by doing it always with his eye on the market, and on his bottom line.[11]

Egenolff and the educational market

Let us just start with some general observations about Egenolff's publications. Among the five hundred books that Egenolff saw through the press between 1528 and 1555, very few show any evidence of having relied on commissions or on private funding for the

---

9 On the value of Egenolff's estate and for an identification of the properties he owned, see Grotefend, *Christian Egenolff*, 22ff. and especially Reske, *Buchdrucker*, 224–226.

10 When Fugger died in 1520, his estate was valued at about 1.6 million gulden. That means that Egenolff was worth simply 1 per cent of what Jacob the Rich was worth. But let's remember, Jacob the Rich would be what investment bankers today call the 'Über Rich', individuals who make up not 1 per cent of a nation's wealth, but one hundredth of 1 per cent. Today, the richest man in the world is Bill Gates, who checked in with US$ 75 billion in *The 2015 Forbes Billionaire List*. One per cent of $75 billion is $750 million. Taking into account inflation and currency adjustments over 500 years, the purchasing power of Egenolff's 16,000 gulden would not be all that different when compared to the purchasing power of US$750 million today. Clearly Egenolff had the 'Right Stuff' and was doing something right to amass the fortune that he did. Indeed, I would like to thank Andrew Pettegree for confirming my suspicion that Egenolff might well be one of the most financially successful publishers in the Renaissance.

11 The ensuing analysis of Egenolff's publications that do not contain music was greatly facilitated by online and printed secondary sources. Of the online sources, by far the most useful was the *Universal Short Title Catalogue* (USTC), hosted by the University of St Andrews. This database (www.ustc.ac.uk, last accessed on 31 January, 2016) allowed me to not only assemble a list of all of Egenolff's publications, but also to sort them by date, language, format, and subject/classification. Moreover, the database enabled me to access remotely digital copies of the Egenolff prints that are available on the World Wide Web. Aside from USTC, I also relied heavily on the German national database sponsored by the Deutsche Forschungsgemeinschaft and the Bayerische Staatsbibliothek: *Verzeichnis der im deutschen Sprachbereich erschienenen Drucke des 16. Jahrhunderts* (VD 16). Using VD16 (www.vd16.de, last accessed on 31 January, 2016) in tandem with USTC, I was able to check the accuracy of earlier printed catalogues and studies of Egenolff's output. Among the secondary literature in print that still remains enormously useful today, see Benzing, 'Christian Egenolff', and idem, 'Die Drucke Christian Egenolffs'. Mention should also be made of the biographical study of Egenolff's life and the useful, but not very accurate, catalogue of Egenolff's works produced by Jäcker, 'Christian Egenolff', 25–46, and idem, 'Verzeichnis', 47–99, in Kulturvereinigung Hadamar, *Christian Egenolff 1502–1555*.

138   JOHN KMETZ

underwriting of a book's publication. This statement seems to be true if only because few of his books are prefaced with long-winded, sycophantic dedications written by an author thanking a current or future employer, or thanking and praising the generosity of a patron. Rather, most are reprints that would appear to have been produced for quick sales, and sales that were particularly focused on what I would like to simply call the educational market, which I see as one market divided in two parts.

The first are those books, mostly in octavo, issued for students who were enrolled in a local Latin school, a trade school or a university. These were not scholarly editions of Jerome and the Church Fathers, nor were they books with Greek and Latin running side by side on a page in a large folio format. These were cheap books, small books, and ones quickly printed. They had titles that often began with such words as 'Enchiridion', 'Isogoge', 'Rudimenta', 'Erotemata', 'Opusculum', 'Unterweisung' or 'Ratschlag' and, as such, were books that served as primers to teach students arithmetic,[12] geometry,[13] Greek,[14] Latin,[15] rhetoric,[16] and just about any other subject that was being taught at the time at a Latin school or university.[17] In a word they were textbooks, and Germans loved them, as indeed the 130 music manuals published by German speakers in the sixteenth century make clear.[18]

The second market consists of books that were practical in nature, not academic. Books that would be, for example, consulted at home by parents to deal with personal health and hygiene,[19] with the preparation and cooking of a meal,[20] with the vagaries of pregnancy,[21] with the daunting task of raising a child,[22] with prophecies and prognostications about the

---

12 See, for example, Johannes Wolf and Sebald Heyden, *Rudimenta arithmetices* (Frankfurt a. M.: Christian Egenolff, 1532), VD16 W 4213.

13 See, for example, Euclides, *Elementale geometricum, ex Euclidis Geometria, à Joanne Voegelin, Haylpronnensi, ad omnium Mathematices studiosorum utilitatem decerptum* (Strassburg: Christian Egenolff, 1529), VD16 E 4164 with a digital copy.

14 See, for example, Johann Lonicer, *Graecae grammaticae methodus, recognita et locupletior reddita, in syntaxi praecipue; per Joannem Lonicerum* (Marburg: Christian Egenolff, 1540), VD16 L 2442 with a digital copy.

15 See, for example, Philipp Melanchthon, *De prosodia de syntaxi grammatica Philippi Melanthonis Latina, iam denuo recognita, et plerisque in locis locupletata* (Frankfurt a. M.: Christian Egenolff 1543), VD16 M 3367.

16 See, for example, Ludwig Fruck, *Rhetoric und Teutsch Formular in allen Gerichts Händlen. Kunst und Regel der Notarien und Schreiber. Titel vund cantzlei Buechlin.* (Strassburg: Christian Egenolff, 1530), VD16 F 3150 with a digital copy; and Sebald Heyden, Nomenclatura rerum, innumeris quàm antea nominibus, cum locupletior, tum castigatior. Formulae colloquiorum puerilium (Frankfurt a. M.: Christian Egenolff, 1532), VD16 H 3386 with a digital copy. It should be noted that the title page of this 1532 Heyden edition contains two woodcuts, one showing two satyrs and the other two putti. These woodcuts are the same two found on the title page of the Paris copy of Egenolff's undated songbook RISM [1535][14] (vdm 25), and identified in Table 7.1 as item no. 7. For a digital copy of the Paris title page see, http://data.bnf.fr/15075961/ christian_egenolff. Unfortunately the woodcuts in the Heyden and those in the music edition show no evidence of damage or wear. Consequently, it is not possible to say if one printing predates another.

17 See Pettegree, *The Book*, Chapter 9, 'At School', 177–199.

18 For a convenient list of the music theory books published by German speakers in the sixteenth century see, Sternfeld, 'Music in the Schools', 113–114; and *RISM*, Series B, vol. 6, pt. 2: *Écrits imprimés concernant la musique* (München-Duisburg: G. Henle Verlag), 1001–1005. Among the numerous studies discussing the contents of these manuals, see Collins Judd, *Reading Renaissance Music Theory*, 82–108.

19 See, for example, Walther Hermann Ryff, *Spiegel und Regiment der Gesundtheit. Fürnemlich auff Land/Gebreuch/Art/und Complexion der Teutschen gerichtet. [. . .] Rechter bericht/breuchliche purgierende Artznei/zur noturfft/ mancherley gestalt/Deßgleichen die furnemsten Species/Confect [. . .] zubereyten und nutzlich zubrauchen* (Frankfurt a. M.: Christian Egenolff, 1544), VD16 R 3990, with a digital copy. The title page of this print contains a wonderful woodcut depicting men and women drinking, eating and bathing outdoors to the accompaniment of a transverse flute.

20 See, for example, *Koch und Kellerei/von allen Speisen und Getraencken/vil guetter künst/Sampt etlichen Notartzneien/Ein nuetzes büchlin* (Frankfurt a. M.: Christian Egenolff, 1544), VD16 K 2511 with a digital copy.

21 See, for example, Eucharius Rösslin, *Ehstands artzneibüch. Schwangerer frawen unnd Hebammen Rosegartenn* (Frankfurt a. M.: Christian Egenolff, 1534), VD16 E 612 with a digital copy.

22 See, for example, Desiderius Erasmus of Rotterdam, *De pueris statim ac liberaliter instituendis* (Strassburg: Christian Egenolff, 1529), VD16 E 3476 with a digital copy.

THE MUSIC BOOKS OF CHRISTIAN EGENOLFF   139

weather that affected farmers and medical doctors alike,[23] or with martial arts and personal defense.[24] Indeed, many of Egenolff's books are quite modern in their conception and presentation, and could easily be displayed today on the shelves of any university bookstore next to the so-called 'Books for Dummies' series, or could be featured at any local store selling printed books, pamphlets or magazines on recreational hobbies, gardening, and personal health and hygiene.

Egenolff the pirate

You would imagine that educational books like these did not necessarily need a privilege, be it holy, Roman, imperial or otherwise. Yet privileges do exist on the title pages of even Egenolff's humbler books; thereby implying that Egenolff believed the privilege was worth something, regardless of whether it served as a deterrent to piracy or simply as a tool to legitimise and market the book. However, if Egenolff did believe that a privilege was a deterrent to the theft of intellectual property, he certainly did not practice what he preached. Indeed, for Christian Egenolff an imperial privilege on a book's title page when the book was not one of his own seemed to carry about as much weight for him as Her Majesty Queen Elizabeth's mark carries for me on a Cadbury's chocolate bar.

Case in point would be Egenolff's scruffy 1533 reprint of Otto Brunfels's *Herbarum vivae eicones*, a magnificent illustrated book, and a monument of botany that was first issued by the Strassburg publisher Johann Schott in 1530.[25] Even though the title page of Schott's folio proudly displays an imperial privilege granted by Charles V, Egenolff simply ignored the six-year privilege and reproduced the illustrations of the plants and their captions with no mention of Schott. Actually by October of 1533, barely six months after Egenolff published his pirated version of the Schott, Schott sued Egenolff for copyright infringement. Yet Egenolff, in his defence, argued that nature could not be copyrighted because plants stood as communal property for any artist.[26] The Schott-Egenolff case resonated in the book publishing industry for quite some time after, and in 1542 Leonhard Fuchs wrote in the preface to his herbal, *De historia stirpium*, that of all of the then available herbals he knew, there were none that had 'more of the crassest errors than those published by Egenolff'.[27] Fuchs even went so far as to attribute Egenolff's sloppy copy to his greed for money. And with Egenolff, that may well be true.

---

23 See, for example, *Propheceien und Weissagungen. Vergangne/Gegenwertige/und Künfftige Sachen/Geschicht unnd Zůfaell* (Frankfurt a. Main: Christian Egenolff, 1548), VD16 P 5065 with a digital copy. On the burgeoning market for such books see, Green, *Printing and Prophecy* and Pettegree, *The Book*, and his discussion on the 'Power of Prophecy', 335–338.

24 See, for example, Hans Lecküchner, *Fechtbuch. Die ritterliche mannliche kunst und handarbeyt fechtens und kempffens. Auß warem ursprunglichen grund der alten beschriben unnd fürgemalt* (Frankfurt a. M.: Christian Egenolff, 1545), VD16 L 877. For a digital copy of the 1558 edition produced by Egenolff's heirs see, VD16 L 878.

25 Otto Brunfels, *Herbarum vivae eicones ad naturę imitationem, summa cum diligentia et artificio effigiatę, unà cum effectibus earundem* (Strassburg: Johann Schott, 1530), VD16 B 8499 with a digital copy; and Eucharius Rösslin, *Kreutterbůch von allem Erdtgewaechs* (Frankfurt a. M.: Christian Egenolff, 1533) VD16 W 4363 with a digital copy. In the Egenolff print, the pair of wood cuts of the satyrs and putti described above in footnote 15 that appear in the undated Paris copy of the Egenolff songbook [c.1535][14] are seen here together again, this time on folio iiii[v] of Egenolff's Kreutterbuch. Actually, I am starting to believe that Nanie Bridgman's hunch for an earlier dating of Egenolff's c.1535 partbooks might well be be correct. For further information also see the chapter and catalogue by Royston Gustavson in this volume.

26 For a transcription of the legal document that Egenolff filed against Schott, see Grotefend, *Christian Egenolff*, 26, Beilage II. On the Schott-Egenolff law suit see, Koerner, *The Moment of Self -Portraiture*, Chapter 10: 'The Law of Authorship', 203–223, especially 215–217.

27 See Kusukawa, 'Leonhart Fuchs', especially 406, and 'Illustrating Nature'.

140   JOHN KMETZ

Let us take for example the forty-five-page booklet that Egenolff published in 1535, the same year he published his first two books of secular polyphony (RISM 1535[10] and RISM 1535[11]).[28] The booklet carries the title *Kunstbüchlin gerechten gründtlichen gebrauchs aller kunstbaren Werckleut*.[29] This little pamphlet of skills cheaply printed on coarse paper, with poor registration, and faulty inking, was released just in time to be offered for sale at the Frankfurt Book Fair that year. Egenolff created the booklet by conflating, or should I say anthologizing, or should I say pirating three previously published, stand alone, manuals. One of those manuals was on metallurgical techniques containing recipes for artists to produce inks and paints (*Artliche Kunst*), the second described techniques for hardening and tempering steel and iron (*Von Stahel und Eysen*), and the third was a booklet on cleaning and dyeing fabrics, or that is to say how to remove spots and stains (*Mackel und Flecken . . . aus zubringen*). It was Egenolff, however, who got the bright idea of combining the three with one of his own pamphlets on alchemy (*Rechter Gebrauch der Alchimei*) to make a new, comprehensive all-purpose manual for household and commercial use.[30]

There is no question that Egenolff took copy from other publishers and that he did it shamelessly. Actually, he even reprinted the *Theuerdank* in 1553, a book that is as imperial and as beautiful as any one book could possibly be, until Egenolff got his hands on it. He shrunk the 1517 first edition from a royal folio to a compact one, doubled up columns of text, and stripped the young emperor of his beautiful Schönsperger typeface. After Egenolff's death, his heirs continued to reprint this allegory of Maximilian's early life no less than four more times, and by 1596, in its final Egenolff incarnation, the *Theuerdank* was finally buried, or should I say liberated, in an upright octavo format that while anything but a good impression of Schönsperger's original was certainly one that now even an impecunious student might own.[31] Indeed, as I mined my way through the collected works of Egenolff, I found him taking, literally, again and again, books released by other publishers and not only reprinting them, but also apparently doing it as quickly and as cost effectively as a baker moved loaves of bread in and out of his oven, as Albrecht Dürer depicted in the pen drawing, illustrated in Figure 7.1, that parodied the publishing industry.

Egenolff's music books in context

That Egenolff was a shrewd businessman is well illustrated by the twelve music books he published in the 1530s, listed in Table 7.1. These books have certainly not gone unnoticed in the musicological community, regardless of their small size. From Eitner,[32] to Riemann,[33] to Moser,[34] Lindenburg,[35] Bridgeman,[36] Staehelin,[37] Lipphardt,[38] Berz,[39] Gustavson,[40]

---

28 Gassenhawerlin (vdm 21) and Reutterliedlin (vdm 22).
29 VD16 R 494. For a digital copy of the title page see http://recipes.hypotheses.org/4251 (last accessed 31 January 2016).
30 Brafman, 'Diary of an Obscure German Artist', 156.
31 For a digital copy of Egenolff's 1553 reprint of the *Theuerdank* (VD16 M 1653) along with the four other reprints published by his heirs after his death, see USTC.
32 Eitner, *Quellenlexikon*, vol. 3, 319.
33 Riemann, *Handbuch*, vol. 2, 21 and 306f.
34 Moser, introductory booklet to *Gassenhawerlin*.
35 Lindenburg, 'Het "Kamper" liedboek'.
36 Bridgman, 'Christian Egenolff'.
37 Staehelin, 'Zum Egenolff-Diskantband' and idem 'Petruccis Canti B'.
38 Lipphardt, *Gesangbuchdrucke*.
39 Berz, *Frankfurt am Main*, 144–156.
40 Gustavson, art. 'Egenolff, Christian'; idem 'Competitive Strategy Dynamics', 191–192 and 199–200; and the article on Egenolff published in this volume.

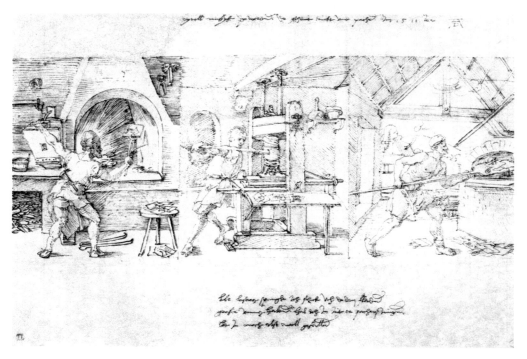

Figure 7.1 Albrecht Dürer, *The Publishing Bakery*, 1511. Pen and ink drawing
Source: Bayonne, Musée Bonnat-Helleu, inv. 1517

Kmetz[41] and Fallows,[42] the Egenolff partbooks have fascinated scholars of music for several generations. This fascination, however, was not primarily because of the unique readings they transmit for previously published repertory, nor because of the unica they preserve. Rather it has been predominantly with the novelty of their size, with the thorny question as to when they were printed, and with the identification of their exemplars.

Let's start with the exemplars. As Table 7.1 shows, five of the twelve sets of partbooks were either exact reprints of other music publishers' works, or were anthologies that reprinted selected works from the anthologies of other music publishers.[43] Having spent the first half of my paper arguing that Egenolff was a 'Master of the Reprint',[44] that he was a pirate, and that he was an astute businessman when it came to all things not musical, it should come as no surprise that his strategy for publishing books of music was exactly the same as his strategy for publishing the hundreds of other books he released that had nothing to do with music. For example, in January of 1532, Egenolff took Erhard Öglin's beautiful upright folio of 1507 featuring Tritonius' musical settings of the Odes of Horace and simply shrank it down to an upright octavo.[45] He dispensed with Öglin's title page and any mention

---

41 Kmetz, 'Closed Market', 181–182.
42 Fallows, 'The Songbooks of Christian Egenolff', and idem 'Songbook at Kampen', 348.
43 This table gives a concise overview of the Egenolff publications. For a detailed description see the catalogue by Royston Gustavson in this volume.
44 On the question of reprints and their frequency in the publication of music, see Bernstein, *Print Culture*, 151–152.
45 In fact, Egenolff could have also worked from the second edition, the *Harmoniae super odis* (Augsburg: Erhard Oeglin, 1507), vdm 108, which Oeglin published a few weeks after the *Melopoiae*, vdm 139, in a smaller, quarto format. A close comparison of Egenolff's publication with the two editions by Oeglin might be able to reveal, which one he followed, but has not been undertaken at this point.

Table 7.1 Selected music books by Egenolff. A summary of dates, titles, sizes, formats and exemplars

	Date; RISM/ *vdm* Number	Short Title/Edition	Size (h × w), cm	Printed area (from *vdm*)	Format	Copy Text
1	1532, January; RISM T 1251, vdm 139	*Melodiae in Odas Horatii*	14.5 × 10.5	11.7 × 6.9	8°	*Melopoiae sive harmoniae*, edited by Conrad Celtis (Augsburg: Oeglin, 1507), vdm 55; or *Harmoniae super odis* (Augsburg: Oeglin, 1507), vdm 108.
2	1532, January; RISM T 1251, vdm 109	*Odarum Horatii Concentus*	14.5 × 10.5	11.7 × 6.9	8°	
3	1535, February; RISM 1535[10], vdm 21	*Gassenhawerlin*	7.5 × 10.5	5.15 × 7.95	16° oblong	
4	1535; RISM 1535[11], vdm 22	*Reutterliedlin*/1st edition	7.5 × 10.5	5.15 × 7.95	16° oblong	
5	1535; vdm 29	*Brabandische Liedlin*	7.5 × 10.5	5.0 × 7.8	16° oblong	Kamper *Liedboek* (Strassburg: P. Schöffer d. J., c.1535 or an unknown Antwerp/Netherlandish printer)
6	c. 1536; vdm 30	*Cantiones vocum trium*	7.5 × 10.5	5.0 × 8.0	16° oblong	*Canti B* (Venice: Petrucci, 1502) or *Quinquagena carminum* (Mainz: Peter Schöffer d. J., 1513),
7	c. 1536; RISM [c.1535][14], vdm 25	*Cantiones vocum quatuor*	7.5 × 10.5	5.2 × 8.0	16° oblong	
8	1536; vdm 689	*Reutterliedlin*/2nd edition	7.5 × 10.5	5.0 × 8.0	16° oblong	
9	1552; RISM [1536][8], vdm 31	*Oberländische Liedlin*	9.5 × 15	6.8 × 10.6	8° oblong	*Fuenff und sechzig teutscher Lieder* (Strassburg: Peter Schöffer d. J., u. Mathias Apiarius, c.1536), vdm 27
10	1552; RISM [c.1535][15], vdm 26	*Newgeborne Liedlin*	9.5 × 15	7.2 × 10.6	8° oblong	
11	1552; RISM [c.1535][12], vdm 23	*Graszliedlin*	9.5 × 15	7.4 × 10.6	8° oblong	
12	1552; RISM [c.1535][13], vdm 24	*Gassenhawer und Reutterliedlin*	9.5 × 15	7.5 × 10.6	8° oblong	Conflation of Egenolff's two earlier music books of the same name

THE MUSIC BOOKS OF CHRISTIAN EGENOLFF   143

of the book's famous editor, Conrad Celtis, and ultimately released the first small, cheap set of partbooks for students learning the Horatian Odes.[46] Following on, it should now also come as no surprise that Egenolff stole from the riches of Petrucci's *Canti B* of 1502 and reproduced dozens of Franco-Flemish songs first released by the famous Venetian.[47] Or better yet, as David Fallows has suggested, perhaps Egenolff didn't steal from Petrucci at all, but rather stole from his fellow German-speaking thief Peter Schöffer the Younger, who reprinted the entire *Canti B* in 1513,[48] and not just parts of it as Egenolff did.[49] If that is the case, we now have thieves stealing from thieves, assuming that these 'honourable' businessmen actually perceived this as theft, or as simply business as usual.[50]

One could criticise Egenolff, as indeed Leonhard Fuchs did, for stealing beautiful books and ultimately destroying their beauty, or for taking popular, practical texts, and producing 'bad' impressions of them. Yet, before we make any decisions as to whether to bury Egenolff or to praise him, let us take a closer look at the size of the books, the quality of the printing, who owned them, what their print run might be, and how much they might cost.

As for their size, no one would disagree that six of the twelve are as small as any oblong format book of music could possibly be. As seen in Table 7.1, six check in at 7.5 centimetres high by 10.5 centimetres wide. Despite the discrepancies in the different catalogues,[51] these six would appear to be in sextodecimo, a format that would make perfect bibliographical sense for books with these dimensions. Having personally examined the Basel copy of the Reutterliedlin, I can assure you that it is in 16mo, given the direction of the chain and laid lines, and the position of the watermark and its twin mark among those lines, as illustrated in Figure 7.2a and Figure 7.2b.[52] The fact that this book is in 16mo means that no less than

---

46 For a pair of wonderful articles on Öglin's *Melopoiae*, see Lodes, '*Concentus, Melopoiae* und *Harmonie*' and Bobeth, 'Die humanistische Odenkomposition'.

47 See Staehelin 'Petruccis Canti B', 125–132.

48 Senn, 'Das Sammelwerk "Quinquagena Carminum"', 183–185. See also Lindmayr-Brandl, 'Peter Schöffer der Jüngere', esp. 298–302.

49 Fallows, 'The Songbooks', 360.

50 Since a privilege on a book's title page was often perceived as meaningless when it came to the question of copyright or should I say the protection of intellectual property, I would have to suspect that Egenolff and Schöffer stole from the riches of other publishers if only because piracy was generally perceived as 'business as usual', regardless of whether a book had a privilege or not.

51 USTC, VD16, RISM and Berz, *Frankfurt am Main*, evidently did not agree on this question.

52 Royston Gustavson, who has examined many copies of these tiny Egenolff music books, has likewise concluded that they are sextodecimos: see Gustavson's article in this volume, as well as his 'Competitive Strategy Dynamics', 191, fn. 30. As how to identify a 16[mo] book see what still remains the indispensable classic of analytical bibliography, Gaskell, *A New Introduction*, 84ff. I choose to reproduce the ox head watermarks from the Basel copy of the second edition of the *Reutterliedlin* (dated December, 1536) so that other scholars might find the identical mark in additional dated books published by Egenolff, regardless of whether they contain music or not. These watermarks can be enormously helpful in dating the books. The watermark and its twin reproduced above in Figures 2a and 2b is ostensibly the same one described in the Salzburg catalogue (vdm.sbg.ac.at) as an 'ox with horns, ears, nostrils, and eyes and with a three-leaf-flower growing out of his head'. (This description is not online.) The catalogue identifies this mark as appearing in five of the Egenolff music prints listed in Table 1 (namely 1, 2, 5, 6, 7 and 8). Of those five, three carry dates (namely, nos. 1 and 2: the first and second editions of *Melodiae in Odas Horatii*, January 1532; and no. 6: the second edition of the *Reutterliedlin*, December of 1536). Assuming that the watermarks are the same, this evidence alone would imply that Egenolff began using this paper, at least in his music books, in 1532 and continued using it until 1536, an observation that is similar to one made by Nanie Bridgman sixty years ago, 'Christian Egenolff', 84–85. While establishing a *terminus post quem* and *ante quem* for Egenolffs consumption of this ox head paper would be helpful, it will not solve the problem of dating. What might help narrow the date range would be to identify concordances for the many woodcuts found on the title and preliminary pages of the undated Egenolff partbooks with the numerous dated Egenolff books that have nothing to do with music, as I indeed noted above. While this avenue of research has yet to be explored, the importance of examining early catalogues as a means of identifying missing dates and titles for Egenolff's music books has, as seen in the article by Royston Gustavson published in this volume.

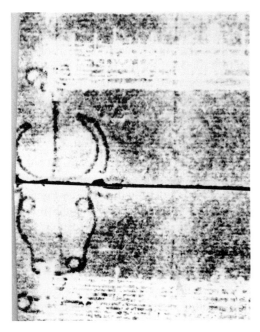 

Figure 7.2a Ox head watermark. Egenolff, *Reutterliedlin*. December 1536 = RISM 1535[11], vdm 689
Source: Universitätsbibliothek Basel, F X 22, fols. 19^r/20^v

Figure 7.2b Ox head twin watermark. Egenolff, *Reutterliedlin*. December 1536 = RISM 1535[11], vdm 689
Source: Universitätsbibliothek Basel, F X 22, fol. 4^r

Figure 7.3 Poor registration of unnested, single impression type. Egenolff, *Gassenhawerlin* (= RISM 1535[10], vdm 21)
Source: CH-Zz Mus. 908, fol. 1^r. Reproduced from the facsimile edited by H.-J. Moser, *Gassenhawerlin und Reutterliedlin* (Augsburg: Benno Filser Verlag, 1927)

THE MUSIC BOOKS OF CHRISTIAN EGENOLFF   145

thirty-two individual pages could be printed on one sheet of paper, sixteen pages on the outer form, and sixteen on the inner form.[53] Obviously, this is a huge saving for the publisher in both time and materials. And if you are Egenolff, using cheap quality paper, deploying single impression type, and not nesting that type (but rather allowing it to shift in the forme, as can be seen in Figure 7.3 where the type moves like a drunken sailor), one can print books very quickly, and very cost effectively.[54] The only way to get around that conveyer belt even quicker would be to simply set up the press once, with only one forme, and print that one forme hundreds, if not thousands of times, as indeed many German printers of broadsheets did, and with many broadsheets containing music, or with texts to be sung to music.[55] Egenolff, however, strangely enough, was not one of them.

As to who bought Egenolff music books, I think it would be safe to say that it would probably not be the same individuals or institutions who purchased, or were gifted, copies of Grimm & Wyrsung's *Liber Selectarum Cantionum* or of Glarean's *Dodecachordon*, two magnificent folio formatters that obviously required funding and were prohibitively expensive.[56] The Egenolff music books, on the other hand, were clearly intended to accommodate the pocket, if not the pocketbook, of an individual looking for cheap print. The fact that so many of the books survive incomplete, and are almost always missing the Tenor partbook, which is where a full text of the songs would have been found, strongly suggests that these books were not owned by professional musicians or collected by well-healed institutions. Rather they were books that were used and abused by fledgling amateurs, as the copy of the *Reutterliedlin*, owned by Basilius Amerbach in 1547, and filled with his juvenile graffiti, suggests. This Egenolff print, along with Georg Rhau's *Wittembergisch deutsch Geistlich Gesangbüchlein*, was used by Piperinus to teach the thirteen-year old Basilius the art of singing between November of 1546 and the summer of 1547.[57] While we have no idea as to how much the Amerbachs paid for the Egenolff print, or how much Piperinus paid, we do know how much the Rhau print cost if only because the title page of the Basel exemplar (CH-Bu kk IV 23–27) carries not only Basilius' dated *ex libris*, but also the cost of the book which was entered in Piperinus' hand, namely 27 schillings, as Table 7.2 shows. In this table I have given you the purchase prices of German music books acquired by Ferdinand Columbus, the illegitimate son of the famous voyager, in the 1520s and 30s,[58] and by Basilius Amerbach and Johannes von Schännis of Zurich in the 1540s and 1570s respectively.[59] There are several things about this list that are worth noting. Clearly, books of smaller format or, more importantly, containing fewer folios are cheaper than larger books containing more folios. No surprise here. What might be a surprise,

---

53 Indeed Royston Gustavson ('Competitive Strategy Dynamics', 191) did the math as well and concluded, as did I, that it would take only 7.5 sheets of paper to print an entire set of partbooks.

54 On cheap print and how to produce it, see van Orden, 'Cheap Print and Street Song' and Watt, *Cheap Print*. For a concise history of books in small formats, see Pascoe, 'Tiny Tomes'.

55 See Schanze, 'Gestalt und Geschichte'.

56 On the *Liber Selectarum*, see Giselbrecht and Upper, 'Glittering Woodcuts and Moveable Music'. See also Schiefelbein, 'Same Same but Different'. On the *Dodecachordon* see, Kölbl, 'Glarean's *Dodekachordon*'.

57 Actually, Basilius Amerbach is the only person I know of from the sixteenth century who owned a copy of an Egenolff book and other music books used by Piperinus to teach Basilius, see Kmetz, *Basel Songbooks*, Chapter 4: 'The Piperinus-Amerbach Partbooks: A Study in Sixteenth-Century Musical Pedagogy', 83–124.

58 The purchase prices paid by Ferdinand Columbus that are listed in Table 7.2 were compiled from the ground-breaking scholarship of Chapman, 'Printed Collections Columbus', and of Boorman, *Petrucci*, 332–334 and 1165–1168.

59 On the 1549 edition of Georg Forster's *Ein Auszbund* [. . .] *Teutscher Liedlein* (RISM 1549³⁵), purchased by the Zurich Burgermeister Johannis von Schännis in Speyer on November 12, 1578, see Kmetz, 'Da Jacob nun das Kleid ansah', 67–70.

146   JOHN KMETZ

Table 7.2 Prices paid for German music books in the sixteenth century

Purchases by Ferdinand Columbus

Author, Title, Year/RISM Nu.	Format/ folios	Where and when purchased	Price (kreutzer) [4 pfg=1 kreutzer]	Price (pfennig)
Music theory				
Glareanus, *Isagoge*, 1516	4°/20ff.	Nuremberg, 1521	5	[20]
Cochlaeus, *Tetrachordum*, 1520	4°/28ff.	Nuremberg, 1521	3	[12]
Rhau, *Enchiridion*, 1520	8°/56ff.	Nuremberg, 1521	10	[40]
Ornithoparcus, *Musice*, 1519	4°/54ff.	Nuremberg, 1521	[7]	28
Quercu, *Opusculum*, 1516/8	4°/54ff.	Nuremberg, 1521	3	[12]
Virdung, *Musica*, 1511	4°/56ff.	Nuremberg, 1521	6	[18]
Koswick, *Compendaria*, 1519	4°/16ff.	Nuremberg, 1521	2	[8]
C. von Zabern, *Ars bene*, 1509	8°/28ff.	Frankfurt, 1522	[1]	4
Burchard, *Hotulus*, 1514	4°/12ff.	Frankfurt, 1522	[1]	4
Faber, *Musica*, 1516	4°/18ff.	Cologne, 1522	[1.5]	6
Bogentanz, *Collectanea*, 1515	4°/26ff.	Cologne, 1522	[2]	8
Twyvel, *Introductorium*, 1513	4°/29ff.	Cologne, 1522	[1]	4
Music				
Schlick, Tabulaturen, 1512[1]	4°/46ff.	Nuremberg, 1521	8	[32]
Arnt von Aich, *In Dissem* [1519][5]	8°/83ff.	Nuremberg, 1521	20	[80]
Walter, *Geystliche* 1525[71]	4°/185ff.	Augsburg, 1531	40	[160]

Purchases by Basilius Amerbach and Johannis von Schännis

Author/editor,Title, Year/ RISM Nu.	Format/ folios	Where and when purchased	Price	Price in pfennig
Walter, *Wittembergisch* 1544[12]	4°/220ff.	Basel, 1546	27 schilling	[270]
G. Forster, *Ein Auszbund* 1549[35]	8°/149ff.	Speyer, 1578	14 batzen	[224]
Reutterliedlin, 1536 (=1535[11])	16°/120ff.	Basel, 1546	unknown	[135?]

The following breakdown of sixteenth-century German currency values was taken from *Three Behaim Boys: Growing Up in Early Modern Germany*, edited by Steven Özment (New Haven, CT & London: Yale University Press, 1990), p. 286, wherein one finds that 1 Gulden = 252 Pfennig; 1 pound = 30 Pfennig; 1 Batzen = 16 Pfennig; 1 Schilling/Groschen = 10 Pfennig; 1 Kreutzer = 4 Pfennig.

however, is that sets of partbooks purchased by Columbus in Germany in the 1520s and 30s are considerably less costly than similar sets of partbooks purchased by Amerbach and Schännis in the 1540s and 70s. Assuming that Columbus, Piperinus and Schännis recorded the purchase price of their books correctly, one would have to conclude that the cost of music books was increasing. While one might argue that the cost rose in direct relationship to rising levels of musical literacy, I am more inclined to believe it was because of the so-called price revolution of the sixteenth century. This economic revolution, wherein the rising costs of goods accompanied by the rising costs for the labour and raw materials to produce those goods, sent prices skyrocketing throughout Europe with the passing of each year, thereby resulting in a century of rampant inflation.[60]

---

60 See Fischer, *The Great Wave*, especially 45–90, where the author discusses market trends and price fluctuations during the fifteenth and sixteenth centuries.

THE MUSIC BOOKS OF CHRISTIAN EGENOLFF 147

With that it mind, it should come as no surprise that Egenolff looked to cut his costs, and his consumers' costs, as much as possible. While I have no evidence to document what anyone in the sixteenth century actually paid for an Egenolff book, I would guess based on the tiny size alone of the Egenolff partbooks in sestodecimo, that Basilius' music teacher paid less than half of what he paid for the larger, oblong quarto published by Rhau in 1546. Half that amount would be about 135 pfennig, which, by the way, would have been what an average journeyman was paid for two days of wages at that time.[61] Consequently, even small, poorly printed books were not that cheap, and, as such, not meant for everyone. And let me assure you the Amerbachs were not everyone. They were a dynastic family of educated elite, who had wealth, power and influence, and had amassed one of the greatest private libraries of the sixteenth century.[62] Yet money didn't grow on trees, even for the Amerbachs, as is made clear by a letter written by Johannes Amerbach, the famous publisher, to his son Bruno, who while enrolled as a student in Paris in July of 1507 wrote his father asking for money. His father's response: 'Perhaps you think I own an ass that coughs up money for me. It doesn't work that way. You know I have not published in two years. We are all living on capital.'[63]

Before we leave the Amerbachs and I give my final impressions of Egenolff as a publisher, businessman, real estate mogul and, as such, a capitalist, I would like to take a moment and look at sixteenth-century manuscripts of polyphonic music that are the same size or similar in size to our Egenolff music books.

As seen in Table 7.3, all of the books preserve a secular repertoire, and with the exception of the one French and the one Belgian source, the repertory, while a mixed bag of French, Italian, and German songs, is predominantly German, and the manuscripts are predominantly of German origin. The four Basel manuscripts, however, are special if only because we actually know a lot about them.[64] They were copied, acquired, and used by their owners while they were teenagers who were either matriculated at the University of Basel, enrolled at a local Basel Latin school, or were working as a goldsmith's apprentice in Augsburg before moving to Basel and becoming a citizen later in life. As for their size and format, which, by the way, are, like Egenolff's music books, oblong sextodecimos, I suspect that Egenolff's Reutterliedlin owned by Basilius Amerbach (and later by his nephew Ludwig Iselin) served as a model of format and of size for their three tiny manuscripts. Actually, I would argue that Egenolff's little sextodecimos served as models for all of the oblong German manuscripts listed in Table 7.3 that date from after 1535, except that Basel F X 21 might well have started life around 1530, namely five years before Egenolff printed his first set of partbooks in 16mo. Nevertheless, I still suspect that Egenolff's tiny, printed music books were much more likely to have been the model of inspiration for manuscript music of the same

---

61 As to the buying power of such currencies of the German-speaking realm as a gulden, pfund, batzen, schilling, groschen, kreutzer or pfennig, see Kmetz, 'Blowing your Horn', 133–141.

62 Amazingly a detailed study of this family has yet to appear in print. By far the best source for documenting their activities as printers, editors, booksellers, humanists, art collectors, university professors, and attorneys remains the family's extensive correspondence. Since 1942 most of the letters have been edited by Alfred Hartmann and by his successor Beat R. Jenny in the ongoing series: *Amerbachkorrespondenz*. For a convenient introduction to the family see Kmetz, *Basel Songbooks*, 3–22.

63 As quoted from the English translation by Barbara C. Halporn (*The Correspondence*, 284, letter no. 198) of the original Latin text (edited in the *Amerbachkorrespondenz*, vol. 1, letter no. 348, 326, lines 21–23), which reads: 'Putas fortassis, quod sit mihi asinus, qui egerens bombis suis mihi cudat pecunias. Non sic formantur, sed ter quinque excipiantur. Scis enim, quod in duobus annis non impressi. Consumimus omnes de capitali.'

64 On the origins and contents of the Basel sources see Kmetz, *Handschriften Basel*, 278–295 (F X 17–20), 296–310 (F X 21), 311–317 (F X 22–24), and 317–322 (F X 25–26).

Table 7.3 Music manuscripts of the same size or are similar in size to Egenolff's music books (*i.e.* 7.5 × 10.5 cm)

Manuscript sigla	Size (cm)	Date	Provenance	Owner	Repertory	Remarks
B-Br MS IV 90	7.8 × 11	c.1511	Bruges	Ludovicus Bloc	Songs	
CH-Bu F X 17–20	7.5 × 10.5	c.1545–60	Augsburg & Basel	Jacob Hagenbach	Songs	
CH-Bu F X 21	7.5 × 10.5	c.1529–79	Basel	Ludwig Iselin	Songs	
CH-Bu F X 22–24	7.5 × 10.5	c.1547	Basel	Basilius Amerbach	Songs	Appendix to 1535[11]
CH-Bu F X 25–26	7.5 × 10.5	c.1574	Basel	Ludwig Iselin	Odes/Songs	
CH-Sfp 30–1	11 × 11	1st half 16th	Unknown	Unknown	Lieder	
CH-Zz 906	7.2 × 10.1	after 1535	Unknown	Unknown	Motets	once bound to 1535[11]
D-Bds 280	9.6 × 7.6	c.1500	Cologne?	Anna von Koln	Songs	Mostly songtexts
D-HB X/2	7.5 × 10.5	1550s	Frankfurt?	Unknown	Songs	Copy of bass: [1535][14]
D-Mbs 4483	10 × 11	c.1515	South German	Unknown	Lieder	
D-Rtt 3/I	9.7 × 15.3	c.1550	South German	Unknown	Songs	
D-Usch 235 (a-d)	10 × 15	2nd half 16th	South German	Unknown	Lieder	
D-Usch 237	9.8 × 14.2	c.1530–40	Central German	Unknown	Songs/Motets	
I-Fn Magl. 57	11 × 8	Mid 16th	French?	Unknown	Songs	
I-Rvat lat 11953	10 × 13	c.1515–30	German	Unknown	Songs	

This list was compiled from data recorded in the *Census-Catalogue of Manuscript Sources of Polyphonic Music 1400–1550*, edited by Charles Hamm and Herbert Kellman. The University of Illinois Musicological Archives for Renaissance Manuscript Studies (Neuhausen-Stuttgart: Hänssler-Verlag, 1979–1988), vols. I–V.

THE MUSIC BOOKS OF CHRISTIAN EGENOLFF   149

size copied after 1535 than the other way around. I say this if only because a print run for any one of the Egenolff books listed in Table 3.1 was certainly nothing less than 500 copies, and I suspect could have easily exceeded 1,000 if the books were marketed in a university town such as Marburg, where Egenolff actually served as the university's official printer from 1538 to 1545. Indeed, given the fact that there are no Egenolff music books that carry dates from the 1540s (only music books from the 1530s and 1550s carry dates), it might well be possible that he printed 1,000 or more copies of each set of partbooks from the 1530s and then simply sold his 1530's stock in the 1540s. By doing this he would have embraced the accounting principle known today as FILO (First In Last Out)[65] and, as such, would have protected his business and its profits from the rising costs that he was incurring for labor and materials during a century plagued by out-of-control inflation. Actually, Basilius Amerbach's copy of the Reutterliedlin, acquired by him in 1547, might well be one of those warehoused books.[66]

Final impressions

Egenolff was unquestionably an astute businessman, and clearly was one of the most financially successful publishers in the sixteenth century, as we have seen by examining many different layers of evidence. There is the evidence drawn from the final accounting of his estate upon his death, the evidence procured from an examination of his books of music, and without music, which shows that he routinely reprinted, edited, or anthologised books issued by other publishers in order to release 'new' books with his name on them. We have also seen that he focused his attention predominantly on educational books, not scholarly ones, the former of which were destined for a student market or for literate parents who were looking to purchase practical books that would help them in their daily lives. Finally there is the bibliographical evidence culled from Egenolff's music books, which makes clear that by using cheap paper, deploying unnested, single impression type, and then featuring that type within the confines of a tiny print frame, Egenolff was able to turn his 'bad', or should I simply call them 'mediocre', impressions of good music, into cheap print with a good return on investment.

All of this evidence supports the title of my paper, and now in my closing remark leaves me wondering whether or not I should bury Egenolff as a shameless capitalist or praise him as an ingenious businessman. As a businessman myself, I say we praise him. He read the market, and he read it well. He, like so many of his German contemporaries who printed music, diversified his portfolio of publications by issuing books in numerous subjects. He did this clearly to protect his assets, his net worth, and, as such, his family. He really took no risks once he had established his business model. He published no big, expensive books needing outside funding from venture capitalists. Rather he seems to have funded most books himself, and then took his gains and reinvested them in real estate, or simply put them back into his business. When he died at the age of 53, he had created the first dynastic printing house in Frankfurt, and he did it not as an ingenious inventor such as Gutenberg who died poor, but rather as a businessman such as Fust, who had the right stuff and died rich.

---

65 See above, footnote 5.

66 For a discussion on the warehousing of books in the Renaissance, see Maclean, *Learning and the Market Place*, 110, 230, 238, and 242–245; and idem, *Scholarship, Commerce, Religion*, Chapter 7, 'Sellers and Purchasers: Markets, Distribution, and Collection-Building', 176–178.

150   JOHN KMETZ

References

Benzing, Josef. 'Christian Egenolff zu Straßburg und seine Drucke (1528 bis 1530)'. *Das Antiquariat* 10 (1954): 88–89 and 92.

Benzing, Josef. 'Die Drucke Christian Egenolffs zu Frankfurt am Main vom Ende 1530 bis 1555'. *Das Antiquariat* 11 (1955): 139–140, 162–164, 201–202, 232–236.

Bernstein, Jane A. *Print Culture and Music in Sixteenth-Century Venice.* Oxford: Oxford University Press, 2001.

Berz, Ernst-Ludwig. *Die Notendrucker und ihre Verleger in Frankfurt am Main von den Anfängen bis etwa 1630: Eine bibliographische und drucktechnische Studie zur Musikpublikation.* Catalogus musicus 5. Kassel: Bärenreiter, 1970.

Blackburn, Bonnie J. 'The Printing Contract for the *Libro primo de musica de la salamandra* (Rome, 1526)'. *Journal of Musicology* 12 (1994): 345–356.

Bobeth, Gundela. 'Die humanistische Odenkomposition in Buchdruck und Handschrift: Zur Rolle der *Melopoiae* bei der Formung und Ausbreitung in eines kompositorischen Erfolgsmodells'. In *NiveauNischeNimbus: Die Anfänge des Musikdrucks nördlich der Alpen*, edited by Birgit Lodes. Wiener Forum für ältere Musikgeschichte 3. Tutzing: Hans Schneider, 2010, 67–87.

Boorman, Stanley. 'Early Music Printing: Working for a Specialized Market'. In *Print and Culture in the Renaissance: Essays on the Advent of Printing in Europe*, edited by Gerald P. Tyson and Sylvia S. Wagonheim. Newark, DE: University of Delaware Press, 1986, 222–245.

Boorman, Stanley. *Ottaviano Petrucci. Catalogue Raisonné.* Oxford: Oxford University Press, 2006.

Brafman, David. 'Diary of an Obscure German Artist with (almost) No Friends'. *Getty Research Journal* 6 (2014): 151–162.

Bridgman, Nanie. 'Christian Egenolff, imprimeur de Musique (A propos du recueil *Rés. Vm7 504* de la Bibliothèque Nationale de Paris)'. *Annales Musicologiques* 3 (1955): 77–177.

Chapman, Catherine Weeks. 'Printed Collections of Polyphonic Music Owned by Ferdinand Columbus'. *Journal of the American Musicologial Society* 21 (1968): 34–84.

Christie, Alix. *Gutenberg's Apprentice.* New York: Harper Collins, 2014.

Clark, Harry. 'Foiling the Pirates: the Preparation and Publication of Andreas Vesalius's *De humani corporis fabrica*'. *Library Quarterly* 51 (1981): 301–311.

Die Amerbachkorrespondenz. Basel: Basel University Library Press.

Eitner, Robert. *Biographisch-bibliographisches Quellenlexikon der Musiker und Musikgelehrten des christlichen Zeitrechnung bis zur Mitte des 19. Jahrhunderts.* Leipzig: Breitkopf & Härtel, 1899–1904.

Fallows, David. 'The Printed Songbook at Kampen'. In *NiveauNischeNimbus: Die Anfänge des Musikdrucks nördlich der Alpen*, edited by Birgit Lodes. Wiener Forum für ältere Musikgeschichte 3. Tutzing: Hans Schneider, 2010, 347–354.

Fallows, David. 'The Songbooks of Christian Egenolff'. In *NiveauNischeNimbus: Die Anfänge des Musikdrucks nördlich der Alpen*, edited by Birgit Lodes. Wiener Forum für ältere Musikgeschichte 3. Tutzing: Hans Schneider, 2010, 355–368.

Fischer, David Hackett. *The Great Wave: Price Revolutions and the Rhythm of History.* Oxford: Oxford University Press, 1996.

Gaskell, Philip. *A New Introduction to Bibliography.* Oxford: Oxford University Press, 1972.

Giselbrecht, Elisabeth and L. Elizabeth Upper (now Savage). 'Glittering Woodcuts and Moveable Music: Decoding the Elaborate Printing Techniques, Purpose, and Patronage of the *Liber Selectarum Cantionum*'. In *Senfl-Studien I*, edited by Stefan Gasch, Birgit Lodes and Sonja Tröster. Wiener Forum für ältere Musikgeschichte 4. Tutzing: Hans Schneider, 2012, 17–67.

Green, Jonathan. *Printing and Prophecy: Prognostication and Media Change, 1450 –1550.* Ann Arbor, MI: University of Michigan Press, 2012.

Grotefend, Hermann. *Christian Egenolff, der erste ständige Buchdrucker zu Frankfurt am Main und seine Vorläufer*. Frankfurt: K. T. Völcker's Verlag, 1881.

Gustavson, Royston. 'Competitive Strategy Dynamics in the German Music Publishing Industry 1530–1550'. In *NiveauNischeNimbus: Die Anfänge des Musikdrucks nördlich der Alpen*, edited by Birgit Lodes. Wiener Forum für ältere Musikgeschichte 3. Tutzing: Hans Schneider, 2010, 185–210.

Gustavson, Royston. 'Egenolff, Christian'. In *Die Musik in Geschichte und Gegenwart*, edited by Ludwig Finscher, Personenteil 6. Kassel: Bärenreiter, 2001, cols. 98–103.

Halporn, Barbara C. *The Correspondence of Johann Amerbach: Early Printing in Its Social Context*. Ann Arbor, MI: The University of Michigan Press, 2000.

Judd, Cristle Collins. *Reading Renaissance Music Theory: Hearing with the Eyes*. Cambridge: Cambridge University Press, 2001.

Kapr, Albert. *Johann Gutenberg: The Man and his Invention*. Aldershot: Scolar Press, 1996.

Kmetz, John. '250 Years of German Music Print (c.1500–1750): A Case for a Closed Market'. In *NiveauNischeNimbus: Die Anfänge des Musikdrucks nördlich der Alpen*, edited by Birgit Lodes. Wiener Forum für ältere Musikgeschichte 3. Tutzing: Hans Schneider, 2010, 167–184.

Kmetz, John. 'Blowing Your Horn in the New Economy, c.1550'. In *Tielman Susato and the Music of his Time: Print Culture, Compositional Technique and Instrumental Music in the Renaissance*, edited by Keith Polk Hillsdale. New York: Pendragon Press, 2005, 133–141.

Kmetz, John. '*Da Jacob nun das Kleid ansah* and Zurich Zentralbiliothek T 410–413: A Well-Known Motet in a Little-Known 16th-Century Manuscript'. *Schweizer Jahrbuch für Musikwissenschaft*, Neue Folge 4/5 (1984/85): 63–79.

Kmetz, John. *Die Handschriften der Universitätsbibliothek Basel. Katalog der Musikhandschriften des 16. Jahrhunderts: Quellenkritische und historische Untersuchung*. Basel: Basel University Library Press, 1988.

Kmetz, John. *The Sixteenth-Century Basel Songbooks: Origins, Contents, Contexts*. Bern: Paul Haupt, 1995.

Koerner, Joseph Leo. *The Moment of Self-Portraiture in German Renaissance Art*. Chicago, IL: University of Chicago Press, 1993.

Kölbl, Bernhard. '"Mitto ad te meos de musica labores": Glarean's *Dodekachordon* and the Politics of Dedication'. In *Heinrich Glarean's Books: The Intellectual World of a Sixteenth-Century Musical Humanist*, edited by Iain Fenlon and Inga Mai Groote. Cambridge: Cambridge University Press, 2013, 47–63.

Kulturvereinigung Hadamar (ed.). *Christian Egenolff 1502–1555: Ein Frankfurter Meister des frühen Buchdrucks aus Hadamar*. Limburg: Glaukos, 2001.

Kusukawa, Sachiko. 'Illustrating Nature'. In *Books and the Sciences in History*, edited by Marina Frasca-Spada and Nick Jardine. Cambridge: Cambridge University Press, 2001, 92–97.

Kusukawa, Sachiko. 'Leonhart Fuchs on the Importance of Pictures'. *Journal of the History of Ideas* 58 no. 3 (July, 1997): 403–427.

Lindenburg, Cornelis. 'Het "Kamper" liedboek'. *Tijdschrift van de Koninklijke Vereniging voor Nederlandse Muziekgeschiedenis* 16/1 (1940): 48–62.

Lindmayr-Brandl, Andrea. 'Peter Schöffer der Jüngere, das Erbe Gutenbergs und "die wahre Art des Druckens"'. In *NiveauNischeNimbus: Die Anfänge des Musikdrucks nördlich der Alpen*, edited by Birgit Lodes. Wiener Forum für ältere Musikgeschichte 3. Tutzing: Hans Schneider, 2010, 283–312.

Lipphardt, Walter. *Gesangbuchdrucke in Frankfurt am Main vor 1569*. Frankfurt am Main: W. Kramer, 1974.

Lodes, Birgit. 'Concentus, Melopoiae und Harmonie 1507: Zum Geburtsjahr des Typendrucks mehrstimmiger Musik nördlich der Alpen'. In *NiveauNischeNimbus: Die Anfänge des Musikdrucks nördlich der Alpen*, edited Birgit Lodes. Wiener Forum für ältere Musikgeschichte 3. Tutzing: Hans Schneider, 2010, 33–66.

152   JOHN KMETZ

Maclean, Ian. *Learning and the Market Place: Essays in the History of the Early Modern Book*. Leiden: Brill, 2009.

Maclean, Ian. *Scholarship, Commerce, Religion: The Learned Book in the Age of Confessions, 1560–1630*. Cambridge, MA: Harvard University Press, 2012.

Moser, Hans Joachim. Introductory booklet to the facsimile edition of *Gassenhawer und Reutterliedlin* Augsburg and Cologne, 1927; reprinted Hildesheim: G. Olms Verlag, 1970.

Pascoe, Judith. 'Tiny Tomes: Literature in Miniature Has a 500-year History, but What's the Appeal of a Volume Too Small to Read?' *The American Scholar* 75, no. 3 (2006): 133–138.

Pettegree, Andrew. *The Book in the Renaissance*. New Haven, CT: Yale University Press, 2010.

Reske, Christoph. *Die Buchdrucker des 16. und 17. Jahrhunderts im deutschen Sprachgebiet*. 2nd, extended edition Wiesbaden: Harrassowitz, 2015.

Riemann, Hugo. *Handbuch der Musikgeschichte*. Leipzig: Breitkopf & Härtel, 1901–1913.

Schanze, Frieder. 'Gestalt und Geschichte früher deutscher Lied-Einblattdrucke nebst einem Verzeichnis der Blätter mit Noten'. In *NiveauNischeNimbus: Die Anfänge des Musikdrucks nördlich der Alpen*, edited by Birgit Lodes. Wiener Forum für ältere Musikgeschichte 3. Tutzing: Hans Schneider, 2010, 369–410.

Schiefelbein, Torge. 'Same Same but Different: Die erhaltenen Exemplare des "Liber Selectarum Cantionum" (Augsburg 1520)'. PhD dissertation, Universität Wien, 2016.

Scholz Williams, Gerhild. 'The Arthurian Model in Emperor Maximilian's Autobiographic Writings *Weisskunig* and *Theuerdank*'. *The Sixteenth Century Journal* 11/ 4 (1980): 3–22.

Senn, Walter. 'Das Sammelwerk "Quinquagena Carminum" aus der Offizin Peter Schöffers d. J.'. *L'arte musicale in Italia* 6 (1964): 183–185.

Silver, Larry. *Marketing Maximilian: The Visual Ideology of a Holy Roman Emperor*. Princeton, NJ: Princeton University Press, 2008.

Staehelin, Martin. 'Petruccis Canti B in deutschen Musikdrucken des 16. Jahrhunderts'. In *Gestalt und Entstehung musikalischer Quellen im 15. und 16. Jahrhundert*, edited by Martin Staehelin. Wolfenbütteler Forschungen 83. Wiesbaden, 1998, 125–131.

Staehelin, Martin. 'Zum Egenolff-Diskantband der Bibliothèque Nationale in Paris. Ein Beitrag zur musikalischen Quellenkunde der 1. Hälfte des 16. Jahrhunderts'. *Archiv für Musikwissenschaft* 23 (1966): 93–109.

Steinmann, Martin. *Johannes Oporinus: Ein Basler Buchdrucker um die Mitte des 16. Jahrhunderts*. Basel: Helbing & Lichtenhahn, 1967.

Steinmetz, Greg. *The Richest Man Who Ever Lived: The Life and Times of Jacob Fugger*. New York: Simon & Schuster, 2015.

Sternfeld, Frederick. 'Music in the Schools of the Reformation'. *Musica Disciplina* 2 (1948): 99–122.

Strieder, Jacob. *Jacob Fugger the Rich: Merchant and Banker of Augsburg, 1459–1525*. New York: Archon Books, 1966.

Van Orden, Kate. 'Cheap Print and Street Song Following the Saint Bartholomew's Massacres of 1572'. In *Music and the Cultures of Print*, edited by Kate van Orden. New York & London: Garland, 2000, 271–324.

Watt, Tessa. *Cheap Print and Popular Piety, 1550–1640*. Cambridge: Cambridge University Press, 1993.

8

The music editions of Christian Egenolff

A new catalogue and its implications[1]

Royston Gustavson

For Grantley McDonald

Introduction

Christian Egenolff is one of the most important music printers in the German-speaking area in the sixteenth century, in part because he was the first German printer to use single-impression movable type to print mensural music (which is much cheaper than the previous double-impression process), and in part because of his editions of *Tenorlieder*. Music, however, formed a very small part of his output, both in terms of total editions (sixteen of more than 600 editions) and of the physical scale of the editions. To place this into perspective, to print one copy of each of his known music editions (excluding the lost *Gesangbüchlin*) would have taken 282 sheets of paper; to print one copy of his 1534 bible (VD16 B 2692) took 290 sheets of paper.

Previous catalogues of Egenolff's music editions have been incomplete, although that by Hans-Christian Müller in 1964 was an outstanding version based on the evidence known at that time.[2] A third of Egenolff's extant editions have until now remained without a known title as the title pages were missing, just over half have had a contested date of printing, and two works have been believed to exist in two editions, whereas there is only one edition, but two issues, of each. The present chapter, based on a first-hand examination of all of Egenolff's music editions, including every known exemplar of ten of the fourteen extant editions, aims to remedy this, so that future work on Egenolff and the music in his editions can rest on a surer bibliographical foundation. The catalogue closes with a number of titles that either do not in fact contain printed music, or the printing of which is hypothesised; these are discussed briefly in the catalogue but not in the text below.

---

1 I am grateful to the following libraries and their staff who allowed me access to original Egenolff editions during my visits: A-Wn, CH-Bu CH-BEl, CH-Zz, D-B, D-Mbs, D-W, D-Z, F-Pn, GB-Lbl, PL-Kj, US-Wc, and to the many libraries that sent me photographs of materials. I am grateful to Grantley McDonald for translations from the Latin, checking some archival materials in Vienna, and for his constant encouragement to write this chapter.

2 Of the previous detailed catalogues of Egenolff's music editions, the most important is Müller, 'Die Liederdrucke', which is drawn on by Berz, *Frankfurt am Main*. Those with brief entries on Egenolff's music editions include RISM and Gustavson, 'Egenolff'. The anthologies are catalogued in Eitner, *Sammelwerke*; and the Lied anthologies are catalogued, with incipits for all voices, in Böker-Heil, *Das Tenorlied*. Catalogues that cover Egenolff's entire output include the group of three articles by Josef Benzing: 'Christian Egenolff', (1954), 'Die Drucke Christian Egenolffs', (1955) and 'Christian Egenolff und seine Verlagsproduktion', (1973); Jäcker, 'Verzeichnis'; and the *Verzeichnis der im deutschen Sprachbereich erschienenen Drucke des 16. Jahrhunderts* (VD16), online at www.vd16.de.

154 ROYSTON GUSTAVSON

Typefaces and woodcuts

Egenolff used only one music typeface throughout his career,[3] despite the staff lines of the individual pieces of type not joining smoothly and the stem lengths being irregular. These features resulted in the pages of music having a rather untidy appearance. This typeface was used neither by other printers,[4] except for two staves in a grammar text,[5] nor by his heirs, except in their very first music edition,[6] after which their editions used a different typeface.[7] As such, it is not necessary to discuss his music typeface further. In his music prints, Egenolff set Latin headings (and sub-headings) in a Roman typeface, and Latin body text, with very rare exceptions, in a so-called Aldine italic in which only the lowercase letters were slanted but the capitals were upright. For languages other than Latin, he typically used a Fraktur for headings, and always used a Schwabacher for body text.[8] On his music title pages he used a variety of ornaments, including three different types of vine leaves – two types of single leaf and one type of trifoliate leaf[9] – and woodcuts including musical instruments, people playing musical instruments, animals, and geometric designs.

1 Tritonius. Odes. 1532

Egenolff's first music edition was a reprint of Öglin's 1507 quarto edition of Petrus Tritonius' settings of Horace's odes (RISM T 1250, vdm 108).[10] Unlike Öglin, who printed all four voices in one volume with the voice parts across a single opening, Egenolff printed the ode-settings in a set of four partbooks. The purpose of the edition was instruction in Latin metre, and like most schoolbooks it is printed in upright octavo.

This edition can be divided into two groups on the basis of two small variations in the typesetting that occur on the title page of the Tenor partbook. The first involves the first two lines of text: in the first group, the title begins *ODARVM Horatij Concentus*; in the second group, it begins *MELODIAE in Odas Horatij*. The second variation is that the title page of the first group has a border around the woodcut, but the second group does not. Apart from these differences, all examined copies of each of the four partbooks are from the same setting of type, and there are no changes to the makeup such as the addition or removal of leaves, therefore both titles belong to the same edition. From a technical perspective, the alterations to the title page are just like any stop-press changes. Egenolff stopped the press during the print run of the first sheet of the Tenor partbook, which contained the title page, and amended this one page of sixteen on the sheet. Fredson Bowers defines the differences

---

3 This typeface is described in Berz, *Frankfurt am Main*, 127–129.

4 Krummel, 'Early German Partbook Type Faces', 81, who did not note the Braubach as he did not include grammar texts.

5 Philipp Melanchthon, *Grammatica graeca* (Frankfurt a.M.: Peter Braubach, 1541; exemplar at GB-Lbl Hirsch IV.1518), with one stave of music on each of fols. A6^r and A7^r (VD16 M 3500; vdm 665). Berz, on p. 129, classifies this as a different typeface to Egenolff's, but the two typefaces appear identical to me. Braubach's 1544 edition of this title (VD16 M 3502), according to Berz (p. 151), has the music printed from woodblocks, not type; I suggest that this implies that Braubach borrowed the type for the 1541 edition. I have not seen the 1542 or 1543 Braubach editions of the *Grammatica graeca*.

6 The *Psalmen, Geistliche gesenge, Kirchen Ordenung und Gebet* of 1565 (RISM VIII DKL 1565^{03}); see also Lipphardt, *Gesangbuchdrucke*, 17.

7 Berz, *Frankfurt am Main*, 22–24, and 133–136 where he discussed the music typeface found in all but their very first music edition (see fn. 6 above); Berz' discussion does not consider their first edition as it only came to his attention after his study was completed ('Nachträge', 280).

8 These typefaces have been categorised and discussed by Johnson, *Christian Egenolff*.

9 Vervliet, *Vine Leaf Ornaments*, p. 69, no. 8 (single leaf), p. 79, no. 13 (trifoliate leaf), and p. 112, no. 43 (single leaf).

10 Gustavson, *Competitive Strategy Dynamics*, 204–205.

THE MUSIC EDITIONS OF CHRISTIAN EGENOLFF   155

between states as 'Alterations which do not affect makeup and which were performed in the type-pages of a forme, whether intentionally or unintentionally, while it was printing'.[11] However, there is what Bowers calls an 'ideal copy', that is, a version of the book that the printer considered to be the most correct or that best represents the book. Here this does not exist, as there are two ideal copies, one for each title. Bowers defines 'issue' as follows:

> The publisher or bookseller of a separate issue should issue the book in some different form from the common issue, that this different form is specified in a press-altered title and is not merely an unpurposed variant state within his share of the edition, and finally that the form should reflect the different circumstances of issue or should be contrived for reasons affecting sale.[12]

Here there is a press-altered title, but technically the two versions are identical in form. Although there is no physical difference, there is one of perception. The different titles cause the purchaser to perceive the partbooks in different ways, one as a music edition and one as a poetry edition, and so the different titles were 'contrived for reasons affecting sale'. Brian McMullin has kindly considered this question for me and, based on the evidence of the title pages, is of the view that the *Odarum* and the *Melodiae* are separate, simultaneous issues rather than just being different states of the title page.[13]

Despite the two different titles, this is one edition that exists in two issues. As the woodcut on the title page of the *Odarum* is in a better condition than in the *Melodiae*, and the title pages of the Discantus and Bassus partbooks all read *Odarum Horatii concentus*, it can be inferred that the title-page of the *Odarum* was printed before that of the *Melodiae*. Because of the different titles, this edition has been catalogued as two separate editions in most bibliographies, at least since Gesner's *Pandectae* of 1548.[14]

The order of printing of the partbooks is unusual. The signatures in Egenolff's prints were always in the order single uppercase, then single lowercase, then other combinations. Therefore, the Tenor was printed first, then the Bassus. We need to draw on other evidence for the order of the two other partbooks. The final leaf of the Discantus is blank, but that of the Altus, while blank on the recto, has a full-page woodcut of two musicians on the verso. This implies that the Altus partbook is last, with the woodcut on the final page. The order is therefore TBDA. In all other sets of Egenolff partbooks where the order is known or can be inferred, it is TDBA. Although the BD are in reverse order here, the Altus is in its invariable position at the end.

2–4, 6–8 The extant sedecimos 1535–1536: overview

This group of editions is characterised by their format, oblong sedecimo. This is a very unusual format for printed music, and I know of no other editions in this format from the first half of the sixteenth century.[15] Each sheet of paper produced sixteen leaves or thirty-two pages, producing editions so small they could fit into a shirt pocket. These books were designed to be cheap. A complete set typically required only a few sheets of paper.

---

11 Bowers, *Principles*, 46.

12 Bowers, *Principles*, 101.

13 Brian McMullin, email of 25 January 2017.

14 Conrad Gesner, *Pandectarum . . . libri XXI* (Zurich: Christoph Froschauer, 1548), 83ʳ for the *Melodiae* and 84ᵛ for the *Odarum* (VD16 G 1699); see also Bernstein, 'The Bibliography', 147 (No. 144) and 154 (No. 231).

15 Laurent Guillo (email of 17 July 2015) informs me that the Genevan printers Simon Du Bosc and Guillaume Guéroult printed a series of books of motets or spiritual songs books in oblong sedecimo: RISM 1554¹²⁻¹³, 1555¹³⁻¹⁴, 1555¹⁶⁻¹⁷, 1556¹⁰⁻¹¹, [1558]⁸, [1559]⁴⁻⁵, C 2684–2685.

156   ROYSTON GUSTAVSON

The amount, and hence cost, of typesetting was reduced by supplying only the first stanza of each song in the Tenor partbook of the German- and Flemish-texted editions and incipits alone in the other nineteen partbooks, and there were no dedications or other preliminary texts.

Until now, only three of these editions have had a known title and date; only the Discantus partbooks, lacking the title and date, of the other three editions were believed to be extant. The most important contribution of this chapter is the identification of the titles of these three editions and the date of one of the editions by drawing on the *Bibliothecae Traiectinae Catalogus* (Utrecht: Rhodius, 1608), and the identification of the Tenor partbooks of the other two editions in the Schweizerische Landesbibliothek in Bern.

For more than two decades, I have been searching through early catalogues for references to early music prints. In the *Bibliothecae Traiectinae Catalogus*, three titles, in the section 'Libri Musici', all published at Frankfurt, caught my eye:

CANTIONES III. VOC. [fol. Qq1ᵛ]
Cantiones ſelectiſſimæ LXVIII. zu Francfurt. [fol. Qq2ᵛ]
CANTIONES IV. VOC. [fol. Qq2ᵛ]
Cantiones quatuor vocum, zu Francfurt. bis. [bis = Tenor] [fol. Qq3ʳ]
Brabandiſche Liedlin/zu Franckfurt. 1535. [the next entry on fol. Qq3ʳ].

A search on these titles in Google Books led me to a reference to the 'Cantiones selectissimae LXVIII' in a book celebrating the fiftieth anniversary of the Schweizerische Landesbibliothek.[16] A search of that library's catalogue brought up the Tenor partbook of that title, which is bound with the Tenor of the four-voice *Cantiones*. The title page of the four-voice *Cantiones* names Egenolff as printer, which is final proof of the long-accepted arguments that these are Egenolff prints. His extant sedecimo editions are therefore:

2   *Gassenhawerlin*, February 1535
3   *Reutterliedlin*, 1535
4   *Brabandische Liedlin*, 1535
6   *Reutterliedlin*, second edition, December 1536
7   *Cantiones vocum quatuor*, undated
8   *Cantiones selectissimae LXVIII vocum trium*, undated [hereafter *Cantiones vocum trium*].

We shall first discuss why these constitute a group, and what can be gleaned about the order in which they were printed. We shall then comment on each in turn.

Four of these titles (2, 3, 7, 8; and 6, which is a reprint of 3) consistently commence with new music, then reprint works sourced from German editions of the 1510s.[17] This shared pattern suggests that these collections were all compiled by the same editor. Three of the four songbooks on which the editor of Egenolff's sedecimo songbooks drew were printed by Peter Schöffer the Younger,[18] the other by Arnt von Aich:

---

16 Wissler, 'Die Musikalien', 89.

17 See Moser, introductory booklet to *Gassenhawerlin*; Bridgman, 'Christian Egenolff'; and Staehelin, 'Petruccis Canti B'.

18 Until the discovery of the Egenolff Tenor partbook it could not be determined whether Egenolff used Petrucci's *Canti B* or Schöffer's reprint, the *Quinquagena carminum*, as his source, as only the Tenor of Schöffer's edition is extant. Schöffer copies Petrucci very closely, however there are a very small number of differences,

[Liederbuch 3–4 St.] (Mainz: Peter Schöffer the Younger, 1513) RISM 1513², vdm 13
Quinquagena carminum (Mainz: Peter Schöffer the Younger, 1513), not in RISM, vdm 15
[36 Lieder] (Mainz: Peter Schöffer the Younger, 1517) RISM [c.1515]³, vdm 16
In dissem Buechlyn fynt man LXXV hubscher lieder (Cologne: Arnt von Aich, [1514/1515])
RISM [1519]⁵, vdm 17.

Egenolff reprints them as follows:

Gassenhawerlin: Nos. 17–20 = [36 Lieder] 18, 22, 29, 30; Nos. 21–28 = [Liederbuch 3–4
St.] 7, 8, 9, 13, 32, 46, 50, 54; Nos. 29–34, 37–39 = *In dissem Buechlyn*, Tenor partbook
2, 3, 5, 6, 50, 62, 40, 51, 35
Reutterliedlin Nos. 19–25 = [36 Lieder] 3, 11, 20, 27, 28, 35, 36; Nos. 26–27 = [Liederbuch
3–4 St.] 35, 51; Nos. 28–31, 33, 36 = *In dissem Buechlyn*, Tenor partbook 12, 20, 49, 45,
38, 46
Cantiones vocum quatuor Nos. 18–33 = *Quinquagena carminum* 7, 9–11, 13, 16, 15, 17–21,
25, 28, 31, 34
Cantiones vocum trium Nos. 14–25 = *Quinquagena carminum* 39–40, 42–51 (all of the three-
voice pieces).

The only sedecimo for which no earlier source print is known is the *Brabandische Liedlin*,
but I argue below that this too was a reprint, but of an entire earlier edition, rather than
drawing together material from several editions. It is also interesting that Egenolff gave
his songbooks titles only in German and Latin, even though the *Brabandische Liedlin* contains
works in Flemish and the *Cantiones vocum quatuor* contains mostly French chansons. The
unusual word order for the two Latin-titled editions, 'vocum [number]' rather than
'[number] vocum', further strengthens the argument that those two editions were edited
together.

A second feature that implies that the sedecimos are, or include, a group is the signatures.
The signature, which is essential for correct binding of a book, appears on the bottom right
hand of the front (recto) side of a leaf. It identifies the gathering to which each bifolium
belongs, and the specific place of that bifolium within that gathering. Egenolff normally
signed gatherings with a single uppercase letter. In editions that required more than a single
alphabet, for example in very long books, he differentiated groups of gatherings by using
first a sequence of uppercase letters, then lowercase, then other combinations, such as double
lowercase. When producing a set of partbooks, Egenolff needed to differentiate the partbooks so that the printed sheets would not become mixed up with each other, and to do
this he used the same idea: different combinations of uppercase and lowercase letters. We
can see this in the partbooks of the 1532 ode collection (Cat. 1), where the signatures are:

Uppercase: Tenor
Lowercase: Bassus
Double lowercase: Discantus
Uppercase and lowercase: Altus

---

and here Egenolff follows Schöffer. To give three examples, Egenolff fol. C6ʳ, stave 4, notes 8–9 are SB, dotted
SB in Egenolff and Schöffer but M M SB M in Petrucci; fol. C6ᵛ, stave 1, note 4 is a SB in Egenolff and Schöffer
but M M in Petrucci; Egenolff and Schöffer fol. D4ʳ, stave 1, have no repeat sign but there is one after the
brevis in Petrucci.

158   ROYSTON GUSTAVSON

The Waldis *Psalter* (Cat. 16), which although a single volume has enough leaves to require more than one alphabet, is signed uppercase, then lowercase, then double lowercase for the preliminaries, including index, which were printed last. Each title of the sedecimos had its partbooks signed using a single sequence. However, the style of signature used for each title differentiates it from the others:

> Uppercase: *Gassenhawerlin*, Feb. 1535; *Brabandische Liedlin*, 1535
> Lowercase: *Reutterliedlin*, 1535 (reprinted in 1536)
> Double lowercase: *Cantiones vocum trium*, undated
> Uppercase and lowercase: *Cantiones vocum quatuor*, undated.

Unless the different titles were printed either simultaneously or, more likely, sequentially, there would be no reason to differentiate them from each other by this method. If all five titles were a set, then it would be unexpected that two – the *Gassenhawerlin* and *Brabandische Liedlin* – use the same signature pattern of single uppercase, as there are many signature patterns that were available but not used (for example, double uppercase). We can infer that one of these two prints is not part of the 'set'. The *Gassenhawerlin* and *Reutterliedlin* are surely a pair owing to their method of compilation, a claim strengthened by their being reprinted in 1552 in a combined edition as the *Gassenhawer und Reutterliedlin*. As the *Reutterliedlin* is the only title signed with single lowercase, we can infer that its pair was the *Gassenhawerlin* and therefore that the *Brabandische Liedlin* is not part of the set. In addition to the duplication of the uppercase signatures there are other reasons, discussed below, why the *Brabandische Liedlin* is unlikely to be part of the 'set' of partbooks consisting of the other sedecimos. As noted earlier, there is no established signature pattern that allows us to determine whether uppercase+lowercase was used before or after double lowercase. To order the two volumes of *Cantiones* within the catalogue, I turn to evidence from other prints. The *Quinquagena carminum* commences with a section for four-voice works and concludes with a section for three-voice works; the sections are also differentiated by an index for four-voice works and an index for three-voice works. The *Liber selectarum cantionum* (Augsburg: Grimm & Wyrsung, 1520; vdm 18) and the *Novum et insigne opus musicum* (Nuremberg: Formschneider, 1537; vdm 35) both commence with six-voice works, then move on to five-voice works, then conclude with four-voice works. Based on this contemporary practice, our Catalogue orders the print with the larger number of voices first, followed by that for the smaller number of voices. This is consistent with Egenolff naming himself as the printer on the title page of the *Cantiones vocum quatuor*, but not on the title page of its companion, the *Cantiones vocum trium*.

The ornaments used in the printing link some of the editions. The *Gassenhawerlin* and *Cantiones vocum trium* have woodcuts of birds, the most musical of animals, on their title pages; although the woodcuts are of different birds, they are from the same set. The *Cantiones vocum quatuor* and the second edition of the *Reutterliedlin* each have the same woodcuts of a lute and a bagpipe, with the former also having a hurdy-gurdy and the latter a viola da gamba from what appear to be the same 'set' of woodcuts; these two editions also use Vine Leaf 43 on their title pages, whereas Vine Leaves 8 and 13 are used in the three prints that bear the date 1535, namely the *Gassenhawerlin*, the first edition of the *Reutterliedlin*, and the *Brabandische Liedlin*.

The watermarks give further clues. None of the partbooks of the 1535 *Reutterliedlin* has a watermark. The 1535 *Gassenhawerlin* has crowns and a lily. All of the other sedecimos have one or more oxheads, detailed in the catalogue, and in each edition there is at least one paper in which the oxhead is over a posthorn. The only other print that bears the date 1535, the *Brabandische Liedlin*, has (i) an oxhead over which is a letter T, and (ii) an oxhead under which is a small posthorn and over which is a clover leaf; both of these watermark types are included in Piccard's catalogue with their source given as a non-music Egenolff print, the *Chronica* (VD16 E 57, exemplar at D-Sl HB b 368), the colophon of which is dated August 1535. Most interesting is that one paper, an oxhead with a letter T over it and a large posthorn under it, appears in both volumes of the *Cantiones* and in the second edition of the *Reuttterliedlin*.

The poor survival-rate of these sedecimos means that the surviving exemplars provide relatively little additional evidence about their interrelationships. None of the extant editions is complete. Of the twenty-three partbooks that originally constituted these six editions, eight are completely lost, one is fragmentary, and only one survives in more than one exemplar. We can therefore make few assumptions based on the surviving copies. While the presence of three non-German texted editions in the *Bibliothecae Traiectinae Catalogus* would seem to provide evidence that further identifiable exemplars existed in the past, there is good evidence that the exemplars listed in the Utrecht collection are those now held in Paris. The former owner of the Paris partbooks was a nineteenth-century collector in Utrecht, Jan Jacob Nahuys (1801–1864), whose stamp is found on the title pages. The names of two earlier owners inscribed in the books, 'J. Goude' and 'Jan van Dijck' are also Dutch. It is likely then that the exemplar formerly in the Utrecht collection is that now in Paris. The Zwickau exemplars of the *Gassenhawerlin* and *Reutterliedlin* are bound together in an early binding, while those of the *Cantiones* partbooks in Bern are bound together in a modern library paper and cardboard binding. But as noted earlier, these are the only sedecimo polyphonic music editions from the first half of the sixteenth century, and so they could not be bound with any other editions available on the market at that time. Consequently, these tiny editions were more likely than others to go missing, which also means that there may be other, lost editions (including a second edition of the *Gassenhawerlin*).

The minimum possible period over which the extant and postulated sedecimos could have been printed may help to determine the minimum dating parameters. First, we need to consider the print run. Evidence presented by Heartz, Agee, Lewis, Blackburn and others suggests that musical editions were generally printed in runs of 500 or 1000.[19] This is consistent with the conclusions of Gaskell, who writes that the standard unit of work for the operator of a printing press was a token of 250 sheets, resulting in 'a strong tendency for edition sizes to be exact multiples of this'.[20] To be conservative in our calculations, we will assume a print run of 1000. One copy of each of the sedecimos would require sixty-seven sheets of paper and the setting of 134 formes of type. According to McKenzie, the operator of a press could print at a maximum some 3000 impressions per day, six days per week.[21] If the print run were 1000 copies and the seven editions were printed consecutively, the printing of the 134 formes would at maximum working speed take forty-five working days or seven and a half weeks. We also need to consider the rate of typesetting. McKenzie writes that an experienced typesetter could typeset up to 10,000 to 12,000 letters per day.[22]

---

19 Heartz, *Pierre Attaingnant*, 120–122; Agee, 'A Venetian Music Printing Contract', 59–64; Lewis, *Antonio Gardano*, 87–89; and Blackburn, 'The Printing Contract', 347.

20 Gaskell, *A New Introduction*, 124.

21 McKenzie, 'Printers', 8.

22 McKenzie, 'Printers', 8.

160   ROYSTON GUSTAVSON

Counting the number of pieces of type on Bassus C1 and C2, we get an average of 122 pieces of type per page. These books, set in sedecimo (sixteen pages per forme) thus had some 2000 pieces of type per forme. A compositor could thus set five or six such formes per day. A compositor who produced five formes a day would take twenty-seven working days to typeset 134 formes. As each forme would be printed soon after it was typeset (as there was always a limited supply of type), printing these seven sets of sedecimos sequentially could have been completed in not more than seven and a half weeks.

To conclude: evidence suggests that four of the sedecimos form a set, with the *Brabandische Liedlin* not being part of the set. The two *Cantiones* editions are not dated, but as part of a set their date will be identical to that of the dated volumes from the same set. If they were printed with the first edition of the *Reutterliedlin* and *Gassenhawerlin*, they will be dated 1535. If they were printed with the second edition of the *Reutterliedlin* (and a lost second edition of the *Gassenhawerlin*), they will be dated 1536. There is little to link the *Cantiones* prints with the 1535 editions, but they are linked to the 1536 editions by the common use of the woodcuts of musical instruments, the use of vine leaf 43, and the overlap of watermarks. The evidence leads to the conclusion that the *Cantiones* editions were printed in about December 1536. I shall now turn to comments on the individual editions.

2–3 *Gassenhawerlin and Reutterliedlin. 1535*

I have argued above that the first two sedecimos printed by Egenolff were the *Gassenhawerlin* and *Reutterliedlin*. Each required only seven and a half sheets of paper. These two books, which are similar in content and appealed to the same market, were published as two separate titles, suggesting that the market was price-sensitive. To publish them as a combined edition, as Egenolff did in 1552, would have doubled the price. Unfortunately, the Discantus partbook of the 1535 edition of neither the *Gassenhawerlin* nor *Reutterliedlin* survives. Möller identified these prints, described as having 'vier kleine partes', in a 1617 catalogue of the Ratsschulbibliothek in Zwickau. In 1877 Eitner described all partbooks as present, but in 1896 Vollhardt noted that the Discantus partbooks were missing.[23] It is perhaps surprising that the Discantus partooks went missing, rather than the Tenor as it contained the full texts. Curiously, the missing Discantus partbook of the *Novum et insigne opus musicum* in the Bischöfliche Zentralbibliothek in Regensburg (shelfmark A. R. 58–61) also went missing in the late nineteenth century; inserted in its Contratenor partbook is a letter from J. J. Maier in Munich requesting to borrow the Discantus partbook, presumably to assist him with cataloguing the music collection of what is now the Bayerische Staatsbibliothek. As Munich has only the later combined edition of the *Gassenhawerlin* and *Reutterliedlin*, it is possible that Maier also requested to borrow the Discantus of these editions from Zwickau.

4 *Brabandische Liedlin. 1535*

The title and date of this print were unknown until I identified both in the *Bibliothecae Traiectinae Catalogus*. The date of the edition has long been debated, especially because of its relationship to the so-called 'Kamper Liedboek', printed beautifully by a double-impression process, but of which only fragments remain. Scholars had assumed that the 'Kamper Liedboek' was a reprint of the Egenolff edition until in 2001 I argued that it was the other way around.[24] The fragments include neither title nor date; they had been dated

---

23 Möller, 'Notenkataloge', 17; Eitner, *Sammelwerke*, 34–35; and Vollhardt, *Musik-Werke Zwickau*, 66.
24 Gustavson, 'Egenolff', 101.

THE MUSIC EDITIONS OF CHRISTIAN EGENOLFF   161

*c.*1541 until David Fallows re-dated them to *c.*1535.[25] From the secure dating of the *Brabandische Liedlin* to 1535 we can infer that these two editions were each reprinted independently from an earlier, lost edition. The earlier edition surely included texts for each song, as texts are underlaid in the surviving fragments of the 'Kamper Liedboek', and were probably included in the Tenor of the Egenolff edition. The surviving Egenolff Discantus, signed G–K^{8}L^4 (36 leaves) includes only text incipits; the lost Tenor, almost certainly signed either A–E^{8}F^4 (44 leaves) or A–F^8 (48 leaves) had an additional 8 or 12 leaves, which is most likely explained by inclusion of one stanza of text for each song.

Egenolff inexplicably omits one of the songs included in the 'Kamper Liedboek', 'Alsoe sy seet'. There is no obvious reason for this, as it is not duplicated in any of the other sedecimo editions. I suggest that there was physical damage to the exemplar used as the basis for Egenolff's edition such that this Lied had to be omitted. Another Lied, 'Druck en verdriet' (no. 29), also appears in the *Cantiones vocum quatuor* (no. 7), although there are minor differences in the readings, including the retention of the so-called 'Landini cadence' in the latter.

There are three characteristics of this print that differentiate it from the other sedecimos. First, it appears to have reprinted an entire earlier edition, rather than being a compilation of earlier editions. Second, there is a duplication of one song between this and one of the other sedecimos, and we would not expect a duplicate song in a set. Third, it duplicates the use of capital letters for the signatures used by one of the other sedecimos. Together, these raise questions about the relationship of the *Brabandische Liedlin* to the other sedecimos, and lead to the conclusion that it was not part of the 'set' of four editions.

5 The lost Gassenhawerlin. [Second edition]. [c. December 1536]

A second edition of the *Reutterliedlin* is extant (Cat. 6 below), but there is no known second edition of the *Gassenhawerlin*. These two titles were printed as a pair in both their first edition in 1535 and their combined edition in 1552, which suggests that they may have been printed as a pair in a second edition. The signature patterns of Cat. 6, 7 and 8 below suggest that a print signed with single uppercase letters is missing from the 1536 series, and the 1535 edition of the *Gassenhawerlin* had that signature pattern. As such, it is hypothesised that there is a lost 1536 edition of the *Gassenhawerlin*.

6 Reutterliedlin. [Second edition]. December 1536

The commercial success of the *Reutterliedlin* may be inferred from the printing of a second edition the following year. The 1536 edition contains many small differences in typesetting.

7 Cantiones vocum quatuor. [c. December 1536]

The title of this edition was unknown in the literature on Egenolff and to modern bibliography until now. The sole surviving copy of the Tenor partbook of this title and of the *Cantiones vocum trium* (see Cat. 8 below) entered the Schweizerische Landesbibliothek in Bern in the 1890s from a private collection,[26] but has gone unnoticed by scholars since then. Despite its title, the songs in the *Cantiones vocum quatuor* are almost all in French. This reminds us of the lost *Viginti cantiunculae Gallicae quatuor vocum*, first published by Schöffer

---

25 Fallows, 'Songbook at Kampen', 352.

26 Email dated 06 August 2015 from Andreas Berz, Information Services, Swiss National Library. It was not located by RISM Switzerland in their major project of cataloguing early music in Swiss libraries, and so is included in neither Schanzlin, 'Musik-Sammeldrucke', nor RISM.

162   ROYSTON GUSTAVSON

in 1530 (vdm 895). David Fallows has considered whether Schöffer's edition may have been another of the sources used in the compilation of this Egenolff edition.[27] The woodcuts on both the title page and in the print are of musical instruments, not singers; given that there are incipits only, with no full texts, this may have signalled that the print was intended for performance on instruments rather than for singing.

8 Cantiones vocum trium. [c. December 1536]

Although there have been important studies of this edition, including one by Bridgman and two by Staehelin,[28] Egenolff's edition of three-voice songs has been virtually ignored in the literature on the *tricinium*, presumably because until now it was thought that only a single printed partbook had survived. The location of a complete Tenor partbook in Bern, joining the long-known Discantus partbook in Paris and the manuscript copy of thirty-one of the *tricinia* from the Bassus in Heilbronn (D-HB X/2, nos. 1–31)[29] means that thirty-one of the *tricinia* are now complete in Egenolff's readings. Hopefully, this will ignite further interest in this source.

The edition opens with 'Ich hab mich recht gehaltē' by 'H. Heyg' (Hans Heugel), which is dated '15 Februarij: Anno 1535' in a manuscript copied by Heugel.[30] According to Cramer, dates in the Heugel manuscripts indicate dates of composition, not dates of copying.[31] Moser hypothesised that Heugel was Egenolff's musical adviser.[32] However, Müller dismissed this hypothesis, pointing to the fact that only two of Heugel's more than seventy known Lieder appear in Egenolff's collections.[33] Gottwald suggested that the manuscript revives the discussion as to whether Heugel was Egenolff's musical advisor.[34] However, on the balance of the evidence, I suggest that this can be ruled out.

Overview of Egenolff's 'First Period': 1532–c. December 1536

Egenolff's first eight music editions appeared between 1532 and 1536, with no further music editions for more than a decade. They each required only a few sheets of paper (between 7.5 and 15 sheets per title) and hence were cheap. They all consist of secular polyphony. There is no monophonic music. There is no sacred music (apart from a very small number of songs in mostly secular anthologies). They characteristically reprinted earlier volumes complete, or were primarily compiled from earlier volumes. The languages of the texts were varied: Latin, German, French and Flemish. Apart from the Tenor of the *Gassenhawerlin*,

---

27 Fallows, 'Songbooks of Christian Egenolff', 361 and 368.

28 Bridgman, 'Christian Egenolff', Staehelin, 'Zum Egenolff-Diskantband' and Staehelin, 'Petruccis Canti B'.

29 This was postulated in Staehelin, 'Zum Egenolff-Diskantband,' 94–95, and is strengthened by the new evidence of the composer ascriptions which in the printed edition are only in the Tenor partbook. A comparison of the composer attributions in the Heilbronn manuscript with those in the Egenolff Tenor produces an almost perfect match. The only exception is that the very first work in the manuscript, which is attributed to 'Adrianus Wilhart' but which in the printed edition (no. 47) has no composer attribution; the same work gives a longer text incipit, 'Cedant par moy' in the manuscript than the 'Cedant' in the printed edition. The positioning of this work as the opening piece of the manuscript suggests that it was already known to the copyist. A scan of the Heilbronn manuscript is available online at https://stadtarchiv.heilbronn.de/fileadmin/daten/stadtarchiv/online-publikationen/06-musikschatz.pdf.

30 D-Kl 8° Ms. Mus. 53b, fol. 40^v, online at http://orka.bibliothek.uni-kassel.de/viewer/image/1292414993290/85/; see Siegele, *Die Musiksammlung Heilbronn*, 47.

31 Cramer, *Johannes Heugel*, 18 and 163–65.

32 Moser, *Gassenhawerlin*, 2.

33 Müller, 'Die Liederdrucke', 217.

34 Gottwald, *Manuscripta Musica*, 793.

Reutterliedlin and presumably the *Brabandische Liedlin*, the other nineteen song partbooks only contained text incipits, presumably to save costs. Even where there was a full text, it was not underlaid to the music: an incipit appeared at the beginning of the music and the text appeared in a block at the end of each Lied. It is unclear why Egenolff suddenly stopped printing music at this time, as his other printing activities continued unabated. One possibility is competition. Öglin, Schöffer, and Arnt von Aich printed several Lied anthologies between 1512 and 1517. There was a long hiatus, interrupted only by Johann Walther's *Geistliche Gesangbüchlein* (1524, 1525; vdm 110 and 111), until after the introduction of single impression music printing in Germany in 1532. Hans Ott published his *121 Newe Lieder* in 1534 (vdm 20). Schöffer published his *65 Lieder* in c.1536 (vdm 27), which still used the technique of double impression that he had perfected. It was into this newly invigorated market that Egenolff put forth his 1535 editions. He was clearly successful, as he printed the two *Cantiones* editions and reprinted the *Gassenhawerlin* and *Reutterliedlin* in 1536, the same year in which Ott published the second volume of his Lied anthology, under the title *Schöne auszerlesne Lieder* (vdm 425). Petreius printed Georg Forster's two-volume Lied anthology in 1539 and 1540 (vdm 48 and 53), and reprinted it in 1543. In 1544, Berg & Neuber printed Hans Ott's third Lied collection (vdm 1027), and Petreius released Wolfgang Schmeltzel's collection (vdm 1026). The same happened for collections of three-voice works. There was a suddenly increased demand for the *tricinium* in southern Germany from the late 1530s, reflected in the publication of Formschneider's *Trium vocum carmina* in 1538 (vdm 41), Kugelman's *Concentus novi trium vocum* in 1540 (vdm 52), Petreius' *Trium vocum cantiones centum* in 1541 (vdm 1021), and Rhaw's *Tricinia* in 1542 (vdm 1023). It would appear that in the face of this competition, Egenolff turned his attention away from music for more than a decade, until his 'Second Period' of music printing from 1550 to 1553.

9 The lost Gesangbüchlin. Before August 1550

The lost *Gesangbüchlin* from 1550 (or very improbably the late 1540s) is very unlike the editions of the first period as it was an edition of sacred music. It is known only from a letter from Erasmus Alber to Hartmann Beyer dated 24 August 1550:

> Please ask Egenolph to send me his little book of songs, which he published so that the common people might sing them in church. Amongst these are some of my own too. I shall organise that all forty of my songs be printed together. If Egenolph wishes, I shall send them to him to be printed. [. . .] There are still some letters (as Heinrich writes) in his house, which were amongst my books. Have them all packed up so that they can be sent to me, as well as my translation of Aesop [fabulę meę], and with them Egenolph's little song book [gesangbuchlin].[35]

The dating of this edition is contested. Bill dates it to 1550, the year in which the letter was written, but Lipphardt, questioning Bill's methodology dates it to 1546–1549; Bill subsequently questioned Lipphardt's interpretation.[36] Since the 'fabulę meę' surely refers

---

35 Erasmus Alber to Hartmann Beyer, 24 August 1550 (in D-F Ms.Ff.H.Beyer A 17, see: http://kalliope-verbund.info/DE-611-HS-66573), ed. in Schnorr von Carolsfeld, *Erasmus Alberus*, 205: 'Egenolphum roges vt mittat mihi libellum suarum Cantilenarum: quas edidit pro vulgo in templis cantandas: in quibus et meę aliquae sunt: curabo enim vt omnes meę Cantilenę numero 40: simul imprimantur. Si Egenolphus vult: mittam ei imprimendas. [. . .] Es sind noch brieffe (sicut scribit Henricus) in seinem Hause, die vnter meinen bücheln gewest, die last alle zusamen packen das sie mir geschickt werden, vnd fabulę meę darzw sampt Egenolphi gesangbuchlin.' I am grateful to Grantley McDonald for the translation. This passage was also cited and discussed by Bill, *Das Frankfurter Gesangbuch*, 12–13; and Lipphardt, *Gesangbuchdrucke*, 206–207.

36 Bill, *Das Frankfurter Gesangbuch*, 12; Lipphardt, *Gesangbuchdrucke*, 47, 206–207; and Bill, 'Besprechung', 191.

164   ROYSTON GUSTAVSON

to Alber's adaption of Aesop's fables, *Das buch von der Tugent vnd Weißheit/ nemlich/ Neunvndviertzig Fabeln* (Frankfurt a.M.: Peter Braubach, 1550 [VD16 A 553]), we can conclude that the *Gesangbüchlin* may also have been published in 1550. Alber's hymn texts were published frequently, usually without printed music. However, some editions that included hymn texts by Alber also included printed music, such as the *Psalmen . . . mit Christlichen Gesengen gemehrt* published by Egenolff's heirs (RISM VIII DKL 1565^{03}). Although the nature of this *Gesangbüchlin* cannot be determined with confidence, it is probable that it contained music, like the 1565 edition published by Egenolff's heirs.

10 Spangenberg. Hymni. 1550

The *Hymni ecclesiastici duodecim* (1550) is a Latin translation by Reinhard Lorichius of Johann Spangenberg's *Zwölff Christliche Lobgesenge* (1545), a collection of well-known hymn texts set to music, each followed by a commentary.[37] It should be noted that only Spangenberg's commentaries were translated into Latin: the German hymn texts underlaid to the printed music remained in German. The single edition of the *Hymni* appeared in two separate issues, the technical justification for which is the same as that for the 1532 odes (Cat. 1 above). Like the 1532 odes, this was surely for marketing purposes to make the edition attractive to multiple audiences.

The first issue, the *Postilla* issue, is titled, in translation, 'Postil. The Gospels and the Epistles for Sundays and Feast Days throughout the year . . . Also Hymns of the Highest Feasts'. It is a 2000-page pedagogical work set out in question and answer format, subdivided into four sections: (i) the Gospels for Sundays throughout the year, (ii) the Epistles (*Epistolae*), (iii) the Gospels for Feast Days throughout the year (*De festis praecipuis*), and (iv) the Hymns (*Hymni*). Each of these sections was printed with its own title page and colophon, its own series of signatures beginning with A, and its own foliation beginning with 1 (excluding the *Hymni* which is not foliated). The third section, *De festis praecipuis*, is signed in double lowercase (commencing aa), clearly differentiating the pages from those of the other sections, just as the lack of foliation in the *Hymni* differentiates its pages from those of the other sections. As such, the *Postilla* could be sold as a single title, or as four separate titles, or as combinations of titles. Of the four titles, only the *Hymni* contains printed music. It consists of sixty leaves, including a blank leaf at the end, and so appears in some bibliographies as containing fifty-nine leaves. It has its own series of signatures, A–G^{8}H^4, but neither pagination nor foliation. At the end of the edition (H3^r) is the date 1550. Although the *Postilla* represents only a single issue of a single edition, the *Hymni* was available as the fourth section of the *Postilla*; or as part of a separate two-section *De festis praecipuis*, which names the *Hymni* on its title page ('Item, hymni ecclesiastici . . .'); or separately as the *Hymni*. For clarity, although only the *Postilla* appears in the catalogue as a separate issue, the *De festis praecipuis* and *Hymni* are noted as part of the entry as different ways in which the issue was made available.

The second issue is distinguished by typographical changes to the title page of the *Hymni*. As with the 1532 odes, the print run of the sheet containing the title page was stopped part way through and the name of a separate work, the *Funebres*, was added. Examination of the title pages of the first and second issues of the *Hymni* reveals that this addition was decided before printing of the first issue began, as most of the title page used the same

---

37 The discussion of this print draws on, but supersedes, that in Gustavson, 'Competitive Strategy Dynamics', 205–206.

THE MUSIC EDITIONS OF CHRISTIAN EGENOLFF   165

setting of type. For example, on both title pages, the first *c* in *Ecclesia* is slightly higher than the second *c*. Egenolff has packaged this product in a number of different ways, one of which, the *Hymni* alone, was as a music edition. This is clearly clever marketing.

11 Nigidius, ed. Odes. 1551

In 1548, Melchior Sachse in Erfurt published Petrus Nigidius' *Isagogicus rerum grammaticarum libellus in usum rudium puerorum*, which closed with a section of nine polyphonic ode settings (Y7ʳ–Z8ʳ).[38] Egenolff republished this edition, but divided it into two separate editions: one, the *Isagogicus* (VD16 N 1745), containing the verbal text and the other, the *Geminae undeviginti odarum Horatii melodiae*, containing a massively expanded edition of the music which, in addition to six odes from the Sachse edition, contains the Tritonius Odes of 1532 (Cat. 1), the settings of the same texts by Michael from fols. F3ᵛ–I4ʳ of Theobald Billican, *De partium orationis inflexionibus* ([Augsburg: Ruff], 1526),[39] and an additional thirty-two ode settings. This splitting of the Sachse edition into two separate editions is typical of Egenolff, as it allowed purchasers to select either both, or just one, of the editions according to their interests. Additionally, Egenolff's edition in partbooks means that performance required just one set of partbooks, rather than four copies of Sachse's text and music edition.

The dedication of both editions is dated August 1550 and signed 'Marpurgi, ex ædibus pædagogij' (*Isagogicus* fol. A3ᵛ, *Geminae* fol. A3ʳ). However, although the *Isagogicus* is dated 1551 and the Altus partbook of the *Geminae* is dated June 1551, the Tenor partbook is dated May 1552. It is improbable that the Tenor was printed a year after the Altus, and so the year printed in one of the partbooks is evidently incorrect. It is very unusual for a set of partbooks to have a colophon other than in the Tenor, but here there is additionally a colophon in the Altus. A possible reason is that as the signatures in the edition are sequenced Tenor (A–G), Discantus (H–K), Bassus (L–N), Altus (O–P). The final page of the Altus was the final page of the edition and so included a colophon where it would typically be found in a book: at the end of the final gathering. Indeed, sets of partbooks of this edition were in some cases bound together in a single volume ordered TDBA (as was also frequently the case for the 1532 odes above). The sequencing of the signatures is consistent with the month in the Tenor, May, preceding that in the Altus, June. It may be concluded that the year 1552 given in the Tenor partbook is incorrect, and the year 1551 in the Altus intended as a correction.

12–15 The octavo Lied anthologies: overview

Egenolff published four Lied anthologies in oblong octavo format. None of the Tenor partbooks survives; none of the other partbooks transmit the date of publication, and partbooks for only two of the anthologies transmit the title. Three of the anthologies were dated in RISM to 1535, and the other to 1536. Müller realized that two of them, the *Gassenhawer und Reutterliedlin* and the *Graszliedlin*, included fourteen and three Lieder respectively

---

38 The 1548 edition printed in Erfurt by Melchior Sachse d. Ä. is not in the VD16. That the edition contains polyphonic music has been known in the literature since at least the nineteenth century from Schmidt, *Geschichte der Pädagogik*, p. 159: 'worin . . . mehrstimmig gesetzte Gesänge zur Einübung der Metra sich finden.' The only known extant exemplar is D-OB F 341; the exemplar at D-Kl Philol. 420. 8° was destroyed in 1941. As D-OB is closed until 2018 owing to renovations, I am grateful to Sonja Tröster for sharing her photographs of the music in this print with me.

39 VD16 G 1564 and H 4957; vdm 137. Although the 1526 edition of Michael's odes is often cited as lost, it was identified as this Billican edition a century ago by Henry Thomas, 'Musical Settings', 83. Further on Michael's ode-settings, see the chapter by Sonja Tröster in this volume.

166   ROYSTON GUSTAVSON

from Ott's 1544 anthology (RISM 1544[20]), and so must post-date Ott's edition.[40] Several pieces of evidence, taken together, allow us to provide a title for the two editions that lack a title, and a date for each.

The first piece of evidence is a catalogue of the books available from Egenolff's heirs at the 1579 Frankfurt book fair, which lists books printed by both Egenolff himself and by his heirs. The catalogue exists in two forms: a manuscript submitted to the *Bücher-kommission* in Vienna, and a printed broadsheet, 'CATALOGVS LIBRORVM, HAEREDVM TY⸗‖POGRAPHIAE EGENOLPHICAE FRANCOFORTI AD MOENVM. ‖ [at end:] M. D. LXXIX. ‖'.[41] Günter Richter, who discussed and transcribed the manuscript and identified most of the editions, concluded that the manuscript was prepared before the printed version.[42] I have re-transcribed the music titles in the manuscript. In addition to the 'Horatij Melodiæ 8ᵘᵒ' (fol. 44ʳ; our Cat. 11) and the 'Pſalter geſangsweiß 8ᵘᵒ' (fol. 45ᵛ; our Cat. 16), it includes the following list on fol. 47ʳ:

> Gaſſenhawer. 8ᵘᵒ.
> Newgeborne/ 8ᵘᵒ.
> Oberlendiſche 8ᵘᵒ.   } Liedlein
> Graſliedlein 8ᵘᵒ.
> Geiſtliche gaſſenhawer
> Chriſtliche liedlein

Richter identifies the first as our Cat. 15, does not identify the second or third, identifies the fourth as our Cat. 14, and the last two as our Cat. F and Cat. G, Heinrich Knaust's *Gassenhawer, Reuter, und Bergliedlin, Christlich, moraliter, unnd sittlich verendert*, printed without music by Egenolff's heirs. Richter bases his identification of the Knaust on earlier entries in the Catalogue under 'Germanica Ihn der Theologj' which he transcribes as 'Christliche gassenhauer Knastij 8ᵘᵒ' and 'Christliche Lieder Knaustij 8ᵘᵒ' (fol. 45ʳ).

The printed broadsheet includes the same items, the 'Horatij melodiæ, in 8' among the 'Varii libri latini', the 'Pſalter geſangsweiſe/in 8' among the 'Germanica in der Theologi', and the following titles among the 'Allerhandt Teütsche Bücher':

> Liedlin { Chriſtliche Liedlin.
>   Gaſſenhauwer.
>   Geiſtliche Gaſſenhauwer.
>   Graßliedlin.
>   Neuwgeborne.
>   Oberlåndiſche.

Here the titles in the bracket are given in alphabetical order, but in the manuscript there is no discernible internal ordering, which supports Richter's argument, noted above, that the printed version post-dates the manuscript version. These two book lists both include two unidentified Lied editions, the *Newgeborne* and the *Oberlåndiſche*. I have suggested elsewhere that these two titles could refer to the two Egenolff Lied octavos without a title,

---

40 Müller, 'Die Liederdrucke', 29, 73.
41 The manuscript is at A-Whh RHR Bücherkommission im Reich 1–36, online reference at www.archivinformationssystem.at/detail.aspx?ID=3278329. The broadsheet is at D-Mbs Einbl. VIII,7 bc.
42 Richter, 'Christian Egenolffs Erben', 806–812 and 865–873.

THE MUSIC EDITIONS OF CHRISTIAN EGENOLFF   167

the [56 Lieder] and the [65 Lieder], but that it could not be determined which was which.[43] Müller also considered this question, but after weighing the evidence he concluded that at least one, if not both of these Lied editions have been lost.[44] Information not known when either of us was writing settles this question.

Richard Charteris, in his book on the music collection of Johann Georg von Werdenstein, transcribed the 1592 inventory prepared for the sale of Werdenstein's music collection to Duke Wilhelm V of Bavaria, now in the Bayerische Staatsbibliothek.[45] Almost all of the editions from Werdenstein's collection are still extant in Munich, and so Charteris compared the Werdenstein catalogue against the library's present holdings, and identified Werdenstein's 'Oberländiſche Neẅe Liedlein 65. Franckfŭrt. 1552. 8°. ‖ partes 4'[46] as Mus.pr.46, which is in its original binding. The identification of a title for Mus.pr.46 had not previously been made as the Tenor, which contained the title and presumably the publication details, was missing by 1795.[47] Where multiple items were bound together, the Werdenstein catalogue only lists the first, but Mus.pr.46 includes two of the three other editions named in the Egenolff catalogues, the *Graßliedlin* and the *Gassenhawer Liedlin*. There can therefore be no doubt that the first print in Mus.pr.46 is Egenolff's *Oberländische Liedlin* referred to in the 1579 Catalogues.

There is yet another reference to the *Oberländische Liedlin*. Uhland noted that an 'Oberländiſche Liedlein' was recorded in the systematic catalogue [volume 3, fol. 94ᵛ] of the Church Library (now the Nicolaus-Matz-Bibliothek) in Michelstadt compiled in 1630, but that it was missing.[48] This reference has been noted by others, including Müller, who cited a fuller transcription by Walter Albach as 'Oberländische neue Liedlein unterschiedlicher Autorum'.[49] However, none of the transcriptions of this catalogue entry has included a key piece of information. All of the bound items in the catalogue are numbered, and this entry appears between number 58 and a duplicated number 58 as the last of a group of three editions under the heading 'Vngebunden' as '65. Oberlendische Neẅe Liedlein, vntersc[hied]‖licher autorum.'[50] Previous scholars erroneously assumed that the '65' is the entry number of the book in the catalogue, but it is part of the title. Thus, Müller did not make the connection between the 'Oberländische neue Liedlein' and the [65 Lieder]. He also knew that the title of the Schöffer edition that Egenolff reprinted was the 'Fünff vnd ‖ ſechzig teütſcher ‖ Lieder/ vormals ‖ im̄ truck nie uß ‖ gangen. ‖' (vdm 27) which is a very different title, and apart from the number of songs there is no identifying link between the two.

As the [65 Lieder] is the *Oberländische Liedlin* and the [56 Lieder] is the only remaining unidentified Lied edition in the 1579 Egenolff catalogues, then by a process of elimination the latter edition is surely the *Newgeborne Liedlin*.

---

43 Gustavson, 'Egenolff', 99–100.

44 Müller, 'Die Liederdrucke', 30–32.

45 Charteris, *Werdenstein*, 58–199.

46 D-Mbs Cbm Cat. 121 t, fol. 64ᵛ, No. 7, which I transcribed from microfilm; see also Charteris, *Werdenstein*, 178.

47 Johann Baptist Bernhart, 'CATALOGVS LIBRORVM MVSICORVM TVM MANVSCRIPTORVM TVM IMPRESSORVM, IN ELECTORALI BIBLIOTHECA BAVARICA MONACENSI ASSERVATORVM', preface dated 29 July 1795, manuscript, B-Br Fétis 5179, at 233–234.

48 Uhland, *Alte hoch- und niederdeutsche Volkslieder*, 979, fn.* [sic].

49 Müller, 'Die Liederdrucke', 32.

50 I am grateful to Erwin Müller, Nicolaus-Matz-Bibliothek, for sending me colour scans of the section 'Libri Musici', email of 22 October 2015, and to Grantley McDonald for assisting me with the transcription.

168   ROYSTON GUSTAVSON

Like the sedecimo Lied anthologies, these editions were planned systematically. While the *Oberländische Liedlin* is a complete reprint of a set of partbooks printed by Schöffer in the mid 1530s, we know little of the precursor or precursors to the *Newgeborne Liedlin*. Between them, the *Oberländische Liedlin* and *Newgeborne Liedlin* contain five Lieder included in the 1535 editions of the *Gassenhawerlin* and *Reutterliedlin*, but which were removed in the combined 1552 edition of the *Gassenhawer und Reutterliedlin*.[51] From this we can infer that the editing of the *Oberländische Liedlin* and *Newgeborne Liedlin* was finalised before the editor's decision to remove them from the *Gassenhawer und Reutterliedlin*. The deletion of duplicate works from the combined reprint was deliberate as buyers would resent duplication among volumes. Lieder from Ott's 1544 anthology *Hundert vnd fünfftzehen guter newer Liedlein* were incorporated into two of the four editions: fourteen (of eighteen added Lieder) into the reprint of the *Gassenhawer und Reutterliedlin*, and three at the end of the *Graszliedlin*, which links these two editions. They are also linked as they are the only two of these four editions that have the title of the collection printed on the title page of each partbook, whereas the *Oberländische Liedlin* and *Newgeborne Liedlin* follow the norm and have the title printed only in the Tenor. Taken together, all of this implies that the *Gassenhawer und Reutterliedlin, Oberländische Liedlin, Newgeborne Liedlin* and *Graszliedlin* belong to the same complex or 'set'.

A very unusual typographical feature shared by these editions is the presence of a signature on the title page of each partbook (except presumably the lost Tenor); these are the only instances from this period in Germany of which I am aware that a signature appears on the title pages of the Discantus, Altus and Bassus partbooks. Single capitals are used for the signatures of three of the editions, but the *Gassenhawer und Reutterliedlin* uses lowercase letters. If the *Newgeborne Liedlin* and *Oberländische Liedlin* were the first two of these editions to be printed, then the signatures imply that the *Graszliedlin*, which uses capital letters, was printed before the *Gassenhawer und Reutterliedlin*.

The watermark evidence implies that these four editions were printed sequentially. Four different papers are found among the partbooks:

1   Oxhead, surmounted by a clover leaf, between two chain lines. Both the eyes and the nostrils of the Oxhead are on the outside of the face. This watermark, not in Piccard,[52] is found in every partbook of every edition except the Altus of the *Graszliedlin*. (Owing to paper degradation, the watermarks in the Altus in D-Mbs, if present, are unreadable);

2   Oxhead with eyes, ears, and horns curving inwards on a chainline surmounted by a letter T, similar to Piccard 2.X.257, 541, 542. This paper is found in the *Oberländische Liedlin* (Discantus), *Newgeborne Liedlin* (Discantus, Altus), *Graszliedlin* (Altus, Bassus), and *Gassenhawer und Reutterliedlin* (Discantus, Altus, Bassus);

3   a glove surmounted by a single-stem five-petal flower, Piccard XVII.1184 (Maastricht 1532), found only in the *Newgeborne Liedlin* (last gathering of the Bassus [Q]) and the *Oberländische Liedlin* (first gathering of the Discantus [J], second gathering of the Altus [Y, only in PL-Kj], and first and third gatherings of the Bassus [P, R]). The dating of this paper is inconsistent with the other dating evidence and must not be

---

51 Gassenhawerlin No. 3 = 65 Oberländische Newe Liedlin No. 23; Gassenhawerlin No. 8 = 65 Oberländische Newe Liedlin No. 13; Gassenhawerlin No. 15 = Newgeborne Liedlin No. 6; Reutterliedlin No. 1 = 65 Oberländische Newe Liedlin No. 28; Reutterliedlin No. 16 = Newgeborne Liedlin No. 11.

52 Piccard, *Die Wasserzeichenkartei Piccard*, revised online at www.piccard-online.de/.

THE MUSIC EDITIONS OF CHRISTIAN EGENOLFF   169

dismissed without compelling counter evidence, but here there is compelling counter evidence. For example, the dating of some of the Lieder and the copying of Lieder from a 1544 edition means that a date of 1532 is impossible. Egenolff purchased materials from other printers who had gone bankrupt, such as Steiner, and so it is possible that this paper had been purchased from another workshop;

4   unwatermarked paper.

The appearance of the unusual paper 3 at the end of the *Newgeborne Liedlin* and beginning of the *Oberländische Liedlin* suggests that they were printed sequentially, in that order. The mixture of the other papers is consistent with the hypothesis that the four editions were printed within a short time of each other. A complete set consisted of 676 leaves of octavo, equivalent to 84.5 sheets of paper, or 169 formes. Given the calculations of typesetting given above, one typesetter could have set all four editions in thirty-four working days and one printer could have printed 1000 copies in fifty-seven working days. As it has been established that the *Oberländische Liedlin* was printed in 1552, we may assign a date of [1552] to the other editions on the basis of the watermark evidence.

A final piece of evidence is the fact that all four editions are bound together in the two known surviving exemplars, in Munich (missing Tenor) and Krakow (Altus only). Although one example of this is not worthy of mention, that there are no surviving copies of any of these prints that are not bound together as a four-title print is worthy of mention. While this is not compelling, it is consistent with the other evidence.

The Werdenstein catalogue dates the *Oberländische Liedlin* to 1552, and we can infer that the other three Lied editions were also printed in 1552 on the basis of the compilation of the anthologies, the watermarks, and evidence from the binding. That the four editions were still available from Egenolff's heirs twenty-seven years after publication is not without precedent. The *Thesaurus musicus* (RISM1564[1]–1564[5]) printed by Montanus & Neuber in 1564 was still listed for sale by their heirs in the *Catalogus librorum excusorum in officina Gerlachiana* [1582].[53]

Taken together, the evidence is compelling: the [65 Lieder] can be identified as the *Oberländische Liedlin* printed in 1552, and the [56 Lieder] as the *Newgeborne Liedlin*, printed immediately before the *Oberländische Liedlin*. It suggests that the *Graszliedlin* and *Gassenhawer und Reutterliedlin* were printed sequentially after these, and so can also be dated to [1552]. I now turn to brief comments on each of these editions.

12 Newgeborne Liedlin. [1552]

The first detail for consideration is the spelling of the title, as the two sources differ very slightly:

Newgeborne Liedlein (manuscript Egenolff catalogue)
Neuwgeborne Liedlin (printed Egenolff catalogue)

We can draw on the spelling of the titles of the two titled editions from this set, *Gassenhawer und Reutterliedlin* and the *Graszliedlin*, to determine our preferred spelling. The first difference, the 'u' before the 'w' in the printed catalogue, does not appear in the titled Lied editions, and so the 'u' is disregarded. The second difference, the second 'e' in Liedlein,

---

53 See the facsimile inserted between 136 and 137 of Ameln, 'Ein Nürnberger Verlegerplakat'.

170   ROYSTON GUSTAVSON

does not appear in the titled Lied editions, and so the second 'e' is disregarded. As Egenolff's catalogues use highly abbreviated titles, the Tenor partbook may have had a fuller title.

The *Newgeborne Liedlin* does not reproduce any known earlier edition. It contains fifty-six Lieder. Forty-six are *unica* and ten are known from concordances to be by Mathias Greiter. Müller suggests that many of the *unica* in this edition were also composed by Greiter who may have been Egenolff's musical adviser.[54] Schmid, in his monograph on Greiter, regards Müller's evidence as insufficient.[55] The title 'Newgeborne' is unusual, but does appear in an Egenolff edition from 1534: *Vom Newgebornenn Endtchrist: Newe Zeitung des groszen Meyß vonn Rodiß/ dem Christlichen volck überschickt* (VD16 ZV 15559). It was evidently intended as a variation on titles such as Ott's *Hundert vnd ainundzweintzig newe Lieder* (1534 [VD16 ZV 26800]), a trend pushed even further by Forster's *Frische teutsche Liedlein* (1553 [VD16 ZV 18757]), which emphasises that the songs it contained were very new and thus highly fashionable.

13 Oberländische Liedlin. [1552]

This edition is a reprint of an earlier collection by Schöffer. The first detail for consideration is, again, the exact title of the edition, which is very different to that of Schöffer's original. Sources record four variant versions of the title:

> *Oberlendiſche Liedlein* (manuscript Egenolff catalogue)
> *Oberlåndiſche Liedlin* (printed Egenolff catalogue)
> *Öberländiſche Newe Liedlein 65.* (Werdenstein catalogue)
> *65. Oberlendiſche Neŭe Liedlein, vnterſc[hied]‖licher aŭtorum.* (Michelstadt catalogue).

As the spelling 'Liedlin' is invariably used in Egenolff's extant Lied editions, it is adopted here. There is no evidence to support the choice between 'Oberlåndiſche' and 'Oberlendiſche', and so the source that used 'Liedlin' is followed. The Egenolff catalogues reduce titles to one or two words. The fuller titles in the Werdenstein and Michelstadt catalogues, both including '65' and 'Newe/Neue', are surely closer to Egenolff's title. In the Werdenstein catalogue, the entry immediately preceding the 'Öberländiſche Newe Liedlein 65' is 'Teütſche Lieder 121' which refers to Ott's *Hundert vnd ainundzweintzig newe Liede*; as the scribe reverses the position of the number in the Ott, it may be assumed that the same was repeated in this, the following entry. The Michelstadt catalogue is therefore followed in placing '65' at the beginning, which is also consistent with the source edition. This raises the question of whether '65' was given in numerals or words. Entry 35 of the Michelstadt catalogue is David Köler's *Zehen Psalmen Davids* (RISM K 1227) but the entry in the catalogue commences '10'. As such, if our title commenced 'Fünff vnd ſechzig' (the spelling in the source edition) it would have been changed to '65' in both of these catalogues. Egenolff used numerals in the title of Cat. 8 but 'undeviginti' in Cat. 11; and Arnt von Aich used numerals in his Lied anthology, but most other printers spelled out numbers, especially when a number commences the title. Although this question must remain open, on the balance of probabilities I suggest that it was spelled out. For the choice between 'Newe' and 'Neue', Egenolff in other editions uses 'w', for example in the titles of Cat. 16 and Cat. E below. Although this edition does not contain the word

---

54 Müller, 'Die Liederdrucke', 182–200.
55 Schmid, *Mathias Greiter*, 84–85.

THE MUSIC EDITIONS OF CHRISTIAN EGENOLFF   171

'Neue/Newe', the spelling of words such as 'frewte' (Discantus, K5^v) and 'trewen' (Discantus, K8^v, L3^v) is again consistent with the choice of 'Newe'. The proposed title is therefore *Fünff vnd sechzig Oberländische Newe Liedlin* (abbreviated as *Oberländische Liedlin*).

As noted earlier, this edition reprints Schöffer's *Fünff vnd sechzig teütscher Lieder/ vormals im truck nie ußgangen*. Egenolff changed the title, replacing the statement that these songs had never previously appeared in print with the word 'new', presumably to make it attractive to the market despite that fact that it was not true. The word *Oberländische* refers to the fact that many of the composers represented, such as Senfl, came from the uplands of southern Germany or Switzerland. The title pages of the Discantus, Altus and Bassus partbooks carry only an ornamental letter, the first letter of the voice designation of the respective partbook. As this practice is not found in any other Egenolff partbooks, it was evidently copied from the Schöffer partbooks, which do likewise.

14 Graszliedlin. [1552]

The *Graszliedlin* contains a series of twenty-five *unica* followed by three Lieder from Ott's 1544 anthology (RISM 1544^{20}, nos. 13, 50 and 59), presumably to minimise the number of empty pages at the end of the partbooks. As there are still blank pages at the end of the Discantus, Altus and Bassus partbooks, it may be assumed that the lost Tenor partbook was full.

15 Gassenhawer und Reutterliedlin. [1552]

The *Gassenhawerlin* and *Reutterliedlin* were republished as a combined edition. Each was already slender in sedecimo format, and the new octavo format would have seen the Discantus, Altus and Bassus partbooks reduced to twelve leaves each. This is probably why they were republished as a combined, enlarged edition, just as the odes were in 1551. Thirteen of the eighteen new Lieder appear after the works reprinted from the sedecimo edition of the *Gassenhawerlin* and before those from the *Reutterliedlin*. The editor kept different settings of the same text together. Consequently, the series of thirteen Lieder referred to above includes twelve from Ott's anthology and a setting from another source of a text also set in Ott's collection.[56] In addition to omitting five Lieder that also appear in the *Oberländische Liedlin* and the *Newgeborne Liedlin*, as discussed earlier, the editor omitted two other Lieder. *Reutterliedlin* No. 3 (*Laboret dominus*) was surely omitted as the text is in Latin but the other texts are in German. There is no obvious reason for the omission of *Gassenhawerlin* No. 24 (*O all mein hoffnung*), for which neither the text nor the music are duplicated in these Lied anthologies.

16 Waldis. Psalter. 1553

In the following year, 1553, Egenolff printed his most extensive music edition, Burkhard Waldis' *Der Psalter Jn Newe Gesangs weise vnd künstliche Reimen gebracht*, a 558-page octavo containing 150 melodies. This work was never reprinted.[57] It is Egenolff's only music edition

---

56 A concordance between the number of the added pieces in the *Gassenhawer und Reutterliedlin* with those in the Ott *115 guter newer Liedlein* is: 24=18, 40=5, 41=19, 42=42, 43=43, 44=47, 46=48, 47=53, 48=70, 49=73, 50=75, 51=76, 52=77, 86=72. It will be noticed that 45 is not from Ott, but it sets the same text as 44, 'Ich armes meydlin klag mich sehr'. Ott 72, a setting of 'Freundtlich und mild' (Isaac), is inserted at 86 immediately following an anonymous setting of the same text at 85.

57 The best study of this work remains Horn, *Der Psalter des Burkard Waldis*. As Egenolff's only true first edition that exists complete, it has been edited in full in Stalmann, *et al.*, eds, *Die Melodien bis 1570*. See also Lieb, 'Zur Edition'.

172   ROYSTON GUSTAVSON

with a title page printed in two colours (red and black), and the only one printed on paper from Egenolff's own mill, on which the watermark reproduces his printer's mark.

Overview of Egenolff's 'Second Period': *c.*1550–1553

Egenolff's second period had similarities to, and differences from the first. He produced eight musical editions in each period. In the first period, four of the eight were complete reprints of earlier volumes and the other four re-printed works from earlier editions, but during the second, only one (the *Oberländische Liedlin*) was a complete reprint and two, the *Gassenhawer und Reutterliedlin* and Nigidius *Odarum*, were expanded versions of editions from his first period. The *Hymni* is a translation into Latin of a German edition, and so it is partway between a reprint and a new edition. The Waldis *Psalter*, and (perhaps) the *Newgeborne Liedlin*, *Graszliedlin* and lost *Gesangbüchlin* are first editions. All of the editions from the second period are in octavo format, unlike those from the first period in which seven of the eight were in sedecimo format. The editions of Lieder in the second period were also generally larger in scale. In the sedecimo editions, only the Tenor of the German- and presumably Flemish-texted editions contained a full text, which was printed immediately following each piece of music, whereas the other songbooks had only an incipit. However, the songbooks of the second period all have at least one stanza underlaid in all voices. As there had been no change in technology to reduce the costs of printing, we may suppose that either Egenolff's target market was no longer so price-sensitive, or that texts had become so standard in all partbooks that to omit them would undermine the demand for the edition – both of which are driven by commercial considerations. In the first period, Egenolff included editions in Flemish and French as well as German and Latin, but in his second period he restricted the languages in his editions to German and Latin, which suggests that in his market books in these languages sold best. This is consistent with Kmetz's finding that German music editions sold almost exclusively within the German-speaking area.[58] Most significantly, three titles from this period contain monophonic German sacred music: the *Gesangbüchlin*, the *Hymni* (the commentaries are in Latin but the hymn texts set to music are in German), and the *Psalter*; Egenolff printed neither monophonic music nor editions of sacred music in his first period. It is striking that Egenolff printed no sacred Latin polyphony, a mainstay of his competitors Petreius, Rhaw and Ott, in either period. The identity of Egenolff's musical editors or advisors remains unknown. There is insufficient evidence to substantiate the hypotheses that Heugel, Greiter or Alber worked for Egenolff in this capacity. However, given that the two short periods of his musical output (1532–1536 and 1550–1553) were separated by a long gap, it may be that he employed different musical editors during each period.

We do not know why Egenolff returned to music printing, but it is reasonable to assume that this was partly commercial, and partly at the instigation of his editor. Commercially, if we look at his competitors in music printing, Hans Ott died in 1546, Peter Schöffer the Younger in 1547, Georg Rhau in 1548, and Johannes Petreius in early 1550. After 1539, Formschneider's music output consisted only of two lute tablatures and Isaac's *Choralis Constantinus*. This left only the great printing firm of Berg & Neuber, founded in 1542, as a major competitor, and it may have been the strength of that firm and the sheer volume of its music publications, especially its Lied publications commencing in 1549, that saw the

---

58 Kmetz, '250 Years of German Music Printing', 182–183.

ending of Egenolff's second period in 1553. The catalogues of 1579 imply that this second period was not financially successful: six of the eight editions, including all five editions of polyphonic music, were still listed as available for purchase from Egenolff's heirs more than two decades after his death.

To conclude, this new catalogue of Egenolff's musical output has many implications. First, it postulates a revised dating for seven of the editions. This will affect the accepted dating of some of the compositions that they contain. Second, it identifies two partbooks previously believed lost that contain a number of *unica* for which we now have an additional voice, and for thirty-one of the pieces in the *Cantiones vocum trium* we now have complete versions of Egenolff's edition. From a bibliographical perspective, the catalogue provides titles for five previously unnamed editions. This greater precision, such as the exploration of the similar phraseology of the Latin titles of two of the editions, helps us better to conceptualise the contents and interrelationships between these editions. Furthermore, this catalogue clarifies that there was only one edition each of the 1532 odes and the 1550 hymns, although there were two issues of each edition. This finding illuminates Egenolff's marketing strategies. One of the most pressing concerns of those studying Egenolff as a music printer – dating the editions and placing them into chronological order – has now been largely resolved. But as this article demonstrates, further finds in historical and modern catalogues, archives or libraries may further refine the present catalogue. Future studies of this key German music printer can use this new catalogue as a basis to focus on the musical aspects of his output.

174 ROYSTON GUSTAVSON

Catalogue of the music editions of Christian Egenolff[1]

Note on the catalogue entries

Where Egenolff's typesetter inserted a space before a punctuation mark, or did not add a space after a punctuation mark, this is retained in the transcription. Egenolff's italic typeface had upright capitals; where a section begins with a word or words in capitals and continues in italic and the capital is the same size fount, the indication of italic is placed before the word/s in capitals. The transcription of q[ue] is q;.

Key

Authors: PND = Personennamendatei

Titles: Vine Leaf [number] = Vervliet, *Vine Leaf Ornaments*; *Herbarum* = Egenolff, *Herbarum*; *Modelbuch* = Egenolff, *Modelbuch*

Watermarks: Briquet = Briquet, *Les filigranes*; Piccard = Piccard, *Wasserzeichenkartei*; Piccard-online = www.piccard-online.de

Exemplars: *examined firsthand; ^examined in digital copy; ?the exemplar is listed in a reliable source but the holding library did not respond to a request to reconfirm its holding

---

1 I am grateful to the following individuals who answered my questions about their library's holdings of Egenolff prints: Izabela Baron, Oddział Zbiorów Muzycznych, Biblioteka Uniwersytecka we Wrocławiu (email of 29 June 2016); Andreas Berz, Information Services, Swiss National Library (email of 7 August 2015); Barbara Bobak, Kunstbibliothek, Staatliche Museen zu Berlin – Preußischer Kulturbesitz (emails of 21 July and 22 November 2016); Marie-Françoise Bois-Delatte, Coordination des Fonds patrimoniaux, Bibliothèques municipales de Grenoble (email of 10 June 2016); Dr Joachim Brand, Bibliotheksdirektor, Kunstbibliothek, Staatliche Museen zu Berlin – Preußischer Kulturbesitz (email of 1 July 2016); Susan Clermont, Music Division, Library of Congress (emails of 2 June 2016 and 11 January 2017 and especially for the digital scans of print E)); Abigail Connick, Rare Book and Manuscripts Library, University of Illinois at Urbana-Champaign (email of 12 January 2017); Thomas Csanády, Abteilung für Sondersammlungen, Karl-Franzens-Universität Graz (email of 10 June 2016); Claudia Davidts, Stadtarchiv und Wissenschaftliche Stadtbibliothek Soest (email of 11 January 2017); Thomas Drugg, Östersund Library (email of 11 January 2017); Jean Christophe Gero, Musikabteilung, Staatsbibliothek zu Berlin (email of 15 June 2016); François-Pierre Goy, Département de la Musique, Bibliothèque nationale de France (email of 7 June 2016); Gregor Hermann, Wissenschaftlicher Mitarbeiter, VD16/Musiksammlung/Nachlässe, Ratsschulbibliothek Zwickau (email of 14 June 2016); Sophie Hoffmann, Dezernat Historische Bestände / Benutzung, Universitäts- und Landesbibliothek Münster (email of 11 January 2017); Christine Hoppe, Bibliothek Michaeliskloster, Hildesheim (email of 1 February 2008); Raschida Mansour, Lesesaal Handschriften, Universitätsbibliothek Johann Christian Senckenberg Bockenheimer (email of 10 June 2016); Gerhard Mittermeier, Abteilung Benutzungsdienste, Bayerische Staatsbibliothek (email of 5 July 2016); Erwin Müller, Nicolaus-Matz-Bibliothek, Michelstadt (email of 22 October 2015, and especially for attaching digital scans of the openings containing the music prints); Jürgen Neubacher, Staats- und Universitätsbibliothek Hamburg Carl von Ossietzky (email of 10 June 2016); Nicholas Rogers, Archivist, Sidney Sussex College, Cambridge (email of 14 October 2016); Eva Rothkirch, Abteilung Historische Drucke, Staatsbibliothek zu Berlin (emails of 20 June and 5 July 2016); Kerstin Schellbach, Abt. Handschriften, Alte Drucke und Landeskunde, Sächsische Landesbibliothek: Staats- und Universitäts-bibliothek Dresden (email of 22 June 2016); Martina Schmidt-Spandern, Sondersammlungen, Universitätsbibliothek Kassel Landes- und Murhardsche Bibliothek der Stadt Kassel (email of 27 June 2016); Sophie Schrader, Abteilung Handschriften und Alte Drucke, Bayerische Staatsbibliothek (email of 4 July 2016); Joseph Eytan Shemtov, Rare Book Department, Free Library of Philadelphia (emails of 6, 7, 8, 16, 25 June 2016); Christophe Vellet, Responsable du patrimoine imprimé, Bibliothèque Mazarine (email of 7 July 2016); to Sarah Adams, RISM United States of America (email of 24 June 2016); to the following libraries and their staff for their help during my visits to examine Egenolff prints in their collections: A-Wn, CH-Bu, CH-BEl, CH-Zz, D-B, D-Mbs, D-W, D-Z, F-Pn, GB-Lbl, PL-Kj, and US-Wc; and to the following libraries for preparing for me digital scans of Egenolff prints that they hold: CH-Bu, CH-BEl, CZ-Bu, D-Dl, D-MÜu, and GB-Lbl. I thank Nicholas Rogers for correcting my description of the printer's device from 'burning heart' to 'heart amid flames'.

THE MUSIC EDITIONS OF CHRISTIAN EGENOLFF   175

Catalogues: Berz = Berz, *Notendrucker*; Eitner = Eitner, *Sammelwerke*; Müller = Müller, *Christian Egenolff*; RISM = RISM; RISM VIII (DKL) = RISM VIII (DKL); VD16 = www.vd16.de; vdm = www.vdm.sbg.ac.at/

1. Tritonius. Odarum Horatii Concentus. 1532.

There is one edition only of this book, but there are two simultaneous issues that are differentiated by the two states of the title page of the Tenor partbook: the first issue begins *Odarum*, and the second issue begins *Melodiae*. The issue of exemplars missing the title page of the Tenor cannot be determined.

Issue 1 (State 1 of the title page):

Author: Tritonius, Petrus (PND 100649416)

Title: [Roman] O D A R V M Horatij Concentus, ‖ [italic] Cum quibuſdam alijs Carminum generibus. ‖ EARVNDEM Argumenta, Genus, ac ratio: Vnà ‖ cum inſignioribus & Odis, & Sententijs. ‖ [Vine Leaf 8] [Roman] TENOR⌃ ‖ [italic] EMPTORI BIBLIOPOLA. ‖ Forſitan hos rides,Emptor, me uendere cantus, ‖ Putidaq; hæc, dicis, quis, niſi ſtultus, emat? ‖ Haud equidem ignoro,ſic toto uiuitur orbe, ‖ Vt paßim ſapiens quilibet eſſe uelit. ‖ Si tamen ut ſtultus nunc quiſq; eſt, ſic emat ista, ‖ Crede mihi, exiguo tempore diues ero. ‖ [woodcut, 63 × 52mm, of man playing a five-stringed Groß Geige] ‖ Francofordiæ, Chr. Ege. ‖

Title of other partbooks:

> ODARVM HORATII ‖ CONCENTVS. ‖ [Vine Leaf 8] BASSVS⌃ ‖ HORATIVS, ‖ [italic] Me pinguem, & nitidum bene curata cute uiſes ‖ Cum ridere uoles Epicuri de grege porcum. ‖ [woodcut of a fly ('Flieg', *Modelbuch*, 13ᵛ)] [woodcut of a spider ('Spinn', *Modelbuch*, 14ᵛ)] ‖

> ODARVM HORATII ‖ CONCENTVS. ‖ DISCANTVS ‖ [italic] Hic inter Lyricos ſublimi uertice uates ‖ Sydera ſumma ferit: ſeu dulcia furta puellæ, ‖ Cantat, amicitias, conuinia [sic], prælia, paces, ‖ Siue Lycambeis lacerat latratibus hoſtem, ‖ Impetit aut uario corruptos carmine mores. ‖ [woodcut of a unicorn ('Einhorn', *Herbarum*, 260)] [woodcut of a stag ('Hirtz', *Herbarum*, [261])] ‖

> CARMINVM ‖ HORATII, ‖ [Vine Leaf 8] ALTVS⌃ ‖ P E R S I V S S A T. I. ‖ [italic] Omne uafer uitium ridenti Flaccus amico ‖ Tangit, & admißus circum præcordia ludit, ‖ Callidus excußo populum ſuſpendere naſo. ‖ [woodcut of a camel ('Cameel', *Herbarum*, 260)] [woodcut of a woodpecker ('Specht', *Herbarum*, 264)] ‖

Colophon (Tenor, C8ᵛ): [italic] FRANCOFORDIAE, Apud Christianum ‖ Egenolphum. Menſe Ianuario. ‖ An. M. D. XXXII. ‖

Format: upright octavo

Collation and signatures:

> T: 24 leaves, A–C⁸; $5 signed in uppercase Roman letters and lowercase italic Roman numerals (-A1, A2)

> B: 12 leaves, a⁸b⁴; $5 signed in lowerase Roman italic letters and lowercase italic Roman numerals (-a1, b4)

> D: 12 leaves, aa⁸bb⁴ (bb4ʳᵛ blank); $5 signed in double lowercase Roman italic letters and lowercase italic Roman numerals (-aa1, bb4)

> A: 12 leaves, Aa⁸Bb⁴ (Bb4ʳ blank, Bb4ᵛ woodcut); $5 signed in uppercase then lowercase Roman italic letters and lowercase italic Roman numerals (-Aa1, Bb4)

176 ROYSTON GUSTAVSON

Watermarks: (i) Piccard-online 81387 (oxhead; over it: a serpent on a Greek cross); (ii) Piccard-online of type 77429–34, 37, 40, 42 (oxhead; over it: a serpent on a Roman cross); (iii) Piccard-online of type 73672 (oxhead; over it: a letter T; under it: a symbol, see Piccard and, for the symbol only, Briquet 15429); (iv) not in Piccard: oxhead, with rectangular ears and horns, no markings inside face (e.g. no eyes or nostrils); over it: a letter T?; (v) oxhead; over it: a clover leaf (as the mark is in the inner margin the binding means that mark cannot be identified more accurately); (vi) appears to be a glove? (D-Z, gathering B)

Exemplars: D-W 2.33 Musica (2); *GB-Lbl (T missing C1–8; D missing bb1–4; B missing b4) K.1.e.19; *PL-Kj (formerly D-B) Mus.ant.pract. E 80

Reprint of: *Harmoniae Petri Tritonii* (Augsburg: Öglin, 1507), RISM T 1250 (vdm 108)

Catalogues: RISM T 1251 / TT 1251. VD16 H 4959. Eitner 1532d. Müller 1. Berz 1. vdm 109.

Notes: Care must be taken not to confuse this edition with Frisius' *Brevis Musicae Isagoge* (1554, RISM F 2002; ²1555, RISM F 2003) as the title page of the DAB partbooks reads (here, the Discantus): ODARVM HORATII ‖ CONCENTVS. ‖ DISCANTVS. ‖ and there is no publication information in partbooks other than the Tenor. For example, the Altus partbook at GB-Mr R213961 is the Frisius edition. Our Altus partbook, Bb4ᵛ, has a woodcut of a woman playing a harp and a man playing a lute.

Issue 2 (State 2 of the title page, which is as for State 1 except):

Title commences: [Roman] M E L O D I AE in Odas Horatij. ‖ [italic] Et quædam alia Carminum genera. ‖ [otherwise as for State 1 except that the woodcut of the musician lacks the border and some hatching lines]

Exemplars: B-Br Fétis 2.208 A (RP); D-BAs 22/L.mus.o.38#1; ^D-Dl (Tenor) Lit.Rom.A.1483; D-LEdb Museum/Studiensammlungen/Klemm: III 21, 21a; *D-Z (Tenor bifolia A1/8, A2/7, B2/3 only) Mus. 139.6; *F-Pn Rés. Vm¹ 194; *GB-Lbl Hirsch III.1129 (missing Altus, bb4); I-Rc (Tenor) VOL MISC.76 5. Current location not traced:² Stadtbibliothek Elbing; private library of Georg Wolfgang Panzer; Sotheby 1939 (Tenor; 'woodcut on title daubed with colour')

Catalogues: RISM T 1251 correctly has issue 2 as a variant of issue 1. VD16 H 4958. Not in Eitner. Müller 2. Berz 2. vdm 139.

EXEMPLARS OF UKNOWN ISSUE (TITLE PAGE OF TENOR IS MISSING)

*F-Pn (formerly F-Pc) Rés 1166; US-NHub 2012 782 (Bassus only, missing b1–4)

GHOST EXEMPLARS

F-G (B) F.205 Rés. CGA is the 1551 edition (Cat. 11 below); F-Po (RISM TT 1251) is a typographical error for F-Pc (the exemplar now at F-Pn Rés 1166);³ US-PHf (ST) cannot be located by the library.⁴

---

2 *Stadtbibliothek Elbing*, 219; Panzer, *Annales typographici*, 52; Sotheby, *Catalogue Arkwright*, 16, lot 69.

3 I am grateful to François-Pierre Goy, Département de la Musique, Bibliothèque nationale de France, for this information (email of 6 June 2016).

4 Emails from US-PHf of 6, 7, 8, 16, 25 June 2016; and email from RISM US on 24 June 2016. The only other music print before 1700 listed in RISM A/1 in this library, the Hofhaimer odes (RISM HH 6246, vdm 47), also cannot be located there.

THE MUSIC EDITIONS OF CHRISTIAN EGENOLFF   177

2. Gassenhawerlin. 1535.

Author: [anthology, editor unknown]

Title: [Fraktur] Gaſſenhawerlin. || [Roman] TENOR⌃ || [Vine Leaf 13] || [Schwabacher] Franckfurt am Meyn /Bei Chriſtian Egenolff. ||

Title of other partbooks:
> [(Eitner, p. 35:) [woodcut of a chicken (presumably 'Henn' or 'Hane', *Modelbuch*, 13ᵛ)] || DISCANTVS⌃ || [Vine Leaf 13] ||]
> [woodcut of an owl ('Kautz', *Modelbuch*, 13ʳ)] || [Roman] BASSVS⌃ || [Vine Leaf 13] ||
> [woodcut of a peacock ('Pfau', *Modelbuch*, 13ᵛ)] || [Roman] ALTVS⌃ || [Vine Leaf 13] ||

Colophon (Tenor, F8ʳ): [Schwabacher] M. D. XXXV. || Jm Hornung. ||

Format: oblong sedecimo signed and gathered in eights

Collation and signatures: all signed in Schwabacher uppercase letters and lowercase Roman numerals:
> T: 48 leaves, A–F⁸, $5 (-A1)
> [D: 24 leaves, G–I⁸, $5 (-G1)]
> B: 24 leaves, K–M⁸, $5 (-K1, K2)
> A: 24 leaves, N–P⁸, $5 (-N1)

Watermarks: (i) Piccard Crown I.V.8b, gatherings A (CH-Zz, D-Z), O (D-Z); (ii) Piccard of the type crown I.VII.105, gatherings C, E (CH-Zz), F, L (D-Z); (iii) Piccard of the type lily XIII.I.235–238, gathering C (D-Z)

Exemplars: *CH-Zz (T) Z. Mus. 908; *D-Z (ATB; D is described in Eitner but missing by 1896[5]) 69.2.14–16 (formerly LXXXII, 2)

Reprint of: nos 17–34 reprinted from RISM [c.1515][3] (vdm 16), RISM 1513[2] (vdm 13), and RISM [1519][5] (vdm 17)

Catalogues: RISM 1535[10]. VD16 G 487. Eitner 1535d. Müller 3. Berz 3. vdm 21.

3. Reutterliedlin. 1535.

Author: [anthology, editor unknown]

Title: [Fraktur] Reutterliedlin. || [Vine Leaf 8] [Roman] TENOR⌃ || [Schwabacher] ¶ Zu Franckenfurt am Meyn/ Bei || Chriſtian Egenolff. || ★ ||

Title of other partbooks:
> [(Eitner, p. 35:) DISCANTVS | darunter eine Arabeske]
> [Vine Leaf 8] [Roman] BASSVS⌃ || [Vine Leaf 13] || [rectangular woodcut ornament] ||
> [rectangular woodcut ornament] || [Vine Leaf 8] [Roman] ALTVS⌃ || [Vine Leaf 13] ||
> [rectangular woodcut ornament] ||

Colophon (Tenor, f8ʳ): [Schwabacher] M. D. XXXV. ||

Format: oblong sedecimo signed and gathered in eights

---

5 Vollhardt, *Musik-Werke Zwickau*, 66.

178   ROYSTON GUSTAVSON

Collation and signatures: all signed in Schwabacher lowercase letters and lowercase Roman numerals:
T: 48 leaves, a–f⁸, $5 (-a1) [mis-signing a2 and a3 in uppercase]
[D: 24 leaves, g–i⁸, $5 (-g1)]
B: 24 leaves, k–m⁸, $5 (-k1, m4)
A: 24 leaves, n–p⁸, $5 (-n1)

Watermarks: no watermarks in any partbook

Exemplar: *D-Z (ATB; D is described in Eitner but was missing by 1896) 69.2.14–16 (formerly LXXXII, 2)

Reprint of: nos 19–31 reprinted from RISM [c.1515]³ (vdm 16), RISM 1513² (vdm 13), and RISM [1519]⁵ (vdm 17)

Catalogues: RISM 1535¹¹. VD16 G 487. Eitner 1535e. Müller 4. Berz 4. vdm 22.

4. Brabandische Liedlin. 1535.

Author: [anthology, editor unknown]

Title: [[Fraktur] Brabandiſche Liedlin ‖ [Vine Leaf 13] [Roman] TENOR⌃ ‖]

Title of other partbooks:
[Vine Leaf 13] ‖ [Roman] DISCANTVS⌃ ‖ [square decorative woodcut including two satyrs each playing a pipe, 29 × 29mm] [square decorative woodcut including two putti, 29.5 × 29.5mm] ‖

Colophon: [Franckfurt 1535, from *Bibliothecae Traiectinae Catalogus*]

Format: oblong sedecimo signed and gathered in eights

Collation and signatures: all signed in Schwabacher uppercase letters and lowercase Roman numerals:
T: [either 48 leaves, A–F⁸ or 44 leaves, A–E⁸F⁴, $5 signed (-A1)]
D: 36 leaves, G–K⁸L⁴, $5 signed (-G1, G4, L4)

Watermarks: (i) Piccard-online, of the type 72937 (oxhead, with eyes and nostrils; over it: a letter T), gathering G; (ii) Piccard-online, of the type 71773 (oxhead—the head is convex, and the horns are attached rather than continuous—with eyes and nostrils; over it: a clover leaf; under it: a smaller posthorn [NB a slightly different mark to that in Cat. 7 and 8 below]), gathering J

Exemplar: *F-Pn (D only) Rés. Vm⁷ 504(2), probably the exemplar formerly in the Utrecht City Library (Bibliotheca Traiectina)

Reprint of: unknown earlier music edition from which the Kamper Liedboek (NL-Kga Ms. 212) was also reprinted

Catalogues: RISM [c.1535]¹⁴. Not in VD16. Not in Eitner. Müller 7. Berz 7. vdm 29.

Notes: Title and date known from BIBLIOTHECÆ TRAIECTINÆ CATALOGVS (Utrecht: Salomon Rhodius, 1608), LIBRI MVSICI, CANTIONES IV. VOC., Qq3ʳ. This title was formerly thought to have been a reprint of the Kamper Liedboek, but the confirmed date of 1535 means that both editions represent independent reprints of an earlier lost volume. Previously known in the literature as [36 flämische Lieder] or [Lieder zu 3 & 4 Stimmen] or [36 songs in Flemish] or [36 Lieder ohne Titel]

THE MUSIC EDITIONS OF CHRISTIAN EGENOLFF   179

5. Gassenhawerlin. [c. December 1536].

A lost second edition of the *Gassenhawerlin* is hypothesised to have been printed as part of a set with editions 6–8 below.

6. Reutterliedlin. December 1536.

Author: [anthology, editor unknown]

Title (inferred): [[Fraktur] Reutterliedlin. ‖ [Vine Leaf 43] [Roman] TENOR⌃ ‖ [Schwabacher] ¶ Zu Franckenfurt am Meyn/Bei ‖ Chriſtian Egenolff. ‖ ★ ‖]

Title of other partbooks:
[Roman] DISCANTVS⌃ ‖[Vine Leaf 43] ‖ [woodcut of six-string viola da gamba and bow] ‖
[Roman] BASSVS⌃ ‖ [Vine Leaf 43 ‖ [woodcut of six-string viola da gamba and bow] ‖
[Roman] ALTVS⌃ ‖ [Vine Leaf 43] ‖ [woodcut of six-string viola da gamba and bow] ‖

Colophon (Tenor, F8ʳ): [Schwabacher] ¶ Jm Chriſtmonat. M. D. XXXVI. ‖

Format: oblong sedecimo signed and gathered in eights

Collation and signatures: all signed in Schwabacher lowercase letters and lowercase Roman numerals:
T: 48 leaves, [a]–f⁸, $5 signed ([-a1], f3)
D: 24 leaves, g–i⁸, $5 signed (-g1)
B: 24 leaves, k–m⁸, $5 signed (-k1, k4, m4)
A: 24 leaves, n–p⁸, $5 signed (-n1)

Watermarks: (i) Piccard-online 73680 (oxhead, with eyes and nostrils; over it: a letter T; under it: a larger posthorn), gatherings f, i, n; (ii) oxhead; over it: a clover leaf, gatherings g, l, p

Exemplars: *CH-Bu (DAB) F.X.22–24; *CH-Zz (Tenor e2–f8 only) Z. Mus. 908

Reprint of: Cat. 3 above

Catalogues: RISM 1535[11] does not note that there was a second edition and catalogues these partbooks as being of the first edition. Not in VD16. Not in Eitner. Müller 5. Berz 5. vdm 689.

Notes: Woodcuts of instruments excluding title page: lute, DA[T]B verso of title page; bagpipe, DATB verso of final leaf.

7. Cantiones vocum quatuor. [c. December 1536].

Author: [anthology, editor unknown]

Title: [woodcut of a bagpipe player, 49 × 22mm] [woodcut of a fiddle player, 49 × 22mm] [between them:] CANTIONES ‖ VOCVM ‖ QVATVOR. ‖ TENOR⌃ ‖ [Vine Leaf 43] ‖ [italic] Chri. Egenolph. ‖

Title of other partbooks:
[woodcut of a bagpipe player] [woodcut of a fiddle player] [between them:] DISCAN⸗‖TVS⌃ ‖ [Vine Leaf 43] ‖

180   ROYSTON GUSTAVSON

Colophon: none

Format: oblong sedecimo signed and gathered in eights

Collation and signatures: all signed in uppercase then lowercase Schwabacher letters and lowercase Roman numerals:
    T: 48 leaves, Aa–Ff⁸, $5 signed (-Aa1)
    D: 48 leaves, Gg–Mm⁸, $5 signed (-Gg1)

Watermarks: (i) Piccard-online 73680 (description at Cat. 6 above), gatherings b, c, e; (ii) Piccard-online, of the type 71773 (description at Cat. 4 above), gatherings h, j, m

Exemplars: *CH-BEl (T only, missing Ff8; first gathering misbound Aa1, Aa8, Aa2–7) Ma 3549; *F-Pn (D only) Rés. Vm⁷ 504(1), probably the exemplar formerly in the Utrecht City Library (Bibliotheca Traiectina)

Reprint of: nos. 18–33 reprinted from *Quinquagena carminum* (Mainz: Peter Schöffer the Younger, 1513), vdm 15, not in RISM

Catalogues: RISM [c.1535]¹⁴. Not in VD16. Not in Eitner. Müller 6. Berz 6. vdm 25.

Notes: previously known in the literature as the [39 Chansons, 3 flämische Lieder und 1 Motette] or [43 Chansons ohne Titel] or [Lieder zu 3 & 4 Stimmen] or [43 songs in four voices]; title page woodcuts are by Hans Sebald Beham (Hollstein, *Hans Sebald Beham*, 253, nos. P. 1241 and P. 1242); woodcuts of instruments excluding title page: lute, verso of title page (DT); hurdy gurdy, recto of final leaf (D; presumably T); bagpipe, verso of final leaf (D; presumably T).

8. *Cantiones vocum trium. [c. December 1536].*

Author: [anthology, editor unknown]

Title: CANTIONES SELE⸗‖CTISSIMÆ LXVIII. VOCVM ‖ TRIVM⌐ ‖ TENOR⌐ ‖ [woodcut of a blackbird ('Amsel', *Herbarum*, 264)] [woodcut of a linnet on a branch ('Henfling', *Modelbuch*, 13ʳ)] ‖

Title of other partbooks: not known [title page of D missing]

Colophon: none

Format: oblong sedecimo signed and gathered in eights

Collation and signatures: all signed in double lowercase Schwabacher letters and Roman numerals:
    T: 80 leaves, aa–kk⁸ (kk8ᵛ blank), $5 signed (-aa1, cciiii; mis-signing bbiii as Ibiii, ccii as cc; aaiii signed in italic)
    D: 80 leaves, ll–vv⁸ (vv8ʳᵛ blank?), $5 signed (-[ll1]; mm, nn4, pp4 signed in italic)

Watermarks: (i) Piccard-online 73680 (description at Cat. 6 above), gatherings a, d (ii) Piccard-online, of type 71773 (description at Cat. 4 above), gathering e; (iii) oxhead, centred on a chain line, with eyes and nostrils; over it: a clover leaf; under it: nothing; as the mark is across the binding of four leaves a more precise identification is not possible, gathering g, k, m, o, q, v; (iv) oxhead, between two chain lines, with eyes and nostrils, horns turned outwards, nothing over or under it, gathering s

THE MUSIC EDITIONS OF CHRISTIAN EGENOLFF   181

Exemplars: *CH-BEl (T only) Ma 3549; *F-Pn (D only, missing title page) Rés. Vm⁷ 504(3), probably the exemplar formerly in the Utrecht City Library (Bibliotheca Traiectina); a manuscript copy of thirty-one tricinia of the lost Bassus is at D-HB X/2, nos. 1–31

Reprint of: nos. 14–25 reprinted from *Quinquagena carminum* (Mainz: Peter Schöffer the Younger, 1513), vdm15, not in RISM

Catalogues: RISM [c.1535]¹⁴. Not in VD16. Not in Eitner. Müller 8. Berz 8. vdm 30.

Notes: Previously known in the literature as the [68 Tricinia] or [Lieder zu 3 & 4 Stimmen] or [68 Lieder ohne Titel] or [68 songs in three voices].

9. Gesangbüchlin. [1550].

That this Gesangbüchlin was printed is known from a letter from Erasmus Alber to Hartmann Beyer, 24 August 1550, preserved at D–F Ms.Ff.H.Beyer A 17, ed. Schnorr von Carolsfeld, *Erasmus Alberus*, 204–206 (see above, p. 163). The letter also refers to Alber's *Fabulae* (Frankfurt a.M.: Peter Braubach, 1550; VD16 A 553) which suggests that the Gesangbüchlin was likewise printed in 1550. It remains possible that this lost edition did not include any printed music, but as the 1565 edition by Egenolff's heirs contained printed music it is likely that this edition did. It is not in RISM VIII (DKL), VD16, Eitner, Müller, or Berz; vdm 403. Lipphardt (see Cat. C below) postulates other lost editions of the Gesangbüchlin.

10. Spangenberg. Hymni. 1550.

There is only one edition of the *Hymni*, but it appeared in two separate issues (as distinct from re-issues). Each issue makes the *Hymni* available in a different form, anthologised with other titles. The '*Postilla*' issue included the *Hymni* as part of a set of four titles and explicitly named the *Hymni* on the title page of the first. Within this set, titles III and IV were available separately as a set of two titles (note that the title page of III, *De festis praecipuis*, explicitly names IV, the *Hymni*, on its title page); and title IV, the *Hymni*, was also available separately. These, however, do not constitute separate issues as the individual titles are identical in each and all combinations were available for purchase at the same time. That the exemplars of title I (468 leaves) are usually bound separately from titles II–IV (460 leaves) may be explained by their size making binding in a single volume of octavo difficult to use. The second issue, the '*Funebres*' issue, had the print-run of title IV stopped part way through and its title page amended to include the name of a different work, the *Funebres* (as such, this a second state of the title page).

'Postilla' issue

Author: Spangenberg, Johann (PND 123624878)

Title: [I] POSTILLA ‖ EVANGE-‖LIA, ET EPISTOLAE, QVAE IN ‖ Ecclefia,toto Anno,Dominicis & Feftis ‖ diebus proponuntur,per Quæftio-‖nes,piè ac fynceriter explicata, ‖ & imaginibus exornata. ‖ [italic] EADEM Euangelia,& Precationes,quas ‖ Collectas uocant,quibus utitur Ecclefia, ‖ Carmine Elegiaco reddita. ‖ ITEM, Hymni Ecclefiaftici, fummis Feftiuita-‖tibus cantari foliti,Annotationibus pijs expla-‖nati. Autore IOAN. SPANG. ‖ Herdeßiano, Theologo. ‖ [printer's device: a heart amid flames on a square altar] ‖ F R A N C. Apud Chr. Egen. ‖

[II] EPISTO-‖LAE, PER TOTVM ‖ ANNVM, DOMINICIS DIEBVS IN ‖ Ecclefia legi folitæ,per Quæftiones ex-‖plicatæ,Autore IOAN. SPANG. ‖ Herdeffiano, Theologo. ‖ [printer's device

182 ROYSTON GUSTAVSON

a heart amid flames on a square altar] ‖ [italic] FRANC. Apud Chr. Egenolphum ‖ Hadamarium. ‖

[III] DE FESTIS ‖ PRAECIPVIS, EVAN-‖GELIA. ITEM, HYMNI ECCLESIA-‖ſtici, Summis feſtiuitatibus ab Eccleſia ſo-‖lenniter cantari ſoliti. Annotatio-‖nibus pijs,ſyncerè explicati, ‖ Autore IOAN. SPANG. ‖ Herdeſſiano,Theo-‖logo. ‖ [printer's device: a heart amid flames on a square altar] ‖ [italic] FRANC. Apud Chr. Egenolphum ‖ Hadamarium. ‖

[IV] H Y M N I ‖ ECCLESIASTICI DVODECIM, SVM≈‖mis Feſtiuitatibus ab Eccleſia ſolenniter ‖ cantari ſoliti, Annotationibus pijs expla-‖nati. Autore M. IOANNE SPANGEN-‖BERGIO. Recens è Germanico ſermo-‖ne, Latino redditæ,Per REINAR-‖DVM LORICHIVM Ha-‖damarium. ‖ ‖ [printer's device: a heart amid flames on a round altar] ‖ [italic] FRANC. Apud Chr. Egenolphum. ‖

Colophon:
[I] (Nn4ʳ = 467ʳ [*recte* 468ʳ]): [italic] F R A N C. Apud Chr. Egen. ‖ An. M. D. L. ‖
[II] (i4ʳ): [italic] An. M. D. L. ‖
[III] (tt4ʳ): [italic] FRANCOFORTI, Apud Chr. Egenolphum ‖ Hadamarium. Anno ‖ M. D. L. ‖
[IV] (H3ʳ): [italic] An. M. D. L. ‖

Format: all in upright octavo

Collation and signatures:
[I] 468 leaves, A–Z⁸a–z⁸Aa–Mm⁸Nn⁴ [Nn4ᵛ blank], $5 signed in Roman italic letters and Arabic numerals in three series: uppercase, lowercase, then uppercase and lowercase (-A1, Nn4; misprinting V3 as V5, Z2 as Z, a2 as Z2; the following signed in Roman: g4, n3, o, p5, q5)
[II] 252 leaves, A–Z⁸a–h⁸i⁴ [i4ᵛ blank], signed in Roman italic letters and Arabic numerals in two series: uppercase then lowercase (-A1, i4)
[III] 148 leaves, aa–ss⁸tt⁴ [tt4ᵛ blank], signed in Roman italic double lowercase letters and Arabic numerals, $5 signed (-aa1, tt4)
[IV] 60 leaves, A–G⁸H⁴ [H3ᵛ–H4ᵛ blank], signed in Roman uppercase letters and Arabic numerals, $5 signed (-A1, H3, H4)

Foliation:
[I] [1] 2–384, 384–166 [*recte* 467], [468] in Arabic numerals (-1, 3, 4, 165, 186, 467 [*recte* 468]; misprinting 327 as 732, 378 as 387, 401 as 402, 466 [*recte* 467] as 166; CC1ʳ misnumbered 384 instead of 385, with the misnumbering carried throughout the edition)
[II] [1] 2–152 [*recte* 252] in Arabic numerals (-4, misfoliating 103 as 10, 251 as 151, 252 as 152)
[III] [1] 2–147 [148] in Arabic numerals (3 misfoliated as 5, 48 as 84, 56 as 58, 64 as 94, 76 as 66, 142 as 542)
[IV] No foliation

Watermarks:
[I], [II], [III] not examined
[IV] none in A-Wn

Exemplars (all known exemplars of titles I–IV included): *A-Wn SA.76.E.47 (Title IV only); ?CZ-D (formerly deposited in CZ-Bu; Titles III, IV, II); D-Berlin, Kunstwissenschaftliche

THE MUSIC EDITIONS OF CHRISTIAN EGENOLFF   183

Bibliothek, Staatliche Kunstmuseen zu Berlin, Gris 662 kl (Title I only); ^[III and IV only] D-Dl Theol.ev.past.358.w,misc.1+2+3 (Titles II, III, IV, preceded by a German-texted Spangenberg edition; IV is missing H2–H4); D-DÜl PRTHEOL-1–700 (Titles II, III, IV); ?D-KALb (Title II only); ^D-Mbs Hom. 2107 w (Title I only, missing Cc1 which has the duplicate folio number; purchased 2015); ^[II and IV only] D-MÜu G+2 6313 (Titles III, II, IV); D-SO 5 Ff 7.6 (Title II only, not bound with any other editions); GB-Cssc Y.6.19 (Titles II, III, IV); S-ÖS Zetterström 20–14 (Title II only, not bound with any other editions); US-U IUA11649 (Titles I, III, IV). Status not known: formerly Sotheby (Titles I, II, III, IV).[6] Lost (Kriegsverlust): D-B Dy 12296 (Title I only).

Reprint of: Title I of 1545 Egenolff edition (VD16 S 7996); Title II of 1544 Egenolff edition (VD16 ZV 14582); Title III of 1545 Egenolff edition (VD16 S 7998); Title IV is a new Latin translation by Reinhard Lorichius of *Zwölff Christliche Lobgesenge* (Wittenberg: Georg Rhaw, 1545), RISM VIII (DKL) 1545[13], VD16 S 8096, vdm 1290.

Catalogues:
> [I]–[IV] No catalogues give as a unit.
> [I] Not in RISM VIII (DKL). VD16 ZV 30601. Not in Eitner. Not in Müller. Not in Berz. Not in *vdm*.
> [II] Not in RISM VIII (DKL). Not in VD16. Not in Eitner. Not in Müller. Not in Berz. Not in *vdm*.
> [III]+[IV] RISM VIII (DKL) 1550[11]. Not in VD16. Not in Eitner. Not in Müller. Not in Berz. Not in *vdm*.
> [IV] Not in RISM VIII (DKL). Not in VD16 (but see Cat E. below). Not in Eitner. Müller 13. Berz 20. vdm 1150.

_____. *'De festis/Hymni' available separately*

Titles III and IV above were available separately; note that the *Hymni* is referred to on the title page of III.

Exemplars: no extant exemplars contain only these two titles; where both exist in a single binding, they are also bound with Titles I and/or II.

_____. *'Hymni' available separately*

Title IV above was available separately.

Exemplars: the only exemplar of Title IV that is not bound with one or more of Titles I–III is A-Wn SA.76.E.47, however whether this exemplar was purchased separately, or was purchased with other titles above and at some later time became separated from them, cannot be determined.

'Funebres' issue

Title: [I] H Y M N I ‖ ECCLESIASTICI DVODECIM, SVM⸗‖mis Feſtiuitatibus ab Ecclefia folenniter ‖ cantari foliti, Annotationibus pijs expla-‖nati. Autore M. IOANNE SPANGEN-‖BERGIO. Recens è Germanico fermo-‖ne, Latino redditæ, Per REINAR-‖DVM LORICHIVM Ha-‖damarium. ‖ ‖ [italic] Accefferunt Funebres conciones quindecim, unà ‖ cum

_____

6 *Music and Manuscript Music, London, May 21, 2004* (London: Sotheby, 2004), lot 158, was a single volume in contemporary vellum, clasps missing, of three Spangenberg titles all printed in 1550 by Egenolff: *Postilla. Evangelia et Epistolae; Epistolae, per Totum Annum; De Festis Praecipuis . . . Hymni ecclesiastici duodecim.*

184 ROYSTON GUSTAVSON

Thematis,ultra LX.ad quæ funebrium Oratio-‖num Argumenta commodè adplicari,& ad coronam ‖ Chriftianam in uita defunctorum fepulturis,uti≠‖liter poterunt haberi.Eodem Autore. ‖ [printer's device: a heart amid flames on a round altar] ‖ FRANC. Apud Chr. Egenolphum. ‖

[II] [Vine leaf 13] FVNE/‖BRES CONTIONES QVIN-‖decim: E facrarum Literarum fontibus ‖ depromptæ. Quæ ad Coronam Chri-‖ftianam,in uita defunctorum Se-‖pulturis,utiliter poterunt ‖ haberi. ‖ [italic] ACCESSERVNT ‖ THEMATA, PAVLO PLVS SE-‖xaginta,Ex ueteris Testamenti facrario congesta: ‖ ad quæ Funebrium orationum argumenta,commo-‖dùm poterunt adplicari. ‖ Quæ iampridem omnia ‖ M. IOAN. SPANGENBERGIVS, Ger-‖manico fermone confcripfit: Iam autem re-‖cens Latinitate donauit REINAR-‖DVS LORICHIVS ‖ Hadamarius. ‖ [Roman] ITEM, ‖ Medicina Animæ,De Morte commentationes, ‖ atque confolationes. Collectore eodem REIN-‖HARDO Lorichio Hadamario. ‖ [italic] FRANC. Chr. Egen. ‖

Colophon:
    [I] [identical to IV above]
    [II] (F8ʳ): M. D. XLVIII. ‖

Collation and signatures:
    [I] [identical to IV above]
    [II] 48 leaves, A–F^8 (F8^v blank), \$5 signed in Roman uppercase letters and Arabic numerals (-A1)

Foliation:
    [I] [identical to IV above]
    [II] [1] 2–48 in Arabic numerals

Watermarks:
    [I] none in GB-Lbl
    [II] not examined for watermarks

Exemplars (only exemplars that include Title I are included because Title II, a non-music title, was printed in 1548 anthologised with a non-music title): ^CZ-D (formerly deposited in CZ-Bu with the shelfmark CH-0002.695,pŕív.); D-HImk GBA 1550 (formerly in D-HVkms); D-W A: 394.44 Quod. (4); D-Z 25.7.9.(8/9) (formerly XXV.VII.9); *GB-Lbl Hirsch III.1104

Catalogues: RISM VIII (DKL) 1550^{10}. VD16 S 8097 (Title I), S 7814 and ZV 23858 (Title II). Not in Eitner. Not in Müller. Not in Berz. vdm 1383.

11. Nigidius, ed. Odarum. 1551.

Author: Nigidius, Petrus (PND 119774550), ed.

Title: GEMINAE ‖ VNDEVIGINTI ODARVM ‖ HORATII MELODIAE, QVA-‖tuor Vocibus probè adornatæ, cum fele-‖[italic]ctißimis Carminum,partim facrorum,partim pro-‖phanorum,concentibus: additis circa finem alijs item ‖ cantionibus, matutinis, meridianis, & ferotinis: Pæ-‖dagogijs rectè inftitutis, ac fcholis quibuflibet ‖ pro exercenda iuuentute literaria ‖ accommodatißimis. ‖ [Roman] CANDIDO LECTORI. ‖ [Italic] Vis animum uarijs diftractum fiftere curis, ‖ Humano languet dum tibi more grauis. ‖ Hunc pete iucundum pulchra ratione libellum, ‖ Et cedent mœfto tædia lenta tibi. ‖ [printer's device: a heart amid flames on a square altar] ‖ [Roman] FRANC. Apud Chri. Egenolphum. ‖

THE MUSIC EDITIONS OF CHRISTIAN EGENOLFF 185

Title of other partbooks:

DISCAN≠‖TVS. ‖ [italic] Quale canunt, niuei moribundo gutture Cygni, ‖ Tale mihi tenero carmen ab ore uenit. ‖ Diſcite me pueri faciles,teneræq̃; puellæ, ‖ Guttura præcipuè nam mihi ueſtra placent. ‖

BASSVS. ‖ [italic] Vox mea ceu fuſco metuenda tonitrua cœlo, ‖ Grande melos craſſo gutture digna canit. ‖ Dumq̃; ſuis numeris aliæ tolluntur in altum, ‖ Me ſubmiſſa graui murmura uoce iuuant. ‖

ALTVS. ‖ [italic] Eſt ſua uox alijs,me leniter ire per altum, ‖ Et reliquis mixtam uocibus eſſe iuuat. ‖ Per quaſcunq̃; feror celeri modulamine uoces, ‖ Officio tardis non licet eſſe meo. ‖

Colophon:

[Tenor, G7ʳ]: [italic] FRANCOFORTI, APVD CHRI≠‖ſtianum Egenolphum Hadamarium. ‖ Anno M. D. LII. ‖ Menſe Maio. ‖

[Altus, P8ᵛ] [italic] FRANCOFORTI, APVD CHRI-‖ſtianum Egenolphum. Anno ‖ M. D. LI. ‖ Menſe Iunio. ‖

Format: upright octavo

Collation and signatures: all partbooks signed in Roman uppercase letters and lowercase Arabic numerals:

T: 56 leaves, A–G⁸ [G8ʳᵛ blank]; $5 signed (-A1, mis-signing A3 as G3, and F5 as G5)
D: 20 leaves, H–I⁸K⁴; $5 signed (-H1, K4)
B: 20 leaves, L–M⁸N⁴ [N3ᵛ–N4ᵛ blank], $5 signed (-L1, N4)
A: 16 leaves, O–P⁸; $5 signed (-O1)

Watermarks: (i) Piccard-online, somewhat similar to 54238 (crown, between two binding wires, with double contoured superstructure with pearls, over which is a double contoured cross, over which is a single contoured star), T in A-Wn, D-Mbs, and F-Pn; (ii) unwatermarked, all gatherings in DAB in A-Wn, D-Mbs, and F-Pn

Exemplars: *A-Wn (DT) SA.77.F.11; D-ERu H00/PHL-VIII 524; D-GRu 542/Dh 536; D-HB I/3; D-LEm II. 3. 3; *D-Mbs 8 Mus.pr.145; DK-Kk 170, 271; F-G (B) F.205 Rés.; *F-Pn (TB) Rés. VM¹ 195; US-Cn Case minus VM 1580.N68g. Lost: F-Pm 8° 22177 (identified as missing in April 1955). Ghost: Sotheby 1939[7]

Reprint of: Cat. 1 above, expanded by odes from F3ᵛ–I4ʳ of Theobald Billican, *De partium orationis inflexionibus* ([Augsburg: Ruff], 1526; VD16 G 1564 and H 4957, vdm 137) and 38 ode settings (noting that ode 40 consists of three different settings, and ode 45 of two different settings) from other sources including six from Y7ʳ–Z8ʳ of Petrus Nigidius, *Isagogicus rerum grammaticarum libellus* (Erfurt: Melchior Sachse d. Ä., 1548).

Catalogues: RISM 1551¹⁷. VD16 H 4961. Eitner 1551a. Müller 14. Berz 21. vdm 1384.

Notes: Some sets of partbooks are bound together TDBA (D-HB, DK-Kk, US-Cn)

---

7 Sotheby, *Catalogue Arkwright*, p. 16, lot 70, Suprema vox (AA–DD8) is misidentified as this Egenolff print; it is the Frisius print (RISM F 2002 or F 2003).

186   ROYSTON GUSTAVSON

12. *Newgeborne Liedlin. [1552].*

Author: [anthology, editor unknown]

Title: [[Fraktur] Newgeborne Liedlin. [Roman] TENOR. ||]

Title of other partbooks:
   [Roman] DISCAN≠||TVS. || || [Schwabacher] G ||
   [Roman] BASSVS. || || [Schwabacher] M ||
   [Roman] ALTVS. || || [Schwabacher] R ||

Colophon: not extant [date inferred from Cat. 13 below]

Format: oblong octavo

Collation and signatures: all signed in Schwabacher uppercase letters and lowercase Roman numerals; note that the DBA title pages are signed:
   T: [48 leaves, A–F^8]
   D: 40 leaves, G–L^8 (L7^v–8^v blank), $5 signed
   B: 40 leaves, M–Q^8 (Q7^v–8^v blank), $5 signed
   A: 36 leaves, R–V^{8}X^4 (X3^v–4^v blank), $5 signed (-X4)

Watermarks: (i) Not in Piccard; oxhead between two chain lines surmounted by a clover leaf, the eyes and nostrils outside the face; (ii) Piccard, of type 2.X.257, 541, 542 (oxhead on a chainline surmounted by a letter T); (iii) Piccard XVII.1184 (a glove surmounted by a single-stem five-petal flower); (iv) unwatermarked

Exemplars: *D-Mbs (DAB) Mus.pr.46#Beibd.2; *PL-Kj (formerly D-B) (A only) Mus.ant.pract. G 305 [2]

Reprint of: status not known

Catalogues: RISM [c.1535]^{15}. Not in VD16. Eitner 1535d. Müller 10. Berz 10. vdm 26.

Notes: Title from A-Whh RHR Bücherkommission im Reich 1–36, 47^v; and D-Mbs Einbl. VIII, 7 bc. Previously known in the literature as the [56 Lieder ohne Titel] or [Liederbuch]

13. *Oberländische Liedlin. 1552.*

Author: [anthology, editor unknown]

Title: [[large ornamental capital] T || [Fraktur] Fünff vnd ſechzig Oberlåndiſche Newe Liedlin ||]

Title of other partbooks:
   [large ornamental capital] D || [Schwabacher] J ||
   [large ornamental capital] B || [Schwabacher] P ||
   [large ornamental capital] A || [Schwabacher] X ||

Colophon: [1552]

Format: oblong octavo

THE MUSIC EDITIONS OF CHRISTIAN EGENOLFF 187

Collation and signatures: A–Z signed in Schwabacher uppercase letters and lowercase Roman numerals, a–c signed in Schwabacher lowercase and lowercase Roman numerals; note that the DBA title pages are signed:

T: [64 leaves, A–H⁸], [$5 signed]
D: 48 leaves, J–O⁸ (O7ᵛ–8ᵛ blank), $5 signed (-L4)
B: 44 leaves, P–T⁸V⁴ (V4ᵛ blank), $5 signed (-V4)
A: 48 leaves, X–c⁸ (c7ʳ–8ᵛ blank), $5 signed

Watermarks: (i) Not in Piccard; oxhead between two chain lines surmounted by a clover leaf, the eyes and nostrils outside the face; (ii) Piccard, of type 2.X.257, 541, 542 (oxhead on a chainline surmounted by a letter T); (iii) Piccard XVII.1184 (a glove surmounted by a single-stem five-petal flower); (iv) unwatermarked

Exemplars: *D-Mbs (DAB) Mus.pr.46; *PL-Kj (formerly D-B) (A only) Mus.ant.pract. G 305 [3]. Lost: D-Michelstadt Nicolaus-Matz-Bibliothek (see catalogue of 1630, vol. 3, 94ᵛ); possibly Montbéliard.[8] Ghost: RISM lists a Vagans in *GB-Lbl (K.8.i.9) but that exemplar is the Schöffer edition

Reprint of: Schöffer & Apiarius RISM [1536]⁸, vdm 27

Catalogues: RISM [1536]⁸ catalogued with the Schöffer edition under a subheading *Rééd. sans titre*. Not in VD16. Eitner1536a. Müller 9. Berz 9. vdm 31.

Notes: Title and date in D-Mbs Cbm Cat. 121 t, 64ᵛ, entry 7; title in D-Michelstadt Nicolaus-Matz-Bibliothek, catalogue of 1630, vol. 3, 94ᵛ; short title in A-Whh RHR Bücherkommission im Reich 1–36, 47ᵛ, and D-Mbs Einbl. VIII,7 bc. It is possible that the number '65' was on the title page in numerals. Previously known in the literature as [65 Lieder]

14. Graszliedlin. [1552].

Author: [anthology, editor unknown]

Title: [[Fraktur] Graſzliedlin ‖ [Roman] TENOR. ‖]

Title page of other partbooks:
[Fraktur] Graſzliedlin. ‖ [Roman] DISCAN-‖TVS. ‖ ‖ [Schwabacher] C ‖
[Fraktur] Graſzliedlin. ‖ [Roman] BASSVS. ‖ ‖ [Schwabacher] E ‖
[Fraktur] Graſzliedlin. ‖ [Roman] ALTVS. ‖ ‖ [Schwabacher] G ‖

Colophon: not extant [date inferred from Cat. 13 above]

Format: oblong octavo

Collation and signatures: all signed in Schwabacher uppercase letters and lowercase Roman numerals; note that the title pages of the DBA are signed:

T: [16 leaves, A–B⁸], [$5 signed]
D: 16 leaves, C–D⁸ (D8ʳᵛ blank), $5 signed
B: 16 leaves, E–F⁴ (F8ᵛ blank), $5 signed
A: 16 leaves, G–H⁸ (H8ʳᵛ blank), $5 signed

---

8 Meyer, 'Un inventaire Montbéliard', 128, but which from the dates of the other items is more likely to be the Schöffer edition: 'Item vier getruckte Partes mit Lieder . . . da das erst *Veil Jch gros gunst.*'

188   ROYSTON GUSTAVSON

Watermarks: (i) Not in Piccard; oxhead between two chain lines surmounted by a clover leaf, the eyes and nostrils outside the face; (ii) Piccard, of type 2.X.257, 541, 542 (oxhead on a chainline surmounted by a letter T); (iii) unwatermarked

Exemplars: *D-Mbs (DAB) Mus.pr.46#Beibd.3; *PL-Kj (formerly D-B) (A only) Mus.ant.pract. G 305 [4]

Reprint of: final 3 lieder (26–28) reprinted from RISM 1544[20], vdm 1027

Catalogues: RISM [c.1535][12]. Not in VD16. Eitner 1535d. Müller 11. Berz 15. vdm 23.

15. Gassenhawer und Reutterliedlin. [1552].

Author: [anthology, editor unknown]

Title: [[Fraktur] Gaſſenhawer vnd Reutterliedlin. ‖ [Roman] TENOR. ‖]

Title of other partbooks:
   [Fraktur] Gaſſenhawer vnd Reutterliedlin. ‖ [Roman] DISCAN-‖TVS. ‖ ‖[Schwabacher] 1 ‖
   [Fraktur] Gaſſenhawer vnd Reutterliedlin. ‖ [Roman] BASSVS. ‖ ‖ [Schwabacher] ſ ‖
   [Fraktur] Gaſſenhawer vnd Reutterliedlin. ‖ [Roman] ALTVS. ‖ ‖ [Schwabacher] bb ‖

Colophon: not extant [date inferred from Cat. 13 above]

Format: oblong octavo

Collation and signatures: all signed in Schwabacher lowercase letters and Roman numerals; note that the title pages of the DBA are signed:
   T: [80 leaves, a–k⁸]
   D: 56 leaves, l–r⁸ (r8^{rv} blank), $5 signed
   B: 52 leaves, s–z⁸aa⁴ (aa3^r–4^v blank), $5 signed (-aa3, aa4)
   A: 56 leaves, bb–hh⁸ (hh7^r–8^v blank), $5 signed

Watermarks: (i) Not in Piccard; oxhead between two chain lines surmounted by a clover leaf, the eyes and nostrils outside the face; (ii) Piccard, of type 2.X.257, 541, 542 (oxhead on a chainline surmounted by a letter T); (iii) unwatermarked

Exemplars: *D-Mbs (DAB) Mus.pr.46#Beibd.1; *PL-Kj (formerly D-B) (A only) Mus.ant.pract. G 305 [1]

Reprint of: Cat. 5 and Cat. 6 above, removing seven pieces including five Lieder that were published in Cat. 12 and Cat. 13 above and one piece in Latin, and adding eighteen pieces, including fourteen from RISM 1544[20], vdm 1027

Catalogues: RISM [c.1535][13]. VD16 G 488. Eitner 1535d. Müller 12. Berz 16. vdm 24.

Note: a rectangular print, 80 × 89mm, consisting of two rectangular woodcuts of instrumental musicians by Hans Sebald Beham with the words 'Gaſſenhawer vnd Reutterliedlin.' between them (Hollstein, *Hans Sebald Beham*, 254, nos. P. 1243 and P. 1243α) is believed to be extant in only a single exemplar (Bremen, Kunsthalle, Inv.Nr. 1905/214).[9] The Bremen exemplar

---

9 I am grateful to Christien Melzer, Kustodin Kupferstichkabinett: Zeichnung und Druckgraphik 15.–18. Jahrhundert, Kunsthalle Bremen, for the physical description of the Kunsthalle's copy of this leaf (email of 17 May 2017).

THE MUSIC EDITIONS OF CHRISTIAN EGENOLFF   189

has been heavily trimmed, the leaf measuring 91 × 94mm. Given the size of the print, that its verso is blank, that the chain lines in the paper, which has no watermark, run horizontally and so it could have been cut from an oblong octavo, and that the text is printed using the same typeface as that used on the title pages of the extant partbooks of Cat. 15, it is possible that this print was cut from the title page of the missing Tenor partbook.

16. Waldis. Psalter. 1553.

Author: Waldis, Burkhard (PND 118628666)

Title: [Fraktur, red] Der Pſalter/‖ Jn Newe Geſangs wieſe/‖ [Schwabacher, black] vnd künſtliche Reimen ‖ gebracht/durch ‖ [red] Burcardum Waldis. ‖ [black] Mit ieder Pſalmen beſondern Melodien/ ‖ vnd kurtzen Su͂marien. ‖ [woodcut, 61 × 56mm, of King David kneeling and looking up, with his harp on the ground directly before him, with Jesus looking at him] ‖ [red] Zu Franckfurt/Bei Chr. Egenolff. ‖

Colophon: [l7ᵛ = 271ᵛ] Getruckt Zu Franckfurt ‖ am Meyn/Bei Chriſti⸗‖an Egenolff. Anno ‖ M. D. Liij. ‖ Jm Mayen. ‖

Format: upright octavo

Collation and signatures: 280 leaves, aa⁸A–Z⁸a–l⁸ (18ʳᵛ blank), $5 signed (-aa1) in Schwabacher uppercase letters and lowercase Roman numerals

Foliation: [8 unfoliated leaves] [1] 2–271 [272] in Arabic numerals (the number 128 is printed upside down, 213 misnumbered 113)

Watermarks: (i) Egenolff's printer's mark; (ii) unwatermarked

Exemplars: A-Gu I 52096; A-Wn SA.79.F.73; D-B Eh 2510 (formerly in the private library of Karl Hartwig Gregor von Meusebach); D-B Slg Wernigerode Hb 2595 (missing title page; formerly in the private library of Karl Zeisberg zu Wernigerode); D-F Handschriftenabteiling Ausst. 270; D-Gs 8 P GERM II, 2813 RARA; D-HAu Dd 5347; ^D-Mbs Res/B.metr. 261 (purchased 2013 from Antiquariat Kainbacher to replace destroyed exemplar; replacement catalogued using identical shelfmark); D-S Sch.K.M.oct.Wal 250/30; D-W Tc 51; D-W YA 6.8° Helmst; D-WGp 8ETh406–1; D-WRz 14, 5: 1 [b]; *D-Z 29.4.25 (formerly CVIII,6); DK-Kk Th. 23968 8°; *GB-Lbl Hirsch III.1139; *GB-Lbl 3436.f.32; I-Rvat Stamp.Pal.V.319(int.3); PL-WRu 540708; RUS-Mrg mk16v (formerly D-Dl Hymn.323.h); US-R M1490.W163. Destroyed [Kriegsverlust]: D-Hs PO VIII 10; D-Kl cant.sacr. 8 Nr. 73; D-Mbs Res/B.metr. 261. Status not known: St Anna, Augsburg, catalogue of 1620; private library of Herr Baumgarten[10]

Reprint of: this is a first edition

Catalogues: RISM VIII (DKL) 1553⁰⁶. VD16 B 3316. Not in Eitner. Müller 16. Berz 23. vdm 1385.

Notes: a version of Egenolff's printer's mark, a heart amid flames, both red, on a square altar, is on aa8ᵛ

---

10 Schaal, *Das Inventar St. Anna*, 83; *Bibliothecae Baumgartenianae* (Halle: Joh. Justin Gebauer, 1765), 69, item 598.

190 ROYSTON GUSTAVSON

Appendix

Music acoustics

A. Schreiber. Rechenbüchlin. [1534 or 1535].

Author: Schreiber, Heinrich (PND 11949132X)

Title: [Fraktur] EYn new künftlich be⸗‖[Schwabacher]hend vnd gewiß Rechenbüch⸗‖lin vff alle Kauffmanfchafft. ‖ Nach [bracket] ‖ Gemeynen Regeln de tre. ‖ Welfchen practic. Regeln falfi. ‖ Etlichen Regeln Coffe. ‖ Proportion des gefangs / in Diato⸗‖nio außzutheylen monochordū / Or‖gelpfeiffen/vnd andre Jnftrument/ ‖ durch erfindung Pithagore. ‖ . . . ‖ [italic] M. Henricus Grammateus. ‖ [between two woodcuts] Chri. ‖ Ege. ‖

Colophon: none

Exemplars: ^A-Wn 72.M.35.(2); D-DÜl HUG21; D-Ngm [Postinc.] 8° H. 2650; PL-WRu 453297; US-NYcub Plimpton 511 1535 Sch 6

Catalogues: VD16 S 4145

Comments: The section on music, 'Arithmetica applicirt oder gezogen uff die edel kunst Musica' on H8^v–J6^r, includes a typeset illustration of Guido's gamut on J5^r. The date 1535 appears in book-keeping examples on J8^r, K6^r, and L1^r, suggesting publication in 1534 or 1535. The edition is a reprint; an earlier edition was printed by Johann Stuchs in Nuremberg c.1520 (VD16 S 4144; RISM VI/1, 374). Egenolff's heirs reprinted the title in 1572 (VD16 S 4147; Richter, 'Christian Egenolffs Erben', col. 966, no. 337).

B. Schreiber. Rechenbüchlin. [1543 or 1544].

Author: Schreiber, Heinrich (PND 11949132X)

Title: [Fraktur] Ein new künftlich be⸗‖[Schwabacher]hend vnd gewiß Rechenbüchlin/ ‖ vff alle Kauffmanfchafft. ‖ Nach [bracket] ‖ Gemeynen Regeln de Tri. ‖ Welfchen practic. Regeln falfi. ‖ Etlichen Regeln Coffe. ‖ Proportiō des gefangs in Diatonio/ ‖ außzutheylen monochordum / Or⸗‖gelpfeiffen /vñ andre Jnftrumēt/ ‖ durch erfindung Pythagore. ‖ . . . ‖ M. Henricus Grammateus. ‖ [two woodcuts] ‖

Colophon: none

Exemplars: D-FRu T 680; ^D-Mbs Res/Math.p. 182; D-TRs D 118: 1 an; I-Rvat Stamp.Pal.V.359; US-BEb tHF5644.S4 1544

Catalogues: VD16 S 4146

Comments: A reprint, with almost identical layout, of Cat. A above. It does not name Egenolff but has the same woodcuts including those on the title page. The example on fol. L1^r has the date 1544 suggesting publication in 1543 or 1544.

'Ghost' music edition

C. [Psalmen und Geistliche Gesänge. 1535.]

Author: [anthology, editor unknown]

Title [from Lipphardt]: [Psalmen und Geistliche Gesänge]

Colophon: not known

Exemplars: none known

Catalogues: RISM VIII (DKL) 1535[01]

Comments: Lipphardt, *Gesangbuchdrucke*, pp. 25–26, 178–180, hypothesised the existence of this edition, through careful reasoning, as an earlier, lost, edition of Cat. 9 above, but there is no empirical evidence that it existed. Even if it were printed, there is no evidence that it was printed by Egenolff. Lipphard (p. 18) himself notes that Gülfferich printed the music in his 1546 edition of Veit Dietrich's *Agendbüchlin* from woodblocks, and so there was no need to restrict possible printers to those with a music font, nor indeed to printers in Frankfurt. Lipphardt postulates further lost editions from 1544 and 1555 (pp. 180–183). Bill's review of Lipphardt's book (Bill, 'Besprechung') raises questions about Lipphardt's arguments. The lack of empirical evidence and the ultimately unconvincing hypothetical arguments lead to the classification of this edition as a 'ghost'.

Text-only editions that have been cited as (possible) music editions

D. Duodecim Hymni. [1550 recte 1570].

Author: Spangenberg, Johann (PND 123624878)

Title: [Roman] DVODECIM ǁ HYMNI ǁ ECCLESIASTICI ǁ SVMMIS FESTIVITATIBVS AB ǁ Ecclefia folenniter cantari foliti, Annota-ǁtionibus pijs explanati, à [italic] M. IOAN. SPAN ǁGENBERGIO: [Roman] Iam verò è Germanico ǁ Latinè redditi per [italic] REINARDVM ǁ LORICHIVM HADA-ǁ[Roman]marium. ǁ [printer's mark: heart amid flames on a square altar] ǁ [italic] FRANC. Apud Hæred. Chr. Egenol. ǁ

Colophon [H8r]: FRANC. apud Hæredes Chriftiani ǁ Egenolphi. Anno ǁ 1570. ǁ

Exemplars (partial list only): ^D-Mbs Hom. 1510#Beibd.1; D-W A:1240.27 Theol. (4) ['Unvollständig, nur bis Bl. H7 vorhanden']; F-Sn E.161.034,3; RUS-Mrg mk16v [formerly D-Dl]. Ghost: VD16 S 8098 at A-Wn [SA.76.E.47] is not this edition but the first issue of Cat. 10 above

Catalogues: VD16 S 8098. Berz, p. 154, states that this edition does not contain music.

Comments: VD16 S 8098 dates the edition [1550], presumably initially using the incomplete exemplar at D-W which is missing the colophon, and at a later time drawing on Cat. 10 above, which is however a different edition, for publication information. This edition was not printed by Christian Egenolff, but by his heirs. It exists in two issues, one by itself and one appended to Spangenberg's *Epistolae* (1570), VD16 ZV 14069; see Richter, 'Christian Egenolffs Erben', cols 960–961, entry 314.

E. Eilff schöner newer Lieder. [1552].

Author: [anthology, editor unknown]

Title: [Decorative woodcut ornament that extends across the entire width of the printed area] [Fraktur] Eilff Schöner ǁ [Schwabacher] newer Lieder. ǁ [a list the eleven lieder, each item in the list on a separate line, in the following format: number in Arabic numerals, followed by the first line of the text, then 'etc.'] ǁ Gedruckt zu Franckfurdt ǁ am Mayn ǁ

Colophon: none

Exemplar (unicum): ^US-Wc MT5.5.H45 1550 Case

Catalogues: VD16 E 994, Müller 15, Berz 22.

192 ROYSTON GUSTAVSON

Comments: This edition was listed in a 1931 auction catalogue.[11] On the basis of the title and place of publication alone, it has been noted in the literature as a possible Egenolff music edition. The copy auctioned in 1931, now in US-Wc, contains text only, and no printed music. There is also evidence that the edition, which does not name the printer, was not printed by Egenolff. The same title page ornament and typefaces appear in Andreas Pfeilschmidt, *Ein hübsch vnnd Christlich Spiel* (Frankfurt a.M: Jost Gran, 1555 (RISM VIII DKL 1555[11], VD16 P 2369); on the relationship between Egenolff and Gran, see Gustavson, 'Senfl in Print', pp. 292–296. On the balance of probabilities this edition is by Gran.

F. Geistliche Gassenhawer. [1571].
G. Christliche Lieder. [1571].

Author: Knaust, Heinrich (PND 119011743)

Title: [Fraktur] Gaſſenhawer/Reuter ‖ vnd Bergliedlin/ ‖ [red] Chriſtlich/ ‖ [Roman] moraliter, [Fraktur] vnnd ‖ ſittlich verendert/da ‖ [Schwabacher, black] mit die böfe ergerliche weiß/ ‖ vnnütze vnd ‖ ſchampare Liedlin/auff den Gaſſen/ Fel⸗‖de Häuſern/ vnnd anderßwo /zuſingen/ ‖ . . . ‖ [red] Durch Herrn Henrich Knauſten ‖ [black] der Rechten Doctor/vnd Keyſer⸗‖lichen gekrönten Poeten/rc. ‖ . . . ‖

Colophon (H8r = 64r): [Schwabacher] Getruckt zu Franckfort ‖ am Meyn/ Bey Chriſtian ‖ Egenolffs Erben/im Jar ‖ [Roman] M. D. LXXI. ‖

Exemplars: ^D-B Eh 2940; I-Rvat Stamp.Pal.V.444; I-Rvat Stamp.Pal.V.675. Destroyed (Kriegsverlust): D-Kl cant 8° 23

Catalogues: VD16 K 1407, Berz 28.

Comments: These two titles appear one after the other in the Egenolff catalogues of 1579 (A-Whh RHR Bücherkommission im Reich 1–36 and D-Mbs Einbl. VIII,7 bc) and are discussed in Müller, *Christian Egenolff*, pp. 30–32 but not included in his catalogue, and in Richter, 'Christian Egenolffs Erben,' col. 810 with a bibliographical description at cols. 962–963, No. 321. Richter argues, as accepted here, that the two entries refer to the same edition, the *Gaſſenhawer/Reuter ‖ vnd Bergliedlin*, which contains no printed music.

---

11 *Bibliothek George Nestle-John: Frankfurt am Main (1839–95) . . . Versteigerung . . . Dienstag, den 6. Oktober 1931* (Frankfurt a.M.: Joseph Baer, 1931), 58–60, lot 116, online at http://digi.ub.uni-heidelberg.de/diglit/baer1931_10_06a/0071. Given that the binding consists of six unrelated prints, the identification of this particular exemplar in later catalogues can be made with complete certainty. At some time it entered the library of Alfred Cortot (it has his bookplate). It reappeared in *Music and Continental Books and Manuscripts London, 09 June 2010* (London: Sotheby, 2010), lot 74, online at www.sothebys.com/fr/auctions/ecatalogue/lot.74.html/2010/music-and-continental-books-and-manuscripts-l10402, at which time it was purchased by US-Wc.

References

Agee, Richard. 'A Venetian Music Printing Contract and Edition Size in the Sixteenth Century'. *Studi Musicali* 15 (1986): 59–65.

Ameln, Konrad. 'Ein Nürnberger Verlegerplakat aus dem 16. Jahrhundert'. In *Musik und Verlag: Karl Vötterle zum 65. Geburtstag*, edited by Richard Baum and Wolfgang Rehm. Kassel: Bärenreiter, 1968, 136–142.

Benzing, Josef. 'Christian Egenolff und seine Verlagsproduktion'. *Aus dem Antiquariat* 9 (1973): A348–352.

Benzing, Josef. 'Christian Egenolff zu Straßburg und seine Drucke (1528 bis 1530)'. *Das Antiquariat* 10 (1954): 88–89 and 92.

Benzing, Josef. 'Die Drucke Christian Egenolffs zu Frankfurt am Main von Ende 1530 bis 1555'. *Das Antiquariat* 11 (1955): 139–140, 162–164, 201–202, 232–236.

Bernstein, Lawrence. 'The Bibliography of Music in Conrad Gesner's Pandectae (1548)'. *Acta musicologica* 45 (1973): 119–163.

Berz, Ernst-Ludwig. *Die Notendrucker und ihre Verleger in Frankfurt am Main von den Anfängen bis etwa 1630: eine bibliographische und drucktechnische Studie zur Musikpublikation*. Catalogus musicus 5. Kassel: Bärenreiter, 1970.

Bill, Oswald. '*Besprechung*: Walther Lipphardt. *Gesangbuchdrucke in Frankfurt am Main vor 1569*'. *Jahrbuch für Volksliedforschung* 21 (1976): 190–192.

Bill, Oswald. *Das Frankfurter Gesangbuch von 1569 und seine späteren Ausgaben*. Marburg: Görich & Weiershäuser, 1969.

Blackburn, Bonnie J. 'The Printing Contract for the *Libro primo de musica de la salamandra* (Rome, 1526)'. *The Journal of Musicology* 12 (1994): 345–356.

Böker-Heil, Norbert, Harald Heckmann, and Ilse Kindermann, eds. *Das Tenorlied: Mehrstimmige Lieder in deutschen Quellen 1450–1580*. 3 vols. Catalogus musicus 9–11. Kassel: Bärenreiter, 1979–1986.

Bowers, Fredson. *Principles of Bibliographical Description*. Princeton, NJ: Princeton University Press, 1949.

Bridgman, Nanie. 'Christian Egenolff, imprimeur de musique (A propos du recueil *Rés. Vm⁷ 504* de la Bibliothèque nationale de Paris)'. *Annales Musicologiques* 3 (1955): 77–177.

Briquet, Charles-Moïse. *Les Filigranes: Dictionnaire historique des marques du papier dès leur apparition vers 1282 jusqu'en 1600*. 4 vols. Paris: Alphonse Picard, 1907; rpt. Amsterdam: The Paper Publications Society, 1968.

Charteris, Richard. *Johann Georg von Werdenstein (1542–1608): A Major Collector of Early Music Prints*. Sterling Heights, MI: Harmonie Park Press, 2006.

Cramer, Susanne. *Johannes Heugel (c.1510–1584/85): Studien zu seinen lateinischen Motetten*. Kassel: Gustav Bosse, 1994.

[Egenolff, Christian]. *Herbarum, arborum, fruticum, frumentorum ac leguminum. Animalium præterea terrestrium, volatilium & aquatilium. . . .* VD16 H 2193. Frankfurt a.M.: Egenolff, 1546.

[Egenolff, Christian]. *Modelbuch aller Art*. VD16 M 5710. Frankfurt a.M.: Egenolff, 1535.

Eitner, Robert. *Bibliographie der Musik-Sammelwerke des XVI. und XVII. Jahrhunderts*. Berlin: Leo Liepmannssohn, 1877.

Fallows, David. 'The Printed Songbook at Kampen'. In *NiveauNischeNimbus: Die Anfänge des Musikdrucks nördlich der Alpen*, edited by Birgit Lodes. Wiener Forum für ältere Musikgeschichte 3. Tutzing: Hans Schneider, 2010, 347–354.

Fallows, David. 'The Songbooks of Christian Egenolff'. In *NiveauNischeNimbus: Die Anfänge des Musikdrucks nördlich der Alpen*, edited by Birgit Lodes. Wiener Forum für ältere Musikgeschichte 3. Tutzing: Hans Schneider, 2010, 355–368.

Gaskell, Philip. *A New Introduction to Bibliography*. Oxford: Oxford University Press, 1972.

Gottwald, Clytus. *Manuscripta Musica*. Die Handschriften der Gesamthochschulbibliothek Kassel, Landesbibliothek und Murhardsche Bibliothek der Stadt Kassel 6. Wiesbaden: Harrassowitz, 1997.

Gustavson, Royston. 'Competitive Strategy Dynamics in the German Music Publishing Industry 1530–1550'. In *NiveauNischeNimbus: Die Anfänge des Musikdrucks nördlich der Alpen*, edited by Birgit Lodes. Wiener Forum für ältere Musikgeschichte 3. Tutzing: Hans Schneider, 2010, 185–210.

Gustavson, Royston. 'Egenolff, Christian'. In *Die Musik in Geschichte und Gegenwart*, edited by Ludwig Finscher, Personenteil 6. Kassel: Bärenreiter, 2001, cols. 98–103.

Gustavson, Royston. 'Senfl in Print: The *Einzeldrucke*'. In *Senfl-Studien 2*, edited by Stefan Gasch and Sonja Tröster. Wiener Forum für ältere Musikgeschichte 7. Tutzing: Hans Schneider, 2013, 257–307.

Heartz, Daniel. *Pierre Attaingnant, Royal Printer of Music: A Historical Study and Bibliographical Catalogue*. Berkeley, CA: University of California Press, 1969.

Hollstein, Friedrich Wilhelm. *Hans Sebald Beham*. German Engravings, Etchings and Woodcuts *c.*1400–1700 3. Amsterdam: Hertzberger, 1954.

Horn, Max. *Der Psalter des Burkard Waldis: Ein Beitrag zur Geschichte des deutschen Kirchenliedes im XVI. Jahrhundert*. Halle: Ehrhardt Karras, 1911.

Jäcker, Carsten. 'Verzeichnis aller in der Offizin Christan [*sic*] Egenolffs entstandenen Bücher'. In *Christian Egenolff 1502–1555: Ein Frankfurter Meister des frühen Buchdrucks aus Hadamar*, edited by Kulturvereinigung Hadamar. Limberg: Glaukos, 2002, 47–97.

Johnson, Alfred Forbes. 'Christian Egenolff of Frankfort [*sic*] and his Types'. *Print: A Quarterly Journal* 2 (1941): 91–100.

Kmetz, John. '250 Years of German Music Printing (c.1500–1750): A Case for a Closed Market'. In *NiveauNischeNimbus: Die Anfänge des Musikdrucks nördlich der Alpen*, edited by Birgit Lodes. Wiener Forum für ältere Musikgeschichte 3. Tutzing: Hans Schneider, 2010, 167–184.

Krummel, Donald. 'Early German Partbook Type Faces'. *Gutenberg-Jahrbuch* 60 (1985): 80–98.

Lewis, Mary S. *Antonio Gardano: Venetian Music Printer 1538–1569: A Descriptive Bibliography and Historical Study. Volume 1: 1538–1549*. New York: Garland, 1988.

Lieb, Ludger. 'Zur Edition sämtlicher Schriften des Burkard Waldis'. In *Editionsdesiderate zur Frühen Neuzeit: Beiträge zur Tagung der Kommission für die Edition von Texten der Frühen Neuzeit*, edited by Hans-Gert Roloff. Amsterdam: Rodopi, 1997, 37–50.

Lipphardt, Walther. *Gesangbuchdrucke in Frankfurt am Main vor 1569*. Frankfurt a.M.: Waldemar Kramer, 1974.

McKenzie, Donald Francis. 'Printers of the Mind: Some Notes on Bibliographical Theories and Printing-House Practices'. *Studies in Bibliography* 22 (1969): 1–75.

Meyer, Christian. 'Un inventaire des livres et des instruments de musique de la chapelle des Comtes de Montbéliard (1555)'. *Fontes artis musicae* 38 (1991): 122–129.

Möller, Eberhard. 'Die beiden ältesten Notenkataloge der Ratsschulbibliothek Zwickau'. In *Im Dienst der Quellen zur Musik: Festschrift Gertraut Haberkamp zum 65. Geburtstag*, edited by Paul Mai. Tutzing: Hans Schneider, 2002, 13–26.

Moser, Hans Joachim. Introductory booklet to *Gassenhawerlin und Reutterliedlin zu Franckenfurt am Meyn. Bei Christian Egenolf [sic] 1535: Faksimileneuausgabe*. Augsburg: Filser, 1927.

Müller, Hans-Christian. 'Die Liederdrucke Christian Egenolffs', 2 vols, PhD dissertation, Christian-Albrecht-Universität Kiel, 1964.

Panzer, Georg Wolfgang. *Annales typographici ab anno MDI ad annum MDXXXVI continuati, vol. 7*. Nuremberg: Zeh, 1799.

Piccard, Gerhard. *Die Wasserzeichenkartei Piccard im Hauptstaatsarchiv Stuttgart*, 17 vols. Stuttgart: Kohlhammer, 1961–1997, revised online at www.piccard-online.de/.

Richter, Günter. 'Christian Egenolffs Erben 1555–1667'. *Archiv für Geschichte des Buchwesens* 7 (1967): cols 449–1130.

RISM. *Répertiore International des Sources Musicales*, Series A1, *Einzeldrucke vor 1800*, edited by Karl-Heinz Schlager *et al.*, vols 1–15 [vol. 10 not published]. Kassel: Bärenreiter, 1971–2003. Series B/I *Recueils imprimés XVIe–XVIIe siècles*, edited by François Lesure. Munich: Henle, 1960.

RISM VIII (DKL). *Das deutsche Kirchenlied: Kritische Gesamtausgabe der Melodien*, edited by Konrad Ameln, Marcus Jenny, and Walther Lipphardt. Vol. 1, part 1, *Verzeichnis der Drucke*, Répertoire International des Sources Musicales B/VIII/1. Kassel: Bärenreiter, 1975.

Schaal, Richard. *Das Inventar der Kantorei St. Anna in Augsburg.* Catalogus musicus 3. Kassel: Bärenreiter, 1965.

Schanzlin, Hans Peter. 'Musik-Sammeldrucke des 16. und 17. Jahrhunderts in schweizerischen Bibliotheken'. *Fontes artis musicae*, 4.1 (1957): 38–42.

Schmid, Manfred Hermann. *Mathias Greiter: Das Schicksal eines deutschen Musikers zur Reformationszeit.* Aichach: Mayer, 1976.

Schmidt, Karl. *Die Geschichte der Pädagogik in weltgeschichtlicher Entwicklung und im organischen Zusammenhange mit dem Culturleben der Völker*, vol. 3. Cöthen: Paul Schettler, 1861.

Schnorr von Carolsfeld, Franz. *Erasmus Alberus: ein biographischer Beitrag zur Geschichte der Reformationszeit.* Dresden: Ehrlemann, 1893.

Siegele, Ulrich. *Die Musiksammlung der Stadt Heilbronn.* Heilbronn: Stadtarchiv Heilbronn, 1967.

Sotheby. *Catalogue of a Selected Portion of the Well-Known Collection of Old and Rare Music and Books on Music The Property of Godfrey E. P. Arkwright, Esq., Crowshott, Highclere, Newbury.* London: Sotheby & Co., 1939.

Stadtbibliothek Elbing. *Katalog der Stadtbibliothek zu Elbing*, vol. 2. Elbing: Reinhold Kühn, 1894.

Staehelin, Martin. 'Petruccis Canti B in deutschen Musikdrucken des 16. Jahrhunderts'. In *Gestalt und Entstehung musikalischer Quellen im 15. und 16. Jahrhundert*, edited by Martin Staehelin. Wolfenbütteler Forschungen 83. Wiesbaden: Harrassowitz, 1998, 125–131.

Staehelin, Martin. 'Zum Egenolff-Diskantband der Bibliothèque Nationale in Paris'. *Archiv für Musikwissenschaft* 23 (1966): 93–109.

Stalmann, Joachim, Karl-Günther Hartmann and Hans-Otto Korth, eds. *Die Melodien bis 1570: Melodien aus Autorendrucken und Liederblättern*, 2 vols. Das deutsche Kirchenlied III,1,1. Kassel: Bärenreiter, 1993.

Thomas, Henry. 'Musical Settings of Horace's Lyric Poems'. *Proceedings of the Musical Association 46th Session* (1919–1920): 73–97.

Uhland, Ludwig. *Alte hoch- und niederdeutsche Volkslieder*, vol. 1, part 2. Stuttgart: Cotta, 1845.

Vervliet, Hendrik D. L. *Vine Leaf Ornaments in Renaissance Typography.* New Castle, DE: Oak Knoll Press, 2012.

Vollhardt, Reinhard. *Bibliographie der Musik-Werke in der Ratsschulbibliothek zu Zwickau.* Leipzig: Breitkopf & Härtel, 1896.

Wissler, Gustav. 'Die Musikalien'. In *Fünfzig Jahre Schweizerische Landesbibliothek 1895–1945.* Bern: [Schweizerische Landesbibliothek], 1945, 87–94.

Part IV

Music printing and intellectual history

9

The cult of Luther in music[1]

Grantley McDonald

Several studies have confirmed the truism that the Reformation could not have taken place if not for the easy availability of print. The triangular relationship between print, the Reformation, and music is less obvious. The sudden demands of the Reformation on the presses of Germany and on the attention and resources of German readers and book buyers temporarily suppressed the production of certain kinds of printed musical sources. For example, while seventeen editions of the missal, most containing music, were printed for the diocese of Passau between 1491 and 1522, none were produced after this period.[2] The presence of similar patterns in other German dioceses suggests that this was not due simply to coincidence or a saturation of requirements. Rather, the kinds of music being printed changed in response to the onset of the Reformation. Beginning in 1524, there was an explosion of editions providing music for the Lutheran rite: liturgical books for the use of the clergy, monophonic hymn books for the use of the congregation, and books of polyphony for the choir. Moreover, Lutheran and Roman Catholic controversialists alike used music to spread propaganda, as Rolf Wilhelm Brednich, Rebecca Wagner Oettinger and others have shown.[3]

Printed material tends to be of two kinds: ephemeral (or occasional), and archival, that is, material intended to be consulted more than once. Print increased the availability and quantity of both kinds of source, ephemera particularly strongly.[4] Since propaganda is usually topical and timely, it is naturally somewhat ephemeral. However, collectors who preserved ephemeral material for later consultation helped it cross over into the realm of the archival. It is principally the fortuitous activity of such early collectors that has preserved ephemeral pamphlets until our time.[5]

The present paper will examine five ephemeral or occasional editions containing music that have hitherto escaped detailed examination. As we shall see, they vividly reflect the ways in which printed music helped form the public image – or rather, images – of Martin Luther. These pieces reflect on several landmarks in Luther's life as well as on the religious reforms he provoked. The first, *Ad Martinum Lutherum captivum lamentatio*, is a reaction to Luther's apparent abduction to the Wartburg in 1521. The second, *Epithalamia Martini Lutheri Wittenbergensis*, describes Luther's marriage in 1525 as the latest in a series of outrages against the monastic vows to which he had sworn. The third, *Eyn erschreglicher und doch widderumb*

---

1 For Elisabeth Giselbrecht, in fond memory of our library adventures. Research for this paper was made possible by funding from the Austrian Science Fund (FWF) for the project P24075–G23.
2 Weale and Bohatta, *Bibliographia liturgica*, 131–136.
3 Brednich, *Liedpublizistik*; Wagner Oettinger, *Music as Propaganda*.
4 Eisermann, 'Auflagehöhen von Einblattdrucken', 143.
5 Griese, 'Sammler und Abschreiber'.

kurtzweylliger und nutzlich gesangk, depicts Luther as the tool of Satan and his demons, who rejoice at his attacks on the authority and traditions of the Roman church. The fourth and fifth pieces, Leonhard Kettner's *Nu hört jr Christen newe meer* and Caspar Othmayr's *Mein himlischer vatter*, set Luther's last words to music. These two pieces, written within a few months of Luther's death on 18 February 1546, depict his last moments as suffused with pious tranquillity, in contrast to the stories spread by Roman Catholic apologists, in which the dying Luther was described as tortured by demons. These musical pamphlets present highly partisan interpretations of Luther, depicting him either as a saint or as a tool of the devil. The music thus serves a similar function to visual images that were likewise spread through the medium of print, such as Hans Baldung Grien's woodcut of Luther as an inspired, prophetic saint (Figure 9.1), or the title woodcut to a polemic by Petrus Sylvius, which depicts Luther as an accomplice of the devil (Figure 9.2).

These pieces contain several recurrent details that reveal much about the authors' motivations. The persistent imagery of saints and demons in the texts provides insight into the perceived cosmic consequences of Luther's rebellion. These pieces are written in various musical styles and genres, with analogies in the various registers of Reformation debate, which extended from learned and reasoned theological argumentation to abusive name-calling. The variety of musical genres, and the form in which the music is presented – either as broadsheets, pamphlets or individual pieces within collections of polyphony – suggests

Figure 9.1 Hans Baldung Grien, *Luther as an Augustinian friar*, from *Acta et res gestae, D. Martini Lutheri, in Comitijs Principum Vuormaciae, Anno M D XXI*. [Strasbourg]: [Johann Schott], [1521], (VD16 ZV 62), fol. A1ᵛ
Source: München, Bayerische Staatsbibliothek, Res/H.ref. 750 k

Figure 9.2 Title page from Petrus Sylvius, *Luthers vnd Lutzbers eintrechtige vereinigung*. [Leipzig]: [Michael Blum], 1535 (VD16 P 1310), fol. A1[r]
Source: Staatliche Bibliothek Regensburg, 999/4 Theol.syst.675(3)

conclusions about the intended audience for these pieces, and the circumstances of their performance.

Ad Martinum Lutherum captivum lamentatio

The first piece we shall consider is a polyphonic lament on the supposed abduction of Luther in early May 1521. After Luther was placed under imperial ban at the Diet of Worms, Duke Friedrich the Wise of Saxony had a band of men intercept his party in a feigned attack. Luther was then brought to safety in the Wartburg, a fortress near Eisenach, where he would live in disguise for the next ten months. As news of Luther's apparent abduction spread in May 1521, his supporters reacted with horror, uncertain of his fate. On 17 May 1521, Albrecht Dürer wrote in his diary:

> I don't know if he is still alive, or if they have murdered him. He has suffered this fate on account of Christian truth and because he punished the unchristian papacy [...]. O God, if

202 GRANTLEY MCDONALD

Luther is dead, who will proclaim the Gospel to us so clearly? O God, what might he yet have written for us in ten or twenty years? O you pious Christians, help me to mourn this God-given man properly, and pray that God send us another enlightened man.[6]

An anonymous poet expressed similar sentiments in the following Latin verses:

Heu heu quae nobis te sors doctissime ademit?
    Quae te praehendit invida?
Quis te livor edax rapuit dulcissime? Quid sic
    Martine anhelos deseris?
Sicne tibi servata fides, servataque iura?
    Hei veritas quid sustines?
Parce precor praedae raptor, satis est rapuisse.
    Heus parce, parce occidere.

Alas, what fate has taken you, o learned man, from us?
    What envious fate has grasped you away?
What destructive spite has taken you, o sweetest man?
    Why do you thus desert your fervent followers?
Is this how you preserve your faithfulness, and observe your vows?
    Alas o truth, what a blow have you taken!
O captor, show mercy to your prey, I pray; it is enough to have taken him;
    Spare, o spare from taking his life.

The title of the poem, 'A lamentation for the captive Martin Luther', is subtly undercut by the choice of metre. Laments were normally written in elegiac couplets or hexameters. By contrast, this poem is written in a rare metre, the second Pythiambic, which comprises distichs of a hexameter followed by an iambic dimeter. This metre is generally found not in laments but in epodes, a species of invective poem. *Heu heu quae nobis te sors* expresses not merely loss. The grieving poet blames Luther for vanishing, characterising this as a betrayal of the trust his followers had placed in him; Luther's disappearance had led to a state of civil disquiet comparable to that lamented by Horace in his own bitter epodes. This subtle choice of metre, chosen carefully to reflect the poet's conflicted emotional state, and the classicising Latin diction (for example, the collocation 'livor edax' is borrowed from Ovid) suggest that the poem was probably written in the humanist milieu of the universities or urban sodalities, from which Luther drew much of his early support.[7]

An anonymous polyphonic setting of this poem for four voices was printed on a broadsheet (Figure 9.3, Example 9.1).[8] The music is set in the third and fourth tones, widely acknowledged in the sixteenth century as appropriate for lamentation. The quality of the music is consistent with the proposed origin of the poem; the writing is generally competent and at times quite effective, but is not the work of a first-rate composer. The music appears to have been written specifically for this text. At some points the word-setting is relatively syllabic, and fits closely with the music. If the piece were a contrafact, then the text of the model would necessarily have been written in the same unusual metre, and cast in similar units of sense. Given the rarity of the metre, this is perhaps unlikely.

---

6 Dürer, *Tagebuch*, 1:170–171: 'Und lebt er noch oder haben sie jn gemördert, das ich nit weiß, so hat er das gelitten umb der christlichen wahrheit willen und umb das er gestrafft hat das unchristliche pabstumb [. . .]. O Gott, ist Luther todt, wer wird uns hinfurt das heilig evangelium so clar fürtragen! Ach Gott, was hett er uns noch in 10 oder 20 jahrn schreiben mögen? O ihr alle fromme christen menschen, helfft mir fleissig bewainen diesen gott geistigen menschen und ihn bitten, das er uns ein andern erleuchten mann send.' See also Steiff, 'Entführung Luthers', 210–212. All translations are my own.
7 Steiff, 'Entführung Luthers', 211.
8 D-Tu Ke XVIII 4.2° Nr. 20, vdm 159.

Figure 9.3 *Ad Martinum Lutherum captivum lamentatio*. [Strasbourg]: [Johann Knobloch the Elder], [c.1521], (vdm 159)
Source: Universitätsbibliothek Tübingen, Ke XVIII 4.2°, Nr. 20

Neither the date nor the printer's name are mentioned on the sheet, but on the evidence of the type, the edition has been assigned to Johann Knobloch of Strasbourg.[9] This does not necessarily mean that the piece was written in Strasbourg; Knobloch could have pirated a sheet printed somewhere else. Nevertheless, the piece was evidently written during Luther's time on the Wartburg (May 1521 to February 1522), probably early in that period, before it became clear that Luther was still alive. The notes are printed from woodcut. Except in the case of books consisting entirely of mensural notation or chant, woodcut was still the most common way of printing music in Germany at this time. While Dürer expressed

---

9 Röckelein *et al.*, *Die lateinischen Handschriften*, 80–81.

204 GRANTLEY MCDONALD

his distress in private, the medium of print allowed this poet and composer to publicise Luther's suspicious disappearance, to reflect on its significance, to express their personal reaction to this event, and even, as the last couplet would have it, to try to influence the outcome of the situation.

The only known copy of this broadsheet survived because it was bound into a manuscript by Conrad Hager, pastor of Renningen during the Reformation, whose collection represents one of the most important sources of the broadsheets now preserved in the university library in Freiburg.[10] The sheet was obviously used; at a couple of points, notes that are unclear in the woodcut have been touched up in ink, such as the broken stem on the first minim in the discantus. Collectors such as Hager evidently valued such ephemera even after their 'news content' was no longer relevant. Preserving evidence of reactions to the reformer's life was a way of participating in the event as it happened, and commemorating it after it was past.

Epithalamia Martini Lutheri Wittenbergensis

The second piece we shall examine was written in response to Luther's wedding in 1525. When urged by his friends to marry, Luther protested that he, as an outlaw under imperial ban, might be taken and executed at any time. Such uncertainty was an unfair burden to expect a wife to bear. When a group of fugitive nuns appeared in Wittenberg shortly after Easter 1523, Luther was able to arrange marriages for all except one, Katharina von Bora. At last he was prevailed upon to marry her, and the ceremony duly took place on 13 June 1525. Cranach's workshop created a series of double portraits of Luther and Bora in order to emphasise the lawfulness of the wedding.[11] To the enemies of the Reformation, the marriage of an Augustinian friar to a runaway Carthusian nun provided yet more proof that Luther had abandoned ecclesiastical discipline at the urgings of his intemperate passions. Lyndal Roper has recently shown that a fascination with Luther's appetites, both culinary and sexual, played an important role in the creation of his public image on both sides of the confessional divide.[12]

Luther's opponent Hieronymus Emser, shocked by his marriage to Bora, wrote a collection of three satirical epithalamia (wedding songs) for Luther and for Johannes Hess, Lutheran preacher at St Mary Magdalene's church in Breslau, who married Sara Jopner on 8 September 1525.[13] The first poem in the collection, subtitled 'Hymn of the groomsmen' (*Hymnus paranymphorum*), is set to music (Figure 9.4).[14] Emser's 'Hymn of the groomsmen' ironically celebrates the marriage of Luther and Bora, and includes a jubilant enumeration

---

10 *Huguitius Ortulus grammatice*, D-Fu Mc 6 (olim Q 161); Steiff (1888), 211; Brinkhus, 'Bücherstiftung Hagens', esp. 15–16; Röckelein *et al.*, *Die lateinischen Handschriften*, 80.

11 Leppin and Schneider-Ludorff, *Luther-Lexikon*, 117.

12 Roper, 'Martin Luther's Body'.

13 Köstlin, 'Johann Heß', 218–219.

14 *EPITHALAMIA ‖ MARTINI LVTHERI Vuittenbergensis, IOANNIS HES‖SI Vratislauiensis, ac id genus nuptiatorum* ([Dresden]: [Hieronymus Emser], [c.1525]), vdm 738. Some sources (including VD16) attribute this collection to Johannes Cochlaeus, but Cochlaeus attributed it to Hieronymus Emser; see Johannes Cochlaeus, *COMMENTARIA ‖ IOANNIS COCHLAEI, DE ACTIS ‖ ET SCRIPTIS MARTINI LVTHERI SAXONIS* [. . .] (Mainz: Behem, 1549), VD16 C 4278, 118: '[Lutherus] omnia ista dissimulans, Monialem duxit uxorem, ac laetas celebrauit publice nuptias, incoestu & uotifragio sacrilegas, ac tot milibus occisorum funestatas. In quas sane nuptias satis elegans (ut amoeni erat uir ingenij) aedidit carmen Hieronymus Emserus. Quod & Quatuor vocum concentu decorauit [. . . He cites from the *Epithalamia*]. Hęc pius Emserus, in quem multi iuuenes Poëtę Vuittebergenses iampridem frustra conspirauerant. In mortem enim usque constantissime uir ille piam patrum religionem contra eos defendit.' Further, see Ruland, 'Epithalamia Martini Lutheri', Wiedemann, *Johann Eck*, 557–565; Clemen, 'Beiträge zur Lutherforschung 3', 113–114.

Figure 9.4 *Epithalamia Martini Lutheri Wittenbergensis*. [Dresden]: [Hieronymus Emser], [c.1525] (VD16 ZV 21361, vdm 738), fol. A1ʳ
Source: Forschungsbibliothek Gotha, Schloss Friedenstein, Cant.spir 8° 01323

of other married Protestant clergy, including Hess, Pellicanus and Bugenhagen. Yet Emser satirically undercut the event and questioned the motivations of its participants. Surpassing the good-natured ribaldry characteristic of the classical epithalamium, the groomsmen sing that Luther acted only to satisfy his itching member ('pruriente mentula'), and rejoice that they were now free to indulge in every kind of unspeakable wickedness ('licet nobis | Omne nephas'). This wild abandon is seen as the ultimate outcome of Luther's disdain for authority: 'Let kings, popes and emperors disapprove [. . .], let us laugh even at the saints of Christ, and destroy their images' ('Infamare licet reges | Papamque cum Caesare [. . .] | Sed et ipsos irridemus | Christi sanctos, et delemus | Eorum imagines'). Luther and Bora mocked the monastic discipline to which they had earlier sworn: 'Hence o cowl, farewell o habit, Bye-bye prior, guardian, abbot, along with your obedience' ('I cuculla, vale cappa | Vale Prior, Custos, Abba | Cum obedientia'). This wedding chorus is set to stirring music in a catchy homophonic style, and each stanza concludes with the cry, 'with joy' ('cum iubilo'), in an arresting hemiola pattern (Example 9.3).

The second poem in the collection is in mock-heroic hexameters. It begins with an invocation to the Muse, who is to tell of the strange marriage of Luther, this 'insane monk,

206   GRANTLEY MCDONALD

who mingles sacred and profane, who stirs up crowds and riots, who subverts every norm of order and the faith' ('[. . .] Insano monacho, qui miscet sacra profanis, | Qui turbas, motusque ciet, qui subruit omnem | Ordinis, & fidei normam [. . .]'). This, according to Emser, was the result of Luther's dangerous ambition: 'He farts at the highest peaks, and touches the sacred heights' ('[. . .] oppedit et ipsis | Verticibus summis, et sancta cacumina tangit'). The scatological humour of this poem is not simply gratuitous or puerile, but expresses vividly the horror aroused by Luther's sacrilege, as Piotr Wilczek has argued.[15] The third poem calls on the Furies to attend the wedding of Hess.

Emser's 'hymn of the groomsmen' is not an entirely new work, but is based on the *Rhythmus die divi Martini pronunciatus* ('rhythmical song performed on St Martin's day') by the Bolognese humanist Antonio Urceo Codro (1446–1500):

> Io Io Io Io,
> Gaudeamus Io Io,
> Dulces Homeriaci, Io Io,
> Noster vates hic Homerus,
> Dithirambi dux sincerus
> 　　Pergraecatur hodie, Io Io.
>
> *Io, io, io, io,*
> *Let us rejoice, io, io,*
> *Sweet disciples of Homer, [. . .]*
> *This our poet Homer,*
> *The genuine leader of the dithyramb,*
> 　　*Today rejoices with Greek abandon [. . .].*

The refrain *Io io* and the reference to the dithyramb indicate that the song was intended as a kind of bacchanal.[16] Codro's *Rhythmus* was popular in Germany and Poland, and was reprinted at least six times north of the Alps. Some of the German editions contain a four-voice setting that may have become attached to the poem only once it had left Italy (Example 9.2).[17] Codro's *Rhythmus* was particularly popular at Wittenberg in the early sixteenth century. It was reprinted there twice (1511, 1513), and was sung at the thirtieth birthday party of the Wittenberg humanist Christoph Scheurl in November 1511, where the guests included Georg Spalatinus.[18] It also formed the basis for a dithyramb by Jacob Locher on the election of Charles V in 1519.[19]

---

15 Wilczek, *(Mis)translation and (Mis)interpretation*, 79–101, esp. 88.

16 Creizenach, 'Das "Gaudeamus"', 204.

17 Antonio Urceo Codro, *In hoc Codri volumine ‖ hec continentur. ‖ Orationes. seu sermones ‖ vt ipse appellabat. ‖ Epistole ‖ Silue ‖ Satyre ‖ Egloge ‖ Epigrammata* (Venice: Liechtenstein, 1506), USTC 990166, fols. 66ʳ⁻ᵛ (no musical notation); *ANTHONII CODRI VRCEI ‖ Rhythmus die diui Martini ‖ pronunciatus [. . .]*, ed. Herman Trebelius (Wittenberg: Grunenberg, 1511), vdm 95; *RHYTMVS CODRI VRCEI DIE ‖ DIVI MARTINI PRONVNCIATVS* ([Worms]: [Gregor Hofmann], [c.1542–1553]), vdm 94; *Antonij Codri Vrcei rhythmus ‖ die diui Martini pronunciatus [. . .]*, ed. Hermann Trebelius (Wittenberg: Grunenberg, 1513), vdm 93; *RITHMVS CODRI VRCEI POETE ET ORA‖TORES VNDEQVAQVE DOCT‖ISSIMI IN DIE DIVI MARTINI ‖ PRONVNCIATVS* (Erfurt: Hans Knappe the Elder, 1514), vdm 645; *RHYTHMVS CODRI FESTIVISSIMVS. ‖ CARMEN MORI VRBANSSIMVM. I ‖ LVSVS CAMICZIANI VERISSIMVS* (Leipzig: Melchior Lotter, 1519), VD16 ZV 15128; not in *vdm*; no musical notation; *EXHORTATIO ‖ GVLIELMI BREYDSCHNEIDERII, IVRE=‖consulti Herbipoleñ. in amoeniora stu=‖dia [. . .]* ([n. p.]: [n. p.], 1526) VD16 ZV 2455; not in *vdm*; no musical notation; *ANTONII CO‖DRI VRCEI [. . .] opera, quae extant, omnia [. . .]* (Basel: Henrich Petri, 1540); not in *vdm*; no musical notation, 415–420. In the Zwickau copy of Frank's edition (VD16 ZV 15128), music is added by hand; see Clemen, 'Andreas Frank von Kamenz', 107. I could not locate any copies of the following edition listed in Estreicher et al., *Bibliografia polska*, 32:63: *Hymnus faceciis, urbanitate et hilaritate plenus, in honorem Bachi et potatorum omnium ab Autore editus* ([Vienna? Kraków?]: Hieronymus Vietor, 1528).

18 D-Ngm Cod. 306, fol. 92ʳ; digest in Bauch, 'Zu Christoph Scheurls Briefbuch', 422.

19 Heider, *Spolia vetustatis*, 206–208.

THE CULT OF LUTHER IN MUSIC   207

Emser's parody follows Codro's original quite closely, assimilating its dithyrambic refrain (*Io, io*), its metrical structure (the so-called *Stabat Mater* strophe) and the triple rhythm of the musical setting, though the music itself is different (see examples 9.2 and 9.3):

Io Io Io Io
Gaudeamus cum iubilo,
Dulces Lutheriaci [. . .].
Noster pater hic Lutherus,
Nostrae legis dux sincerus,
    Nuptam ducit hodie [. . .].

Io, io, io, io,
Let us rejoice with gladness,
Sweet disciples of Luther [. . .].
This our father Luther,
The genuine leader of our law,
    Today takes a bride [. . .].[20]

The idea of writing a parody of Codro's *Rhythmus* may have occurred to Emser because of the association of St Martin's day and Martin Luther, or because of the popularity of Codro's *Rhythmus* at Wittenberg. The idea of adapting Codro's poem as an epithalamium may likewise have suggested itself to Emser because a poem celebrating the wedding of Georg Schiltel was included in the 1519 Leipzig edition of Codro's text.

The inclusion of musical notation in Emser's pamphlet suggests that the piece was intended to be sung, probably in a convivial gathering of students or humanists such as the *dulces Homeriaci* bidden to sing Codro's *Rhythmus*. Ingrid Rowland has shown that groups of humanists sometimes participated in spirited drinking sessions, during which they would recite and improvise satirical and often shockingly obscene poems criticising the sexual excesses of the clergy.[21] Emser's *Epithalamia* may have been sung at just such a gathering. Once printed, such poems could be read and sung at multiple gatherings in different places, thus forging group identity through the recognition and abuse of a common enemy.

The sole independent edition of Emser's *Epithalamia* comprises a single sheet of poor-quality paper in quarto format. The music is printed from woodblocks, legibly but without much elegance. There is little attempt to align the voice parts. This was evidently not intended as a luxury edition. The edition is unsigned, but its types belonged to Emser's press in Dresden, which produced a number of polemical pieces against Luther in the 1520s, including another one with music that protested against Luther's rejection of St Benno.[22]

Emser's satires on the weddings of Luther and Hess were evidently quite popular. The text (without the music) was reprinted as an appendix to a 1527 edition of the correspondence between Luther and Henry VIII, edited by Johann Eck.[23] The entire

---

20 The dependence of Emser's *Hymnus paranymphorum* on Codro's *Rhythmus* was pointed out by Creizenach, 'Das "Gaudeamus"', 204; see also Malagola, *Antonio Urceo*, 410–412.

21 Rowland, 'Revenge'.

22 ενκωμιον [sic] *in diuum Bennonem.*‖ *Ach Benno du vil heilger man* [. . .].‖ αντιφρασισ [sic] *in Bennomasticem.*‖ *Ach Luter du vil bößer man* ([Dresden]: Emser, 1524), vdm 167. See Wagner Oettinger, *Music as Propaganda*, 52–53, 81–88, 129, 205, 213–214, 231.

23 *EPISTOLA* ‖ *MARTINI LVTHERI AD HENRI*‖*CVM.VIII.ANGLIAE AC FRAN=*‖*ciae Regem etc. In qua ueniam petit eorum* ‖ *quae prius stultus ac praeceps in eundem* ‖ *regem effuderit: offerens pali=*‖*nodiam se cantaturum.* ‖ *RESPON*‖*SIO DICTI INVICTISSIMI ANGLIAE* ‖ *ac Franciae regis* [. . .] ‖ *EPITHALAMIA festiua in Lutherum,*‖ *Hessum et id genus nuptiatorum,* ed. Johann Eck (Ingolstadt: [Peter Apian and Georg Apian], 1527), VD16 L 4622, fols. D1ʳ–8ʳ. The gathering containing the *Epithalamia* is absent from many of the copies I inspected.

208   GRANTLEY MCDONALD

pamphlet, including the music, was also copied into a manuscript collection of anti-Reformation propaganda written by Lorenz Truchsess von Pommersfelden (1473–1543).[24] Lother Mundt has argued convincingly that the *Epithalamia* influenced Simon Lemnius' *Monachopornomachia*.[25] Indeed, the poems would be cited in anti-Lutheran propaganda for centuries to come.[26]

Eyn erschreglicher und doch widderumb kurtzweylliger und nutzlich gesangk

The third edition we shall consider is another satirical piece, 'A frightful and yet amusing song of the Luciferian and Lutheran church', published as part of a new year's message for 1526 by the Roman Catholic controversialist Petrus Sylvius.[27] Sylvius' song was a direct response to two contrafacts that appeared in the wake of the Diet of Worms. In 1521 or 1522, one of Luther's supporters wrote the contrafact *Invicti Martini laudes intonant Christiani* ('Christians sing aloud the praises of the invincible Martin'), a parody of the Easter sequence *Victimae paschali laudes*, which was to be sung to the same melody.[28] Sylvius objected to the fact that this poem implicitly placed Luther on the same level as Christ. He also noted that another parody, this time of the vernacular Easter Leise *Christ ist erstanden*, was sung at Nuremberg in 1524, to the same melody as the original:

> Martinus hat gerathen/ man sol die pfaffen brathen.
> Die mönnich vntterschüren/ Die Nonn inß. N. füren. kyrioleiß.[29]

Hoffmann von Fallersleben, *Gaudeamus igitur*, reports having seen this text in a sixteenth century manuscript; its location is now unknown.

24 D-Mbs Clm 24163, fols. 294ᵛ–297ᵛ; see Löbbert, 'Nachlass Lorenz Truchsess von Pommersfelden', esp. 127–132. The secondary literature on this chorus contains some errors. Löbbert, 'Nachlass Lorenz Truchsess von Pommersfelden', 131–132, referring to Renner, 'Gaudeamus omnes', 199–202, states that the melody of Emser's *Epithalamia* is based on the 'Introitus-Antiphon [sic] zum Allerheiligenfest', that is, *Gaudeamus omnes*, but this is not the case. Renner's article also contains some errors. He interpreted the snippet of the introit *Gaudeamus omnes* in a woodcut in Brant's *Narrenschiff* as a distortion of the chant melody for satirical effect. In the *Liber usualis*, the source Renner takes as authoritative, *Gaudeamus* has the pitches c–d–d–a–bb♮–a. The *Narrenschiff* woodcut has the notes c–d–d–a–c–a, which Renner interprets as a 'shocking' alteration that would be obvious to all. However, this melodic feature was typical of the German chant dialect. The reading of *Gaudeamus omnes* given in the *Graduale Pataviense* (Vienna: Winterburger, 1511), vdm 272, fol. 162ʳ, agrees perfectly with that found in the woodcut. On this feature of the German chant dialect, see Hiley, *Western Plainchant*, 573.

25 Mundt, *Lemnius und Luther*, 1:105–108.

26 See for example Johann Nass, *Quinta centuria, das ist/ das fünfft Hundert/ der Euangelischen Warheit* (Ingolstadt: Alexander Weissenhorn, 1570), VD16 N 105, fols. 365ʳ⁻ᵛ; Maurice Hylaret, *Sacrae decades quinquepartitae* (Paris: Sébastien Nivelle, 1587), USTC 138169, 1:190–191; Johannes Theophilus Klibnitz, *Christliches Sendschreiben an* [. . .] *Johann Georgen/ dem Andern/ Hertzogen zu Sachsen* (Vienna: Leopold Voigt, 1671), VD17 12:111610F, fols. F4ʳ⁻ᵛ; Johann Nikolaus Weisslinger, *Friß Vogel oder Stirb!* (Strasbourg: Dietrich Lerse, 1722), not in VD18, 65; Eusebius Engelhard, *Lucifer Wittenbergensis, oder der Morgen-Stern von Wittenberg* (Landsberg: Johann Lorenz Singer, 1749), VD18 10787917, 2:125–129.

27 *Eyn erschreglicher* ‖ *vnd doch widderumb kurtzweylliger vnd nutzlich gesangk* ‖ *der Lutziferischen vnd Luttrischen kirchen/ auff dy* ‖ *nachfolgend weyse durch eyn Euangelische vnd* ‖ *Apostolischen Prister ytzt zum nawen Jar* ‖ *der Christenheyt tzu heyl vnd seligkeyt* ‖ *auß gegangen.* ‖ [music] ‖ *Martinus hat gerathen Das Ri Rum Ritz.* ‖ *Man sal die pfaffen brathen Das Ri rum Ritz etc.* ‖ *M. R Syl.* ‖ *M.D.xxvj.* ([Leipzig: Nickel Schmidt], 1526), vdm 695. Sylvius summarises this book in: *Von den letzten Funff* ‖ *buchern M. Petri Syluij* [. . .] (Leipzig: Nickel Schmidt, 1528), VD16 P 1307, fol. C4ᵛ. An extract from text is edited in Neumann, *Geistliches Schauspiel*, 2:214–218. Further on Sylvius, see Seidemann, 'Die Schriften des Petrus Sylvius', esp. 13–15, 288–289, 302–306.

28 Clemen, 'Invictas Martini', showed that this parody first appeared as an appendix to *Sendtbrieff. D. Andree Boden: von Carolstadt meldende seiner Wirtschafft/ Newe getzeyt vonn pfaffen vnnd mönchenn zu Wittemberg außgangen* (Wittenberg: [n. p.], [1522]), D-Dl Hist.eccl.E.243,16, not in VD16; later editions: VD16 B 6189–6194, ZV 2156.

29 Petrus Sylvius, *Summa vnd schutz der* ‖ *waren Euangelischen lere/ vnd der* ‖ *gantzen Göttlichen schrifft/ auffs newe gedrückt/ gemehrt/* ‖ *vnd gebessert* [. . .] ([Leipzig]: [Nickel Schmidt and Valentin Schumann], 1529), VD16

THE CULT OF LUTHER IN MUSIC   209

Martin has bidden that the priests should be roasted, the monks burned, and the nuns sent into the whorehouse. Kyrie eleison.

Sylvius answered these parodies with two of his own. In response to *Invicti Martini laudes* he wrote *Convicti Lutheri fraudes exhorrent Christiani* ('Christians shudder at the deceptions of the defeated Luther').[30] He countered *Martinus hat gerathen* with:

Christ hat gerathen/ vnd ernstlich gebothen.
Die Priesterschafft zu ehren/ vnd folgen ihrer lehren.
ky[rieleis].[31]

Christ has bidden and earnestly commanded
that we should honour the priesthood and follow its teaching.
Kyrie eleison.

At New Year 1526, Sylvius published a pamphlet entitled *On the identity of the Lutheran and Luciferian churches*, in which he pointed out twenty-one similarities between the Lutheran church and the devil.[32] He may have been prompted to write this work as a response to a 1523 dialogue by Erasmus Alberus, in which Luther debates two devils dressed in monks' cowls.[33] As a companion piece to this tract, Sylvius published a satirical song in which the devil and his hosts rejoice at the song *Martinus hat gerathen* and the harm it has done to the true church. In the preface, Sylvius explained that he was prompted to write this song by reports of the 'dumb Lutheran youth' who sang this blasphemous parody in beer halls. The song comprises a dialogue between an 'infernal chorus' ('der Hellische Chor') and Satan. The text was to be sung to a simple, mocking melody that, Sylvius tells us, was customarily used in plays when the infernal spirits sang to Lucifer.[34] Sylvius reproduced the melody in mensural notation on the frontispiece of his pamphlet (Figure 9.5). Although the melody given by Sylvius is of the simplest kind, it is historically important, for it represents the only known notated example of the music sung in the devils' chorus, a stock scene in mediaeval religious drama.[35]

The demons sing that Luther is Satan's brother, who has fallen away from his vows and is now mired in lust and sin. Moreover, he attempts to seduce Christians from the right way, bringing to pass whatever Lucifer can invent ('Was Lutzifer kan erdencken | Das kan

---

P 1300, Appendix, fols. A1ᵛ–2ʳ: 'Darauff heb ich mit meynen ohren gehöret das sie auch vor [A2ʳ] fünff iarn geßungen haben/ den nachfolgenden vnchristlichen deutschen text vff die weiß des österlichen geßanges/ Christ ist erstanden [. . .]. Welcher Text als ichs von glawbwirdigenn gehorth/ hab/ ist erstlich geßungen worden in der löblichen vnd Christlichen stadt vortzeyten genanth Nurnbergk.' Sylvius, *Eyn erschreglicher* (1526), fol. A2ʳ, gives the readings: 'Der Luther hat geratten' and 'Dy nonnen yns freyhauß furen'.

30 Sylvius, *Summa vnd schutz*, fol. A2ʳ.

31 Sylvius, *Summa vnd schutz*, fol. A4ʳ.

32 Petrus Sylvius, *Von der eynigkeit ‖ der Luttrischen vnd Lutziferischen kirche vnd/‖ von yhrer gleychformiger arth vnd eygenschafft ‖ [. . .]* (Leipzig: Schmidt, Nickel, 1526), VD16 1309.

33 [Erasmus Alberus], *Ain schoner Dialogus von Martino ‖ Luther vnd der geschickt pottschafft auß der helle die falsche ‖ gaystligkayt vnd das wortt gots belangen ‖ gantz hubsch zu lesen* ([Erfurt]: [Michael Buchführer], 1523), VD16 A 1524.

34 Sylvius, *Eyn erschreglicher* (1526), fol. A1ᵛ: 'So ich dan offt gehöret hab/ wie die Thumme Lutrische iugent in etlichen stedten/ ßo sy in byrheusern bey der kweßrey den hellischen geistern meßhalten/ pflegen tzu verachtung der Christlichen geistligkeyt tzu syngen den teuffels gesangk/ Luther hat gerathen &c. auff den thon und weyse wie die hellischen laruen pflegen tzu syngen yhren Lutzifer ßo man yrgent ein spil übet. Nemlich Lutzifer in dem Throne/ das Ri Rum Ritz &c. vnd nicht vnbekumlich/ dan wie die kirche ist/ Also sal auch sein der gesangk/ Der text/ die nothen und dy ßenger. Derhalben auff das dy Lutrische kirche/ vnd solchs teuffels gesinde/ sampt mit der Lutziferischen kirche/ eintrechtig vereyniget muchten mit eynander tzu gleych singen/ So hab ich auff dy selbige weyße noch mehr text gemacht/ darynn des Luthers vnd Lutzifers vereynigunge wird noch volkomlicher erklert.'

35 Neumann, 'Zeugnisse mittelalterlicher Aufführungen', 1:114–115.

Figure 9.5 Petrus Sylvius, *Eyn erschreglicher und doch widderumb kurtzweylliger und nutzlich gesangk.* [Leipzig]: [Nickel Schmidt], 1526 (VD16 ZV 12265; vdm 695), fol. A1ʳ
Source: Halle, Universitäts- und Landesbibliothek Sachsen-Anhalt, AB 153250 (6)

Luther auß schencken'). Satan's interventions are written in a different metre, and were perhaps spoken rather than sung. Some of Sylvius' claims were evidently not true, such as the notion that Luther advocated the abolishment of liturgical music ('Alles syngen vnd klingen | Das sall man gantz abdingen'). Despite all its crude satire and exaggeration, Sylvius' poem nevertheless expresses the fears and anxieties of those who remained true to the Roman church. Luther, they believed, encouraged the simple folk to disdain the praise of God and obedience to authority. He taught that bells, monstrances and chalices were to be melted down, and nuns sexually corrupted. Such actions could only bring the traditions of the church to ruin.

Sylvius' pamphlet comprises a single sheet, printed in quarto. The musical notation is cut quite carefully in wood. The printer did not identify himself, though Sylvius published most of his pamphlets with Nickel Schmidt following his move to Leipzig in August or September 1525. The typography of this edition is consistent with Schmidt's workshop. Curiously, Schmidt is known to have been a Lutheran; in 1524, he signed a petition requesting that the Leipzig city council allow Lutheran services in the city. However, his own evangelical faith evidently did not preclude him from printing tracts attacking Luther. Few printers in Leipzig could afford to turn away paid work in the 1520s, when the industry in the city was on the verge of collapse. Schmidt probably told himself that if he did not print Sylvius' pamphlets, one of his competitors would.[36]

Like Emser's *Epithalamia*, Sylvius' poem draws attention to Luther's perceived infractions of ecclesiastical order, and aims to forge group spirit by identifying and mocking a common enemy. In 1535, Sylvius reprinted a revised edition of his 1526 work on the Satanic nature of the Lutheran church, including the devil's chorus as an appendix, with the music printed

---

36 Reske, *Buchdrucker*, 518.

THE CULT OF LUTHER IN MUSIC   211

from the same woodcut as the earlier edition. This later edition also has a title woodcut that depicts Luther and Satan holding hands to swear a compact (see Figure 9.2). The depiction of Luther, resting his left hand on a book as if to confirm the pact, derives from images from the Cranach workshop. Luther credulously extends his right hand while Satan offers only his left, thus deceiving Luther himself. Furthermore, the composition also recalls the iconography of a betrothal portrait, a monstrous marriage from which only ill could spring. In a parody of the iconography of Gregory the Great and the dove of the Holy Spirit, a small demon lifts the corner of Luther's doctoral biretta and whispers into his ear. The notion that Luther had entered into a pact with the devil was intended to disarm Luther's own identification of the Roman Catholic church as the antichrist.[37]

Nu hört jr Christen newe meer and *Mein himlischer vatter*

In early 1546, Luther travelled to Eisleben to adjudicate a dispute between rival factions in the ducal house of Mansfeld. There he suffered an attack of angina followed by cardiac arrest early on the morning of 18 January 1546. Justus Jonas, a theologian from Wittenberg who accompanied Luther on the journey, and Michael Coelius, pastor at Mansfeld, immediately sent an account of Luther's last days to Johann Friedrich of Saxony, including a transcript of his last words:

> Da hat der herr doctor angefangen zu betten.
> Mein himlischer vatter/ ewiger barmherziger Got/ du hast mir deinen lieben sohn/ vnsern herrn Jhesum Christum offenbart/ den hab ich gelert/ den hab ich bekant/ den liebe ich/ vnd den ere ich vor meinen lieben heilandt vnd erlöser/ welchen die gotlosen verfolgen/ schenden vnd schelten/ nim mein selichen zu dir.
> In dem reth er in die drei mal/
> In manus tuas commendo spiritum meum, redemisti me deus veritatis. Ja also hat Got die welt geliebt.[38]

> *Then Dr [Luther] began to pray: 'My heavenly father, eternal, merciful God, you have revealed to me your dear Son, our Lord Jesus Christ. I have taught about him, I have confessed him, I love him, and I honour him as my dear Saviour and Redeemer, whom the godless persecute, defile and abuse. Take my little soul to you.' Then he spoke three times: 'Into your hands I commend your spirit. You have redeemed me, o God of truth. God so loved the world, etc.'*

This account spread quickly, and at least a half a dozen manuscript copies are extant.[39] It received an even broader readership when it was printed in the pamphlet *Drey Schrifften vonn des Eerwirdigen Herren Doctor Martin Luthers Christlichem abschied vnnd Sterben/ auch Eerlichem begrebnuß* ([Augsburg]: [Steiner], 1546), in which Luther's prayer is highlighted through typographical means. This source evidently derives ultimately from the fair copy, since it includes an endorsement in Jonas' hand added to that copy, which assured the recipient that he had dictated the letter and that he and Coelius were present for the full duration of these events ('der bei disen allen gewesen'). A desire to have news from trustworthy eyewitness reports was a natural feature of early news networks, even before print, as Andrew Pettegree has shown.[40]

---

37 Langemeyer *et al.*, *Bild als Waffe*, 163.
38 The draft is in Annaberg, Schulbibliothek; the fair copy is in D-WRl Reg. N 182, fols. 19ʳ–22ᵛ, here at fols. 20ᵛ–21ʳ, ed. Schubart, *Berichte*, 4–5. The diminutive 'selichen' in the Weimar ms is changed to 'Seel' in the early editions.
39 These sources are listed in Schubart, *Berichte*, 1. See also Pettegree, *Brand Luther*, 306–307.
40 Pettegree, *The Invention of News*, 2.

212   GRANTLEY MCDONALD

After writing to the duke, Jonas wrote another letter to his colleagues in Wittenberg. On the morning of 19 January 1546, Philipp Melanchthon announced the contents of Jonas' letter to his class in Wittenberg, as one of his auditors related:

> He told us that he had been advised to do so by the other professors for the reason that we, informed about the truth of the matter, might not embrace the many fictitious stories surrounding Luther's death which they knew would circulate here and there.[41]

While the idealised death described in the mediaeval *ars moriendi* emphasised the efficacy of the sacrament of extreme unction and the power of the administering priest, the various accounts of Luther's death that circulated in manuscript, and soon after in print, became a new Protestant norm that stressed the saving power of individual faith.

The Nuremberg cantor Leonhard Kettner wrote a versified account of Luther's death that ran through at least eleven editions between 1546 and 1549, in Upper German and Low German, chapbooks in octavo format, printed from a half-sheet. The edition printed at Wittenberg by Georg Rhau has a woodcut portrait of Luther on the cover, and contains the musical notation of the melody to which the ballad was to be sung: Johann Agricola's hymn *Ich ruf zu dir, Herr Jesu Christ*. (Most of the other editions simply specified this melody on their title pages without supplying the notation.) Kettner's versification of Luther's last words stretches over four stanzas. His account is clearly based on Jonas' report, from which it borrows words and even entire phrases. Direct verbal borrowings are indicated here in italics:

O Got *Vater*/ Herr Jesu Christi/ sprach er mit rechtem hertzen:‖:
Hilf mir jtzund zu dieser frist/ vnd wende meinen schmertzen/
Dein Son hastu mir offenbart/
 Von dem hab ich geleret/
 In geehret/
Darinn kein müh gespart/
 Also Bapsts lehr zerstöret.

Herr/ dein wort ich gepredigt hab/ *welchs die Gottlosen schenden*:‖:
Hab dauon nicht gelassen ab/ niemand kund das verwenden/
Du bist mein Herr mitten im tod/
 Mein Erlöser/ mein Heiland/
 Thu mir beystand/
O Herr/ O lieber Gott/
 Mach mir jtzt dein Reich bekant.

Denn *so* hastu *geliebt die Welt*/ das du für Vns hast geben:‖:
Dein Son wer zjhm sein glauben stelt/ sol hab das ewig leben/
Zu dir/ Herr ich mein Hoffnung setz/
 Herr dir thu ich vertrawen/
 Auff dich bawen/
Das sag ich zu der letzt/
 Dein angsicht las mich schawen.

---

41 Johannes Pollicarius, ed., *HISTORIA ‖ DE VITA ET ACTIS ‖ REVERENDISS. VIRI D. MART.‖ Lutheri, uerae Theologiae Doctoris, bo-‖na fide conscrip-‖ta, à ‖ PHILIPPO MELANTHONE* [. . .] (Erfurt: Gervasius Sturmer, 1548), VD16 M 3416, E1ʳ–2ᵛ; also ed. in Schubart, *Berichte*, 22–24, from the 1549 reprint. This collection contains a number of documents relating to Luther's life and death, including Melanchthon's biography of Luther, an account of Luther's appearance at the Diet of Worms, and commemorative poems by Pollicarius and Georg Fabricius, collected by Johannes Pollicarius, pastor at Weissenfels. Pollicarius' preface is signed 20 October 1547.

Zum bschlus/ sprach er/ *Herr in dein hend/ ich dir meine Seel thu senden*:‖:
Der wölstu gebn ein seligs end/ dein gnad nicht von mir wenden/
Herr mich allein befihl ich dir/
  In deim Nam will ich sterben/
  Vnd ererben/
Was du hast zugsagt mir/
  Dein ewig Reich erwerben.[42]

'O Father God, Lord Jesus Christ,' he spoke with right heart, 'Help me now and turn away my pain.
You have revealed your Son to me, I taught of him and honoured him, saving no pains, and thus destroyed
the Pope's doctrine.
Lord, I preached your Word, which the godless defile, and did not desist, and no one could refute that.
You are my Lord in the midst of death. My redeemer, my saviour, bear me up! O Lord, o dear God,
show me your kingdom now.
For you so loved the world, that you gave your Son for us, that whoever believes in him should have
everlasting life. In you, o Lord, do I trust and build. And at the last I say, let me see your face.'
And at the end he spoke, 'Lord, into your hands I commend my spirit. Give me a blessed end, and do
not turn your grace away from me. Lord, I commit myself to you alone. I want to die in your name
and inherit what you have promised me: to gain your eternal kingdom.'

The report of Luther's death, as made by eyewitnesses and implicitly endorsed through the fact that it was published at Wittenberg, travelled through Germany in Jonas' prose account and Kettner's ballad, carried along on the back of a familiar melody. Kettner's ballad was reprinted as late as 1549, and Jonas' account as late as 1555, long after the event had ceased to be news. Such postponed editions suggest that readers valued the accounts of Jonas and Kettner as a new kind of *ars moriendi*.

The news of Luther's death prompted an outpouring of grief among his followers. The composer Caspar Othmayr wrote a Latin poem in elegiacs reflecting on the event:

Per quem salvifici redierunt dogmata Christi,
  Hic vermes (ut habent fata) Lutherus alit.
Tutus ab insidiis, et casu tutus ab omni,
  Spiritus in coelis vivit, et astra videt.

Luther, through whom the teachings of our Saviour Christ returned,
  Here feeds the worms, as fate demands.
Safe now from all intrigues and all reverses of fortune,
  His spirit lives in the heavens, and beholds the stars.

Othmayr also set this text to music, once again in the third and fourth tones (transposed).[43] Typical of Othmayr's humanistic approach is his close attention to verse metre. The piece was printed in a set of partbooks containing only two pieces, both relating to the death of Luther.[44] The polyphonic lament is closely related to the literary genre of the classical epicedion and the mediaeval *planctus* or *déploration*. In late sixteenth-century Germany, musical laments are often found in conjunction with funeral sermons, which were invariably

---

42 Leonhard Kettner, *Von D. Mar‖tini Luthers sterben/ Ein ‖ schön new Lied/ darinn kürtz∗‖lich begriffen/ was er jn der letz∗‖ten zeit geredt/ sehr tröstlich ‖ allen Christen* [. . .] (Wittenberg: Rhau, 1546), vdm 1037, fols. A2ᵛ–3ʳ; further editions: VD16 K 846; K 848; K 849; K 850; K 851; K 852; ZV 26007; ZV 22180; ZV 8922; ZV 21593. Brednich does not list the Wittenberg edition. Kettner's poem is not noted in Schubart, *Berichte*.
43 Othmayr's versification is reasonably correct, apart from the infelicitous caesura in v. 2.
44 *EPITAPHIVM ‖ D. MARTINI LVTHERI,‖ A GASPARE OTMAIER ‖ Musicis Elegijs redditum.‖ TENOR* (Nuremberg: Berg and Neuber, 1546), vdm 1038.

accompanied by celebratory and commemorative poems on the deceased. Melanchthon's funeral sermon for Luther, often printed with Jonas' letter describing Luther's death, was one of the first examples of this genre. Othmayr's short collection thus straddles two print genres: the printed collection of polyphonic music, and the printed funeral sermon. This double function is clear on the title page, in which the generic function EPITAPHIVM and the name of the subject D. MARTINI LVTHERI vie for typographical prominence with the voice designation TENOR.

The other piece printed in Othmayr's collection *Epitaphium D. Martini Lutheri* is a polyphonic setting of Luther's last prayer, as reported in Justus Jonas' initial letter to Johann Friedrich. (Most other printed editions rely on slightly later reports, and give a slightly different text of the prayer.) Othmayr's five-voice setting, set once again in the third and fourth tone, transforms a narrative element from Jonas' report into an element of musical structure. According to Jonas, Luther three times spoke the words, 'Into thy hands I commend my spirit; you have redeemed me, o God of truth.' This text, taken from Psalm 30:6, was the *responsorium breve* for compline. Othmayr took the relevant chant as his cantus firmus, repeating it three times, as in Jonas' account. Its appearance is highlighted by the introduction of e-flats in the other voices, to accommodate the b-flats in the cantus firmus (Example 9.4).

Othmayr's collection thus contains two pieces united by their theme, but distinct in other ways. The first piece is in Latin, and is free-composed. The second is in German, but contains a cantus firmus in Latin. This latter piece thus renders Luther's own vigorous bilingualism, which has been explored by Birgit Stolt.[45] Othmayr's purpose in publishing a setting of Luther's last words is perhaps not immediately obvious. It might be argued that this setting had the function of spreading the report of Luther's death. However, by the time he came to write this piece, this was not exactly breaking news. It seems more likely that the piece has a commemorative or even devotional function, like those editions of the reports of Luther's death that appeared years after the event. Furthermore, humanist composers enjoyed setting the last words (*novissima verba*) of famous personages, a summa of their life, a musical analogue to the death mask or deathbed portrait. Settings of *Dulces exuviae*, the last words of Dido as reported in Vergil's *Aeneid*, constitute a subgenre among sixteenth-century secular motets.[46] Othmayr was attracted by the idea of summarising an individual's personality and achievements in a self-contained motto-composition or *symbolum*, and in 1547 he published a volume of thirty-four such motto-pieces, including one for Luther.

Besides this commemorative function, it is suggested that this setting of Luther's last words also has an apologetic, even polemical function. Evidence for this contention may be found in Othmayr's next collection, *Cantilenae aliquot elegantes ac piae* (Nuremberg: Berg & Neuber, 1546).[47] The preface, dated 6 October 1546, was contributed by Veit Dietrich, Lutheran pastor in Nuremberg. Dietrich referred to Jonas' report of Luther's last days. He was dismayed by the response of Roman Catholic controversialists to the reformer's death, especially the sarcastic references to Luther as the 'prophet of Germany'. (Dietrich is probably referring to Georg Witzel's 1546 tract *The reasons for the long-standing calamity*

---

45 Stolt, *Die Sprachmischung in Luthers Tischreden*.

46 Strunk, 'Vergil in Music', p. 489; Guentner, 'Dulces exuviae in Sixteenth Century Music'.

47 *CANTILENÆ ‖ ALIQVOT ELEGAN-‖TES AC PIAE, QVIBVS HIS TVR∂‖bulentis temporibus Ecclesia Christi utitur.‖ Musicis harmonijs ornatæ, à Gaspare Othmayer* (Nuremberg: Berg & Neuber, 1546), vdm 1039.

48 Georg Witzel, *CAVSA ‖ TAM DIVTVRNAE ‖ CALAMITATIS ECCLE‖SIASTICI STATVS ‖ IN GERMANIA.‖ D. Gersonites Landauus* (Cologne: Quentel's heirs, 1546), VD16 W 3889, fols. B3^r-v.

THE CULT OF LUTHER IN MUSIC 215

of the state of the church in Germany.[48]) Dietrich defended Luther's prophetic status against such attacks, comparing his prophetic gifts to those of Elijah. In Dietrich's opinion, hymns such as *Erhalt uns Herr* and *Verleyh uns freiden* revealed their prophetic significance in the chaos following Luther's death. Dietrich praised Othmayr's settings of these hymns, describing him a 'learned musician' ('eruditus Musicus') and 'a very diligent student of true piety' ('pietatis verae perstudiosus').[49] Given that Othmayr asked Dietrich to contribute this preface, we can probably assume that they shared similar views about the importance of vindicating Luther's memory against the calumnies of his opponents.

But perhaps we can go even further. The mediaeval tradition of the *ars moriendi* emphasised that the attitude, actions and words of the dying, as well as the intercession of their friends and the attending priest, would decide whether their soul would be dragged down to hell by demons, or ushered on to purgatory by angels. For decades following Luther's death, Roman Catholic controversialists circulated rumours about this event that reflected their own theological preoccupations. Tommaso Bozio (1591) wrote: 'Luther's servant, who later converted to the true faith, affirmed that Luther, after eating a hearty dinner, was that same night agitated by despair and the furious onslaught of a demon, and hanged himself.'[50] Nicolaus Serarius (1599) went even further:

> Though it is clear that Luther was carried off in a sudden and unprepared death, others are of another opinion, but many people believe that he was slain by his evil demon, since the physicians called to attend him either said that they did not know what his illness was, or pretended that it was a stroke.[51]

Such sudden death, bereft of the assistance of priest or sacraments, was just about the worst thing a Roman Catholic theologian could imagine. The assumption made by Bozio and Serarius that Luther was driven to his death by demons is consistent with the imagery, both verbal and iconographical, of Sylvius' broadsheet. Accordingly, I suggest that Othmayr's intention was not simply to commemorate and mourn Luther's death. Rather, like Melanchthon announcing Luther's death to his students, Othmayr wished to anticipate rumours that Luther's death was violent, frightening and moreover *demonic* by emphasising the tone of serenity, deep faith and faithfulness to the Scriptures, evident both in Jonas' account of Luther's final prayer and in Othmayr's music. The same impression of peaceful departure is given by the multiple images of Luther's deathbed portrait manufactured in the Cranach workshop after an eyewitness sketch by Lucas Furtenagel, and distributed widely.[52] In many of these portraits, the reformer's unmistakeable features are surrounded by a kind of halo or nimbus created by the pillow on which his head rests.

---

49 Dietrich's preface is reprinted in Othmayr, *Ausgewählte Werke*, 5–6.

50 Tommaso Bozio, *DE SIGNIS ‖ ECCLESIAE DEI ‖ LIBRI XII* [. . .] (Rome: Donangeli, 1591), USTC 816657, 2:514: 'Lutherum cùm vespere lautè coenasset, ac laetus somno se dedisset, ea nocte suffocatus interiit. Audiui haud ita pridem compertum testimonio sui familiaris, qui tum puer illi seruiebat, & superioris annis ad nostros se recepit, Lutherum sibimet ipsi laqueo iniecto necem miserrimam attulisse; sed datum protinus cunctis domesticis rei consciis iusiurandum, ne factum diuulgarent, ob honorem adiecere Euangelij.' The story was later related by Cornelius a Lapide, *Commentaria in epistolas canonicas* (Lyon: Prost, 1627), 364.

51 Nicolaus Serarius, *IN SACROS ‖ DIVINORVM ‖ BIBLIORVM ‖ LIBROS,‖ TOBIAM, IVDITH,‖ ESTHER, MACHABAEOS,‖ Commentarius* [. . .] (Mainz: Lippius, 1599), VD16 ZV 1810, 112: 'Lutherum vero subitanea & improuisa morte sublatum cum liqueat, alij quidem aliter, sed plurimi suo à cacodaemone peremtum existimant, cum vocati ad eum Medici morbum vel ignorare se faterentur, vel apoplexiam fingerent.'

52 Dresden, Staatliche Kunstsammlungen, inv. GG1955; Hannover, Niedersächsisches Landesmuseum, inv. KM107; Karlsruhe, Staatliche Kunsthàlle, inv. 0121.

216 GRANTLEY MCDONALD

Conclusion

All the settings discussed here present a picture of Luther that is highly subjective and moulded to polemical ends. The Luther who emerges is not a regular man, but one who dwelt on the level of the saints – or demons. The deployment of such imagery was partly Luther's own invention. He constantly referred to the papacy as the Antichrist, a title taken from the book of the Apocalypse. Many of his best known hymns, such as *Christ lag in Todes Banden*, contain violent imagery of cosmic strife. Such imagery implied that the Reformation of the church (or its deformation, depending on one's own perspective) had cosmic consequences. Each of the pieces we have examined presents a different image of Luther. Each make claims to credibility, but each is carefully crafted and even distorted to a greater or lesser degree in order to represent the interests of those who imagined him capering below with the demons, or resting peacefully in anticipation of the Last Day.

References

Bauch, Gustav. 'Zu Christoph Scheurls Briefbuch'. *Neue Mitteilungen aus dem Gebiet historisch-antiquarischer Forschungen* 19 (1898): 400–456.

Brednich, Rolf Wilhem. *Die Liedpublizistik im Flugblatt des 15. bis 17. Jahrhunderts*. 2 vols. Baden-Baden: Koerner, 1975.

Brinkhus, Gerd. 'Die Bücherstiftung Konrad Hagens für die Universität Tübingen im Jahre 1559: Eine Studie zum ältesten erhaltenen Bestand der Tübinger Universitätsbibliothek'. *Bibliothek und Wissenschaft* 14 (1980): 1–109.

Clemen, Otto. 'Andreas Frank von Kamenz'. *NASG* 19 (1898): 95–115.

Clemen, Otto. 'Beiträge zur Lutherforschung 3.VII'. *Zeitschrift für Kirchengeschichte* 36 (1916): 113–122.

Clemen, Otto. 'Invictas Martini laudes intonent Christiani'. *Archiv für Reformationsgeschichte* 2 (1904/5): 685–690.

Creizenach, Theodor. 'Das "Gaudeamus" und was daran hängt'. *Verhandlungen deutscher Philologen und Schulmänner* 28 (1873): 203–207.

Dürer, Albrecht. *Tagebuch*, in *Schriftlicher Nachlass*. Edited by Hans Rupprich. 3 vols. Berlin: Deutscher Verein für Kunstwissenschaft, 1956–1969.

Eisermann, Falk. 'Auflagehöhen von Einblattdrucken im 15. und frühen 16. Jahhundert'. In *Einblattdrucke des 15. und frühen 16. Jahrhunderts: Probleme, Perspektiven, Fallstudien*, edited by Volker Honemann *et al.*, Tübingen: Max Niemeyer, 2000: 143–177.

Estreicher, Karol Józef Teofil. *Bibliografia polska*. Kraków: Wyd. Tow. Naukowego Krakowskiego.

Griese, Sabine. 'Sammler und Abschreiber von Einblattdrucken. Überlegungen zu einer Rezeptionsform am Ende des 15. und Anfang des 16. Jahrhunderts'. In *Humanismus und früher Buchdruck*, Pirckheimer-Jahrbuch 11, edited by Stephan Füssel and Volker Honemann. Nuremberg: Carl, 1996: 43–69.

Guentner, Francis J. 'Dulces exuviae in Sixteenth Century Music'. *The Classical Journal* 68 (1972): 62–67.

Heider, Andreas. *Spolia vetustatis: Die Verwandlung der heidnisch-antiken Tradition in Jakob Baldes marianischen Wallfahrten*. Munich: Herbert Utz, 1999.

Hiley, David. *Western Plainchant: a Handbook*. Oxford: Oxford University Press, 1993.

Hoffmann von Fallersleben, August Heinrich. *Gaudeamus igitur: eine Studie*, 2nd edn. Halle: Schwetschke, 1872.

Köstlin, Julius. 'Johann Heß, der Breslauer Reformator'. *Zeitschrift des Vereins für Geschichte und Alterthum Schlesiens* 6 (1854): 97–131, 181–265.

Langemeyer, Gerhard, Monika Arndt, and Jürgen Döring, eds. *Bild als Waffe: Mittel und Motive der Karikatur in fünf Jahrhunderten*. Munich: Prestel, 1985.

Leppin, Volker and Gury Schneider-Ludorff, eds. *Das Luther-Lexikon*. Regensburg: Bückle & Böhm, 2014.

Löbbert, Bernhard. 'Über den schriftlichen Nachlass des Lorenz Truchsess von Pommersfelden (1473–1543)'. *Archiv für mittelrheinische Kirchengeschichte* 60 (2008): 111–132.

Malagola, Carlo. *Della vita e delle opere di Antonio Urceo detto Codro studi e ricerche*. Bologna: Garagni, 1878.

Mundt, Lothar. *Lemnius und Luther: Studien und Texte zur Geschichte und Nachwirkung ihres Konflikts (1538/39)*. Bern: Peter Lang, 1983.

Neumann, Bernd. 'Zeugnisse mittelalterlicher Aufführungen im deutschen Sprachraum: eine Dokumentation zum volkssprachigen geistlichen Schauspiel'. PhD dissertation, Universität Köln, 1979.

Neumann, Bernd. *Geistliches Schauspiel im Zeugnis der Zeit*. Munich: Artemis, 1987.

Othmayr, Caspar. *Ausgewählte Werke, Zweiter Teil*. Edited by Hans Albrecht. Frankfurt: Peters, 1956.

Pettegree, Andrew. *Brand Luther: 1517, Printing, and the Making of the Reformation*. New York: Penguin, 2015.

Pettegree, Andrew. *The Invention of News: How the World came to know about itself*. New Haven, CT: Yale University Press, 2014.

Renner, Hans-Georg. 'Gaudeamus omnes. Ein früher musikalischer Spaß? Anmerkungen zur närrischen Musik bei Sebastian Brant'. *Annuaire de la Société des amis de la Bibliothèque de Sélestat* 2006: 199–202.

Reske, Christoph. *Die Buchdrucker des 16. und 17. Jahrhunderts im deutschen Sprachgebiet*. Wiesbaden: Harrassowitz, 2007.

Röckelein, Hedwig, Berndt von Egidy, Joachim-Felix Leonhard and Gerd Brinkhus. *Die lateinischen Handschriften der Universitätsbibliothek Tübingen, Teil 1: Signaturen Mc 1 bis Mc 150*. Wiesbaden: Harrassowitz, 1991.

Roper, Lyndal. 'Martin Luther's Body. The "Stout Doctor" and His Biographers'. *American Historical Review* 115 (2010): 350–384.

Rowland, Ingrid D. 'Revenge of the Regensburg Humanists, 1493'. *Sixteenth Century Journal* 25 (1994): 307–322.

Ruland, Anton. 'Die Original-Ausgabe der "Epithalamia Martini Lutheri"'. *Serapeum* 19 (1858): 7–10.

Schubart, Christoph. *Die Berichte über Luthers Tod und Begräbnis. Texte und Untersuchungen*. Weimar: Böhlau, 1917.

Seidemann, Johann Karl. 'Die Schriften des Petrus Sylvius'. *Archiv für Litteraturgeschichte* 5 (1876): 6–32, 287–310.

Steiff, Karl. 'Zur Entführung Luthers auf die Wartburg'. *Theologische Studien aus Württemberg* 9 (1888): 210–212.

Stolt, Birgit. *Die Sprachmischung in Luthers Tischreden. Studien zum Problem der Zweisprachigkeit*. Uppsala: Almqvist & Wiksell, 1964.

Strunk, W. O. 'Vergil in Music'. *Musical Quarterly* 16 (1930): 482–487.

Wagner Oettinger, Rebecca. *Music as Propaganda in the German Reformation*. Aldershot: Ashgate, 2001.

Weale, William Henry James and Hanns Bohatta. *Bibliographia liturgica: Catalogus missalium ritus latini ab anno MCCCLXXV impressorum*. London: Quaritch, 1928.

Wiedemann, Theodor. *Johann Eck, Professor der Theologie an der Universität Ingolstadt*. Regensburg: Pustet, 1865.

Wilczek, Piotr. *(Mis)translation and (Mis)interpretation: Polish Literature in the Context of Cross-Cultural Communication*. Frankfurt am Main: Peter Lang, 2005.

Appendix

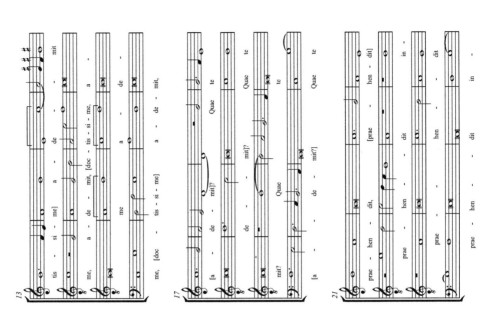
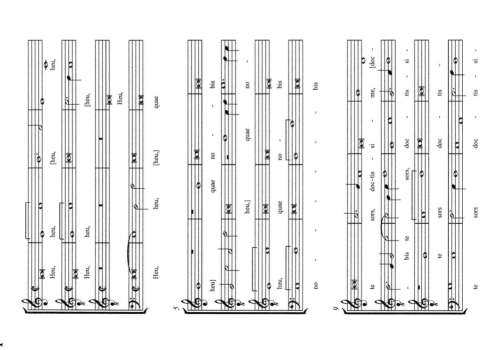

Example 9.1 Anon., *Ad Martinum Lutherum captivum lamentatio* (1521)

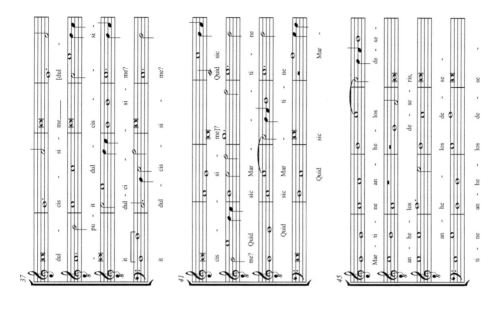
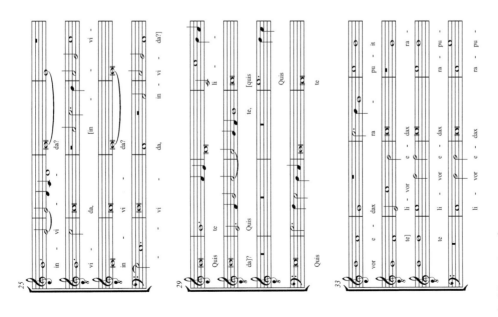

Example 9.1 continued

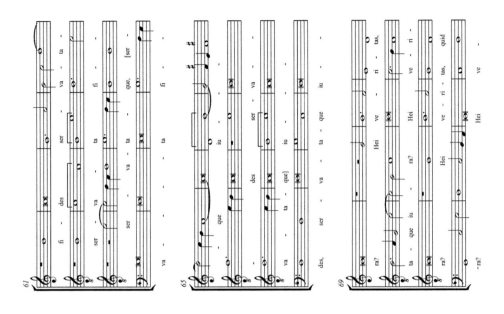
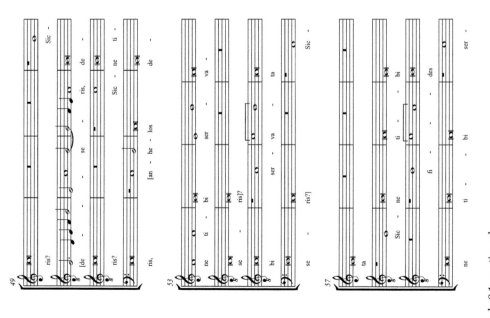

Example 9.1 continued

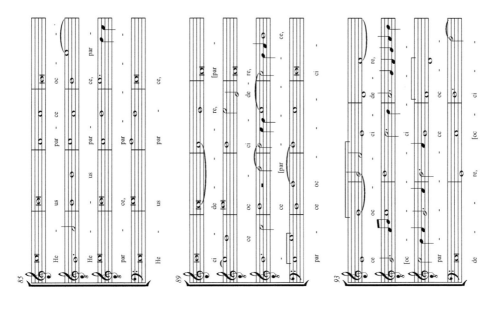
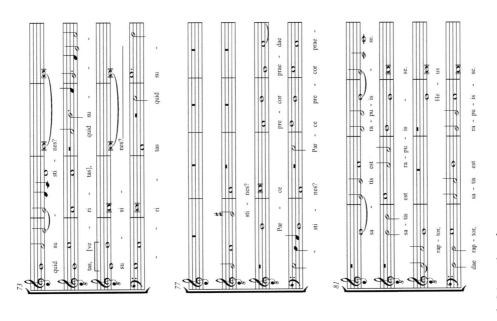

Example 9.1 continued

Example 9.2 Anon., *Rhythmus die divi Martini pronunciatus* (1511)

Example 9.3 Hieronymus Emser, *Hymnus paranymphorum* (1525)

Example 9.1 continued

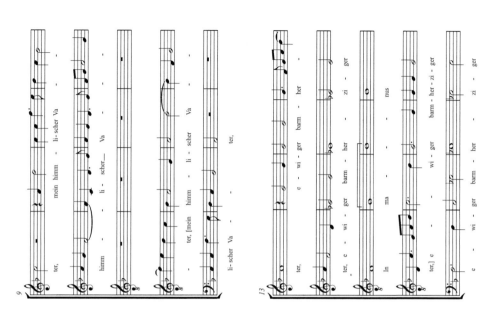

Example 9.4 Caspar Othmayr, *Mein himlischer vatter* (1546), beginning

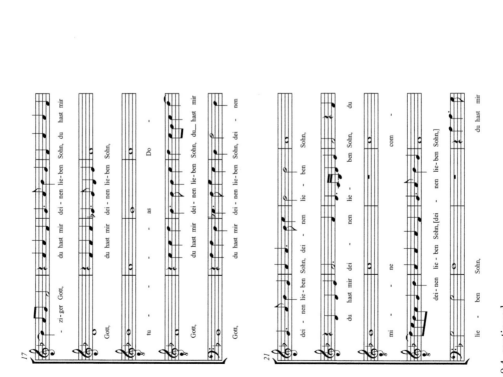

Example 9.4 continued

10

Theobald Billican and Michael's ode settings in print

Notes on an exceptional transmission[1]

Sonja Tröster

In the German-speaking lands, the transition from the fifteenth to the sixteenth century was marked by a remarkable surge of humanistic ideas. This also affected the production of a specific genre of music: the humanist ode setting. The most prominent works of this genre share a set of basic parameters. First, they originated in collaboration between a humanist and a composer. Second, they generally comprised settings of the same corpus of poems, drawn principally from Horace's *Carmina*, and usually for four voices. Finally, most of these collections appeared in print. The phenomenon was initiated by the archhumanist Conrad Celtis, who encouraged Petrus Tritonius (Peter Treibenreiff) to compose four-voice settings of the Horatian texts, thereby realising their metrical quantities in sound. Those settings, among the first polyphonic music to be printed from moveable type north of the Alps, were produced by Erhart Oeglin in a prestigious folio edition and a corrected 'practical edition' in quarto.[2] Joachim Vadian (Watt), Celtis' successor as teacher at the *Collegium poetarum* in Vienna, inspired Wolfgang Grefinger to set texts from Prudentius' *Cathemerinon* to music.[3] In the preface to Grefinger's *Cathemerinon*, Rudolf Agricola the Younger announced that a similar publication of settings of Horatian odes would soon appear, but this collection is not known today.[4] Another twenty years later, Simon Minervius (Schaidenreisser), apparently guided by Celtis' wish, approached Ludwig Senfl to set Tritonius' melodies anew.[5] The resulting *Varia carminum genera* appeared in 1534.[6] Five years later, the products of the collaboration of Johannes Stomius (Mühling) and Paul Hofhaimer, as well as a now-lost collection of Horatian settings by Benedict Ducis were published.[7]

A further collection of humanist ode-settings arising from the collaboration of lesser-known personalities appeared shortly after the middle of the sixteenth century, as a set of partbooks edited by Petrus Nigidius (Ney) and printed by Christian Egenolff in 1551. As the opening pieces in this compendium, Nigidius presents Tritonius' settings of the nineteen metres employed in Horace's *Carmina* alongside with settings of the same texts by a

---

1 The publication of this article is deeply indebted to Grantley McDonald, who devoted many hours to 'polishing' my English. My thanks go also to Laura Macey for her helpful comments.

2 *Melopoiae sive harmoniae tetracenticae* (Augsburg: Erhard Oeglin, 1507), vdm 55 and *Harmoniae super odis Horatii Flacci* (Augsburg: Erhard Oeglin, 1507), vdm 108. Cf. Lodes, 'Concentus', Bobeth, 'Odenkomposition'.

3 *Cathemerinon* (Vienna: Hieronymus Vietor, 1515), vdm 84. Cf. Graf-Stuhlhofer, 'Vadian als Lehrer'.

4 McDonald, 'The Metrical *Harmoniae*'.

5 McDonald, 'The Metrical *Harmoniae*'.

6 *Varia carminum genera* (Nuremberg: Hieronymus Formschneider, 1534), vdm 97.

7 *Harmoniae poeticae Pauli Hofheimeri* (Nuremberg: Johannes Petreius, 1539), vdm 47. Cf. Hofhaimer, *Ausgabe sämtlicher Werke, vol. III, Harmoniae poeticae*. Benedictus Ducis' *Harmoniae in Odas Horatii* (Ulm: Johannes Varnier, 1539), vdm 144, is only known from Conrad Gesner's writings, cf. Bernstein, 'The Bibliography of Music', 147, 154.

226   SONJA TRÖSTER

composer named Michael. After each setting by Tritonius, Nigidius generally writes: 'eadem per Michaëlem N.' In order to justify this combination, Nigidius explains the story of Michael's ode settings in the *epistola dedicatoria*, and how the repertoire came into his hands:

> In 1526 Aldo Manuzio's compendium was published, together with music for the nineteen metrical genera used in Horace's odes, elegantly made to train young students. The task was carried out quite skilfully by the most illustrious man Theobald Billican, who was the first to make a summary of Aldus' instruction from his larger work. Moreover, he encouraged the illustrious composer Michael to compose the music. At length copies of this work, first printed at Augsburg, began to circulate five years later at Marburg.[8]

This passage in the preface has caused some misunderstandings in the musicological literature. The following citation in *Die Musik in Geschichte und Gegenwart* provides an example of such misconceptions: '[. . .] Odensammlungen von dem Marburger Kleriker Michael N. (Vdg. [=Venice] 1526, verloren; Marburg 1531) [. . .]'.[9] In the preface, Nigidius explains that Michael was a cleric from Augsburg. The allusion to Aldo Manuzio refers to his *Institutionum grammaticarum*, an influential Latin grammar book of the time, and not to Manuzio in his function as a printer based in Venice.[10] The edition of ode settings mentioned by Nigidius in the preface to the 1551 collection was actually published in Augsburg, and a few copies are known today.[11] This 1526 publication is a textbook on Latin grammar edited by the humanist Theobald Billican that includes twenty-one ode settings of Horatian texts. Nigidius refers to the composer only by his first name Michael,[12] as Billican could not remember the surname. Adolf Layer tentatively identified this Michael with Michael Rautenweiler, who was from 1523 onwards a vicar at the cathedral in Augsburg.[13] But as no further information on Michael Rautenweiler is available, the identification remains conjectural.[14] The second edition from 1531, which Nigidius mentions as well, is also known today.[15] A further reprint of the ode settings was produced at Marburg in 1533.[16]

These findings mean that Michael's metrical ode settings of nineteen Horatian poems were published in four editions over a time span of twenty-five years. As far as we know,

---

8 Petrus Nigidius, *Geminae undeviginti odarum Horatii melodiae* (Frankfurt am Main: Christian Egenolff, 1551), VD16 H 4961, A2ʳ: 'Exiit in publicum Aldi Manutij compendium anno à natali Christiano 1526. unà cum modis undeviginti Odarum Horatianarum, ad iuventutem exercendam eleganter factis, dexterè admodum id negotij tum procurante clarißimo Viro Theobaldo Billicano, qui & ipse primus epitomen Aldinam ex ingenii opere concinnanit [sic], atque Michaëlem Symphonetam egregium ad modulorum compositionem incitavit. Ea exemplaria Augustæ primùm excusa, tandem post quinquennium denuo Marpurgi invulgari cœperunt . . .' A digital reproduction of the copy in D-Mbs is accessible at urn:nbn:de:bvb:12-bsb00082119–7. Translation by Grantley McDonald.

9 Schmidt-Beste and Hartmann, 'Ode'.

10 *Institutionum grammaticarum libri quatuor* (Venice: Aldo Manuzio, 1508) (Edit16 CNCE 36171).

11 Theobald Billican, *De partium orationis inflexionibus* ([Augsburg]: [Simprecht Ruff], 1526), vdm 137. Copies in: A-Wn: MS11111–8°, D-GOl: Phil 8° 01461/04 (02), D-Mbs: Mus.th. 2784, GB-Lbl: C.71.cc.2.

12 Most likely, the N. is not an abbreviation but stands for the unknown surname, see Simon, *Billican*, 155.

13 Layer, *Fuggerzeit*, 30 and Simon, *Billican*, 156.

14 That Billican did not remember – or pretended not to remember – the last name of a musician he approached and probably even worked with twenty-five years earlier might not only be seen as a case of poor memory. Billican perhaps did not want to disclose the identity of this musician due to confessional or other reasons. In that case it could even be possible that the first name of the composer was not Michael.

15 *De partium orationis adcidentibus, compendium Aldi* (Marburg: [Franz Rhode], 1531), vdm 138, VD16 ZV 10366; unique copy in D-ASsb.

16 *De partium orationis adcidentibus compendium Aldi, unà cum versificatoria Ioannis Murmellij* (Marburg: Franz Rhode, 1533), vdm 141; unique copy in D-MGu. I am grateful to Grantley McDonald for bringing this reprint to my attention.

Table 10.1 Overview of the publications containing Michael's ode settings

Theobald Billican, *De partium orationis inflexionibus* ([Augsburg: Simprecht Ruff], 1526), vdm 137
- twenty-one ode settings inserted between two parts of a Latin grammar
- music printed from type, double impression
- only the respective text sections are underlaid to the music

De partium orationis adcidentibus, compendium Aldi (Marburg: [Franz Rhode], 1531), vdm 138
- twenty-two ode settings at the end of a Latin grammar
- music printed from woodblock
- description of the metre as well as complete texts

De partium orationis adcidentibus compendium Aldi, unà cum versificatoria Ioannis Murmellij (Marburg: Franz Rhode, 1533), vdm 141
- reprint, following closely the 1531 edition

Petrus Nigidius, *Geminae undeviginti odarum Horatii melodiae, quatuor vocibus probè adornatæ, cum selectißimis carminum, partim sacrorum, partim prophanorum, concentibus: additis circa finem alijs item cantionibus, matutinis, meridianis, & serotinis: Pædagogijs rectè institutis, ac scholis quibuslibet pro exercenda iuventute literaria accommodatißimis* (Frankfurt am Main: Christian Egenolff, 1551/52), vdm 1384.
- seventy-four musical settings, mainly ode settings
- music printed from type, single impression
- published in four partbooks

only Tritonius' ode settings reached a comparable presence in print. What makes these findings even more significant for a study of printing cultures is the fact that three different printing techniques were employed to print the music in the various editions:

- type, double impression (1526)
- woodblock (1531 and 1533)
- type, single impression (1551).

In the following I will present briefly the context of each publication and focus on the integration of the music part in the book, the differences in repertoire and readings, as well as the aesthetics of the editions.

Augsburg 1526

Theobald Billican (Gerlacher) studied in Heidelberg and was an eyewitness at Luther's Heidelberg disputation in 1518.[17] He adopted many ideas of the Reformation, and during the 1520s was one of its fiercest proponents. At the time the grammar book containing the ode settings was published, he held the post of preacher in the imperial town of Nördlingen. Billican was also a devoted teacher, and his Latin grammar was designed for the students of Nördlingen's Latin school. The book is based on Aldo Manuzio's *Rudimenta grammatices Latinae linguae* (1501), which for its part is based on works by Aelius Donatus.[18] Johann Baptist Rhumelius, a former student of Billican, initiated the edition and provided a preface, addressed to the students using the book. A further indication of the intended audience of

---

17 Simon, *Humanismus.*
18 Simon, *Humanismus*, 152–154.

228   SONJA TRÖSTER

the book is the reference to Sixt Faber (Schmid), rector of the Latin school in Nördlingen at the time.[19]

Between the two parts of the grammar book, twenty-one musical settings of nineteen Horatian texts are printed in staff notation. They appear without any further title or indication of what follows. The texts are the same as those set by Tritonius, which provide an example of every verse metre that occurs in Horace's *Carmina*. The first two odes each receive two settings. All settings are set for three equal high voices and a lower one, notated in either c2- or c3-clefs, which seems ideal for a school situation in which the master sang the lowest voice and the children the upper voices. In the following descriptions I will nevertheless use the standard voice designations discant, alto, tenor and bass to describe the voice parts.

The music is laid out in choirbook format: each page has two voices of two staves each, and each opening thus has all four voices, which allows all voices to be sung from the book at the same time.[20] The highest voice – with one exception – is found in the upper part of the verso side, with the tenor below. Surprisingly, in the first seven settings the bass is placed in the top section of the recto page, with the alto on the lower half. This order is reversed in the example for the sixth metre, *Scriberis Vario fortis*. The change in layout on one opening is astonishing because *Scriberis Vario fortis* does not begin on a new page, but starts on the second line only of each voice part, directly on from the preceding piece. Thus, the person singing bass who proceeded from n° 5 (*Quis multa gracilis*) to n° 6 (*Scriberis Vario fortis*) would have to jump from the top staff to the bottom staff on the same page, whereas the person singing the alto would have to move up from the third to the second staff (Figure 10.1).

Each piece is written in a new metre, and each is numbered at the beginning of each voice in Arabic numerals. This is especially helpful when the printer begins a new setting part-way through a line, as he does a few times to save space.[21] Only one line of text – usually equalling one stanza – is underlaid in each voice. This suggests that the students learned either the text or the music by heart, following the music and singing the words from memory, or memorised the music and then sang from an edition of the text.

In this source neither the place of printing nor the printer is named. But there is good evidence that the edition was produced in the workshop of Simprecht Ruff in Augsburg, successor to the printing house of Sigmund Grimm and Marx Wirsung.[22] The woodcut on the title page is very finely executed (see Figure 10.2), and I have been able to find three further editions in which it was used: Christoph Hegendorf, *Uber die erst Epistel Petri* ([Augsburg: Simprecht Ruff], 1525) (VD16 H 1111), Hieronymus von Endorf, *Axiomata oder sitig begerungen* ([Augsburg: Simprecht Ruff], 1525) (VD16 E 1175), and Martin Luther, *De servo arbitrio Martini Lutheri* (Augsburg: [Simprecht Ruff], 1526) (VD16 L 6661).[23] None

---

19 Dorn, 'Die Schulmeister und Cantoren', 40. Faber left Nördlingen in spring 1526, but Rhumelius' dedicatory preface is dated 14 November 1525.

20 This is for example not always possible in a publication edited by Sebastian Forster and Lucas Hordisch in Leipzig (RISM B/I 1533³) whereas Oeglin in his 'practical' edition of *Harmoniae Petri Tritonii* from 1507 pays scrupulous attention to placing all voices on one opening, thereby leaving great sections of the page empty.

21 For example on fol. H2ʳ (*Tu ne quaesieris*).

22 Reske, *Buchdrucker*, 34–35.

23 The woodcut was later also used in other workshops, e.g. for the following editions: Guilielmus Ulinus, *Oratio ad linguae sanctae studiosos* ([Ingolstadt]: [Weißenhorn], 1540), VD16 U 26; *Klag der Armen und Dürfftigen* ([Ingolstadt]: [Weißenhorn], 1577), VD16 K 1201. In the latter the woodcut is no longer used as title page, but as a decorative element.

Figure 10.1 Beginning of *Scriberis fortis* (alto and bass) from Theobald Billican, *De partium orationis inflexionibus*. [Augsburg]: [S. Ruff], 1526 (vdm 137)
Source: München, Bayerische Staatsbibliothek, Mus.th. 2784#Beibd.3, fol. G5[r]

of these editions names the printer, but on the basis of the main text font and the initials used, they have all been assigned to Ruff's workshop by VD16. The italic text font used in Billican's textbook is also found in other books printed by Ruff. Initials in this publication are also present in other editions firmly attributable to Ruff, such as Luscinius' *Loci ac sales mire in festivi* (VD16 N 26), which bears a colophon stating that the book was executed with Simprecht Ruff's types and paid for by Sigmund Grimm.

Thus, the well-known *Liber selectarum cantionum* (RISM B/I 1520[4]), Billican's *De partium orationis inflexionibus*, and a broadsheet with music cut from woodblocks[24] represent the only known musical editions printed in this workshop. The *Liber selectarum cantionum* and Billican's book share some characteristics: in both cases the music is printed from type in double-impression, and in each case the staff lines of recto and verso page of each folio are carefully aligned.[25] The music font follows in many ways the same aesthetic principles in both editions, as the single notes are evenly spaced and the note beams are chamfered at

---

24 Jakob Micyllus, *Sic tua celestes metuant* ([Augsburg]: [Sigmund Grimm], [c.1525]), vdm 201.
25 For a digital reproduction of the D-Mbs copy of the *Liber selectarum cantionum* (Augsburg: Sigmund Grimm & Marx Wirsung, 1520), vdm 18; cf. urn:nbn:de:bvb:12-bsb00083822–1.

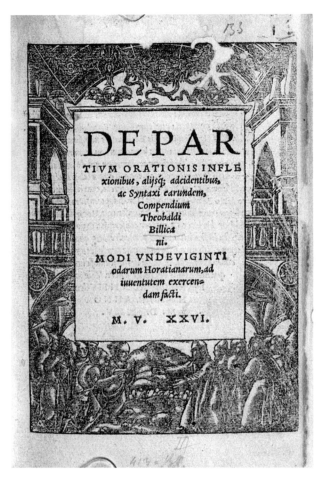

Figure 10.2 Titlepage of Theobald Billican, *De partium orationis inflexionibus*. [Augsburg]: [S. Ruff], 1526 (vdm 137)
Source: München, Bayerische Staatsbibliothek, Mus.th. 2784#Beibd.3

the end. Likewise, the b-flats look very much the same, the longae have a very long beam, and the staff lines are continuous rather than being printed from a series of shorter pieces. Finally, the shape of the c-clef is the same. I will return to this detail later.

On the other hand, there are also differences between the two editions. First is the size of the font, determined of course by the fact that the ode settings are printed in octavo and the *Liber selectarum cantionum* in folio. Furthermore, the custodes are of different shapes. Moreover, the humanist settings contain only a limited range of note values and shapes: there are no ligatures, no coloration, no breves, and no note values smaller than the semiminim. Only two settings are supplied with a mensuration sign (*tempus imperfectum prolatio minor*), and one has rests. The printer uses no vertical lines, for example at the end of a section or a piece. In the 1526 edition, the staves and the notes are often poorly aligned (see Figure 10.1). Consequently, although the overall appearance of the printed music is very elegant, it does not always fulfil the required function, as the pitch of a given note is in many cases ambiguous. In short, it seems that the edition of ode settings was prepared with less care than the *Liber selectarum cantionum*.

Marburg 1531

Five years after this edition, as Nigidius mentions in his preface, the grammar was reprinted with minor changes, and without explicit mention of Billican. The printer of this edition, Franz Rhode, is not named, but at the end of the book the place of printing (Marburg) and the date are given.[26] The title now describes the book as a 'compendium' by Aldo Manuzio. In the edition it is printed along with Johannes Murmellius' *Artis versificatoriae rudimenta* (first edition: VD16 M 7012 including VD16 M 6871 and P 1544). While the dedicatory preface only mentions the Marburg pedagogues, Nigidius tells us that the editors of this edition were Caspar Rudolphi and Reinhard Lorichius (Lorich, Hadamarius).[27] At the time, both held posts at the University of Marburg, founded four years earlier in 1527. Caspar Rudolphi, professor of dialectic, was also rector of the Paedagogium in Marburg. It seems that he had previous knowledge of Billican's book and probably even possessed a copy, as he was a teacher in Nördlingen before his appointment at Marburg.

Michael's ode settings from the 1526 edition are reprinted along with this Latin grammar, which deviates in a few passages from Billican's version. This time they are placed not in between the two parts of the grammar book, but at the end of the volume. Further aspects of the presentation of the ode settings were also changed.

This section of the book now has a separate title: *Odarum Horatianarum genera undeviginti, cum modis earundem, ad iuventutem exercendam in fine adiectis* (Figure 10.3). Each ode is introduced with a heading and an 'argumentum' as well as a description of the metre. This tradition of presenting each metre seems to have begun in editions of Horace printed in Italy, as for example in *Q. Horatii Flacci poemata* (Florence: Filippo Giunta, 1514). As far as I can establish, such explanations first appeared in the German-speaking lands in an edition of Horace's *Carmina* printed in Basel in 1520 (VD16 H 4851).[28] In the 1531 Marburg edition, the introduction to each metre and each ode is followed by the complete text of the ode. The music of the ode setting is then given, underlaid with one line of text. As far as I know, this is the first time that ode settings were printed in such an explanatory pedagogical context. But in later publications this form of presentation occurs frequently, as for example in the ode collection by Forster and Hordisch printed at Leipzig in 1533,[29] and in Johann Reusch's *Melodiae odarum Georgii Fabricii*, printed at Leipzig in 1554.[30]

The 1531 Marburg edition also contains a few changes in the musical repertoire. The first two odes are each illustrated here by only one setting: for the ode *Maecenas atavis* only the first setting from the 1526 edition is reprinted; the Sapphic ode *Iam satis terris* is illustrated with a new three-voice setting absent from the earlier edition. Three further settings for three voices are added at the end of the edition: *Livor tabificum malis venenum, Adeste Musae maximi proles Iovis* (both from *Symposium duodecim sapientium*, n° 143 and 142),[31]

---

26 Möncke, 'Marburger Drucke', 102 (n° *40g). Reske, *Buchdrucker*, 653.

27 Rudolphi (*1501 Cannstadt, † 1561 Marburg) was teacher in Waiblingen, Lauingen and Nördlingen, from 1530 onwards he was appointed rector of the Paedagogium in Marburg. 'Rudolphi, Caspar', in *Hessische Biografie* www.lagis-hessen.de/pnd/119807629 (last updated: 12.2.2014). Lorichius (*1510 Hadamar, † after 1564 Bernbach) was the first professor of dialectic at Marburg. For the year 1532 he is also documented as teacher at the Paedagogium. Monika Rener and Wilhelm Kühlmann, 'Lorichius, Reinhard', in *Verfasserlexikon – Frühe Neuzeit in Deutschland 1520–1620* (Berlin, Boston: De Gruyter, retrieved 24.2.2016, from www.degruyter.com/view/VDBO/vdbo.vl16.0272.

28 From fol. 9^r onwards. Copies in D-Mbs A.lat.a. 245 and 246.

29 Three editions can be distinguished, all known as RISM B/I 1533³. See vdm 19, 453, 608.

30 RISM A/I R 1210. See Heidrich, 'Musik und Humanismus', esp. 104–106.

31 Friedrich, *Das Symposium*, esp. 75–76 (texts), 350–382 (commentary). The author attributes the anthology to Lucius Caecilius Firmianus Lactantius, see 479–508.

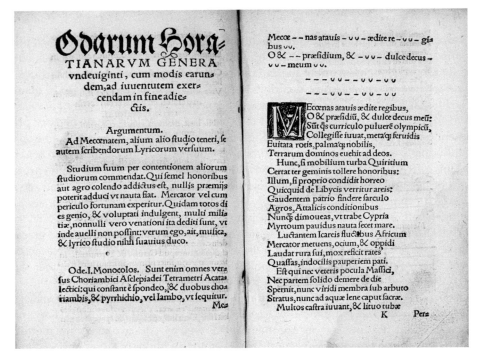

Figure 10.3 First pages of music section from *De partium orationis adcidentibus, compendium Aldi*. Marburg: [Franz Rhode], 1531 (vdm 138)
Source: Stiftsbibliothek Aschaffenburg, 4500/U-242, Bb. 2, fol. [lviii]ᵛ–K[i]ʳ

and *Hanc tua Penelope* (Ovid, *Heroides* I). The first two pieces are for three equal high voices, whereas the lowest voice in the third one is in the tenor range. Unlike the other settings, these are underlaid with only one line of text. Furthermore, they have neither heading nor indication or introduction to the metre. For those last three settings the cutter of the music evidently had another model to copy from. Now mensuration signs are provided for all pieces and a different form of g-clef appears.

The music in the 1531 Marburg edition looks very different from that in the Augsburg edition, primarily because the music in the Marburg edition is printed from woodblock. Nevertheless, many details indicate that this edition was dependent on the earlier Augsburg edition. As in the Augsburg edition, the printer tried to display the music in such a way that all four voices could be sung from one opening. Often the voices are laid out exactly as in the 1526 edition, but for practical reasons, the printer sometimes used a different layout, in which all voices appear on one page, with only one staff each (see Figure 10.6, example with three voices). Since this edition has more text, it was not always possible to set out the complete piece over a single opening, and sometimes a piece is distributed over two openings. Layout was thus determined by whether or not the music could be printed on a single opening. In the first five pieces, the voices are generally laid out with the alto following the bass. In the pieces that follow, beginning with *Scriberis Vario fortis* (n° 6), the bass is arranged underneath the alto. This change of arrangement occurs at the same place in the 1526 and 1531 editions, which suggests that the latter is based on the former.

There are many other hints that the printer Rhode was working from a copy of the Augsburg 1526 edition. For example, the clefs are cut in a similar way to the font of the type:

the 'rabbit-teeth' form of the c-clef used by the Grimm and Wirsung workshop (see Figures 10.1 and 10.4.) was not commonly found in music type. Oeglin's c-clefs resemble a ladder,[32] which is also true for later editions from Augsburg by Melchior Kriesstein. In his 1513 song book,[33] Schöffer uses a kind of ladder, as do all the Nuremberg printers. But the 'rabbit-teeth' c-clef used by Ruff seems to have been particularly popular among Augsburg printers of the 1520s. Melchior Ramminger and Hans Steiner also use it in some of their publications.[34]

The shapes of the g-clefs are likewise similar in both the 1526 and the 1531 edition of Michael's ode settings, as well as the extravagant custos (see Figures 10.4 and 10.5). A further significant similarity between the two editions is found in the setting of *Lydia dic per omnes*. The custos in the tenor voice of the 1526 edition is placed upside down on the staff, as otherwise it would protrude into the text or even the music of the staff above. The cutter of the 1531 edition has copied this quite faithfully, although the problem could have been solved in different ways in music printed from woodblock.

Other examples of this faithful copying from the earlier model can be found throughout the book. It seems that even within the text passages, the printer tried to imitate an initial of the 1526 edition.[35]

In summary, as music printing from woodblocks requires fewer technical skills and precision on the side of the printer to produce a functional music edition, the 1531 edition of Michael's ode settings is probably a more practical edition than the aesthetically more appealing Augsburg edition. Many passages in the 1526 book in which the pitches are ambiguous can be read without hesitation in the later edition. But apart from this practical aspect, it seems that the blockcutter was not familiar with reading music and by no means an expert in music printing. The line-breaks in the music are often the same as in the 1526 edition, which is in part due to the verse pattern of the odes. But in cases in which the line-breaks deviate, and the cutter thus had no reliable model, rather than determining the placement of custodes himself, he simply refrained from using any, as for example in n° 14 (*Ibis liburnis*) (Marburg 1531, fol. [Nviii]ʳ). Mistakes in the first edition that were faithfully copied into the 1531 edition also indicate dependence on the model. For example, in n° 1 (*Maecenas atavis*), the second verse has an erroneous c2-clef in the alto, and in n° 5 (*Quis multa gracilis*) the cutter copied an erroneously placed custos before the last verse in the alto.

Marburg 1533

In 1533, only two years later, a further edition containing Michael's ode settings appeared in Marburg.[36] This time the place of printing and the printer Franz Rhode are named.[37] The contents as well as the overall appearance of this publication closely resemble the 1531 edition, which suggests that the first Marburg edition was likewise printed by Franz Rhode.

---

32 *Harmoniae super odis Horatii Flacci* (Augsburg: Erhard Oeglin, 1507), vdm 108, digitised copy D-Mbs: urn:nbn:de:bvb:12-bsb00011101–5.

33 [Songs for 3–4 voices] (Mainz: Peter Schöffer d. J., 1513), vdm 13, digitised copy D-Mbs: urn:nbn:de:bvb: 12-bsb00074659–9.

34 *Etlich Cristliche lyeder* (Augsburg: Melchior Ramminger, 1524), vdm 178, digitised copy D-Mbs: urn:nbn:de:bvb:12-bsb00071754–7).

35 Compare the Q-initial in Augsburg 1526, [D7]ᵛ with the one in Marburg 1533, [E8]ᵛ.

36 A description of the edition is in Bredehorn, *Marburger Frühdrucke*, 137–139.

37 Dommer, *Die ältesten Drucke*, 35 (n° 46). Concerning Franz Rhode see (5)–(11).

Figure 10.4 *Lydia dic per omnes* from Theobald Billican, *De partium orationis inflexionibus*. [Augsburg]: [S. Ruff], 1526 (vdm 137)
Source: München, Bayerische Staatsbibliothek, Mus.th. 2784#Beibd.3, fol. [G7]ᵛ

The content of this edition is the same as in the 1531 edition, but as is already visible on the title page, all text passages, which are set from moveable type, are newly composed.[38] This is also true for the text underlaid beneath the music. The music itself, on the other hand, is mostly printed from the same woodblocks used in the earlier edition. Only in a few cases did new blocks need to be cut, probably because the original ones were lost or damaged.

Given this conformity, it seems surprising that, whereas in the 1531 edition the music section begins on a verso page, in the 1533 edition it begins on a recto page. However, this discrepancy is already compensated at the end of the first ode setting, through the rectification of an error in the earlier edition, the inadvertent omission of a whole page containing the ending of *Maecenas atavis*. Although a custos at the end of each system directs the singer to the following note, the music is interrupted in the 1531 edition by a heading and by text relating to the second ode setting. This mistake is amended in the 1533 edition, and the missing staves fill a page of their own, so that recto and verso sides of the two editions are in concordance again.

---

38 Compare the digitised copy in D-MGu under http://archiv.ub.uni-marburg.de/eb/2015/0075.

Figure 10.5 *Lydia dic per omnes* from *De partium orationis adcidentibus, compendium Aldi*. Marburg: [Franz Rhode], 1531 (vdm 138)
Source: Stiftsbibliothek Aschaffenburg, 4500/U-242, Bb. 2, fol. Mii^v

However, some mistakes in the 1531 edition remained uncorrected, and in the few cases in which new blocks had to be cut, new errors are sometimes introduced. For example in *Livor tabificum malis venenum* (1531: Pv^r; 1533: T[v]^r) the first system of the discantus in the 1533 edition is newly cut and one mistake is faithfully copied: the seventh note seems to be c^2 rather than the printed b^1, which results in a dissonance with the a^1 in the bass. Moreover, in the 1533 edition this note is erroneously missing a stem (Figures 10.6–10.7). To judge from the visual appearance, it seems that the craftsman responsible for recutting this staff was annoyed by the ornate g-clef and the delicate custos of his model, and drew them in a much plainer style. A few blocks in the 1533 edition also show traces of damage, such as the first system of the bass of *Petti nihil me*, where the lower part of the c-clef is missing (Sii^r).

Students at the Paedagogium were probably required to purchase this book, and the first Marburg edition was soon out of stock. This necessitated a reprint only two years after the 1531 edition. Either the printer Franz Rhode or the Marburg pedagogues will have kept the woodblocks of the musical examples in store, thus facilitating the reprint. All text passages printed from moveable type, on the other hand, had to be set anew.

Figure 10.6 *Livor tabificum* from *De partium orationis adcidentibus, compendium Aldi*. Marburg: [Franz Rhode], 1531 (vdm 138)
Source: Stiftsbibliothek Aschaffenburg, 4500/U-242, Bb. 2, fol. [Pv]^r

Figure 10.7 *Livor tabificum* from *De partium orationis adcidentibus compendium Aldi, vnà cum versificatoria Ioannis Murmellij*. Marburg: Franz Rhode, 1533 (vdm 141)
Source: Universitätsbibliothek Marburg, 095 IVb C 552 h, fol. [Tv]^r

Frankfurt 1551

Michael's ode settings were released for the fourth and last time in Petrus Nigidius' *Geminae undeviginti odarum Horatii melodiae*, printed by Christian Egenolff in Frankfurt am Main (RISM B/I 1551[17]).[39] This publication was printed in four partbooks and, as already mentioned, Michael's ode settings are given alongside Tritonius' settings of Horace. Astonishingly, this latest edition provides the majority of available information on the composer Michael and the circumstances of the earlier editions. The editor of this publication, Petrus Nigidius, was a teacher at the Paedagogium in Marburg from 1532–1539.[40] After ten years of teaching at the town school in Cassel he returned to Marburg as rector of the Paedagogium in 1549. As such he was a colleague of Theobald Billican, who enrolled at Marburg University in 1544 and in 1546 acquired a post as lecturer. Billican was even appointed as rector of the University in 1548, though this success was short-lived, as he was suspected of espionage for the Roman Catholic side.[41] In the preface of the 1551 edition, Nigidius reports that the ode settings of the 1526 edition were composed on Billican's behalf and under his direction by a certain Michael, who is described as 'an outstanding musician, formerly a singer at the cathedral in Augsburg' ('insignis musicus, psaltes olim templi summi Augustani').[42] He also states that no copies of this book, or of the reprint from 1531, were currently available. Therefore, Nigidius had decided to compile and publish a new Latin grammar for use at the Paedagogium on the occasion of his return to Marburg, entitled *Isagogicus rerum grammaticarum libellus*.[43] Nigidius greatly enlarged the musical section and had it printed as a separate set of partbooks, the *Geminae undeviginti . . . melodiae*. Both publications bear a preface dated August 1550, and both were printed by Christian Egenolff in 1551.[44]

However, the publication of 1551 was not Nigidius' first grammar textbook. Probably as early as 1543 he had already published a Latin grammar, *Isagogicus rerum grammaticarum libellus* (the only extant edition is Erfurt: Melchior Sachse, 1548 [D-OB], vdm 1518).[45] At the back of the volume are nine ode settings for two to four voices, some of them by Tritonius, Heugel and Senfl, printed from woodblock. All these settings reappear in Nigidius' collection from 1551.[46] Although the overall appearance of the music is quite elegant, the compositor was obviously not accustomed to setting up pages containing music.[47] The voices of each piece are laid out on the page in a most impractical way. Indeed, it is impossible to read them simultaneously on one opening, as the turning points of the voices do not coincide.

---

39 On Petrus Nigidius and his publications see Knoke, 'Leben und Schriften'.

40 Koch, *Geschichte des akademischen Pädagogiums*, 15; Engel, *Musikpflege* provides little information and confuses several details.

41 Simon, *Humanismus*, 183–186.

42 RISM B/I 1551[17], A2[v].

43 Leonhardt, 'G2. Petrus Nigidius d.Ä.' and 'Die grammatischen Lehrwerke von Petrus Nigidius d.Ä.'.

44 In a private conversation, Royston Gustavson mentioned that he assumes the date 1552 in the tenor partbook to be a mistake, as a time span of more than one year (the tenor is dated 'ANNO M. D. LII. Mense Maio' and the altus 'Anno M. D. LI. Mense Iunio') would not seem realistic for such a publication. I share his opinion for two further reasons: the prefaces of Nigidius' *Isagogicus* (the edition is dated 1551) and *Geminae* are both dated August 1550, which underlines the affiliation of the two editions; it is possible that Egenolff even started printing the music volume with the tenor partbook, as the last setting *Da pacem Domino* is not included in the index, which is at the beginning of the tenor partbook.

45 See Knoke, 'Leben und Schriften', 99. Sachse is known for his Eulenspiegel editions. Reske, *Buchdrucker*, 219–220.

46 Some of the ode settings reappear with different texts, for example Heugel's setting of *Hanc tua Penelope* is adapted and underlaid with *Vivet Maeonides* (n° 26) in 1551 and *Mercuri facunde* is underlaid with *Ingenium quondam* (n° 31).

47 The only other music edition by Melchior Sachse the elder known today is an edition of *Deudsche Messe und Ordnung Gottesdiensts* from 1526 with Hufnagelnotation in woodcut (vdm 941 and vdm 332).

238 SONJA TRÖSTER

This earlier book was published at a time when Nigidius was still in Cassel and probably had not yet met Billican.[48] Nevertheless, there is one setting among this repertoire that had already been included in Billican's grammar in 1526: there it served as the first setting of *Iam satis terris*. In the 1548 edition Nigidius presents the setting under the heading 'vetus melodia' and underlays it with a different Horatian text: *Mercuri, facunde nepos Atlantis* (Horace, *Carmina* I.10). In 1551 Nigidius chooses yet another text, the ode *Ipse cum solus varios retracto* by the humanist Hermann von dem Busche. This setting will be discussed later.

The reasons why Nigidius chose Egenolff as printer for a new and greatly enlarged edition of his grammar book in 1551 were probably manifold. By the middle of the century, Egenolff was certainly a printer of some renown. He had experience in printing music, and from 1538 to 1542 he maintained a branch of his workshop in Marburg, which stood in close contact with the university.[49] Egenolff used single-impression music type, in which the short sections of staff that form part of each sort are clearly visible. This music edition makes no visual references to the earlier editions of Michael's ode settings. But in each case the note values are retained: in Michael's settings, at the relation of semibreve and minim, and in Tritonius' settings, breve and semibreve.

Compared to the new setting of the music in the Marburg publications, it becomes apparent that a musically educated editor or typesetter was at work. Whereas in the earlier editions only deviations from a standard cut-C mensuration were marked, here each setting now shows a mensuration sign. Furthermore, some errors were amended, and informed alterations were made. For example in n° 9 (*Vides ut alta stet*) the first note in all voices is changed from a semibreve (as in the 1526, 1531 and 1533 editions) to a minim, which shows considerable knowledge of the structure of the Alcaic metre, in which the first syllable of any verse can be short or long, but which in this case is short.

The 1551 edition draws material both from the 1526 Augsburg edition, and from one of the Marburg editions. Nigidius reproduces nearly all of Michael's settings of Horace, only for the first two metres he chooses one of the two settings provided in the 1526 edition (see Appendix).[50] In the first setting of *Maecenas atavis*, an erroneous c2-clef ahead of the second verse in the alto, which had been copied without alteration in 1531, is here corrected to a c1-clef. In n° 3 (*Sic te diva potens*) the final pitch follows the correct reading in 1526, whereas the solution in 1531 causes a dissonance.[51] Cases such as the last one could imply that Egenolff's publication rather follows the Augsburg 1526 edition. But on the other hand some readings seem to imply that the typesetter (or the editor) also knew the musical text of the 1531 or the 1533 edition: the final pitches of n° 12 (*Miserarum*) in Billican's edition are *e* (discantus and tenor) and *a* (alto and bass). In the 1531 edition, the last note of the alto is changed to *g*, which results in a dissonance with the *a* in the bass. Nigidius (or an unknown musical editor) finally changes the pitches of both alto and bass to *g*, which leads to a consonant final interval, but does not correspond with the 1526 edition. At the same time,

---

48 However, it is astonishing that Nigidius seems not to have known either the 1531 or the 1533 edition of the ode settings, as he succeeded Reinhard Lorich, one of the editors of the first Marburg edition, at the Paedagogium. At the time of the 1533 edition Nigidius was rector of the Paedagogium.

49 Gustavson, art. 'Egenolff, Christian', 98.

50 Michael's ode settings as they appear in Nigidius' edition are transcribed – alongside the settings by Tritonius, Senfl, Hofhaimer and others – in Stemplinger, *Das Fortleben*, 68, 75, 93, 102, 107, 112, 121, 125, 140, 147, 278 (distorted), 336, 402, 423, 450, 453, 455, 462, 465. Stemplinger remarks at several instances that the settings must be distorted by the print, and in his transcriptions many errors are to be found.

51 The 'emendation' in 1531 was probably initiated by the dissonant interval between discant and alto on the second last note ($b^1 - a^1$) in the 1526 edition, which was also corrected in the 1551 edition.

THEOBALD BILLICAN AND MICHAEL'S ODES   239

Nigidius drew on repertoire that is uniquely transmitted in either the Augsburg 1526 or the two Marburg editions (see Appendix); for example, the second four-voice setting of *Iam satis terris* from 1526, and the three-voice *Livor tabificum* and *Adeste Musae*, which appear in 1551 as adjacent pieces in the same order as in Marburg 1531.[52] Taken together, these findings suggest that Nigidius provided Egenolff either with a copy of each of both editions, or with manuscript copies derived from both of those publications.

The repertoire

This leads us on to a closer look at the repertoire of Michael's ode settings in the various publications, and the contexts in which this repertoire appears. Although it is often stated in the literature that the Augsburg 1526 edition contains nineteen ode settings, relating to the nineteen metrical genera found in Horace's *Carmina*, this is not correct. As mentioned before, the first and second odes are each illustrated by two different settings. In the two settings of *Maecenas atavis* the tenor is the same, which could mean that the melody was already established or one of the settings was deliberately being imitated. Reharmonisation of pre-existing tenors was a particularity of this genre, as seen in Senfl's reworkings of Tritonius' tenors. Later editions reprint only the first setting of *Maecenas atavis*. Instead of the two settings of *Iam satis terris* given in the 1526 edition, both Marburg editions include a three-voice setting that has no voice in common with any of the two earlier settings. Concerning the settings of this metre, Nigidius reprints the second setting of *Iam satis terris* found in the 1526 edition, and ascribes it to Michael. But he also reproduces the three-voice setting from the Marburg editions, which he assigns to an unknown composer ('Incerti authoris'). For the remaining metres, the transmission of the repertoire is more stable.

Only at the end of the music section, the two Marburg editions add a further three ode settings. These settings differ from the rest in several respects. First, they are for three voices. Second, two of them have a mensuration sign. Third, *Adeste Musae* is given in a different level of note values (breves and semibreves). Finally, the last one, a setting of *Hanc tua Penelope*, is not strictly homophonic: the two lower voices enter a semibreve after the highest voice, but maintain the same metrical scheme. This imitative character is reinforced further, as the middle voice forms a canon at the fourth with the highest voice. I suggest that those three pieces, as well as the three-voice *Iam satis terris*, form a heterogeneous set of settings, probably by a local Marburg composer, and are not related to those by Michael.

The first setting of *Iam satis terris* in the 1526 edition (n° 2a in the Appendix) also shows several conspicuous features. In the 1526 Augsburg edition, the voices are laid out in a different way from the other pieces in this collection: the highest voice, notated with a g2-clef, is placed in the bottom right corner, whereas one of the middle voices (presumably the tenor) is located in the upper left corner. Nigidius included this setting in his two editions, but both times with different texts: with the text *Mercuri, facunde nepos Atlantis* in 1548, and *Ipse cum solus* in 1551. In both of Nigidius' editions, the voices are arranged in a different way from the 1526 edition. Nigidius calls the (presumed) tenor from the 1526 edition discantus, and gives the other three voices an octave lower than they appear in 1526. He designates this setting as an 'old melody' ('vetus melodia'); indeed, it was widely transmitted from the first decade of the sixteenth century onwards. The earliest known concordance is in a manuscript appendix with a short treatise on metres used by Boethius,

---

52 N° 36 and 37. Only the three-voice setting *Hanc tua Penelope*, composed with canon, does not reappear in Nigidius' anthology.

240 SONJA TRÖSTER

now in the University Library of Freiburg, Hs. 450. In this manuscript, dated 1507/08, the setting, which deviates slightly in discantus, alto and bass from the setting in Augsburg 1526, appears there with the text *Novimus quantas dederit ruinas* (Boethius, *De consolatione*, liber 2, metrum 6).[53] An exact match with the setting in Billican's book – apart from the transposition – can be found in Glarean's *Dodekachordon*.[54]

An explanation for the transpositions given by Billican is easily provided. If Billican intended to sing this setting with boys' voices only, he had to move the lower voice parts upward into a range comparable to those of the other pieces in his collection. The effect of these transpositions on the music apparently did not concern him too much, although the obvious functions of the voice parts – especially the discant and tenor movement at cadences – are obfuscated. Despite any confusion of the 'original' function of each voice, they were allocated to the appropriate spaces on the opening. If the Augsburg 1526 edition of ode settings was custom-made by Michael on Billican's behalf, as Nigidius claimed, the necessity of such transpositions of voices would be surprising. The conclusion seems clear: this composition is not to be counted among Michael's ode settings.

The same is probably true for the second of the two settings of *Maecenas atavis* at the beginning of the collection, though in that case I was not able to find a concordance. Those two settings were possibly already known in Nördlingen before Billican requested further ode settings from Augsburg. When he decided to publish the collection, Billican inserted them among Michael's compositions. Nigidius, on the other hand, was most likely aware of the widely disseminated Sapphic setting independently from Billican's publication. He reproduced it in the original transposition, separate from Michael's settings.

Nigidius' 1551 edition gathers a great variety of ode settings. But right at the beginning of the book, Michael's settings of Horace appear next to Tritonius' settings of the same text: 'Horatij Melodiarum, Autoribus Petro Tritonio, et Michaele N.' As far as we know, Michael's Horatian ode settings were one of the earliest attempts (after Tritonius and perhaps Grefinger) to set all the metres used in Horace's *Carmina*. However, Michael does not follow Tritonius' model very closely. He neither cited Tritonius' melodies, as Senfl and Heinrich Textor did,[55] nor does he proceed as pragmatically as Tritonius, who applied identical musical sections for similar elements in different metres.[56] And unlike Tritonius, Senfl, and Hofhaimer, Michael uses semibreve and minim instead of breve and semibreve to represent long and short syllables. Later ode settings, for example those set by Textor using Tritonius' melodies, published by Frisius in Zurich in 1554, tend to use this relation more often than the earlier publications. Another detail that shows Michael's independence from Tritonius' model is to be found in the setting of *Altera iam bellis*. The word order in Michael's setting is different from that in the settings of Tritonius and Senfl. Only Hofhaimer's setting of the same text uses the same word order (and the correlating succession of note values) as Michael.[57]

The title of Nigidius' book of ode settings from 1551 reveals one aspect of the intention of this publication: *Geminae undeviginti odarum Horatii melodiae* ('Twin melodies of nineteen Horatian odes'). Although the remainder of the repertoire equals in number the thirty-eight

---

53 Brinzing, *Neue Quellen*, [20]. A reproduction of the relevant page on [39] (Abb. 2a).
54 Heinrich Glareanus, *Dodekachordon* (Basel: Heinrich Petri, 1547), vdm 1112, 438 (*Ut queant laxis*). Cf. Brinzing, *Neue Quellen*, [20]–[21]; and McDonald, 'Notes on the Sources', 626.
55 Johann Fries, *Brevis musicae isagoge* (Zurich: Frosch, 1554), VD16 F 3000.
56 Compare for example Tritonius' *Maecenas atavis*, *Scriberis Vario fortis* and *Vides ut alta stet*. The opening verses of those settings all share the same music. See also Bobeth, 'Die humanistische Odenkomposition', 75.
57 Bobeth, 'Die humanistische Odenkomposition', 70–71.

THEOBALD BILLICAN AND MICHAEL'S ODES   241

Horatian settings and offers settings by renowned composers such as Isaac, Senfl and Ducis, this is not reflected in the title. By juxtaposing Tritonius' settings in such a prominent way with Michael's, Nigidius conveys a number of points. On one hand, he wanted to show that the Marburg Paedagogium had access to a transregional repertoire, as Tritonius' settings had surely become by the time, judging from the innumerable copies in print and manuscript.[58] On the other, he proclaims that Marburg also had an exclusively regional repertoire that met the same standards. A further aspect of this juxtaposition might be reflected in the different note values employed for Tritonius' and Michael's settings. In the preface Nigidius characterises Tritonius' settings as quite old,[59] which may be intended to imply that Michael's settings represent a comparatively more up-to-date repertoire, the modernity of which becomes visually apparent in the use of smaller note values.

Michael's ode settings do not show the extravagance of Senfl's, which sometimes include a melisma in the form of a ligature on the last syllable of a setting. But his settings are contrapuntally well designed, and certainly served the primarily pedagogical function for which they were intended. After Tritonius' settings, which are the most widely transmitted humanistic ode settings, Michael's settings were reprinted next most often. Nevertheless, they neither had the same influence on the evolution of the genre as those of Tritonius, nor were they so widely received. Their ambit most likely never went far beyond Nördlingen and Marburg.[60] Only one of Michael's settings, *Sic te diva potens*, was included in Lucas Lossius' *Erotemata musicae practicae* (Nuremberg: Johann vom Berg and Ulrich Neuber, 1563), most probably taken over from Egenolff's edition.[61] This music textbook, intended for the school in Lüneburg, has an appendix entitled *Melodiae sex generum carminum*.[62] The named composers are Ducis and Tritonius, and as source for his anthology Lossius seems to have heavily relied on Egenolff's publication. Among the borrowed pieces we find Michael's *Sic te diva potens*. The setting is described as 'melodia carminis gliconici' (fols. B5ᵛ–[B7]ʳ) and it is modified in respect to its note values: dotted notes are introduced to produce the more modern feeling of a regular metre. Lossius also included the first (anonymous) setting of *Iam satis terris* (equals n° 31 *Ipse cum solus* in Nigidius 1551; cf. n° 2a in the appendix) from the Augsburg 1526 edition, albeit in a variant version (only the tenor is exactly the same), which was widely disseminated. Lossius presents it as 'melodia carminis Sapphici,' now with the Christian text *Christe confusae medicina mentis* by the French Neo-Latin poet Jean Salmon Macrin.[63]

---

58 Bobeth, 'Die humanistische Odenkomposition' and Brinzing, *Neue Quellen*, [25]–[29].

59 RISM B/I 1551¹⁷, G2ᵛ: 'modulos antiquiores aliquanto'.

60 A subtle hint of the primarily local destination of the publications can be found under the heading 'De Genitivo' towards the end of the first part of the grammar. In Augsburg 1526, E iiʳ, Nördlingen is mentioned in the context of an example: 'Omne verbum admittit genitivum proprij nominis, significantis locum in quo fit actio, ut vixit Rhomae, natus est Nordlingiaci', whereas the last word of the same sentence in Marburg 1533, F [vi]ʳ reads 'Marpurgi'.

61 Lucas Lossius, *Erotemata musicae practicae* (Nuremberg: Johann vom Berg & Ulrich Neuber, 1563), VD16 L 2767; several reprints: Nuremberg: Ulrich Neuber, 1568, V16 ZV 9880; Nuremberg: Katharina Gerlach, 1574; Nuremberg: Katharina Gerlach & Bergs Erben, 1579, VD16 L 2768; Nuremberg: Katharina Gerlach & Bergs Erben, 1583, VD16 L 2769; Nuremberg: Katharina Gerlach, 1590, VD16 L 2770. I used the Munich copy of the 1563 edition.

62 In the 1563 edition this appendix is even treated as a separate book with a new title page, a list of the contents and a repetition of the date 1563. Consequently, also the signatures of folios start anew with gathering A.

63 Lossius, *Erotemata*, [A7]ᵛ–B[1]ʳ. Lossius also reprints two settings on *Vos ad se pueri* ([B7]ᵛ–C5ʳ), which are already present in Nigidius' edition from 1548. The two settings, originally for two voices, are enlarged by a third discantus. For Macrin's text see Schumann, *Salmon Macrins Gedichtsammlungen*, 324–325.

The relative neglect of Michael's ode settings in modern scholarship is at least partly due to the fact that we know so little about the composer. Moreover, there may be confessional issues in play. Theobald Billican, who initiated the composition of these settings, and whose name is closely linked to them, was an ambiguous figure in the early Reformation.[64] At the beginning of his career in Heidelberg, he was a fervent follower of Luther's ideas, and he married in 1523 at Nördlingen. But at the imperial diet in Augsburg in 1530 he formally returned to the Roman Catholic Church. This attracted great attention in Lutheran circles and Billican was subsequently regarded as a controversial figure. On one hand he was respected for his keen mind and his pedagogical works, but on the other hand Protestant circles suspected him of being a traitor and even a spy. This is probably one reason why Billican's name was no longer mentioned when a reworked edition of his Latin grammar was printed in 1531 for use in the realm of the Protestant university in Marburg.[65] Only one year after Billican's conversion, the editors of the publication wanted to avoid being associated with his name in a printed book. As late as the nineteenth century, Protestant scholars interpreted Billican's alienation from the Reformation as a weakness, and he consequently failed to attract any favourable attention. This notion quite possibly also influenced the Protestant Rochus von Liliencron, when he assessed Michael's ode settings, which were so closely linked to Billican. In his influential article 'Die Horazischen Metren in deutschen Kompositionen des 16. Jahrhunderts', Liliencron transcribed only the settings by Tritonius, Senfl and Hofhaimer, and dismissed Michael's ode settings as less important and for the most part relatively dull.[66]

Leaving this somewhat distorted perspective aside, it is remarkable that institutions such as the Paedagogium in Marburg held this corpus of ode settings in such high esteem that they were deemed worthy of the trouble of printing at least four times. This presence in print is only surpassed by Tritonius' settings, which had a role model function for the composition of four voice settings of metrical texts up to the seventeenth century. The earliest publication of Tritonius' settings was backed by Conrad Celtis, and this publication in turn propagated the fame of the arch-humanist. Probably, it was not even seen primarily as a music book, although the majority of the book is devoted to printed music.[67] Michael's ode settings on the other hand appear in the context of a mere pedagogical publication. Like the accompanying textbook, the settings seem to be composed first and foremost with the concrete audience of schoolboys at Latin schools in mind. Therefore, the Marburg editions are probably the earliest examples in which ode settings are linked so closely with explanatory texts and a description of the metre. There is no question that they were destined for use in the context of a humanistic education. The number of known reprints of Michael's ode settings testifies to the demand for such music at the time. At the same

---

64 Simon, *Humanismus*, esp. 213–216.

65 In Poland and Prussia, on the other hand, Billican's *De partium orationis* seems to have been a standard textbook for a long time, as can be established by the numerous reprints in Cracow and Kaliningrad (at the time called Königsberg): 1537 Cracow: Mathias Scharffenberg (USTC 240245); 1538 Cracow: Hieronymus Vietor (USTC 241081); 1540 Cracow: Hieronymus Vietor (USTC 241143); 1543 Cracow: Hieronymus Vietor (USTC 241312); 1549 Cracow: Hieronymus Scharffenberg (USTC 240246); [1564] Königsberg: Jan Daubmann; 1567 Cracow: Nicolai Scharffenberg (http://dlibra.kul.pl/dlibra/docmetadata?id=14301); 1569 Cracow: Hieronymus Scharffenberg. But this strand of transmission did not include the polyphonic settings; all these reprints lack notation.

66 Liliencron, 'Die Horazischen Metren', 48: 'Ich lasse nun hier die je 19 Odenlieder des Tritonius, Senfl und Hofhaimer in der originalen Notierung in Partitur folgen. Die Sätze des Michael lasse ich fort; sie sind unbedeutender und meistens recht trocken.' In the same year the article was also issued as a separate publication and the appendix with the ode settings appeared as a practical edition to be used at schools.

67 Lodes, 'Concentus, Melopoiae und Harmonie', 42–57.

time its transmission reflects a rarely documented ambition to foster a local repertoire in opposition to a more widely known one, apparent in Nigidius' juxtaposition of Michael's and Tritonius' settings.

Appendix

Table 10.2 Musical contents of the publications containing Michael's ode settings

	Billican, Augsburg: Ruff, 1526	Marburg: Rhode, 1531 and 1533	Nigidius, Frankfurt: Egenolff, 1551 (selection)
1a: *Maecenas atavis*	X	X	X
1b: *Maecenas atavis*	X	–	–
2a: *Iam satis terris*	X	–	= 31: *Ipse cum solus*
2b: *Iam satis terris*	X	–	X
2c: *Iam satis terris* (3vv)	–	X	T: 'Incerti Authoris'
3: *Sic te diva potens Cypri*	X	X	X
4: *Solvitur acris hyems*	X	X	X
5: *Quis multa gracilis*	X	X	X
6: *Scriberis Vario fortis*	X	X	X
7: *Laudabunt alii*	X	X	X
8: *Lydia dic per omnis*	X	X	X
9: *Vides ut alta stet*	X	X	X
10: *Tu ne quaesieris*	X	X	X
11: *Non ebur neque aureum*	X	printed without dotted notes	printed without dotted notes
12: *Miserarum est*	X	X	X
13: *Diffugere nives*	X	X	X
14: *Ibis Liburnis*	X	X	X
15: *Petti nihil me*	X	X	X
16: *Horrida tempestas*	X	X	X
17: *Mollis inertia*	X	X	X
18: *Altera iam teritur bellis*	X	X	X
19: *Iam iam efficaci*	X	X	X
Livor tabificum malis venenum (3vv)	–	X	= 36: 'Trium . . . incerti Autoris'
Adeste Musae maximi (3vv)	–	X	= 37: 'Melodia . . . incerti autoris'
Hanc tua Penelope (3vv)	–	X	–

References

Bernstein, Lawrence F. 'The Bibliography of Music in Conrad Gesner's Pandectae (1548)'. *Acta Musicologica* 45 (1973): 119–163.

Bobeth, Gundela. 'Die humanistische Odenkomposition in Buchdruck und Handschrift: Zur Rolle der *Melopoiae* bei der Formung und Ausbreitung eines kompositorischen Erfolgsmodells'. In *NiveauNischeNimbus: Die Anfänge des Musikdrucks nördlich der Alpen*, edited by Birgit Lodes. Wiener Forum für ältere Musikgeschichte 3. Tutzing: Hans Schneider, 2010, 67–87.

Bredehorn, Uwe. *Marburger Frühdrucke 1527–1566*. Schriften der Universitätsbibliothek Marburg 33. Marburg: Universitätsbibliothek, 1987.

Brinzing, Armin. *Neue Quellen zur Geschichte der humanistischen Odenkomposition in Deutschland*. Nachrichten der Akademie der Wissenschaften zu Göttingen I. Philologisch-Historische Klasse 8; Kleinüberlieferung mehrstimmiger Musik vor 1550 in deutschem Sprachgebiet 5. Göttingen: Vandenhoeck & Ruprecht, 2001.

Dommer, Arrey von. *Die ältesten Drucke aus Marburg in Hessen 1527–1566*. Marburg: Elwert, 1892.

Dorn, Ernst. 'Die Schulmeister und Cantoren in Nördlingen von 1285–1543'. *Historischer Verein für Nördlingen und Umgebung*, 11. Jahrbuch (1927): 36–44.

Engel, Hans. *Musikpflege an der Philipps-Universität Marburg seit 1527*. Marburg: Elwert, 1957.

Friedrich, Anne. *Das Symposium der XII 'sapientes': Kommentar und Verfasserfrage*. Berlin, New York: de Gruyter, 2002.

Graf-Stuhlhofer, Franz. 'Vadian als Lehrer am Wiener Poetenkolleg'. *Zwingliana. Beiträge zur Geschichte Zwinglis, der Reformation und des Protestantismus in der Schweiz* 26 (1999): 93–98.

Gustavson, Royston. 'Egenolff, Christian'. In *Die Musik in Geschichte und Gegenwart*, edited by Ludwig Finscher, Personenteil 6. Kassel: Bärenreiter, 2001, cols. 98–103.

Heidrich, Jürgen. 'Musik und Humanismus an der Fürstenschule St. Afra zu Meissen im 16. Jahrhundert'. In *Musikalische Quellen – Quellen zur Musikgeschichte*, edited by Jürgen Heidrich, Hans Joachim Marx and Ulrich Konrad. Göttingen: Vandenhoeck & Ruprecht, 2002, 97–110.

Hofhaimer, Paul. *Ausgabe sämtlicher Werke*, vol. III, *Harmoniae poeticae (Nürnberg 1539)*, edited by Grantley McDonald. Denkmäler der Musikgeschichte in Salzburg 15. München: Strube Verlag, 2014.

Knoke, Karl. 'Leben und Schriften des hessischen Humanisten Petrus Nigidius'. *Zeitschrift für Geschichte der Erziehung und des Unterrichts* 17 (1915): 77–137.

Koch, Christian. *Geschichte des akademischen Pädagogiums in Marburg*. Marburg: Elwert'sche Universitäts-Buchdruckerei, 1868.

Layer, Adolf. *Musik und Musiker der Fuggerzeit*. Augsburg: Himmler, 1959.

Leonhardt, Jürgen. 'G2. Petrus Nigidius d.Ä.: Isagogicus rerum grammaticarum libellus' and 'Die grammatischen Lehrwerke von Petrus Nigidius d.Ä.'. In *Melanchthon und die Marburger Professoren (1527–1627)*, edited by Barbara Bauer. Marburg: Völker & Ritter, 1999, vol. i, 68–70 and vol. ii, 695–705.

Liliencron, Rochus von. 'Die Horazischen Metren in deutschen Kompositionen des 16. Jahrhunderts'. *Vierteljahrsschrift für Musikwissenschaft* 3 (1887): 26–91.

Lodes, Birgit. '*Concentus, Melopoiae* und *Harmonie* 1507: Zum Geburtsjahr des Typendrucks mehrstimmiger Musik nördlich der Alpen'. In *NiveauNischeNimbus: Die Anfänge des Musikdrucks nördlich der Alpen*, edited by Birgit Lodes. Wiener Forum für ältere Musikgeschichte 3. Tutzing: Hans Schneider, 2010, 33–66.

McDonald, Grantley. 'Notes on the Sources and Reception of Senfl's *Harmoniae*'. In *Senfl-Studien* 2, edited by Stefan Gasch and Sonja Tröster. Wiener Forum für ältere Musikgeschichte 7. Tutzing: Hans Schneider, 2013, 623–633.

McDonald, Grantley. 'The Metrical *Harmoniae* of Wolfgang Gräfinger and Ludwig Senfl in the Conjunction of Humanism, Neoplatonism, and Nicodemism'. In *Senfl-Studien* 1, edited by Stefan Gasch, Birgit Lodes, and Sonja Tröster. Wiener Forum für ältere Musikgeschichte 4. Tutzing: Hans Schneider, 2012, 69–148.

Möncke, Gisela. 'Marburger Drucke der Jahre 1527 bis 1566: Ergänzungen zur Bibliographie Arrey von Dommers'. *Archiv für Geschichte des Buchwesens* 65 (2010): 88–156.

Reske, Christoph. *Die Buchdrucker des 16. und 17. Jahrhunderts im deutschen Sprachgebiet*, 2nd, extended edition Wiesbaden: Harrassowitz, 2015.

Schmidt-Beste, Thomas and Karl Günter Hartmann. 'Ode. Die humanistische Ode'. In *Die Musik in Geschichte und Gegenwart*, Sachteil vol. 7. Kassel etc.: Bärenreiter, 1997, cols. 562–567.

Schumann, Marie-Françoise. *Salmon Macrins Gedichtsammlungen von 1537. Edition mit Wortindex*. Hamburger Beiträge zur Neulateinischen Philologie 8. Münster: LIT-Verlag, 2012.

Simon, Gerhard. *Humanismus und Konfession: Theobald Billican, Leben und Werk*. Arbeiten zur Kirchengeschichte 49. Berlin/New York: Walter de Gruyter, 1980.

Stemplinger, Eduard. *Das Fortleben der horazischen Lyrik seit der Renaissance*. Leipzig: Teubner, 1906.

11

Polyphonic music in early German print

Changing perspectives in music historiography[1]

Andrea Lindmayr-Brandl

'Quid est musica?' This question opens many early works of music theory and leads them to various formulations. Following this medieval tradition, the first chapter of the treatise *Tetrachordum musices* by Johannes Cochlaeus, printed 1511 at Nuremberg, begins with a definition of music. The author does not give just one answer, but offers three definitions drawn from ancient authorities: from Augustine (it is the science of modulating well), from Boethius (it is the ability to weigh differences of high and low sounds by sense and by reason) and from Bacchius (it is the knowledge of melodic species and those things that are related to melody).[2] The same question – what is music? – still echoes in the background of contemporary musicological research. It may remain hidden when we work on details, but as soon as fundamental questions arise, the question emerges again to the light. Today we are aware that this question can be interpreted in a number of ways. First is the ontological approach (What is music at all?), a question Cochlaeus also had in mind. But there is also the question of classification (What should be called music and what not?) as well as other terminological problems (e.g. What do we mean when we use the word 'music'?).

We confronted this third question as we gathered the data for our research project *Early Music Printing in German-Speaking Lands (1501–1540)*. (For more on this project see the Introduction of this volume). Gradually it became clear that it is not music *per se*, but polyphonic art music, both vocal and instrumental, that stands in the centre of musicological study and comprises the backbone of the regnant historical narrative transmitted since the beginning of our discipline. When you browse through any music history book, the chapters on Renaissance music always deal only with the same genres: masses, motets, songs and instrumental pieces. In this well-established story, all other kinds of music are more or less ignored. However, there has never been a serious examination of how well this narrative reflects the historical data, at least as far as this can be determined from the surviving musical sources of the musical life in earlier times. My chapter might be understood as an attempt to achieve a more balanced account of the breadth of sixteenth-century musical experience, as this is reflected in the extant printed sources of notated music.

---

1 Research for this paper was made possible by funding from the Austrian Science Fund (FWF) for the project P24075–G23.

2 Cochlaeus, *Tetrachordum Musices*, 19. The original text reads: 'Quid est musica? Est bene modulandi scientia. Augustinus. Vel est facultas differentias acutorum et gravium sonorum sensu ac ratione perdendens. Boecius. Vel est habitus meli species et ea que circa melos sunt oberservans. Bacheus.' (fol. Aii^r; see also vdm 128).

246 ANDREA LINDMAYR-BRANDL

Polyphonic music sources in the database *vdm*

Our research project has allowed us to question the traditional narrative because it is not focused primarily on repertoire, but on printed objects bearing legible printed music notation, without taking into account what kind of music they transmit. We knew from the very beginning of our project that we would be working not only with polyphony but also with a variety of 'different' kinds of music: short examples in theory treatises and textbooks, tablatures, monophonic songs, humanist ode-settings and dramatic choruses, as well as chant and congregational hymns for liturgical and devotional purposes. As we compiled the data from the standard bibliographies, it became increasingly clear that these 'different' kinds of music were not outliers but constitute the overwhelming majority of what was published during the period under investigation. The forty-three polyphonic music books printed in German-speaking lands in the first four decades of the sixteenth century, catalogued in the RISM volumes A/I and B/I, represent only 14 per cent of the total number of editions including printed music.

Almost three years later, at the end of the first stage of the project, the number of sources containing musical notation in our database has more than doubled to 695 titles.[3] This massive increase in the number of editions was due to the consultation of older repertoire-based and regional catalogues, secondary literature, systematic search in libraries, and the careful distinguishing of editions that had been bundled together into one single title in earlier bibliographies. (Some new editions with musical notation came up by chance, for example when they were bound together with books that were already registered, which we recorded *in situ*.) However, the growth of our data was not the same in different types of sources.[4] The amount by which a given type of source grew usually stood in reverse proportion to musicological interest in specific genres. Figure 11.1 indicates the total number of titles of a given source type, with a light grey beam showing the number of titles identified at the beginning of the project and a dark grey beam for the final result. The categories on the left side are arranged according to the increase, from top to bottom.

Strikingly, the number of known liturgical books containing music multiplied almost two and a half times, compared with the items of this category at the beginning of the project. This phenomenon stands in sharp contrast to the appreciation for this musical repertoire in our field. The musicological community has never spent much interest nor money on producing a catalogue of printed liturgical books containing music, and hence neglects a large part of the production of the sixteenth century (as well as for later times). A prominent exception is the database RELICS, hosted by the University of Michigan.[5] It is still the best place to start with a study of Renaissance liturgical printed books, although based only on volunteer contributions by scholars who mainly work in major research libraries in the United States. However, since this database includes holdings from only a few European libraries, with some additional data supplemented from published bibliographies and library catalogues (such as the fundamental catalogue of Weale, *Bibliographia liturgica*, and Amiet, *Missels et bréviaires imprimés*), it can make no claim to completeness. Moreover, music is not in the focus of this database (nor is it of the catalogues by Weale and Amiet), so that

---

3 All numbers given in the following tables are based on the status of the data in *vdm* from 21 December 2015. See the current version of the database on our homepage: www.vdm.sbg.ac.at.

4 For the classification of the sources types see the Introduction in this volume.

5 http://quod.lib.umich.edu/r/relics/

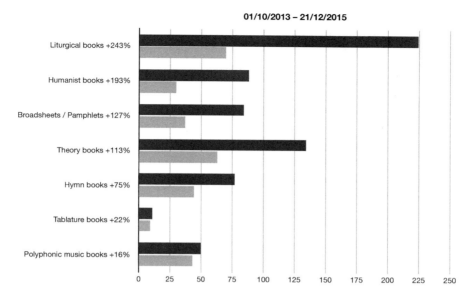

Figure 11.1 Increase of the number of titles known between 1 October 2013 and 21 December 2015 in course of the research project 'Early Music Printing in German-Speaking Lands (1501–1540)'

it is difficult to develop a search routine for titles that contain music.[6] The best way to find new liturgical books containing music is still to go to libraries and check all available items there. Due to this lamentable research situation, one can be sure that there are still many more unknown editions hidden in the stacks.

The second item on our list of rapidly growing source types is humanist books. Their number almost tripled. These books tend to fall through the net of music catalogues since they contain mainly text, with music as an add-on. The few editions registered by RISM either contain a full collection of polyphonic odes, such as the *Harmoniae poeticae* by Paul Hofhaimer (vdm 47), the Horace settings by Tritonius (vdm 55 and 108), and the *Varia carminum genera* by Ludwig Senfl (vdm 97). Some are listed by the author of the chorus and the title of the music, without mentioning the book title or the author of the text. This is the case with the very popular school drama *Scaenica progymnasmata* by Johannes Reuchlin, which is catalogued in RISM A/I under the name of Daniel Megel (M 1739–1748), the composer of the four choruses at the end of each act of the play.[7] This catalogue entry thus ignores the context for which the music was written and does not list a source but a composition.

The next three source types on the list – broadsheets and pamphlets, theory books, and hymn books – increased between 75 and 113 per cent. Only polyphonic music books and tablature books had already been registered with great care before we started our work.

---

6 When one searches 'music' as a keyword, one also gets titles with the description 'no music'. Moreover, it depends on the person who entered the data whether there is information on the presence of music at all.

7 In vdm we count 26 editions, RISM A/I gives 12 editions. The author Megel is already mentioned in the 1498 edition (vdm 73), fol. b3ʳ.

Among the few titles we could add are two tablature books, both derived from historical catalogues with no extant copies: the *Tabulaturae liber ad testudinem secundum Tonos*, listed by the catalogue of the Swiss scholar Conrad Gesner, with intabulations by Johannes Widenhuober (vdm 897); the *Cythare germanice tabulature*, listed in the catalogue of Ferdinand Columbus, printed in Augsburg around 1530 (vdm 898).

Our additions to the already documented polyphonic music books have different explanations:

- Two of them are also only from historical catalogues, without physical traces: the *Brabandische Liedlin*, printed by Christian Egenolff in 1535 (vdm 29) and *Viginti cantiunculae Gallicae*, a collection of French chansons, printed by Peter Schöffer the Younger at Strasbourg in 1530 (vdm 895).
- Another four editions had been known for several years but were either neglected or not distinguished by RISM. Schöffer's reprint of Petrucci's *Canti B* from 1513 (*Quinquagena Carminum*, vdm 15), without RISM number, belongs to the first group;[8] likewise two collections with secular songs by Egenolff, which were until recently only extant in one single Discantus partbook, also not registered by RISM.[9] An example of the second group is a later edition of Egenolff's *Reutterliedlin* (vdm 689). This title was already noticed by Ernst-Ludwig Berz in his painstaking study on early music printers at Frankfurt/Main, but was not distinguished by RISM from the earlier edition of 1535 (B/I 1535[11]).[10]
- Another case is a collection of motets in four and five voices, edited by Georg Forster and printed in 1540 by Johann Petreius at Nuremberg. We distinguished the collection *Selectissimarum mutetarum partim quinque partim quatuor vocum tomus primus* into two separate bibliographical units, with the first one containing the compositions for five voices (vdm 50), the second for four voices (vdm 914).[11]
- Finally, two editions by Christian Egenolff were recently identified by Royston Gustavson: a book with motets for three voices and one for four voices, bound together in the unique known copy, preserved in the Swiss National library at Bern.[12]

Taking into consideration the disproportionate increase of all other source types compared with those containing polyphonic music, it becomes clear why by the end of our search the overall percentage of the latter had dropped dramatically, from 14 per cent of titles to 7 per cent.[13] This low number indicates that in the first four decades of the sixteenth century the printing of polyphonic music in German-speaking lands captured only a minimal share in the full output of printed editions that contained notated music. Printed books that transmitted chant, odes, or Lutheran hymns clearly dominated the market north of the Alps.

---

8 See Lindmayr-Brandl, 'Peter Schöffer der Jüngere', 298–302.

9 They are bound together with another song collection by Christian Egenolff (F-Pn RES VM7–504). See vdm 29, vdm 30 and vdm 25 and Gustavson's chapter in the present book.

10 Berz, *Frankfurt am Main*, 137–6, # 5.

11 The title is listed in RISM B/I under 1540/6. The argumentation for this splitting is presented in Lindmayr-Brandl, 'Early Music Prints'.

12 *Cantiones selectissimae LXVIII, vocum trium* (Frankfurt am Main: Egenolff, *c*.1535–1536), vdm 30 and *Cantiones vocum quatuor* (Frankfurt am Main: Egenolff, *c*.1535–1537), vdm 25. See Gustavson's chapter in the present book.

13 See the percentages of the other source types in the Introduction, p. x.

Chronology

Table 11.1 arranges the number of titles containing printed polyphonic music in German-speaking lands chronologically in blocks of five years, and sorts them according to their repertoire. Editions containing sacred music (masses and motets) and editions containing secular music (mainly German song settings) are displayed separately (see also Table 11.2). Tablature books represent the notated instrumental polyphonic music of the time. Since the focus of this overview is printed music *books*, broadsheets and pamphlets that transmit only single pieces of music, humanist books containing polyphonic choruses, grammar books containing only a few ode settings, and theory and pedagogical books are not included in this table, although larger ode collections that appeared as self-standing music books are included. This repertoire represents a specific German genre of polyphonic music which is highly underestimated by scholars in its social, intellectual, and musical meaning.[14]

A first glance at this table will already indicate that the printing of polyphonic music books in German-speaking lands was a rather late phenomenon, with stiff market competition from the beginning. While the first three decades of the sixteenth century saw only isolated editions of polyphonic music, production accelerated in the 1530s and increased almost threefold in the last five years of this decade. This general development is not only due to a technical shift from the elaborate, time-consuming and expensive double impression process to the relatively quicker and cheaper single impression technique. It is also closely related to social and cultural changes that shook society in its everyday life.

For a more detailed investigation, let us start with the production at the very beginning of the century. Although the first time slot 1501–1505 of the table shows no music books, it is worth mentioning that in the very first year of this period, two printed editions by humanist authors – a pamphlet and a booklet, both carrying individual ode settings – appeared. One was the famous *Ludus Dianae* by the poet laureate Celtis (vdm 59), first performed at Linz, honouring Emperor Maximilian and his wife Bianca Maria Sforza; the other was a praise of the muses (*Laus musarum*, vdm 739) by Georg Spalatinus, then a student of the University of Erfurt, later a committed advocate of the Reformation. In both editions the musical notation is printed from woodcut.

In the next five-year segment we find the first collection of sacred polyphony printed north of the Alps, Gregor Mewes' outstanding collection of four masses by Obrecht, published in Basel, probably in the year 1507.[15] Two other items date from the same year.

Table 11.1 Development of polyphonic printing (number of editions) in German-speaking lands

Time period	First decade		Second decade		Third decade		Fourth decade	
	1501–05	06–10	11–15	16–20	21–25	26–30	31–35	36–40
Ode collections	–	2	–	–	–	1	5	2
Tablature editions	–	–	1	–	3	–	2	5
Secular music editions	–	–	5	1	–	1	4	14
Sacred music editions	–	1	–	1	2	–	3	20
Total	–	3	6	2	5	2	14	41

---

14 For a recent reappraisal of this genre see McDonald, 'Harmoniae'.
15 Lodes, 'Obrecht-Drucke'.

They contain Petrus Tritonius' musical settings of odes by Horace, printed by Oeglin at Augsburg in two closely related editions, the *Melopoiae* and the *Harmoniae*.[16] All three editions used the technique of multiple impression for polyphonic music for the first time in German-speaking lands.[17]

A first boost of secular music in German seems to have occurred in the beginning of the second decade. Here we register two songbooks by Oeglin, two songbooks by Schöffer, and another songbook by Arndt von Aich. Schöffer printed a third songbook in 1517. However, this initiative soon came to an end and was only taken up again in the later 1530s.[18] The only secular book in the years between 1526–1530 dates from the last year of this period: a now lost edition of twenty *cantiunculae* in French, printed by Schöffer at Strasbourg. Most of the other songbooks transmit predominantly German Lied settings.

The printing of sacred polyphony constitutes a different case. Before the start of the Reformation, only two books containing such repertoire were published: the already mentioned Mewes mass book and the extraordinary motet collection *Liber selectarum cantionum*, dedicated to the archbishop of Salzburg, Matthäus Lang. The next two items that appear in the time slot 1521–1525 already have a Lutheran background. They relate to Walter's songbook, containing forty-three polyphonic settings of Lutheran hymn melodies, first printed in Wittenberg 1524 by Klug and reprinted the year later by Schöffer. Nine years later, it was again Schöffer who relaunched the printing of sacred polyphony. In 1534 and 1535 he produced a third edition of the polyphonic hymn book by Walter as well as two collections of music by Sixt Dietrich, a south-German composer who worked in the circuits of the Reformation. These must have been a financial success, since Schöffer produced another edition of Walter's hymn book, and reprinted Dietrich's Magnificat collection some years later. However, a real push forward in printing polyphonic sacred music started as late as 1537. Then the two Nuremberg printers Petreius and Formschneider as well as Georg Rhau in Wittenberg produced several collections containing motets, masses and other polyphonic liturgical music that would make up a stock of sacred compositions for the next decades. In the last four years of our forty-year time span, twenty editions containing polyphonic sacred music were 'brought into light' (as they called it in their figurative language).

All the statistics examined to this point have been based solely on the raw number of editions containing music that were published in this limited geographical area. However, the raw numerical data are not directly proportional to the amount of music within the editions, since the quantity of music contained in any given title might differ strongly from that of another. Moreover, one mass contains much more 'music' than one song or one ode setting, and consequently to assign the same numerical value to various editions without regard to the amount of music they contain does not quite reflect the reality of the situation. To know how much printed music was available in the first decades in German-speaking lands, one has to define the number of compositions for each genre. Such an approach is made possible by the database *vdm*, which gives quite detailed information on each entry, though again it should be stressed that this database does not focus primarily on repertoire, a task that is being fulfilled increasingly by the online RISM database.

---

16 See Lodes, 'Concentus'; also Bobeth, 'Odenkomposition'.

17 The same technique has already been used for about three decades for chant in liturgical books.

18 The new congregations of the Reformation were much more interested in building up a canon of monophonic hymns than fostering sacred polyphonic songs with their profane lyrics. See Lindmayr-Brandl, 'Teutsche Liedlein'.

POLYPHONIC MUSIC IN EARLY GERMAN PRINT   251

Table 11.2 Development of polyphonic printing (number of compositions) in German-speaking lands[a]

Time period	First decade		Second decade		Third decade		Fourth decade		Total
	1501–05	06–10	11–15	16–20	21–25	26–30	31–35	36–40	
Odes	–	38	–	–	–	19	135	46+?	**238+?**
Intabulations	–	–	26	–	65+?	–	88	194+?	**373+??**
Songs /Chansons	–	–	260	36	–	20	194+?	828+?	**1.338+??**
Motets	–	–	–	24	86	–	48	670	**828**
Masses	–	4	–	–	–	–	–	32	**36**

[a] A question mark in the chart means that for an edition it was not possible to give the exact number of compositions that are included since there is no copy extant. Concordances in the repertoire are not considered.

Table 11.2 is structured in the same way as Table 11.1, with an additional distinction between motets and masses. Here the development of printed editions containing polyphonic music in German-speaking lands becomes even clearer. After the slow start in the first decade, with only four masses and thirty-eight ode settings,[19] the second decade is marked by the popularity of German song collections, containing 260 songs; this number drops back to zero at the beginning of the third decade. Intabulations for stringed and keyboard instruments appeared in the tablature books by Arnold Schlick (1512), Hans Judenkünig (1523), Hans Gerle (1532, 1533, 1537) and Hans Neusidler (1536). Although these numbers are too small for a proper statistical analysis, there is nevertheless a perceptible acceleration in the production of printed collections of tablatures towards the end of our period. The relatively high number of odes at the beginning of the third decade is owing to a print revival through Egenolff, who started his career as music printer in the year 1532 with an enlarged reprint of the ode collection by Oeglin, published in two variant versions. Additionally, Nickel Schmidt from Leipzig printed two closely related editions of twenty settings of Prudentius' hymns; and Formschneider printed a volume of thirty-one homophonic quantitative ode-settings by Ludwig Senfl.

The growth in the second half of the fourth decade is not only emphasised by the considerably higher numbers in each columns. It is also remarkable that now the production covers all genres. Only the mass compositions lag behind, beginning as late as 1538 with publications by the three main workshops of the Reformation period: Georg Rhau at Wittenberg, and Johannes Petreius and Hieronymus Formschneider, both at Nuremberg. Overwhelming is not only the number of *Lieder* published in the last five years of our survey, but also the increase in the number of motets printed in this short period, an increase of about fourteenfold, from forty-eight to 670. This specific development will be discussed in more detail later in this chapter.

While the loss of a number of editions means that it is not possible to determine precisely the total numbers of pieces within each genre, the general tendency is nevertheless clear. The most numerous genre of printed music consisted in short vocal secular compositions, mostly German Lied settings, amounting to about 1400 titles. Even when one considers that this total number includes reprints and concordances of the same song, this still represents an impressive amount of music available in print in the fourth decade of the

---

19 Actually the thirty-eight ode settings are nineteen different odes reprinted by the same workshop in the same year.

sixteenth century. No less overwhelming are the 828 motets, a number that rose steeply towards the end of our period. Both genres stand out significantly against the three other types of composition that appear comparatively humble, at least in numerical terms: about 250 ode settings, about 400 intabulations, and thirty-six masses, though it is expected that this last number will grow disproportionately in the following decades.

Polyphonic music printing outside German-speaking lands

Comparing this specific constellation with the situation in the other music printing countries in Europe relativises the development in German-speaking lands. Due to the fact that there are no similar detailed studies on early printed music available from other countries, it is impossible to give the number of printed compositions outside our area. Thus we have to go back to counting editions. In order to facilitate easier comparison, the data from Table 11.2 are transformed into a diagram (Figure 11.2a).

In Italy, Ottaviano Petrucci dominated the first twenty years of polyphonic music printing (see Figure 11.2b). Between 1501 and 1505 he built up a mixed vocal repertoire with series of chansons, frottole, masses and motets. With the publication of the two volumes of *Intabolature* by Spinacino in 1507, lute tablatures entered his range. Other prestigious Italian printers in the coming decades were Andrea Antico, the families Giunta and Scotto, and Antonio Gardano, with Rome and especially Venice as centres of music printing. The number of books containing sacred polyphony exceeds those containing secular compositions, except for a unique drop in the early 1530s. In these years, the first collections of madrigals were published, a genre that boomed in the next decades, and which caused a significant increase in the total number of editions in the last five years of our time span, including intabulations of this repertoire.

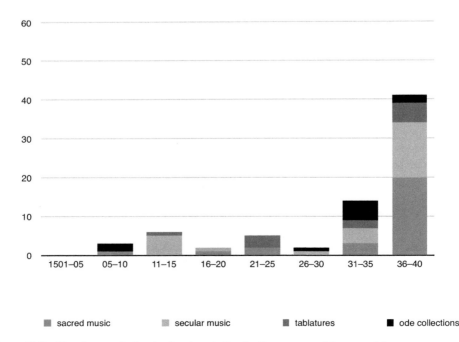

Figure 11.2a Development of polyphonic printing in German-speaking countries

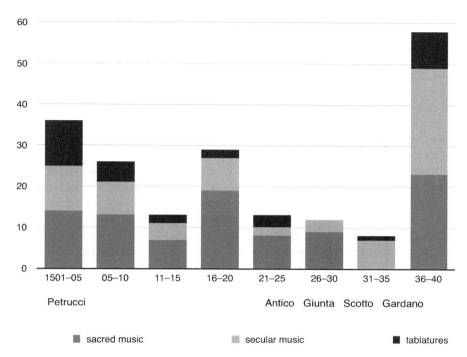

Figure 11.2b Development of polyphonic printing in Italy

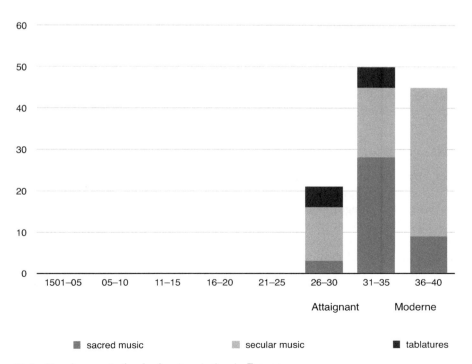

Figure 11.2c Development of polyphonic printing in France

The situation in France was quite different (see Figure 11.2c). The printing of polyphony there began much later, in the year 1528, and was almost entirely concentrated on Pierre Attaingnant in Paris. Only Jaques Moderne in Lyon contributed to a certain extent to the French output. Attaingnant, the first printer who used the single impression technique to print polyphony regularly, opened his rich and manifold programme with a series of chanson collections. In the year 1529 alone he published almost 250 songs in seven books. At the same time Attaingnant began to print tablatures of all genres. Books containing sacred repertoire had a slower start. Apart from two early motet collections, Attaingnant launched a well-organised series of seven printed mass collections in 1532, each book containing three compositions. Additionally, he printed thirteen books of motets. In the last five years of our survey, chanson collections again dominated the French printing market, produced by both workshops in Lyon and Paris. Sacred polyphony was then primarily printed by Moderne.

A comparison of the output of printed polyphony and instrumental music in these three countries shows that the situation in each was quite different. While in Italy there was a more or less steady production from the very beginning of the sixteenth century, and a number of important printing houses each with a substantial output, music printing in France started much later and was dominated only by one or two printers. Both countries produced editions with sacred and secular vocal music as well as tablatures for several instruments. Furthermore it is remarkable that in the last five-year period, 1536–1540, the increasingly popular genres in the vernacular languages – the madrigal in Italy and the chanson in France – dominated the market in both countries. By comparison, the situation in Germany is less coherent. First of all, it is more diverse, since the printed collections of odes were part of the market throughout the entire period. Second, there is no outstanding German printer in the very early times. At best one could name Peter Schöffer, but as an adherent of the new faith he was forced to migrate with his workshop, and had only a modest output compared with his great French or Italian colleagues. Third, no one city dominated music printing in the German-speaking lands, but several places contributed to the output of polyphonic music, with Nuremberg (with twenty-one editions) and Frankfurt am Main (with eleven editions) topping the list.[20] Finally, compared to printers in other countries, those in Germany produced a relatively small number of printed collections of polyphonic music, which appears to be a specifically German phenomenon.

Overall overview

Another approach to music printing in German-speaking lands is the question of the overall chronological development of the numbers of editions that include musical notation. For the restricted categories of titles containing polyphonic music, Table 11.2 already indicated that there was no steady increase in the numbers of titles. Table 11.3, which gives the number of all types of sources over the full time span, underlines this development. While there are 139 titles for the first decade, the number of printed editions increases to 210 in the second decade. Although one would expect a steady increase, there was a relatively strong decline of about 25 per cent in the third decade. In the fourth decade of the century, the number of editions with music increased again remarkably.

---

20 Nuremberg 21, Frankfurt/M. 11, Strasbourg 8, Augsburg 6, Mainz 4, Wittenberg 5, Vienna 2, Cologne 1, Basel 1, Worms 1 (only polyphonic music books and tablatures between 1501 and 1540 are counted).

Table 11.3 Number of editions with printed music notation in German-speaking areas

Time period	1501–10	1511–20	1521–30	1531–40
Number	139	210	167	225

It is suggested here that the drop in the 1520s had something to do with the turmoil of the Reformation.

The printing of polyphony and the Reformation

The traditional narrative that polyphony was in a triumphal procession from the middle of the fifteenth century to the sixteenth was challenged a decade ago by Rob Wegman's book with the provocative title *The Crisis of Music in Early Modern Europe 1470–1530*.[21] Although Wegman was right to upset this narrative, I do not agree with his method of picking out singular events in different places and at different times to construct a general movement against polyphony. One might also be sceptical about his way of using documents that stem from yet other places and other times merging into one coherent narrative in order to show that this trend was followed by a defensive counter-movement of praising this exact genre.[22] Nevertheless, Wegman made us aware that the performance of polyphonic liturgical music was not to be taken for granted in the decades around 1500. In the German Reformation, the opposition to polyphony came to a climax. As much as the Lutheran reformers were interested in introducing monophonic hymns in German for the common people to cover all liturgical domains, they were ideologically inclined to neglect the rich repertory of (Latin) masses, motets and other polyphonic compositions that the old church had developed to this point, at least at the very beginning of the movement.[23] To put it in the drastic words of Wegman: 'The German Reformation marked a turning point in the battle over polyphony. No single event did more to discredit and ultimately defeat the campaign against this art than the Lutheran revolt.'[24] How complex this process was, however, will be indicated in the case study of Nuremberg, one of the most prominent cities in book and music printing.

Polyphonic music printing at Nuremberg

At the beginning of the sixteenth century, Nuremberg was a free imperial city governed by a strong council of patricians who did their job well. The city flourished in commercial business as well as in cultural life and was one of the most populous settlements in Germany. Education was on a high level, and the prosperity of the churches and monasteries was remarkable. Nuremberg embraced the Reformation quite early compared to other German cities. This happened without noteworthy resistance because not only the common people but also the patricians sympathised with Luther's revolutionary ideas, not least because many wished to relieve the city from the powerful authority of the ecclesiastical administration of Rome. In 1524 a Lutheran mass was celebrated in St Sebald and St Lorenz,

---

21 Wegman, *Crisis*.
22 For reviews of this book see James Haar, *Renaissance Quarterly* 60/1: 256–257; Leeman L. Perkins, *Music & Letters* 90/2 (2009), 263–268; Theodor Dumitrescu, 'Wars on Music', *Early Music* 35/1 (2007), 113–115.
23 That the daily practice was not strictly observed has been demonstrated by Herl, *Worship Wars*.
24 Wegman, *Crisis*, 167.

the two main churches of the city, and the Lord's supper was distributed in both kinds. The process of Reformation was complete a year later when the Nuremberg clergy were officially forbidden to say the Roman mass in the parish and monastic churches. What seemed to develop so smoothly was endangered by a conflict of interests as soon as the emperor or one of his agents entered the city. Moreover, Nuremberg had to house the Diet twice in this religiously turbulent period, and was then carefully observed by several representatives of the Holy Roman Empire and the church. The city council was thus frequently torn between the evangelical confession of the town and its loyalty to the Roman Catholic emperor. This resulted in several temporary suppressions of public worship in the new order.[25]

Polyphonic music was seriously questioned by the more radical forces in town. A central reason for this was the claim that the words spoken and sung during the liturgical enactments should be understood clearly and should be in the vernacular language. Polyphonic choral music in the Franco-Flemish style in Latin could obviously not fulfil this demand, although Luther himself did not want to give up this repertoire entirely. Another critical point was the fact that this music genre was traditionally associated with the aristocracy and was distant from the world of the common people who were the focus of the reformers. In their eyes the music was too sophisticated to be accessible for the laity. Furthermore, a financial argument against polyphony was also put forward: people lamented that it was too costly to sustain a polyphonic ensemble (*Kantorei*) to perform this repertoire. One should rather spend this money on the poor. (Erasmus also brought up this argument against polyphony.) Other humanists complained that the students in Latin schools, who contributed substantially to polyphonic singing in Nuremberg's churches, wasted too much time in music rehearsals and performances. They should rather work and study in school. Finally, others condemned the mercenary abuse of paying for polyphonic masses for saints, deceased relatives or for personal prestige or other immoral reasons.

These manifold concerns about music are reflected in the output of printed material produced in the city (see Figure 11.3). Until 1520, Nuremberg printers – notably Georg Stuchs and his son Johann (who published mainly missals), Jobst Gutknecht and Hieronymus

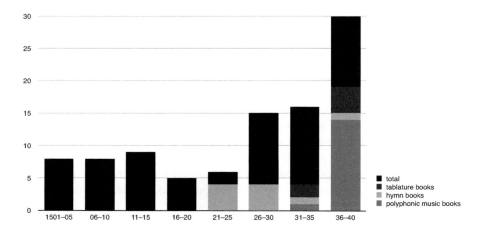

Figure 11.3 Number of editions with printed music notation at Nuremberg

---

25 See Strauss, *Nuremberg*, chapter four: 'Ecclesiastical Affairs and Religion; The Reformation', 154–186. See also Lesting-Buermann, 'Nürnberg' and Schauerte, *Deutschlands Auge & Ohr*.

Höltzel – produced a considerable number of prestigious Roman Catholic liturgical books. They also produced some humanist books, including ode-settings (among them *Ludus Dianae*) and a number of music textbooks, mostly those of the aforementioned school teacher Johannes Cochlaeus. Between 1510 und 1515, Cochlaeus was rector of the Latin school affiliated to St Lorenz. However, the turbulent years between 1517 and 1524 brought a general decline in music printing. Until this point, none of the workshops in the city had produced a polyphonic book with sacred or secular vocal repertoire or instrumental tablatures. This is no surprise. Liturgical books had a specific market in priests, humanist books and music textbooks were intended for students; all three kinds of book were often commissioned and sometimes fully funded. On the other hand, the target group for vocal secular and sacred polyphony was less distinct. Taking into account the aforementioned unstable situation in the practical performance of polyphony within the Reformation movement, printing books with particular liturgical music was a great financial risk – a risk that was not taken by any Nuremberg publisher or printer until the 1530s.

Based on the painstaking study by Bartlett Butler on liturgical music in sixteenth-century Nuremberg, there is evidence that in these early times in certain places the liturgy was still celebrated in a conservative style including reduced polyphonic singing in Latin.[26] In a letter to the Council with recommendations on the use of music in church from 1526, Osiander, one of the driving forces of the Nuremberg Reformation, was not completely opposed to polyphony, which he called 'kunstlich gesang'. But he wanted it to be used in a decent way, 'to serve the word of God and to meet the highest standards of excellence'.[27] Attitudes toward traditional elements in the church were varied and changed in specific churches and over time. This could not prevent a real breakdown. For the years 1525 to 1535 Butler could find no documentary evidence for polyphony in Nuremberg, neither for performance nor for purchase of choral music or payments for copying choirbooks.[28]

This does not mean that there was no music. The focus was then clearly on German hymns. The Nuremberg printers reacted immediately as the need for this repertoire was demanding. Jobst Gutknecht and Hans Herrgott (and his later widow Kunigunde) printed a comprehensive series of hymn books, starting with the so-called *Achtliederbuch* in 1524. In the next eight years several musical editions were published, including church orders for Nuremberg and other cities. All of them contain monophonic songs and chant in German. However, Nuremberg printers had still not produced one polyphonic music book.

The rigorous instructions in the famous Nuremberg church order from 1533 finally seemed to seal the fate of polyphony in this city. However, as a German proverb says: 'Nothing is as bad as it looks.'[29] While this treatise took a long time to be negotiated and published, the practice in the Protestant service swung back to the conservative side. A revival of more traditional forms in liturgy in some churches gave hope to devotees of elaborate choir music. It opened a window for a slow and arduous recovery of polyphony and organ music, supported by the first Nuremberg church administrator ('Kirchenpfleger') Hieronymus Baumgartner and the preacher at St Sebald, Veit Dietrich. In 1534 a Kantorei in St Aegidius was re-established, directed by Johann Rechberger. He was assisted by Wilhelm Breitengraser, rector of the school at St Aegidius and an able composer.[30] Like

---

26 Butler, 'Liturgical Music'.
27 Butler, 'Liturgical Music', 106.
28 Butler, 'Liturgical Music', 405.
29 Die Suppe wird nicht so heiß gegessen wie gekocht.
30 Butler, 'Liturgical Music', 495–497.

a broker at the stock market, the Nuremberg printers predicted this development and delivered the repertoire that would be required in the following years. Parallel to that, they also began to print music for private recreation.

In 1532/33, Hieronymus Formschneider entered into the business of music printing with two volumes of tablatures for string instruments by the Nuremberg lutenist Hans Gerle, followed by two collections of sacred German Lied settings in the next years, both commissioned by Hans Ott.[31] At about the same time, in 1536, Johannes Petreius enriched the market with a set of pedagogical lute books by Hans Neusidler, who also resided in these years in the city. Now two competing printers were involved with polyphonic music, both working with their own music fonts in the new technique of single-impression. Formschneider then added a new tablature by Gerle and started printing liturgical repertoire in 1537. This book was a rich compilation of motets for four to six voices, again published by Hans Ott: *Novum et insigne opus musicum*. It was complemented by a second volume in the next year so that the collection summed up to exactly one hundred motets. Additional to that, Formschneider printed eight Magnificats by Ludwig Senfl, one by each tone. Petreius followed immediately in producing two other collections at the same time: a book with thirty-six psalm-settings, followed by a second volume in the following year, and another book with sixteen motets. The first ordinary mass compositions that were printed in Nuremberg appeared as late as 1539: thirteen masses printed by Formschneider, fifteen masses by Petreius. While Formschneider was only printing on commission, the latter was more independent. Petreius began printing a series of German Lied settings, edited by Georg Forster; he subsequently produced a second volume of German songs, and two more books with selected motets in. Finally it seems that now the spell was broken and polyphonic music found its place in Nuremberg's printing repertoire. In just the last four years of the 1530s, twenty-eight masses and about 300 motets went through the presses of the city and were available for anybody who was interested and could afford it. At least after the middle of the century Nuremberg's church music, including polyphony, had again achieved a high reputation.

Conclusions

Looking back in history and again broadening our view from Nuremberg to other German-speaking areas, we can state that the early Reformation actually fostered music printing, but only specific types of sources: broadsheets and pamphlets, liturgical books, and hymn books. Books with polyphonic music were not in the programme of German music publishers and had to wait until the new church orders were established and the most extreme forces were pushed back in most German cities. However, even at this point polyphonic music was only a fraction of the full output of printed music. And we can be sure that in the early modern period, the notion of 'music' in the mind of the common people meant much more than polyphonic art music, the so called 'kunstlich musik'. It included chant in church, Latin ode settings in schools and universities, monophonic German hymns in the new services and in private homes, and not to forget the great amount of orally transmitted monophony and improvised polyphony for voices and instruments. Vocal polyphonic art music, the heart of our historiography, which survived more or less accidentally through manuscripts and printed editions, was only the tip of an iceberg.

---

31 On the collaboration of Formschneider and Ott see Gustavson, 'Hans Ott'.

References

Amiet, Robert. *Missels et bréviaires imprimés: Supplement aux catalogues de Weale et Bohatta*. Paris: CNRS, 1990.

Berz, Ernst-Ludwig. *Die Notendrucker und ihre Verleger in Frankfurt am Main von den Anfängen bis etwa 1630: eine bibliographische und drucktechnische Studie zur Musikpublikation*. Catalogus musicus 5. Kassel: Bärenreiter, 1970.

Bobeth, Gundela. 'Die humanistische Odenkomposition in Buchdruck und Handschrift: Zur Rolle der *Melopoiae* bei der Formung und Ausbreitung eines kompositorischen Erfolgsmodells'. In *NiveauNischeNimbus: Die Anfänge des Musikdrucks nördlich der Alpen*, edited by Birgit Lodes. Wiener Forum für ältere Musikgeschichte 3. Tutzing: Hans Schneider, 2010, 67–87.

Butler, Bartlett Russell. 'Liturgical Music in Sixteenth-Century Nürnberg. A Socio-Musical Study'. PhD dissertation, University of Illinois at Urbana-Champaign, 1970.

Cochlaeus, Johannes. *Tetrachordum Musices: Introduction, Translation and Transcription*. Edited and translated by Clement A. Miller. Musicological Studies and Documents 23. [Rome]: American Institute of Musicology, 1970.

Gustavson, Royston. 'Hans Ott, Hieronymus Formschneider and the "Novum et insigne opus musicum" (Nuremberg, 1537–1538)'. PhD dissertation, University of Melbourne, 1998.

Herl, Joseph. *Worship Wars in Early Lutheranism: Choir, Congregation, and Three Centuries of Conflict*. Oxford: Oxford University Press, 2004.

Lesting-Buermann, Beate. 'Reformation und literarisches Leben in Nürnberg'. PhD dissertation, Albert-Ludwig-Universität zu Freiburg i. Br., 1982.

Lindmayr-Brandl, Andrea. '"Teutsche Liedlein" im frühen Notendruck: ein neuer Blick'. In *'Teutsche Liedlein' des 16. Jahrhundert: Kongressband 2015*, edited by Achim Aurnhammer and Susanne Rode-Breymann. Wiesbaden (in press).

Lindmayr-Brandl, Andrea. 'Early Music Prints and New Technology: Variants and Variant Editions'. *Fontes artis musicae* 64 (2017), 244–260.

Lindmayr-Brandl, Andrea. 'Peter Schöffer der Jüngere, das Erbe Gutenbergs und die "wahre Art des Druckens"'. In *NiveauNischeNimbus: Die Anfänge des Musikdrucks nördlich der Alpen*, edited by Birgit Lodes. Wiener Forum für ältere Musikgeschichte 3. Tutzing: Hans Schneider, 2010, 283–312.

Lodes, Birgit. '*Concentus*, *Melopoiae* und *Harmoniae* 1507: Zum Geburtsjahr des Typendrucks mehrstimmiger Musik nördlich der Alpen'. In *NiveauNischeNimbus: Die Anfänge des Musikdrucks nördlich der Alpen*, edited by Birgit Lodes. Wiener Forum für ältere Musikgeschichte 3. Tutzing: Hans Schneider, 2010, 33–66.

Lodes, Birgit. 'An anderem Ort, auf andere Art: Petruccis und Mewes' Obrecht-Drucke'. *Basler Jahrbuch für historische Musikpraxis* 25 (2001): 85–111.

McDonald, Grantley. 'The Metrical *Harmoniae* of Wolfgang Gräfinger und Ludwig Senfl in the Conjunction of Humanism, Neoplatonism, and Nicodemism'. In *Senfl-Studien I*, edited by Stefan Gasch, Birgit Lodes, and Sonja Tröster. Wiener Forum für ältere Musikgeschichte 4. Tutzing: Hans Schneider, 2012, 69–148.

Schauerte, Thomas, ed., *Deutschlands Auge & Ohr: Nürnberg als Medienzentrum der Reformationszeit. Eine Ausstellung der Kunstsammlung der Stadt Nürnberg. 24. April bis 31. Oktober 2015. Stadtmuseum Fembohaus. Begleitpublikation*. Schriftenreihe der Museen der Stadt Nürnberg 8, Nürnberg: Tümmel Verlag, 2015.

Strauss, Gerald. *Nuremberg in the Sixteenth Century. City Politics and Life between Middle Ages and Modern Times*. Bloomington, IN and London: Indiana University Press, 1976.

Weale, William Henry James and Hanns Bohatta. *Bibliographia liturgica: Catalogus missalium ritus latini ab anno MCCCLXXV impressorum*. London: Quaritch, 1928.

Wegman, Rob C. *The Crisis of Music in Early Modern Europe, 1470–1530*. New York: Routledge, 2005.

Index

Note: The index uses US and UK spelling. Page numbers in *italic* refer to figures; page numbers in **bold** refer to tables. The plate section is indicated by a P preceding the number, at the end of the relevant entries.

Adeste Musae maximi proles Iovis 231, 232, 239
Ad Martinum Lutherum captivum lamentatio (Knobloch) 199, 201, 202–204, *203*, 218–222
Aich, A. von 156, 163, 170, 250
Alber, E. 163, 164, 172, 181
Amerbach, B. 145, 146, **146**, 147, 149
Amerbach, J. 147
Antwerp printers 1, 71, 75
Arndes, S. 22, 30–33, *32*, **41**
Ars musicorum (del Podio) 54, 56, *57*
Attaingnant, P. 1, 2, 13, 14, 69, 71, 79, 254
Augsburg printers 8, 29–30, *30*, 35

Bamberg printers 26, 29, 35–36
Beck, R. 14
Beckenhub, J. 23, 26–28
Beham, H. S. 180, 188
Beham, L., *Buch von der Astronomie* 92, *93*
Berg & Neuber (printing firm) 163, 172
Beringen, G. 71, 75, 79, *82*
Beringen, M. 71, 79, *82*
Beurhusius, F. 108, 114
Biel, F. 47, 48, 50, 51, 54, 59
Billican, T. 226, 227, 237, 242; *De partium orationis inflexionibus* 229, 229–235, *230*, *232*, *234*, *235*, *236*, 238, 240, 242
Boethius 109, 245; *De consolatione philosophiae* 239–240; *De Musica* 102–103, 110–111
Bozio, T. 215
Brabandische Liedlin (Egenolff) 155–157, 158–159, 160–161, *178–179*, 248
Breviarium Ratisponense (Ratdolt) 92–93
Breviarius Misnensis (Lotter) 130, *130*
Brevis musicae isagoge (Fries) 105, 107, *107*
Brun, P. 47, 48, 54
Buch von der Astronomie (Beham) 92, *93*

Cantilenae aliquot elegantes ac piae (Othmayr) 214
Cantiones vocum quatuor (Egenolff) 155–157, 158–159, 160, 161–162, *179–180*
Cantiones vocum trium (Egenolff) 155–157, 158–159, 160, 162, *173, 180–181*
Carmina (Horace) 225, 228, 231, 239
Cathemerinon (Grefinger) 225
Celtis, C. 143, 225, 242; *Ludus Dianae* 249
Clarissima plane atque choralis musice interpretatio (Prasperg) 90, *91*, *91*
Cochlaeus, J. 14, 245, 257; *Tetrachordum musices* 245
Coci, J. 46, 48, 50, 51, 54
Codro, A. U., *Rhythmus die divi Martini pronunciatus* 206, 207, 222
Colonia, P. de 47, 48, 50
Compendium musicae modulativae (Goetting) *115*, 115–116
Constance Gradual 94
Cranach, L. 132, *133*, 204, 211, 215
Cromberger, J. 47, 48, 50, 51, 56, 58–59
'Cuatro Compañeros Alemanes' 48, 49, 50, 55–56

De consolatione philosophiae (Boethius) 239–240
De dulcissimo nomine Iesu officium (Schöffer) 95, 96–97, *97*, P11, P13
Definitio, divisio musices, & eius subdivisio (Voigt) 110, 111
De Musica (Boethius) 102–103, 110–111
De partium orationis inflexionibus (Billican) 229, 229–235, *230*, *232*, *234*, *235*, *236*, 238, 240, 242
Der Psalter Jn Newe Gesangs weise vnd künstliche Reimen gebracht (Waldis) 158, 171–172, 189
Dietrich, V. 214–215

INDEX

Dirty Bride (Wedding of Mopsus and Nisa), The (Bruegel) 89, P9
Durán, D. M. 55, 56; *Lux bella* 55, 55; *Sumula de canto de órgano* 55, 56
Dürer, A. 140, *141*, 201–202, 203–204

Egenolff, C. 13, 14, 15, 137–140, 147, 149, 153, 172–173, 238, 248, 251; *Brabandische Liedlin* 155–157, 158–159, 160–161, 178–179, 248; *Cantiones vocum quatuor* 155–157, 158–159, 160, 161–162, 179–180; *Cantiones vocum trium* 155–157, 158–159, 160, 162, 173, 180–181; *Der Psalter Jn Newe Gesangs weise vnd künstliche Reimen gebracht* 171–172, 189; *Gassenhawerlin* 144, 155–157, 158–159, 160, 161, 177; *Gassenhawer und Reutterliedlin* 165–166, 167, 168–169, 171, 172, 188–189; *Geminae undeviginti odarum Horatii melodiae* 165, 172, 184–185, 226–227, 237–239, 240–241; *Gesangbüchlin* 163–164, 172, 181; *Graszliedlin* 165–166, 167, 168–169, 171, 172, 187–188; *Hymni ecclesiastici duodecim* 164–165, 172, 173, 181–184; music books 140–145, **142**, 147, 149, 153–156, 162, 172–173, 174–175, 190–192; *Newgeborne Liedlin* 166–170, 172, 173, 186; *Oberländische Liedlin* 166–169, 170–171, 172, 173, 186–187; *Odarum Horatii Concentus* 142, 154–155, 175–177; *Reutterliedlin* 143, *144*, 145, **146**, 147, 149, 155–157, 158–159, 161, 168, 177–178, 179, 248; *Wittembergisch deutsch Geistlich Gesangbüchlein* 145, **146**
Eichstätt printers 24, 25, 35–36
Emser, H. 204; *Epithalamia Martini Lutheri Wittenbergensis* 199, 204–205, 207–208; *Hymnus paranymphorum* 204–205, 206, 207, 222
Epitaphium D. Martini Lutheri (Othmayr) 214
Epithalamia Martini Lutheri Wittenbergensis (Emser) 199, 204–205, 207–208
Erotemata (Faber) 108–110, *109*
Erotemata musicae practicae (Lossius) 113, 241
Erotemata musices in usum scholae Lunaeburgensis (Praetorius) 111, *112*, 113
Evangelistarum quatuor passiones (Lotter) 128, P15, P16
Exemplar in modum accentuandi (Winterburger) 14
Eyn erschreglicher und doch widderumb kurtzweylliger und nutzlich gesangk (Sylvius) 199–200, 208, 209–211, *210*

Faber, G., *Erotemata* 108–110, *109*
Ferrariensis, J. F., *Principium et ars tocius musicae* 104–105
Fludd, R., *Templum musicae* 116

Foeniseca, J., *Quadratum sapiencie* 103–104
Formschneider, H. 172, 250, 251, 258
'Formschneider' typeface 71, *72*, *82*
Freigius, J. T. 108, 114; *Paedagogus* 104, 114
Fries, J. 105–108; *Brevis musicae isagoge* 105, 107, *107*; *Synopsis isagoges musicae* 106, 107; *Synopsis musicae* 105, 107, 108
Froschauer, J. 105
Fuchs, L. 139
Fugger, J. 135, 137
funding 135–136; *see also* sponsorship
Fünff vnd sechzig teütscher Lieder vormals im truck nie ußgangen (Schöffer) 170, 171
Fust, J. 88, 96, 135, 149

Gassenhawerlin (Egenolff) *144*, 155–157, 158–159, 160, 161, 168, 177
Gassenhawer und Reutterliedlin (Egenolff) 165–166, 167, 168–169, 171, 172, 188–189
Geminae undeviginti odarum Horatii melodiae (Nigidius) 165, 172, 184–185, 226–227, 237–239, 240–241
Gesangbüchlin (Egenolff) 163–164, 172, 181
Glockner, T. 46, 48, 50
Goetting, V., *Compendium musicae modulativae* 115, 115–116
Graduale, Constance 94
Graduale Herbipolense (Reyser) P1
Grammatica graeca (Melanchthon) 110
Granjon, R. 75, 79
'Granjon' typeface 75, *76*, *77*, *83*
Graszliedlin (Egenolff) 165–166, 167, 168–169, 171, 172, 187–188
Grefinger, *Cathemerinon* 225
Grimm & Wirsung (printing firm), *Liber selectarum cantionum* 229–230
Guidonian hand 102, 103–104, 105, 111
Gutenberg, J. 2, 3, 14, 84, 135, 149
Gysser, J. 47, 48, 55

Hagenbach, P. 46, 48, 52–53, 56; *Missale mixtum* P6
Hager, C. 204
Hanc tua Penelope 232, 239
Herbst, M. 47, 48, 50
Heugel, H. 162
Heu heu quae nobis te sors 202–204
Horace, *Carmina* 225, 228, 231, 239
Hortulus musices practicae (Lotter) 127, *129*
Hurus, J. 47, 48, 49, 52
Hurus, P. 47, 48, 49, 50, 52, 56, 58; *Missale Cesaraugustanum* P4
Hutz, L. 46, 48, 49, 50, 56
Hymni ecclesiastici duodecim (Egenolff) 164–165, 165, 172, 173, 181–184

262   INDEX

Hymni ecclesiastici duodecim (Spangenberg)
164–165, 181–184
Hymnus paranymphorum (Emser) 204–205, 206,
207, 222

Iam satis terris 231, 238, 239, 241
Ipse cum solus (Nigidius) 238, 239
Ipse cum solus varios retracto (von dem Busche)
238
Isagogicus rerum grammaticarum libellus
(Nigidius) 165, 237–238

Kachelofen, C. 33, 36, **42**, 123
'Kamper Liedboek' 160–161
Keinspeck, M., *Lilium musicae planae* 91
Kettner, L., *Nu hört jr Christen newe meer* 200,
212–213
'Kieffer' typeface 77, *78*, 83
Knobloch, J. 203; *Ad Martinum Lutherum
captivum lamentatio* 199, 201, 202–204,
218–222
*Kunstbüchlin gerechten gründtlichen gebrauchs
aller kunstbaren Werckleut* (Egenolff) 140

Laus musarum (Spalatinus) 249
Leipzig printers 8, 33, 36, 131
Le Roy & Ballard (printing firm) 73, 79
Libellus ad omnes ... circuitus (Lotter) 128, P14
Liber selectarum cantionum (Grimm & Wirsung)
229–230
Lilium musicae planae (Keinspeck) 91
Livor tabificum malis venenum 231, 232, 235, *236*,
239
Lossius, L. 113; *Erotemata musicae practicae* 113,
241
Lotter the Elder, M. 12, 123–124, *124*, **125**,
126–127, *127*, 128–130, 132, 133, 134; *Breviarius
Misnensis* 130, *130*; *Evangelistarum quatuor
passiones* 128, P15, P16; *Hortulus musices
practicae* 127, *129*; *Libellus ad omnes . . .
circuitus* 128, P14; *Missale Brandenburgense*
P17; *Vesperale* 130
Lotter the Younger, M. 123, 124, 132, 133, 134
Lübeck printers 31, *32*
Ludus Dianae (Celtis) 249
Luschner, J. 47, 48, 59
Luther, M. 10, 124, 132, 133, 199–205, *200*, *201*,
209–216
Lux bella (Durán) 55, *55*

Maecenas atavis (Michael) 231, 234, 238, 239,
240
manus see Guidonian hand
Manuzio, A. 227–228, 231; *Rudimenta
grammatices Latinae linguae* 227–228

Margarita philosophica (Reisch) 102, *103*, 104
Mein himlischer vatter (Othmayr) 200, 213,
223–224
Melanchthon, P. 14, 110, 212, 214; *Grammatica
graeca* 110
Mercuri, facunde nepos Atlantis (Nigidius) 239
Michael 225–243; *Maecenas atavis* 231, 234,
238–240; *Sic te diva potens* 241
Missale Brandenburgense (Lotter) P17
Missale Cesaraugustanum (Hurus) P4
Missale mixtum (Hagenbach) P6
Missale Salisburgense (Winterburger) 14
Missale Tarraconense (Rosenbach) 52, *53*
Missale Wormatiense P12
Moderne, J. 1, 71, 79, 254
Musicae erotematum libri duo (Beurhusius)
114
Musices generalis typus (Praetorius) 111,
113–114
music typefaces *see* typefaces

'Nenninger' typeface *76*, 77, *83*
nesting 13, 71
Newgeborne Liedlin (Egenolff) 166–170, 172, 173,
186
Nigidius, P. 225–226, 231, 237, 240; *Geminae
undeviginti odarum Horatii melodiae* 165, 172,
184–185, 226–227, 237–239, 240–241; *Ipse
cum solus* 238–239; *Isagogicus rerum
grammaticarum libellus* 165, 237–238; *Mercuri,
facunde nepos Atlantis* 238–239; *Odarum* 172,
184–185, 238–239
Nu hört jr Christen newe meer (Kettner) 200,
212–213

Oberländische Liedlin (Egenolff) 166–169,
170–173, 186–187
Obsequiale Augustense (Ratdolt) 92, 94, P3
Obsequiale Constantiense (Ratdolt) P10
Obsequiale Eystettense (Reyser) P2
Odarum (Nigidius) 172, 184–185, 238–239
*Odarum Horatianarum genera undeviginti, cum
modis earundem, ad iuventutem exercendam in
fine adiectis* 231, 232
Odarum Horatii Concentus (Tritonius) 154–155,
175–177
Oeglin/Öglin, E. 141, 154, 163, 225, 250, 251
Ornitoparchus, A. 11–12
Othmayr, C. 214, 215; *Cantilenae aliquot elegantes
ac piae* 214; *Epitaphium D. Martini Lutheri* 214;
Mein himlischer vatter 200, 213, 223–224
Ott, H. 15, 163, 170, 172, 258

Paedagogus (Freigius) 104, 114
Parix, J. 46

patronage 13, 15, 22
Pegnitzer, J. 47, 48, 50, 51
Petreius, J. 163, 172, 248, 250, 251, 258
'Petreius large' typeface 70, 73, 77, 79, 82
'Petreius small' typeface 71, 73, 74, 77, 79, 82
Petrucci, O. 1, 2–3, 14, 69, 94, 252
Petzensteiner, H. 28, 33, **38**
'Phalèse Moyenne' typeface 72, 73, 82
plainchant type 32, 32–33
Podio, G. del, *Ars musicorum* 54, 56, 57
Praetorius, C. 111, 113; *Erotemata musices in usum scholae Lunaeburgensis* 111, *112*, 113; *Musices generalis typus* 111, 113–114
Prasperg, *Clarissima plane atque choralis musice interpretati* 90, 91, *91*
Preisegger, W. 117
Principium et ars tocius musicae (Ferrariensis) 104–105
printing press 84, 131
printing process 4, 84–99
Processionarium Predicatorum (Ungut) 54, P5
Prüss, J. 15, 34–35, 36, **43**

Quadratum sapiencie (Foeniseca) 103–104

Ramus, P. 114
Ratdolt, E. 12, 22, 29–30, *30*, 35, **39–40**, 86, 87, 92, 93, 94, P8; *Breviarium Ratisponense* 92–93; colour printing 92–93; *Obsequiale Augustense* 92, 94, P3; *Obsequiale Constantiense* P10
Reformation 4, 8, 10, 131, 199–224, 255, 256, 258
Reisch, G., *Margarita philosophica* 102, *103*, 104
Reutterliedlin (Egenolff) 143, *144*, 145, **146**, 147, 149, 155–157, 158–159, 161, 168, 177–178, 179, 248
Reyser, G. 22, 23, 24, 25, 27–28, **37**; *Graduale Herbipolense* P1
Reyser, M. 22, 24–25, 36; *Obsequiale Eystettense* P2
Rhau, G. 132, 172, 212, 250, 251
Rhode, F. 231–236
Rhythmus die divi Martini pronunciatus (Codro) 206, 207, 222
Richter, G. 166
Rosenbach, J. 47, 48, 49–50, 51, 52; *Missale Tarraconense* 52, 53
Rudimenta grammatices Latinae linguae (Manuzio) 227–228
Ruff, S. 13, 227–229, 233

Sachse, Melchior 165
Savigny, C. de, *Tableaux accomplis de tous les arts* 116–117
'Scale of Guido' ('Scala Guidonis') 104

Schlick, A. 10
Schöffer, P. the Elder 88, 96
Schöffer, P. the Younger 3, 88, 95, 96, 143, 163, 172, 233, 248, 250, 254; *De dulcissimo nomine Iesu officium* 95, 96–97, *97*, P11, P13; *Fünff vnd sechzig teütscher Lieder vormals im truck nie ußgangen* (Schöffer) 170, *171*; *Viginti cantiunculae Gallicae*, 161–162, 248
'Schöffer' typeface 69, *70*, 82
Schott, J. 139
Schwertel, J. 111
Sensenschmidt, J. 22, 26, 27, 28, 29, 33, **38**
Serarius, N. 215
Sic te diva potens (Michael) 241
Spalatinus, G., 206; *Laus musarum* 239
Spangenberg, J. 164–165, 181–184; *Hymni ecclesiastici duodecim* 164–165, 181–184; *Zwölff Christliche Lobgesenge* 164
sponsorship 13, 21–23, *22*, 24, 25
Stoicheiosis harmonica (Voigt) 111
Strasbourg printers 36
Sumula de canto de órgano (Durán) 55, 56
Susato, T. 1
Sylvius, P. 208–209, 215; *Eyn erschreglicher und doch widderumb kurtzweylliger und nutzlich gesangk* 199–200, 209–211, *210*
Synopsis isagoges musicae (Fries) *106*, 107
Synopsis musicae (Fries) 105, 107, 108

Tableaux accomplis de tous les arts (Savigny) 116–117
Templum musicae (Fludd) 116
Tetrachordum musices (Cochlaeus) 245
Theuerdank (Egenolff) 140
Tritonius, P. 154–155, 175–177, 225, 227, 228, 241, 242, 250
typefaces 35, 36, 67–83; dissemination 67–83

Ungut, M. 46, 47, 48, 49, 54; *Processionarium Predicatorum* 54, P5

'Van Ohr' typeface 77, *78*, *83*
Vervliet-Heartz method 67–68
Vesperale (Lotter) 130
Viginti cantiunculae Gallicae (Schöffer) 161–162, 248
Voigt, M., *Definitio, divisio musices, & eius subdivisio* 110, 111; *Stoicheiosis harmonica* 111
von dem Busche, H., *Ipse cum solus varios retracto* 238

Waldis, *Der Psalter Jn Newe Gesangs weise vnd künstliche Reimen gebracht* 158, 171–172, 189

Werdenstein, J. G. von 14, 15, 167, 169
Winterburger, J., 13–15; *Exemplar in modum accentuandi* 14
Wittembergisch deutsch Geistlich Gesangbüchlein (Egenolff) 145, **146**

Wittenberg printers 8, 131, 132
Würzburg printers 22–25, 27–28, 35–36

Zwölff Christliche Lobgesenge (Spangenberg) 164

9781138241053